SPIRITUAL DIVERSITY

in

SOCIAL WORK PRACTICE

The Heart of Helping

Edward R. Canda, Ph.D.
and
Leola Dyrud Furman, Ph.D.

THE FREE PRESS

*f*P

THE FREE PRESS
A Division of Simon & Schuster Inc.
1230 Avenue of the Americas
New York, NY 10020

Designed by MM Design 2000 Inc.

Manufactured in the United States of America

10 9 8 7 6 5 4 3

Library of Congress Cataloging-in-Publication Data

Canda, Edward R.
    Spiritual diversity in social work practice : the heart of helping
    Edward R. Canda and Leola Dyrud Furman.
        p. cm.
    Includes bibliographical references and index.
    1. Social service—Religious aspects. 2. Social workers—
    Religious life. 3. Spiritual life. 4. Spirituality. I. Furman,
    Leola Dyrud. II. Title.
    HV530.C27   1999   99-22123   CIP
    361.3'2—dc21

ISBN 0-684-84411-7

PERMISSIONS ACKNOWLEDGMENTS

We gratefully acknowledge permission to reprint from the following works:

The following portions from Canda, E. R. (Ed.). Special issue on spirituality. *Reflections: Narratives of Professional Helping*, 1(4): Selections from Nakashima, M., Spiritual growth through hospice work, pp. 17–27; selections from Kreutziger, S. S., Spirituality in faith, pp. 28–35; Nguzo Saba, The Seven Principles of Kwanzaa, p. 40, from Karenga, M., Making the past meaningful: Kwanzaa and the concept of Sankofa, pp. 36–46. Used with permission of the publisher.

The poem "If We Nurtured the Soul of Social Work," by Sheridan, M. J. (1997). *Society for Spirituality and Social Work Newsletter* 4(2), 3.

We gratefully acknowledge permission to revise and adapt the following works:

Canda, E. R. (1988). Conceptualizing spirituality for social work: Insights from diverse perspectives. *Social Thought*, 14(1), 30–46.

Canda, E. R. (1988). Spirituality, religious diversity, and social work practice. *Social Casework*, 69(4), 238–247.

Table 8.2. Ethical Considerations for Using Spiritually Based Activities in Social Work, from Canda, E. R. (1990). An holistic approach to prayer for social work practice. *Social Thought*, 16(3), 3–13.

CONTENTS

ACKNOWLEDGMENTS

I thank those people whose caring, spiritual support, and guidance have been crucial to the formation of this book: my wife and partner in all things, Hwi-Ja Canda; my devout and dedicated parents, Frank and Anne Canda; the staff of Shantivanam, the Forest of Peace, who provided a hermitage for writing and an inclusive Catholic community of support; the University of Kansas Keeler Intra-University Exchange Program, for my spring 1997 professorship in the Department of Religious Studies and my very helpful colleagues there, Sandra Zimdars-Swartz and Daniel Stevenson; Ann Weick, dean of the School of Social Welfare at the University of Kansas, for her continuous encouragement; my friend and mentor in East Asian philosophy, Yi Dong-Jun, of Sung Kyun Kwan University in Seoul, Korea; and the professor who did the most to encourage me on the spiritual path of service during my social work student years, Daniel B. Lee, associate dean at the School of Social Work, Loyola University of Chicago. I also am grateful to Cheri L'Ecuyer for her extraordinary secretarial assistance in preparing this book.

—Edward R. Canda

I dedicate this work to my sons, Erik and Jon Furman, whose unfailing faith and belief in me have been inspiring; to my four brothers, Chet, Loiell, Connely, and Clark Dyrud, my life-long friends; and to the memory of my late husband, Philip J. Furman. I thank Cordell Fountaine, associate director of the Social Science Research Institute, University of North Dakota, for assistance in the survey instrument design, mailing, coding, and data entry; John Hoover, director of the Bureau of Educational Research, University of North Dakota, and his research associate, Carol Milner, for data analysis assistance; Robert Koch, social work graduate research assistant; Jani Franz, for editorial assistance; Julie Arnold, for secretarial assistance; Michael Jacobsen, chair of the Department of Social

Work, University of North Dakota, for his encouragement; the Department of Social Work and Alumni Foundation, University of North Dakota, for research grants supporting this project; Kenneth Peterson, my mentor; and my best friend and sister, Gwen Dyrud.

—Leola Dyrud Furman

We both extend our sincere appreciation for the tremendous support and technical assistance in the production of this book to our editor, Philip Rappaport, and the staff at The Free Press; and to those who contributed items from their previous research to development of our survey instrument: Ronald K. Bullis, James Dudley, and Michael Sheridan.

A NOTE TO THE READER

Welcome.
Please enter
the reading of this book
as a journey of discovery and growth.

May you test
what you find herein
by your own deepest wisdom,
by the guidance of those you respect, and
by your daily experience
on the spiritual path of service.

INTRODUCTION

Human beings live not on bread alone.
Matthew 4:4, Christianity
(Jerusalem Bible)

THE HEART OF HELPING

Spirituality is the heart of helping. It is the heart of empathy and care, the pulse of compassion, the vital flow of practice wisdom, and the driving force of action for service. Social workers know that our professional roles, theories, and skills become rote, empty, tiresome, and finally lifeless without this heart, by whatever names we call it. We also know that the people we serve seek spirituality, by whatever names they call it, to help them thrive, to succeed at challenges, and to infuse whatever materials and relationships we assist them with to have meaning beyond mere survival value. We all have many different ways of understanding and finding spirituality. And in social work practice, all these ways come together, knowingly or unknowingly. In this book, we provide a framework of values, knowledge, and skills for bringing the many religious and nonreligious forms of spirituality together in a creative helping process.

Spirituality and religion have become popular topics in the general public. Popular media often have stories about the politics of the Christian Right; moral debates over abortion, homosexuality, and human cloning; breakthroughs in holistic forms of healing and therapy in medicine and psychotherapy; and inspirational lives of world leaders such as Pope John Paul II, the Tibetan Dalai Lama, South African president Nelson Mandela, and the recently deceased Mother Teresa. In the publishing industry, spirituality is one of the fastest-growing sectors of the market. Movies and television documentaries carry many stories about angels, near-death experiences, sexual abuse by clergy, quasi-religious encounters with extraterrestrial beings, religious group suicide, miracles, and religious wars. As we arrive at the millennium, such preoccupations are likely to increase. Yet all this talk about spirituality and religion can cast as much shadow and confusion as light and understanding.

Within the profession of social work is a movement to shed light on the many ways that spirituality affects individuals and society at large. This book presents the state of the art of social work that is respectful and competent in its response to the diverse forms of spirituality that express in clients' lives. Although this movement of spiritually sensitive social work is growing rapidly and gaining influence, many practitioners, students, and educators are yet unaware of it. Others are aware but nervous about it. On the one hand, interest among clients and the popular culture piques some social workers' interest. On the other hand, many social workers are skeptical and suspicious, wondering how to sort out the fool's gold from the real gold. Sometimes students and practitioners are criticized by instructors or supervisors even for broaching the subject. The movement to develop spiritually sensitive approaches to social work reflects all the excitement and controversy to be found in the public arena, professional settings, and private lives of social workers and their clients.

This book draws on a large body of research and writing by social work scholars on spirituality and religion in order to present the state of the art, review the controversies involved, and suggest new possibilities for continued development. Its major contribution is to weave this wide and sometimes scattered material into a comprehensive conceptual framework of values, knowledge, and skills for a spiritually sensitive approach to social work. It draws on our professional heritage, from our roots in religious ideologies and institutions of social service to the most current work in cross-cultural study of religions, transpersonal theory, and spiritually oriented social and environmental activism. It also draws on insights from a wide range of religious, philosophical, and scientific perspectives.

The book incorporates ideas concerning spirituality and religion from social workers in direct practice throughout the country. In 1997, we conducted a national survey of members of the National Association of Social Workers who are engaged in direct practice (we refer to it throughout the book as the National Survey). We obtained a representative sample ($N = 2,069$) with very similar characteristics to the overall NASW membership. This has been the only national survey of practicing social workers on spirituality to date, and it explored a wider range of questions than previous regional studies. We use findings from the survey to discuss the respondents' demographic characteristics and their opinions about addressing spirituality and religion in practice. More information on the details of research methodology and the survey instrument is contained in Appendix B.

This book is intended to be thought provoking and soul searching. It is designed to promote personal and professional growth in the reader. In doing so, it will be challenging and sometimes uncomfortable, but also exciting. The mind, heart, and action of the reader will be engaged. We encourage both intellectual and experiential learning that will lead to spiritually sensitive practice.

At the outset, be reassured (or forewarned, depending on your viewpoint) that this book does *not* present a sectarian view of spirituality or social work. It is not about missionizing or converting anyone to any particular religious faith. Nor is it about stereotyping or putting down any particular religious faith. It is about self-reflection, searching for meaning, sincerely striving to link one's spiritual path (of whatever kind) to professional values and settings. It is about learning to respond sensitively, appreciatively, and competently to the diverse religious and nonreligious forms of spirituality found among the individuals, families, groups, and communities whom social workers have dedicated to serve.

This book proposes a guide for social work practice, but it is only a proposal. We hope that readers will reflect carefully and critically on our framework and then do the most important work of all: develop a personal framework that is congruent with their own values, professional commitments, and areas of practice.

PRINCIPLES THAT GUIDE THE WRITING OF THIS BOOK

We are committed to five principles that have guided our writing: demonstrating value clarity, respecting spiritual diversity, being reflective, supporting strengths and empowerment, and taking a holistic perspective.

Demonstrating Value Clarity

In our writing, we do not claim or wish to be value free or bereft of moral standards. Nor do we wish to pose our own values as absolute or superior truths to be imposed on others. We promote another way for social work that we call *value clarity*.

First, value clarity means that each of us must be clear about our own values and how they shape us. Only in this way can we engage in conscientious self-reflection and growth. Second, whenever appropriate, we need to make our value positions explicit to colleagues and clients, so that we can engage in dialogue, sorting out the value dilemmas and possible conflicts involved. Through dialogue, our formation of values, ethics, and morals can be enriched, broadened, and refined. When educators and practitioners make their value positions explicit, then students and clients can scrutinize them and make choices about whether to agree or disagree. Only then is informed consent possible. In this way, we can examine how our values may affect the course of research or practice, and we can take steps to engage them constructively or to change them.

This does not mean that we should engage in self-revelation merely for our own purposes, out of self-preoccupation or grandiosity. As in all other social work practice, we should engage in self-disclosure at times and in ways that are appropriate to the needs and circumstances of those we serve. But not to self-disclose at all, or to hold major areas of who we are in secrecy, restricts our participation in helping as full human beings. And it replaces the danger of openly imposed agendas with the danger of subtly imposed hidden agendas.

Discussion of religious and spiritual matters intensifies concern about values precisely because people often claim ultimate and absolute truth status for their religiously based opinions. For example, a social worker who believes that his or her religion proclaims with absolute authority that homosexuality is merely a matter of choice for people (and a sinful choice at that) will not be amenable to dialogue and revision of the value position. Scientific evidence or professional admonishments notwithstanding, the social worker may believe it is her or his duty to "fix" the gay or lesbian client through religious conversion or psychotherapeutic manipulations. This kind of rigid thinking is not the exclusive province of religion. Value-rigid positions can be found among ideologues of every stripe, political, theoretical, or religious. The clinician who fervently believes in the dictates of Erik Erikson's stage theory of human development might try to judge every client in terms of developmental tasks achieved and ego functions mastered, no matter what gender, ethnic background, sexual orientation, or type of ability or disability. The community organizer who is a strict classical Marxist might ignore or denigrate the spiritual and religious aspects of community life.

The only workable approach to this problem is to be clear and open about our various value positions and to engage in open respectful dialogue about them. And we need to do this in a way that encourages mutual growth.

This is consistent with the wisdom of a great social activist, Mahatma Gandhi. He believed that there is a divine truth that transcends yet informs all cultures and religions. He also felt that this truth is beyond the ability of anyone to know completely, given our limitations as human beings. Humility was a virtue he praised. He believed that every person and every human group is seeking truth, but that no one has exclusive possession of truth. Even in conflict with oppressors, Gandhi sought to discover his opponents' understanding of truth. He avoided dehumanizing anyone, even as he may have been unjustly persecuted. His philosophy of nonviolence was made dynamic by the principle of *satyagraha*, or truth force. If each person strives continually to understand the truth and opens up to others and helps others in their search for truth, we can all move closer to realization of Truth (Erikson, 1969; Fischer, 1950; Gandhi, n.d.). This is spiritually informed social activism.

This is the position we aspire to in this book. We hope that our own self-disclosures and our juxtapositioning of many different spiritual perspectives will help readers search for truth.

In order to encourage value clarity, we will use two literary devices in writing. One is the traditional academic style of third person, which allows us to present ideas without making personal comments about them. This helps us to present the thinking of others in their own terms and also to adhere to the rigors of academic scholarship. The other device is the narrative style of first and second person. Sometimes we will make explicit where we are giving voice to our joint personal views (*we*) or the views of just one of us (*I*). When writing in the first person, we specify our initials (EC or LF). For example, it seems to us rather awkward and artificial to write "the authors believe . . ." It is more direct simply to say "we believe." We include occasional autobiographical accounts of our personal and professional experiences for two reasons: to illustrate how we strive to integrate spirituality into our lives and work and to expose aspects of our backgrounds and assumptions that shape this book and should be available for critical scrutiny. We hope this encourages you to work out your own integration between the personal and professional aspects of your lives.

Respecting Spiritual Diversity

The social work profession promotes appreciation for all aspects of human diversity. Diversity is often discussed in the social work literature in terms of race, ethnicity, social class, gender, sexual orientation, and disability.

The Council on Social Work Education's (CSWE) curriculum policy statement also identifies that it is important that content on religious and spiritual diversity be included in education (Russel, 1998). Both the NASW and CSWE are opposed to discrimination on the basis of religion or creed. Many different religious or spiritual perspectives shape American society, debate about social policy, and clients' personal beliefs about mental health and social justice (Bullis, 1996; Canda, 1988b & c; Canda & Chambers, 1994; Loewenberg, 1989; Logan, 1990; Lum, 1996; Netting, Thibault & Ellor, 1990; Ortiz, 1991). Genuine respect is more than just tolerance. Respect for diversity should extend to a genuine appreciation for diversity and competence to respond to the diverse backgrounds and situations of clients.

This raises a difficult issue. Some religions propose that their way is the only true and correct way. From these exclusivist religious perspectives, religious diversity is seen as a problem. Variations from their beliefs are viewed as heresies, dangerous deceptions, or at best misguided views that should be missionized and corrected. There are exclusivist versions of all religions, sometimes referred to as militant fundamentalism. From an exclusivist view, the only acceptable kind of social work would be one that is sectarian, based on one's own religious beliefs.

This is not our position. We are committed to inclusiveness in spiritually sensitive social work, and we encourage interreligious dialogue and cooperation for human service. Exclusivists may not be comfortable with this, but we submit our position for consideration by all. Perhaps our greatest challenge is how we can be inclusive of exclusivist spiritual perspectives. For example, there has recently been a debate within the CSWE about whether social work programs in certain religiously affiliated schools should be able to apply for an exemption from the policy on nondiscrimination against people on the basis of sexual orientation (Parr & Jones, 1996; Van Soest, 1996). We do not support any form of discrimination against gay, lesbian, bisexual, or transgendered people. Nor do we support restriction of religious freedom or discrimination on the basis of religion or creed. Our approach is to encourage direct discussion and debate in a respectful manner about such contentious issues and dilemmas. This book will raise difficult dilemmas, and it may provoke as many questions as answers. It will present a variety of spiritual perspectives and contrasting religious views on particular topics. It will provide an introduction to contrasting spiritual perspectives that are influential in American social work and consider also international issues. And it will suggest ways to engage in dialogue and cross-cultural, interreligious experiences.

Being Reflective

In writing this book, we have engaged in a long process of self-reflection in order to link our own personal and professional experiences and to cull out implications for spiritually sensitive practice. In doing so, we changed. Personal engagement in learning is a transformative experience that requires reflectivity, the practice of introspective self-reflection about how one's inner life reflects on the outer world. The capacity for reflection is necessary for the development of insight into self and others and to form empathic and intuitive connection with others.

Our responsibility is to present this book in a way that can encourage and catalyze readers' continuing development. This can be successful only if there is a willingness by each reader to approach the reading of this book as an opportunity for growth. We have written this book with a format that encourages reflectivity in the reader. We include our own self-reflections in autobiographical passages and provide exercises for the reader to engage in self-reflection in response to the text. And we wish to offer here some suggestions for how to read this book in a reflective manner.

The prerequisite for reflective reading is silence—that is, quieting in order to know oneself, the inner stirrings of the heart, and the discerning wisdom of the intellect. This is the starting place for the cultivation of intuition and practice wisdom that makes social work an empathic connection with clients rather than mere technical manipulation and rule enforcement (Keefe, 1996; Krill, 1990; Luoma, 1998). Intuition and practice wisdom involve the ability to respond spontaneously at just the right moment in just the right way to a client. This requires clear awareness focused in the moment.

Reflective silence does not necessarily require absence of external noise or internal mental chatter, but it does require a willingness to become introspective, to "get centered," and to pay gentle consistent attention to oneself and one's situation. The Vietnamese Buddhist meditation teacher, Thich Nhat Hanh (1987, p. 14), referred to this as mindfulness:

> Keep your attention focused on the work, be alert and ready to handle ably and intelligently any situation which may arise—this is mindfulness. There is no reason why mindfulness should be different from focusing all one's attention on one's work, to be alert and to be using one's best judgment. During the moment one is consulting, resolving, and dealing with whatever arises, a calm heart and self-control are necessary if one is to obtain good results. . . .

Mindfulness is the miracle by which we master and restore ourselves. . . . It is the miracle which can call back in a flash our dispersed mind and restore it to wholeness so that we can live each moment of life.

We invite you to pause for a moment before each sitting to read this book. Take a gentle breath, relax, center yourself, and prepare to read with a quiet and clear mind.

Mindful, reflective reading opens the possibility that we will discover passages that seem to jump out at us, as if they were meant just for us. It allows us to reflect sincerely and intelligently on the implications of the reading for our personal and professional development. In effect, mindful reading can become a dialogue between ourselves and the text in which we discover important insights about ourselves and our work with clients.

This is quite contrary to the usual academic way of reading. Often when we read a book for purposes of academic study, we read as if we are doing a weighty chore. We sift the text for facts, analyze and categorize, and try to pick out what we need to know for a class test or a professional licensing exam. Analytical reading is necessary but not sufficient for growth. If we read with brain but no heart, then we can master the facts but miss the implications for our own personal and professional transformation.

The Neo-Confucian tradition of East Asia emphasizes scholarship as a means of cultivating wisdom to apply to social service. The traditional Chinese concept of mind (*shim*) combines the Western ideas of thinking mind and feeling heart. The Korean Neo-Confucian sage (lived 1501–1570), T'oegye, said "What is the meaning of 'thought'? It is seeking the matter out in one's own mind-and-heart and having a personal experience and grasp of it" (quoted in Kalton, 1988, p. 108). Kalton (1988) summarized the Neo-Confucian ideal of learning this way: "This reminds us once again that learning in this context is a spiritual project, and the essential exercise of the mind is not speculative knowledge but personal transformation through a profound personal understanding and appropriation of what is studied" (p. 108).

Reflectivity requires discerning the difference between our own projected biases, fantasies, and assumptions and the world as it is given to us. Reflection offers both promise of insight and peril of distortion (Canda, 1995b). Consider the following metaphor:

As a young boy, I was both fascinated and frightened by windows at night. From within a lit room, I liked to peer into a window, and gaze at the surreal mixture of reflections from within and outside the room. Sometimes, when glimpsing such a window out of the corner of my eye, I thought I saw a terrifying face and my heart would skip a beat. As I'd draw closer to investigate, I would discover that I was frightened by my own face, distorted by the mix of reflections. I realized this was an illusion, but I also felt there really might be something menacing lurking there. This was an important lesson, because it alerted me to be wary of distorted reflections of myself, seen in the faces and actions of clients and students, loved ones and acquaintances. What is menacing is not the reflection itself, but rather my mistaking the reflection for reality. Just like the dark window reflection, our perception of clients is often a confused mix of their reality and our reflections. (p. 3)

This book presents beliefs and helping practices from many spiritual perspectives. It advocates strongly for particular values and questions others. It raises controversies and dilemmas. There is surely something here for everyone to feel agreement or disagreement, comfort or discomfort, as well as confusion and clarity. In reflective reading, your reaction is not a matter of right or wrong. It is crucial first to be aware of your reaction. Second, you need to reflect on where the reaction comes from. A reaction is as much a result of what one brings to the reading as whatever is in the book. So pay gentle but keen attention to your reactions. What do they tell you about your own personal history, professional experience, biases, assumptions, spiritual beliefs and commitments, strengths and limitations? Each strong reaction, favorable or unfavorable, is a message to pay attention to whatever it is in oneself that gives rise to the reaction. When this is understood, the third step is to consider what the reaction implies for continued personal and professional growth. If a limitation of attitude, skill, or knowledge is identified, what can one do to correct the limitation and move beyond it? If a strength or resource within oneself or the environment is newly identified or the appreciation is heightened, how can it be used more effectively?

Supporting Strengths and Empowerment

We support a strengths perspective on social work in general (Saleebey, 1997) and spirituality in social work in particular. Strengths-based social work means that people are viewed as whole beings, with inherent capacities for resilience and creativity. When they seek help for problems, they are never reduced to those problems. Rather, problems are just one facet of their situation, not the defining facet. Problems are opportunities for growth and challenges for creativity. For example, if a person has a severe mental illness, the illness is one aspect of his or her situation. It is not the whole person. The client should never be reduced to a pathology label or negative expectations that come along with it. To define a person or situation only in terms of problems, defects, or deficiencies is to dehumanize that person and to dull our own awareness of the strengths, resources, and resiliencies the person has used successfully to deal with having a disability. These inner strengths and environmental resources need to be the focus of helping in order to support the actualization of people's goals and aspirations rather than merely trying to repair what seems to be broken.

We also believe that empowerment is an important complement to the strengths perspective (Gutierrez, 1990, 1994; Lee, 1994; Solomon, 1987). Empowerment requires that people become aware of obstacles to individual hopes and collective justice. This awareness then becomes shared with others in solidarity, so that mutual support and collective wisdom and action can lead to proactive response. Action for personal and social change is the next step. Awareness is not enough. If a person ventilates painful feelings about injustice, the feelings of hurt and anger may dissipate, but the relief is temporary; there is no lasting benefit. So empowerment requires developing and implementing an action plan for change in oneself and the environment.

Reflectivity is a crucial ingredient for identifying strengths and empowering action. This is why we suggested in the previous section that readers should engage in a reflective process of reading that moves from self-awareness of strengths, limitations, and aspirations to actions supporting personal and professional growth. We also encourage you to discuss your growth process with family, friends, and colleagues, to the extent it is comfortable and secure to do so. Make the most of any spiritual support group or religious community in which you already participate, or develop new ones. Work out explicit plans for further implementation of learning in social work practice. Where obstacles or injustices are identified, perceive them as challenges and opportunities for creative transformative action.

In writing this book, we have focused on the strengths and resources available by incorporating spirituality and religion into social work practice. But we also consider the obstacles and pitfalls that they may involve for people. As with any other aspect of human life, religion and spirituality can be used to support or impede individual fulfillment and social justice. I (EC) once visited the Catholic basilica in Mexico City. For me, this basilica was an intense symbol of the complexity of religion and spirituality. The beautiful religious artwork and architecture were inspiring. The images of Christ's compassion and the gentleness of his mother, Mary, especially as Our Lady of Guadalupe, patron saint of the Americas, illustrate virtues to which I aspire. But at the same time, there is something terrible about the history of the basilica. The guide explained that it was built on the ruins of Aztec sacred temples, destroyed by the conquistadors, in order to show the might and victory of the Spanish colonialists and their church. The very people who were subjugated by this colonialization were forced to build this church on the remains of their desecrated sites. The beauty and grandeur of the basilica cannot be denied. And neither can the inhumanity and injustice of its origin. Both of these qualities coexist in the Catholic church and pose a dilemma for the Catholic faithful, as the contemplative activist monk, Thomas Merton, pointed out (1968). As a member of the Catholic tradition myself, I must confront this paradox openly and honestly.

In various ways, we all face this dilemma. This is not unique to the Catholic church. I have seen similar situations in every religious tradition and spiritual movement I have explored, East and West. Within ourselves and our world there are religious and spiritual experiences, practices, and institutions that provide great solace, strength, beauty, wisdom, and empowerment. But within us and our traditions there are also the harmful manifestations of religion and spirituality. In this book, we acknowledge both, seeking to actualize the strengths and resources of people and institutions, while striving to transform problems and obstacles into challenges and opportunities for working through to ever greater levels of spiritual fulfillment and justice.

Taking a Holistic Perspective

In social work, we often say that we wish to understand the whole person-in-the-environment. It is necessary to learn about the roles of religion and spirituality if we are to have such an understanding. In our conceptualization of spirituality, we will address the inextricable interrelationship between spirituality and the biological, psychological, and social dimensions of human experience.

We also wish to engage the whole person in the process of learning about spirituality and social work. For this reason, we present features of this book that engage the thinking, feeling, sensing, intuitive, and social relational aspects of the reader. We encourage analytical, critical thinking. We evoke feelings through the use of images, metaphors, and self-reflection exercises. We provide guidance for practices that help to cultivate intuition, such as meditation and empathic relating with clients. We examine how spirituality and religion are involved with the wider social and ecological environment. We also consider how various spiritual perspectives understand the nature of ultimate reality, in theistic, nontheistic, animistic, or atheistic terms and what are the implications for human service.

A COMPARATIVE EDUCATIONAL APPROACH

These five principles lead us to use a comparative approach for education about spirituality and religion in social work (Canda, 1989a). Comparative education means examining similarities and differences between perspectives from a variety of vantage points in order to deepen insights. We employ four levels of vantage points. The first vantage point involves examination of different theoretical views of *religion and spirituality as general or universal aspects* of human experience and culture. For example, in Chapter 2, we will consider various conceptions of spirituality and religion, from many different disciplines.

In the second vantage point, we turn from broad generalizations about religion and spirituality to *particular religious and nonreligious expressions of spirituality* as they affect social work practice. For example, in Part II we consider how various contrasting religious and nonsectarian spiritual perspectives provide frameworks for social service. Exploration of these contrasts will provide an introduction to the variety of spiritual expressions and give the reader an opportunity to explore his or her own reactions to them.

We step back further for a third vantage point. We shift from both general theory and particular accounts of spiritual views to examine their *underlying assumptions, strengths, and weaknesses* and how these relate to the experiences, beliefs, and behaviors of students, educators, practitioners, and clients. For example, feminist analysis can examine the patriarchal biases and limitations of religious traditions, in the views of external opponents and faithful adherents. Or we can apply Abraham Maslow's critique of the ways religions promote or impede human development (Maslow, 1968). Our purpose is not to denigrate any belief or to try to prove the superiority of any religious view. Rather, it is to help us reflect respectfully yet critically. For believers in a particular tradition, this can lead to a more sophisticated, mature, and articulated faith (Fowler, 1984, 1996). For both believers and nonbelievers, it encourages the development of new cautions and appreciations, so that the practitioner can be prepared to think carefully about whatever issues clients may bring up.

A fourth vantage point takes a further step back. It looks at the assumptions, values, implications for practice, and communication dynamics that *underlie the reflective process at all levels.* We offer suggestions for experiential and self-reflective exercises that promote insight into the source of personal reactions to material in the book. We encourage careful attention to communication dynamics when this book is used within courses or workshops. For example, in a class discussion, students and educators can reflect on their own assumptions and reactions, where they come from in their personal and professional development, what the implications are for supporting or hampering practice, and how further personal and professional growth can be encouraged to overcome the limitations of assumptions.

PREVIEW OF CHAPTERS

This book is organized in three parts. Part I (Chapters 1–2) presents central values and concepts for spiritually sensitive practice. Part II (Chapters 3–5) explores diverse spiritual perspectives on service and their implications for human service and social work practice. Part III (Chapters 6–9) offers practical guidelines, strategies, and activities for spiritually sensitive social work in action.

Chapter 1 explores fundamental values and ethical principles to guide spiritually sensitive practice. Chapter 2 offers two conceptual models of spirituality and a response to debates about spirituality in our profession.

Chapter 3 reviews the history of spiritual diversity and related controversies in the United States and the social work profession. Chapter 4 presents an introduction to six religious traditions of service: Buddhist, Christian, Hindu, Islamic, Judaic, and shamanistic. Chapter 5 introduces nonsectarian existentialist and transpersonal spiritual perspectives on service. It also compare all eight perspectives and offers suggestions for engaging in dialogue across spiritual perspectives in social work.

Chapter 6 explains how to create a spiritually sensitive context in the helping relationship and in human service organizations. Chapter 7 provides a basis for understanding and assessing spiritual development of individuals throughout the life span. Chapter 8 offers further guidelines to plan and implement practice that supports spiritual transformation and ethical use of religious or spiritual support systems and activities. Chapter 9 provides detailed practical suggestions for employing prayer, meditation, and ritual in social work practice. It also considers the relevance of spiritually sensitive practice for macro social systems and social justice.

This book raises profound spiritual questions in religious and nonreligious guise. They are questions that every social worker must face. So this book is not just about a specialized area of practice or theory; it is about the nature of the helping situation itself. Every social worker is involved in a spiritual journey, in private life as well as in the course of professional work. This book is about that journey, that way of compassion.

EXERCISES

i. How Well Does This Fit?

The introduction presented five principles that guided our approach to writing the book. Reflect back on your reactions to these principles. How do they fit your own views? Did you have any strong reactions of agreement or disagreement? Whatever your reactions, consider what it is about yourself that predisposes you to have these reactions. What does this indicate about your personal experience, professional training, cultural background, and religious or spiritual perspective? Based on these reactions, become aware of what your expectations are for the rest of this book. Do you expect to enjoy the book? Do you expect to feel a sense of conflict with the authors' approach? Finally, put all these expectations aside and promise yourself that you will read with an open mind.

ii. Journaling About Spirituality and Social Work

When quiet time and attention are set aside for regular self-reflection, personal and professional growth can be enhanced significantly. One method for doing this is to keep a growth journal. Journaling provides a format for dialoguing with yourself about your reactions to the reading, insights, and implications about spiritual growth and actions you take to support growth. A journal can be informal and unstructured, consisting of a free-flowing dialogue with yourself. This has the advantage of spontaneity and flexibility. But some structure can also encourage regularity, consistency, and self-discipline. Following is a suggested structure for journaling in response to reading this book. The structure should provide consistency, but it should not hamper creativity. So feel free to modify it as needed.

The main purpose of this format is to encourage systematic self-reflection that moves all the way from awareness of reactions to actions taken to support growth. It is important to start with an accurate reading of the material, but reflective journaling is not just a matter of restating what was said. Reflective journaling incorporates intellectual analysis, but it should not be limited to detached, unfeeling thinking. Mind and heart and action should all be joined.

After reading each chapter, relax and center yourself. Take a few minutes to page back through and recall your reactions, especially reactions of strong agreement or disagreement or any strong feelings and opinions. Identify which aspects of the chapter struck you as having the most significance for your personal and professional growth. If you made notes or underlined text, review those to refresh your memory. Then take fifteen to thirty minutes to write a commentary about your reactions and implications for growth.

A fictitious example will be given for each step. Since this example is fictitious, there is not as much personal detail as would be likely in a real journal entry. Also, there will be great variation of style and content for each person. Find your own level and style of comfort with this journal process. Adapt the following format:

1. Title of the chapter, date read, and date of journal entry

2. Insight in the Reading

State at least one idea contained in the reading. Choose this as your focus for the journal entry. Be sure this is an accurate summary of what you read. Keep it brief—not more than about 50 words.

> *Example:* In the preface, the authors mentioned that one of the greatest challenges to an inclusive approach to spirituality in social work is how to include people who have an exclusive viewpoint and do not wish to dialogue or are not open to change.

3. Self-Reflection

Explain in detail how this is significant to you. Include the following levels of reflection.

    a) What was your immediate reaction at the time of reading? What is your reaction as you think back on it now?

> *Example:* When I first read this, I wondered if they were talking about people like me, a committed Christian. I felt angry and defensive, as though they were insulting me. Now that I think about it, I recall they said rigid, exclusivist thinking could apply to any value

perspective or ideology, so they weren't singling Christians out. But I realize that my feelings are easily hurt when the subject of religion or spirituality comes up in social work settings.

b) Explain what it is about you that predisposes you to this reaction. For example, what is the relevance of this insight to your personal and professional interests; special strengths and talents; any prejudices, biases, or lack of knowledge; significant faith or value commitments; religious upbringing or nonreligious upbringing; cultural heritage and patterns?

Example: I became a born-again Christian four years ago. This made a tremendous impact on changing my life for the better. And after my conversion, I felt called to follow Christ's example by serving others in social work. But I've often been stereotyped and insulted by other social workers as a right-wing fundamentalist. They imply that I shouldn't be a social worker if I have such a strong Christian commitment.

c) Identify specific strengths and limitations of your personal and professional development that are revealed by this self-reflection.

Example: My Christian commitment and support from my church are important sources of strength for me. They give me the energy and motivation to live a life of service. But many of my fellow social workers don't share the same beliefs as me. I can see that this difference is sometimes hard to get past, for both them and me. I understand why I feel defensive, considering my past hurts. But I shouldn't let this get in the way of communicating well with others. I need to figure out how to build on the strength of my faith and also how to join this with the values and ways of communicating within the social work profession.

d) For each strength or limitation identified, list an implication for further growth.

Example: My strength is my faith. I need to explore more how to join my faith with social work.

My limitation is my defensiveness. If someone does question my faith or even criticize my views, I need to learn how to relax and respond clearly. I need to learn how to listen to their concerns with empathy and learn from their position. I also need to learn how to encourage them to listen to me. This way I could have more of a dialogue, and we could learn from each other. This, after all, is consistent with my commitment to Christian love of neighbor and to the social work professional principle of "starting where the person is."

  e) For each implication, list a specific action that you could take to support your growth.

Example: For the strength—I could join the North American Association of Christian Social Workers and attend their meetings. I could also read articles and books about the history of Christian social work and the professional dilemmas and conflicts that sometimes arise around spirituality and social work. I could also learn about a different religious approach to social work, and talk with social workers of this religion, to help me broaden my perspective.

For the limitation—When I meet other Christian social workers, we could form a support group to discuss our experiences in social work, positive and negative. This would provide interesting conversation, mutual support, and an opportunity to work through my feelings. When I meet with the social worker from another religious background, we could discuss how we each try to connect our spiritualities to social work and find not only the differences but also the commonalities between us.

  f) Select at least one action that you commit to carrying out within the next month. Make a promise to yourself in writing to do this. Make a plan for how it can be accomplished.

Example: I will join NACSW within the next two weeks. I will find out when the next regional conference is and attend it. I will also invite my colleague who practices conservative religious Judaism to join me for lunch next week. We've already developed a friendly working relationship and gone to lunch a few times. But the next time, I will ask if it would be all right to talk about our religious backgrounds and how we relate that to social work.

  g) After this action is carried out, create an entry in your journal that discusses what happened, how you felt about it, and what you gained. If new areas for growth are identified from this, repeat the process of taking new actions and reporting to yourself about the results.

Example: I joined NACSW and eagerly await the conference scheduled for next month. I already read a book it published on church-based social work (Garland, 1992). I felt affirmed to find out about the ways social work can be linked to church settings. I am excited to learn more about this.

This afternoon, I had lunch with my Jewish friend. She was surprised that I brought up the topic of religion, but she said she was glad. We had a good conversation. Although we have different faith commitments, we also discovered many commonalities of belief and experience as religiously committed social workers. We plan to discuss this more in the near future.

PART I

CENTRAL VALUES AND CONCEPTS
for
SPIRITUALLY SENSITIVE
SOCIAL WORK

CHAPTER ONE

COMPASSION, THE CALL TO SERVICE, AND ETHICAL PRINCIPLES FOR SOCIAL WORK

> Strive constantly to serve the welfare of the world; by devotion to selfless work one attains the supreme goal of life.
>
> The Bhagavad Gita 3:19, Hinduism
> (trans. Easwaran, 1985).

INTRODUCTION

Recently, much of the world mourned the deaths of two influential women: Diana, princess of Wales, and Mother Teresa of Calcutta. These two women were vastly different. Princess Diana came from a family of privilege and entered the royal corridors of wealth and prestige. She led a life mixed with personal confusion, triumphs, and finally tragic early demise. Mother Teresa came from an impoverished Albanian family, became a Catholic nun, and chose to live with the poorest in her adopted country of India. She died as an elder, among the poorest of the poor, as she wished. But what these two women shared, and what brought them together on occasion, was a commitment to service. Each used her different life circumstances as a medium to help those in need and to help the world see the beauty, strength, and dignity of those who too often are discounted: the homeless; people dying from AIDS, starvation, and neglect; victims of domestic abuse, disease, and land mines; the rejected of society.

Despite controversies and ambiguities surrounding these two women's beliefs and actions, millions of people around the world were moved deeply at their loss. These women's commitment to service and their compassion made them worthy of praise and idealization in the eyes

3

of many. Something in each of us resonates with understanding and appreciation when we encounter genuine human compassion.

As we grow in a sense of connection and responsibility with other people, other beings, and the ground of being, we search for ways to help and heal ourselves and the world. All religious traditions and all people struggle with experiences of suffering, mortality, and death. And all seek means of remedy and transcendence. *Compassion* literally means "passion with others." It is commiseration in empathy with others. It is solidarity of response to suffering.

Spiritually sensitive social work is an expression of compassion. Dass and Gorman (1985) said that when we let this natural compassion express in our work, there is a benefit to ourselves and to others: "The reward, the real grace, of conscious service, then, is the opportunity not only to help relieve suffering but to grow in wisdom, experience greater unity, and have a good time while we're doing it" (p. 16).

Princess Diana and Mother Teresa were helpers from the heart rather than professional social workers. Their lives remind us, as professionally trained social workers, to reflect back on the fundamental humanity and compassion that were within us before the imposition of our formal rules, roles, theories, eligibility requirements, diagnostic schemes, and professional boundaries. By returning to this, we can revitalize our service as professionals.

In this chapter, we explore spirituality more as a matter of heart—the deepest motivations of people that lead us to a path of service and the symbols of compassion that inform service in religious traditions. Finally, we use these insights about compassion to elaborate upon ethical principles for spiritually sensitive social work practice.

THE VIRTUE OF COMPASSION IN PROFESSIONAL SOCIAL WORK

The Profession's Historical Commitment to Compassion

Social work is a normative profession, guided by explicit values, morals, and a code of ethics (Reid & Popple, 1992). Insofar as moral and value systems constitute one of the main components of spirituality, we can say that social work is fundamentally a spiritual profession—one that sets its reason for existence and its highest priorities on service (Siporin, 1982, 1986). Core professional morals, values, and ethics are stated in nonsectarian terms without reference to concepts of the sacred or divinity. However, some social workers link their personal religious values to these professional values (Brackney & Watkins, 1983; Coughlin, 1970). Further, Jewish and Christian values of love of neighbor, charitable service, and justice directly influenced the formation of the profession's values early in our history (Constable, 1983; Leiby, 1985; Siporin, 1983). Our value system is promulgated through professional education of students and enforced through procedures of professional certification, licensure, and ethical adjudication. This demonstrates a very high level of organizational commitment to moral reflection and action. Indeed, the social work profession can be considered to be a nonsectarian spiritual community.

The preamble to the current National Association of Social Workers' Code of Ethics* (1996, p. 1) states:

> The primary mission of the social work profession is to enhance human well-being and help meet the basic human needs of all people, with particular attention to the needs and empowerment of people who are vulnerable, oppressed, and living in poverty. . . . The mission of social work is rooted in a set of core values. These core values, embraced by social workers throughout the profession's history, are the foundation of social work's unique purpose and perspective:
>
> * service
> * social justice
> * dignity and worth of the person
> * importance of human relationships
> * integrity
> * competence

This sounds reminiscent of liberation theology, minus the Christian theological language. This mission, the core values, and the ethical standards that flow from them require social workers to move beyond the bounds of egoism, prejudice, and ethnocentrism (Siporin, 1983). They even require putting the needs and interests of clients and the general welfare of society above one's own needs, as in support for client self-determination. They mandate that people are regarded as having inherent dignity and worth. They call for professionals to place a priority on the interests of the oppressed and to enhance social justice. All of these commitments imply

---

*NASW Code of Ethics (Ethical Principles). Copyright ©1996, National Association of Social Workers, Inc.

a stance of compassion with a transpersonal, that is, ego-transcending, orientation, a profound and challenging spiritual ideal.

Early in the history of the profession, under the influence of religious charitable organizations and the Charity Organization Society, the religious and spiritual implications of this were explicit (Reamer, 1992). Indeed, there was a struggle between different views of compassion or charity. Unfortunately, sometimes charity was (and is) associated with condescending pity, moralistic judgmentalism, and paternalistic control. How far this is from its biblical meaning as love (*caritas,* Latin): "Love is patient and kind; love is not jealous or boastful; it is not arrogant or rude. Love does not insist on its own way; it is not irritable or resentful; it does not rejoice at wrong, but rejoices in the right. Love bears all things, believes all things, hopes for all things, endures all things" (1 Cor. 13:4–7, Revised Standard Version).

Thirty years ago, Salomon (1967) cautioned that social workers should not abandon a moral view of life but also should not fall into moralistic prejudice and judgmentalism. Rather, she recommended that we relate with clients through a spiritual encounter of whole person to whole person, so that both worker and client experience change and healing. Siporin (1982) said that we need to regain moral vision and idealism, whether expressed in religious or secular terms, that combine concern for individual and social well-being. Constable (1983) summarized the ideal as reciprocity between values of social justice, freedom, and opportunity for choice by individuals, and unconditional love and mutual respect.

Reamer (1992) warned about the lures of prestige, wealth, and power or simply a survival-based defensive emphasis on interprofessional competition and turf protection. These lures have grown in the past forty years as the profession has gained in social acceptance and is pressured by federal and state policies, insurance reimbursement regulations, and economic incentives from private clinical practice. In a religious context, these might be called temptations. So Reamer said, "To reclaim its enlightened view of the public good, social work must once again resemble a (secular) calling. One serves—primarily because one cares deeply about matters of social justice—those who are disadvantaged and oppressed, and those who are at risk. Gratification is primarily derived from knowing that one has responded to one of life's principal duties to others" (p. 28).

Social Workers' Personal Commitments to Service

Although many reasons motivate service (Coles, 1993), those who make a commitment for a long time and are able to avoid the pitfalls of cynicism and self-promotion are likely to have a compassionate orientation. This makes sense not only because of the professional values social workers espouse formally, but also because of the personal reasons that many social workers share but seldom discuss openly. The personal reasons stem from why each of us has been motivated to join the profession of social work. Why should we commit ourselves to a profession often derided in media portrayals? Why are we often willing to work long hours in stressful conditions with caseloads beyond belief? What motivates us to a path of service when we live in a society driven largely by consumerism and glorification of economic or political power? We invite readers to reflect on your own experience and to consider how it matches this discussion of social work as a vocation expressing the virtue of compassion. Compare the following vignettes with your experience.

I grew up in a family whose love embraced not only each member, but extended also to the poor and the oppressed. My mother is a school social worker who works with urban youth, mostly immigrants and refugees, and my father is a physician who spends part of his time working at a free clinic. Their example inspired me to pursue a career in social work.

My older brother died from AIDS two years ago. He was a gay activist, well known in his community for championing the rights of gay and lesbian people. As he drew close to death, his courage and continued caring for others inspired me and many other people. Although he was severely ill physically, he had a remarkable sense of spiritual vitality. His family and friends offered much support, but it really seemed more like he was helping us. I decided that I would like to carry on his example by becoming a social worker, with a special interest in hospice programs.

As my meditation practice deepened, I found a quality of peace and clarity that soothed my griefs and pains and gave me the capacity to respond to life's challenges with greater energy and compassion. I realized that my own struggles are mirrored in the struggles of all people and all living beings. In my Buddhist tradition, we take a vow "to save all beings from suffering." In some small way, I hope that my practice as a social worker can help others to find their way from suffering to peace and joy.

When I was a teenager, my parents divorced. My father was abusive and alcoholic. Our family fractured under the strain. At the time, I felt my life was coming to an end. But support from members of my Christian church helped me get through it. Eventually, I found a source of inner strength and resilience that helped me to put the broken pieces of my life back together in a way that is healthier than I ever had as a child. There is something mysterious to me about this "resurrection" experience, but my religious teachings and community support made it possible. Now I would like to help other people find meaning and resiliency through difficult times.

These stories, though fictional, are similar to the accounts we have often heard from social workers in private conversations, class discussions, and autobiographical statements within applications to enter social work programs. Some surveys of social workers show not only that we are more likely than the general public to have experienced abuse, mental disorders, or substance abuse within our families of origin, but also that many of us have seen a way through this, a way toward personal recovery and service for others (Black, Jeffreys & Hartley, 1993). Sometimes a life event or situation wakes a person up to the prevalence of human suffering and generates a drive to help relieve it, not only in self but also in others. This may be something positive, like inspiration from loving parents who demonstrate a commitment to public service. It might be a situation that is painful at first, like a crisis that shatters the foundations of meaning and security but leads eventually to positive personal growth. Some people come to this awareness through a gentle inner stirring, a gradual heightening of awareness and empathy. A person may develop a spiritually sensitive approach to social work when a keen realization of suffering and the possibility of transformation awakens the motivation to help others.

Some of us use religious ideas and metaphors to explain this vocation; some do not. But we expect that this theme of being awakened from egocentrism and defeatism and then feeling called to a path of service and justice may not be uncommon among social workers. This is a spiritual developmental process that puts us in touch with our deepest insights into the meaning and purpose of life. Thus, we respond to a calling. In traditional Christian and Jewish terms, a vocation is a stirring of the heart by the divine to go beyond the limits of the little ego and ordinary social conventions in order to follow a more profound way of life. A vocation is a use of one's talents, abilities, and assets in a life's work that is consistent with God's will (Canda, 1990a).

Social work in its best sense can be considered a spiritual vocation. This does not mean that all social workers follow the beliefs of the Judeo-Christian tradition or that they are religious. Rather, it means that there is an awareness of suffering and the possibility of transformation. It means that there is a motive of compassion to work together with other people to help us overcome obstacles and achieve our aspirations. And it means that spiritually sensitive social workers practice unconditional positive regard for clients and hope in the possibilities of resiliency, reconciliation, and realization of social justice. Of course, it is difficult to "walk this talk."

In a qualitative study, eighteen social work scholars discussed the values that motivated their work in the profession (Canda, 1990c). The interviewees identified themselves as being influenced by seven spiritual perspectives, which were combined for some people: atheist, Christian, existentialist, Jewish, shamanic, theistic humanist, and Zen Buddhist. Three main motivations were expressed: a sense of a mandate to serve, a personal desire to promote social justice, and a quest for personal fulfillment.

Ten respondents said they had a feeling that they are mandated to serve. Some derived this sense of mandate from learned religious or cultural values, such as the Zen Buddhist commitment to help all beings attain enlightenment, Jewish community values for mutual support and social justice, Christian gospel values of love and service, and traditional First Nations Indigenous values of cooperation, sharing, and mutual helping. But some added that this mandate came from a transpersonal or divine source. For example, a Zen practitioner said that compassion and an imperative to help others arises naturally from meditative experiences of one's interconnectedness with other beings. Two Jewish respondents said that they felt mandated to serve out of the awareness that God appointed humanity as custodians of the earth. Four Christians said that they felt a sense of calling from God, sometimes from an early age. One respondent put it this way: "I am impelled not by my own volition, not on making a conscious choice, but that is the way the Lord wants, to use me" (Canda, 1990c, p. 12). Many respondents mentioned that they had a strong personal concern for people who are distressed and oppressed and that this impelled them to action.

All of the respondents said that their experience of personal fulfillment from service motivated them to persevere. Personal satisfactions derived from meeting religious and cultural expectations for service, viewing the beneficial changes in clients' lives as a result of service, and having a career that provides sustenance for their own families. In the experience of these social work scholars, compassionate service creates a situation of mutual benefit for themselves, their clients, and the larger society.

Mitsuko Nakashima (1995), a Japanese-American hospice social worker, gave a detailed account of how her life experiences in Japan and the United States and her family's incorporation of Buddhist, Shinto, and Confucian philosophies and rituals helped direct her into the path of social work:

> I found myself being fascinated with the concept of death and dying in my late teens. My aunt died unexpectedly and soon afterward my grandmother suffered a fatal injury in a car accident. The idea of death, which had been a remote concept to me, rose up to face me. At that time, I already had a belief that a human soul survives the physical body and reincarnates. However, a big question arose: for what purpose do we reincarnate? . . . From my cross-cultural experiences and study in Japan and the United States, I saw that as people grew older and prepared themselves for death, they faced the same kind of challenges despite cultural differences. Many people died feeling that their lives were unfulfilled. . . . Resolution of life issues requires a great deal of introspection in which an individual reviews life experiences and draws meanings from them. The degree of acceptance of one's life determines how peaceful one can feel. Approaching human development solely through consideration of physical, emotional, and social aspects (in most of my social work education) seemed incomplete to me. I believe that spirituality is a nucleus of human existence that directs our thoughts and actions to seek a sense of peace and power by connection to the supreme and holy source of existence, whatever it is called by individuals. . . . Hospice work interested me immediately when I learned about its existence. Because of its regard for the crucial role of spirituality in facilitating the well-being of a person, I intuitively felt that my quest for deepening spiritual self-knowledge could be enriched through hospice social work. . . .

. . . Through hospice work, I am not only helping clients. I am also preparing myself to die the death that will come someday. (pp. 18–19, 27) (Used with permission of publisher.)

Sarah Sloan Kreutziger (1995) told the story of how her journey in and out of and back into Christianity influenced her path into social work:

I am a "heart" more than a "head" person. I am a member of the United Methodist Church, a religious tradition which has historically been known for its "people of the warmed heart." . . . Faith was honed on the legacy of the Social Gospel, or what John Wesley had earlier called, "practical divinity." This is the call to act on behalf of others in response to God's unrelenting love and action in our lives. . . . I had tried for a while to ignore "my Jesus thing." I went into social work because it allowed me "to save the world" as a secular missionary during a long period in early adulthood as I rotated among cycles of agnosticism/atheism/agnosticism. . . . To this day, I'm not sure when my belief in this new found knowledge (Freudianism) began to falter and become hopelessly entangled with my older religious beliefs. I suspect it occurred when I had children. Having children made it more important for me to forge connections between my past and future. Probably a large part of it occurred, however, because I was a lousy atheist in one significant way: I couldn't quit going to church. Despite my best efforts to disengage, I still loved the feel of the church: the rituals, the symbolism, the music, the people, the fellowship, the shared values, "the going into perfection." . . . As a beginning social worker, I found myself relieved, for example, when I discovered my dialysis patients were heavily involved in their churches, especially those patients from rural communities. . . . . My patients forced me to confront my own existential anxieties in order to help them face theirs. I had to move beyond my youth and inexperience and wobbly religious faith in order to fortify my practice and knowledge for their benefit. . . . Most of all, I had to learn to support the courage that comes from staying the course minute by minute, day by day, just as the accumulated wisdom of my religion teaches me to do. (pp. 29, 34) (Used with permission of publisher.)

The stories of Nakashima and Kreutziger illustrate that the call to service is a call to a continuing spiritual journey of growth. As social workers help clients, we are also being helped. The expression of empathy and compas-

sion makes us stretch ourselves into clients' worlds of suffering and meaning, and thereby our own worlds are changed. To the extent that we remain
alert to this continuing call to service as a spiritual journey, we retain a sense
of purpose, excitement, and vitality. This is a very personal and compelling
reason to keep the connection between spirituality and social work alive and
well within our practice as students, practitioners, educators, and
researchers. Mother Teresa put this simply and directly: "The fruit of love
is service. The fruit of service is peace" (Vardey, 1995, p. xxxix).

Next, we would like to tell you some stories about our own spiritual
journeys into social work. In part, this is to give you additional examples
of the routes people may take and the roles of religion and spirituality. But
also we want you to be aware of the spiritual perspectives that shape us,
because they also shape this book. You can then make better-informed
analyses of how our perspectives aid or limit the inclusive approach to
spiritual diversity that we promote. You will see that we have very different personal and professional backgrounds. In writing this book, we have
continued a dialogue that engaged the contrasts and the commonalities
of our spiritual perspectives. We hope that this exemplifies the ideals of
respect and nonjudgmentalism that are so critical in spiritually sensitive
social work.

A Call to Social Work

I (LF) became a social worker because of my religious upbringing and my
personal faith. My Lutheran heritage provided clear messages to guide
me. I feel I was put on earth to serve God and humanity and not to waste
time about it. Whatever my profession, my vocation was to do the will
of God and no excuses. ("And from every one who has been given
much shall much be required" [Luke 12:48, New American Standard
Bible].)

Although my family of origin in northern Minnesota did not have a
great deal of material goods, I knew even when I was young that I was
privileged simply because of having loving parents with a strong religious
faith, along with a large extended family who were concerned about my
spiritual, physical, and emotional well-being. I realized that there were
many who did not have their childhood needs meet. I had been given
much so I must return it . . . but how?

I saw my family's faith lived out every day unchanging, and each
Sunday that same faith was emphasized by others. I remember as a little
girl hearing my uncles or great-uncles and long-time family friends pre-

sent sermons that spoke of heeding the call of God, even if it takes you "to the remotest part of the earth" (Acts 1:8, NASB). Indeed, many of these clergy had heeded the call of God that took them to remote places. A great-uncle and his wife were missionaries in mainland China, and after the communist revolution, in Taiwan. My mother's best friend from college was a missionary teacher in China, and an uncle and his nurse wife were missionaries and health care workers in Madagascar. These clergy friends and relatives wrote often, their letters bearing colorful stamps from around the world. They brought slides of these countries when they were home for visits and told of political upheavals and cultural aspects of the people they served. They provided a rich education regarding human diversity, common human needs, and cross-cultural religious awareness.

As a child, I would sit in the church pew in a little log church that my immigrant Norwegian grandparents helped to build on the Minnesota prairie. I kept wondering when my call from God would come and what it would be. Would I too be called to go to the ends of the earth, learn another language, eat strange food, say good-bye to Mother and Father, and come back to the United States only every seven years like these clergy? I shivered at the thought!

My call came while I was attending a summer Luther League Convention, a gathering of Lutheran Youth. There was a special session on careers. Social work was defined and explained in very simple terms: a profession that works with the poor, with people of color who are experiencing prejudice, with children having problems in schools, with adults having troubled marriages and job loss, and with those with physical or mental illnesses. What became clear to me then was Christ's teaching: "Truly I say to you, to the extent that you did it [charity] to one of these brothers of Mine, even to the least of them, you did it to Me" (Matthew 25:40 NASB). I had seen the evidence of compassion in my family home and through the experiences of missionary relatives and friends. Social work provided a secular avenue for compassionate works. At twelve years old, my call came to become a social worker.

As I went on to college, I was overwhelmed by this call and wondered if I could accomplish this task as well as my heart and soul wanted. My family, my church, and my college showed me that the source of power to follow this call was not in myself ("Do not lean on your own understanding," Proverbs 3:5, NASB), but in my faith in God ("I can do all things through Christ who strengthens me," Philippians 4:13, and "Lo, I am with you always, even unto the end of the age," Matthew 28:20).

It was the experience of knowing people who lived by those words that empowered me and continues to empower me personally and professionally. Since that first awareness of a way I could show compassion to others in a vocation, I studied and trained to become a social worker. For a time, I worked in direct practice in school social work, psychiatric and medical social work, and family and marriage counseling. Then I felt a call that brought me to the academic world to teach and do research about social work, to try to instill in others the deep sense of compassion that I first felt so long ago.

An Awakening of Compassion

I (EC) was raised within a devout Roman Catholic family. My parents have attended daily mass and have been active workers, volunteers, and supporters in their parish as long as I can remember. In my family, being a Catholic meant a lifestyle and worldview much more than just performing a set of religious obligations or attending church on Sunday. I was raised to put spirituality as the first priority in life and to shape my decisions and relationships accordingly.

My family's spiritual perspective emphasized the importance of discerning a vocation through which I could use my talents for the benefit of others and for the glory of God. My parents modeled an ideal of service through their attentive child raising, their assistance for the parish, and in care for their own parents as they became ill. Through religious education from my parents and my Catholic elementary school, I also learned to respect the lives of Jesus and the saints, who gave of themselves selflessly.

I have a vivid memory of an event from the second grade of elementary school that awakened a keen sense of compassion. As a young boy, I played my share of games with violent content, from imitation war to contact competitive sports to killing bugs for fun. To that point, I had had little compunction about these things, except for occasional pangs of guilt or admonitions from my mother.

My second-grade teacher, a Catholic nun, had taken a special liking to me and made special efforts to draw me out of my shyness. What she said and did made a strong impression on me. One spring day, the classroom windows were open. Flies were buzzing around the room, providing distraction and entertainment. Some boys were trying to catch or swat the flies. Sister interrupted class not so much to complain about our misbehavior, but rather to give us a life lesson. She asked us not to harm the flies, because they were her friends. That quite surprised me—that someone could regard these ugly, irritating bugs as friends and serve as their protector. Suddenly I realized that they were living things that merit caring treatment. Sister's friendly pleading woke me up to a sense of compassion that extended out beyond my family and friends to all creatures. The biblical teaching that God made the world and saw it was good suddenly struck home deep in my heart. From that day on, I began to look at things differently.

When I was nearly sixteen years old, I had another awakening to compassion. By this time, I had begun to explore the philosophical teachings of many religious traditions, hoping they would help me understand the nature of things and the purpose of life more broadly than my Catholic upbringing. I was also quite upset about the violence of the Vietnam War, the injustices exposed by the civil rights movement, and the materialistic consumerism I saw rampant around me. Readings of Western and Eastern mystics guided me to develop a personal meditation practice, which helped me to obtain some sense of peace in the midst of this.

My Catholic high school economics teacher assigned a paper based on current economic issues. I chose to read a book by the neo-Marxist psychoanalyst, Erich Fromm, *Marx's Concept of Man* (1966). This book contained Karl Marx's economic and philosophical manuscripts. Considering that Marx was avidly opposed to conventional religions, I was surprised to find a description of communism as an ideal that well fit my sense of Christian love applied to social justice. Marx described the ideal of communism as a society in which all forms of alienation and exploitation between human beings and humans and nature would be overcome. This sounded to me like heaven on earth, or the realization of Christ's beatitudes. Ironically, Marx's words spurred me in a direction that did not fit the conventional thinking of Marxists or capitalists.

One evening, I sat in meditation on my bed, facing a portrait of the Sacred Heart of Jesus, in which Jesus is portrayed with heart exposed, aflame with compassion. I posed the question to myself, "What would it be like for every form of alienation and exploitation to be transcended?" Suddenly my mind opened to a sense of profound communion with the universe in which all separations disappeared. There was a sense of all-pervasive love.

When I pondered this experience later, it was clear to me that my life and cultural conditioning were a far cry from this ideal. I examined the problems, prejudices, and obstacles in my thinking, feelings, and relationships in order to bring myself more into congruence with this sense of union with others. Since society is characterized by many forms of separation, alienation, and suffering, I felt that I should begin to work toward actualizing this unity through social service. But I did not have any practical guidance about how to do this. I was young and confused in many ways, groping toward a light.

This sense of a call to service prompted me to begin volunteer work during summer vacations. For the last two summers of high school, I assisted autistic children in a nearby residential hospital and war veterans at a Veterans Administration psychiatric facility. I was also active in socially concerned student activism at my high school.

In college, I majored in cultural anthropology, especially anthropology of religions, in order to explore how people in various cultures have come to understand the nature of reality and the meaning of life. When I was a senior, an anthropology professor who specialized in Korean culture and religion connected me with a graduate exchange study program at Sung Kyun Kwan University in Seoul, so that I could study East Asian philosophy and religion. My Korean teachers exposed me to the 2,500-year-long Confucian tradition that links scholarly study with political action and social administration. For Confucian scholars, learning is for the sake of cultivating personal wisdom and rectifying society. After fifteen months of study in Korea, I returned to the United States to complete a master's degree in religious studies, focusing on East Asian religions.

Throughout these studies, I saw a common theme among religious traditions East and West. All identified suffering as a fundamental problematic feature of human existence, and all recommended remedies for this problem—some form of helping, healing, salvation, or enlightenment. But it struck me as odd that in the academic study of religion, few scholars went beyond description and analysis of religious phenomena to apply these various approaches to helping in direct service.

After a year of discernment, I realized that the study of religions was not sufficient to meet my calling to a life of service. For this reason, I changed fields to social work. But throughout my M.S.W. and Ph.D. programs and my direct practice, I brought the cross-cultural study of religion and spirituality into social work.

Social work has been a wonderful way for me to link my spiritual call to service with a profession and tradition of service-oriented scholarship. But I found that many other social workers were struggling with a similar desire to link their spiritual vision into professional helping and that there was little guidance in education for how to do so. Once I realized that, I found a way I could be of service to the profession itself. Since I became a professor in 1986, I have dedicated my scholarly research, teaching, and community service to developing a spiritually sensitive approach to social work that would be inclusive and respectful of diverse spiritual perspectives. It has been extremely satisfying to find many other kindred souls since then and to work together from our various spiritual and professional views on this common goal.

Compassion in the Wake of the Flood

Recently my (LF) faith was challenged to further growth as I encountered compassion firsthand as its recipient during a "once-in-two-hundred-years" flood that hit the town of Grand Forks, North Dakota, where I live. In 1997, swollen by winter snowstorms and April snow melt, the Red River inundated Grand Forks. The water forced all of us fifty thousand people from our homes. No other major city in the history of the United States had ever been forced by a natural disaster to evacuate its entire population. There was no time for good-byes or for closures with school friends or graduations. We all were plunged into temporary homelessness, scattering to fifty states and two foreign countries. Everything was closed, including the hospital, a vital link for any community.

Why hadn't we known this would happen? All of the blizzards we had that winter, bringing over a hundred inches of snow and then the deadly ice storm a week and a half before were warning signs. But the Army Corps of Engineers told us not to worry: the dikes would hold; the water would not get any higher than it had in the past; they had everything under control. It was our belief in authority and the inability of the mind to imagine the unimaginable that kept us in denial. This was a profound truth for me. Even though I had studied the defense mechanism of denial and had taught it in my university classes, at this moment I understood its power.

Safe from the flood in my brother's house, I sat glued to the television thinking that we had seen the worst. But then I saw that the downtown was burning. I watched in horror as building after building burned. I saw my bank building in flames, then my attorney's office; the newspaper headquarters was next. The firefighters could not extinguish the fires because there was no pressure in the fire hydrants, and the fire engines could not get through the flooded streets. How ironic to be in the middle of so much water and not to have water available to put out a fire.

The call to compassion during this flood was answered by many people in many ways. Family and friends offered words of consolation. One of my brothers called and left me this old Buddhist adage: "My granaries have burned; I have a clearer view of the moon." In other words, when you lose material things, you have a clearer view of what is really important in life. That was brought home to me by my son Jon's call. He said, "Mom, don't forget you still have your faith, your family, and your friends." Not only were his words comforting, but it was also comforting that he had incorporated my own value system and was now reminding me of what I had always deemed to be important in life.

Two weeks later residents were allowed to return to Grand Forks to view the damage. Hundreds of homes were totally destroyed. The rest, including my own, had silty, foul-smelling water damage in their basements from overland flooding and the river itself. Policemen and national guard members stood all over the city. There was no electricity, water, sanitation, or heat in the entire city, so portable toilets were plunked on street corners. Very few residents moved back to the city until basic services were restored. Instead, we drove into town daily to start the clean-up process.

Our mops and cleaning supplies had disappeared with the flood waters. I drove to the only supermarket still open and saw national guard personnel distributing supplies of water, mops, buckets, and cleaning rags. I wept tears of joy as the Red Cross trucks dispensed rubber gloves, goggles, and disinfectants, and Salvation Army trucks delivered free food and safe drinking water twice a day throughout the whole city. I was reminded of Christ's saying, "For I was hungry, and you gave me something to eat; I was thirsty, and you gave me drink . . ." (Matthew 25:35; NASB), as we daily ate either Salvation Army or Red Cross cuisine.

My life all day long was filled with cement-like mud and smells of rotting food in refrigerators thrown out on the berms. All of Grand Forks was in the same boat. Our homes were very, very cold, and the dampness penetrated through our layers of clothing. Once we had cleaned our basements, we had to haul our debris to the berm. For over a month, miles of berm were piled five to six feet high with what had once been our furnaces, washers, dryers, furniture, drywall, carpeting, and lumber. The sight was heartbreaking.

Often I would hear a great roar and look up to see a DC9 flying into the Grand Forks Airport with supplies and volunteers, whose helping hands gave us hope. I will never forget the first volunteers, who were accountants and financial analysts—flown in free by Northwest Airlines to clean basements of the elderly—police personnel, and firefighters. They wore blue T-shirts that said, "From out of the blue, help comes." These people had read about the flood in newspapers and had seen television footage and were moved to be part of this great struggle. Compassion then pro-vided two blessings: one to the recipient and one to the giver.

Over and over, the people of Grand Forks experienced this great com-passion. One day as I was cleaning, my doorbell rang, and there stood two of my former graduate social work students whom I had taught about compassion in our classes. They had been hired as outreach social workers who went door to door to every home to inquire about social, psycholog-ical, and financial needs. Their visit was comforting and placed me in the new position of receiving their compassion and their services.

A headline in the *Grand Forks Herald* read: "Goodness of God Flows into Grand Forks Churches." Area religious organizations handled flood relief donations exceeding $11 million, which helped people rebuild their lives, their homes, and their places of worship. B'nai Israel Synagogue received support from Jewish congregations in forty-nine states. Regional and national church bodies made donations. Distribution was directed through an interfaith coalition within Grand Forks. Banding together, this interfaith coalition supported a Billy Graham Crusade and door-to-door volunteers who were available to listen to people's concerns and to help them with their spiritual struggles. Never once did they proselytize. "Receiving so much help has been overwhelming," said many clergy and church members. "It's a wonderful display of God's great goodness to us." They voiced the feelings of all. Although we gladly helped each other—and every neighborhood had stories of kindness and pitching in together—it was humbling to receive from other hands.

A school principal had students from forty families living in Federal Emergency Management Agency trailers. She knocked on every door to discuss the transportation needs of each family. This administrator also suffered flood damage to her own home and to her husband's business. She was representative of the many flood heroes who demonstrated boundless compassion to people in need during the flood.

The safety deposit box with my property deeds, kept at my bank, was filled with mud from the floodwaters. Even after experts tried to salvage the deeds, they looked like a tattered heap of brittle paper ready to crum-ble at the least touch. They represented the fragility of material things, and that is the real lesson I learned from this flood. Money, position, and power meant little the night we all evacuated. The only real treasures we have are spiritual ones. I no longer care for possessions. The only constant for me was my faith in the abiding presence of God. When I would look at my property deeds in a heap on a chair in my living room, awaiting a new safety deposit box, I would be reminded: "But lay up for yourselves treasures in heaven, where neither moth nor rust destroys" (Matthew 6:20, NASB).

Each day, I would ask God to give me strength to be compassionate to those around me, even while I was experiencing exhaustion and anger within myself. Shortly after the flood, I came upon Psalm 69, verses 1–3, and marveled at its appropriateness: "Save me, oh God, for the waters have threatened my life. I have sunk in deep mire, and there is no foothold. I have come into deep waters; and a flood overflows me. I am weary with my crying; my throat is parched." We had our feet in the literal mud, but we had also been in the mud of feeling overwhelmed, sinking into the deep mire of depression or anger. We all experienced fatigue from dealing with construction people as we got our homes back in order, from dealing with work and school demands and the day-to-day struggle.

Yet the grace of God gives us hope to endure and to adjust. It gives us compassion to help others. It also provides us the opportunity to receive compassion from others with humility. This flood gave me a deeper understanding of compassion—not just good works to help others but compassion that dignifies the recipient.

SYMBOLS OF COMPASSION IN RELIGIOUS TRADITIONS

In this section, we begin to examine particular religious traditions through their symbols of compassion. This is not to say that people from these traditions always behave in a compassionate manner (that would be very unrealistic), but it is to say that religious traditions identify ideals for compassion that are offered to their adherents. Here, we only touch on these symbols from three widely influential religious perspectives; there is much more depth and detail and variation in these symbols and how they are used. We explore specific religious and nonreligious forms of spiritually based service in Part II.

We hope that these religious symbols of compassion will stir readers' own recollections and meditations on symbols and ideals of compassion that motivate and inspire yourselves. Consider how you respond to each of these symbols. If you feel a sense of comfort and resonance, consider why. What other symbols are important to you? Reflect also on the extent to which you keep these symbols vital to inspire and sustain your practice. If you feel discomfort or unfamiliarity, also consider why. This kind of reaction suggests opportunities for you to explore greater understanding by connecting with people from these religious perspectives. By working through feelings of discomfort and addressing gaps in our knowledge, we can deepen our capacity to empathize with people for whom these symbols are important.

We present symbols from a sample of contrasting religious perspectives: Buddhist, Christian, and shamanic traditions. Buddhism, from Asian origins, can be considered nontheistic in that it does not maintain belief in God in the sense of a personal supreme being, but neither is it concerned to deny it. Christianity, of Middle Eastern origins, is a monotheistic religion that shares with Judaism and Islam belief in a personal supreme being and certain scriptures. Shamanism refers to a wide range of animistically oriented religious systems of spirit-guided healing found throughout the world. These three types of religions share ideals of compassion, but each has a different nuance. By reflecting on the differences, we can expand our own understanding of compassion.

The three illustrations included in this section are intended to convey appreciation for the ideals of compassion found in Buddhism, Christianity, and shamanism. I(EC) photographed these images during spiritual journeys as I sought inspiration in various parts of the world for my path of service. Out of respect for the privacy and values of members of these traditions, I have chosen images from places open to the public and consulted with members to confirm the appropriateness of presenting them.

Kuan Yin, the Bodhisattva of Compassion

Mahayana Buddhism is the most common form of Buddhism found in East Asia, especially China, Korea, Japan, and Vietnam. One of the most widely known schools of Mahayana in the West is Zen (de Bary, 1969). The term *Mahayana* means literally "Great Vehicle," meaning it is a vehicle large enough to move all beings toward enlightenment. In Mahayana, many Zen practitioners take a vow of great compassion that encompasses a commitment to serve all beings, human and nonhuman "Sentient beings are numberless, I vow to save them all."

Bodhisattvas are beings who have attained enlightenment but postpone entering Nirvana until all other beings are enlightened. Thus, devotees may regard them as divine beings and appeal to them for help in special circumstances of need, such as a time of death or crisis. In the Zen context, all Bodhisattvas can be considered symbolic expressions of the Buddha nature of virtue and enlightenment inherent within each person (Venerable Chong Mu, personal communication, Seoul, Korea). Reflection on the ideal and symbol of a Bodhisattva should inspire a person to realize that quality within himself or herself and to express it in action.

Illustration 1.1

The Bodhisattva of Compassion, Kwanseum Bosal: Close-up View of a Buddhist Wood Carving, Kyongju City, Republic of Korea.

(Photograph by Edward R. Canda)

One of the most popular Bodhisattvas is Kuan Yin, also named Kuan Shi Yin (Chinese; Kwanseum, in Korean), the Bodhisattva of Compassion (Bloefeld, 1988; Canda, 1995a). The name of this Bodhisattva means literally "to perceive the sound of the world." The Korean Zen Master, Seung Sahn (personal communication), said that this represents the ideal of having a mind and heart clear and open to perceive the cries of all suffering beings so that we can respond with help. Kuan Yin is an East Asian adaptation of an earlier Indian figure, Avalokitesvara, who is portrayed with male gender (Schuhmacher & Woerner, 1994). Since at least the tenth century, Kuan Yin has been portrayed variously as male, female, or androgynous. In essence, the Bodhisattva is beyond gender distinctions, but may manifest in various forms as needed to help people.

Sometimes Kuan Yin is depicted as having a thousand eyes and hands. This symbolizes a compassionate mind that perceives all suffering and is able to reach out in all directions with help. Kuan Yin is also sometimes shown with twelve heads depicting various aspects of compassion. Often there are eleven faces on a crown above the main face of the Bodhisattva. According to one explanation, three faces symbolize praise for people of good heart (Canda, 1995a). Three faces represent rightful anger toward those who do harm. Three faces smile with encouragement and praise for people who do good. One face in the middle indicates nonjudgmental acceptance of all kinds of people. And one face represents the Buddha of Infinite Light. These eleven faces are above the main face of Kuan Yin, which represents the face of wisdom beyond any of the other conditional compassionate reactions. The ideal here is that compassion may express in many different ways and circumstances, but the direction should always be to help others in a nonjudgmental way. In fact, Kuan Yin is often used to illustrate the ideal of social work in Korean Buddhist settings (Canda, Shin, & Canda, 1993).

The Passion of Jesus

The passion of Jesus is one of the most common devotional themes in Christian theology and art. Christians regard Jesus Christ as God incarnate, joining the fullness of divinity with a complete experience of human suffering and death (Nielsen et al., 1993). In the context of the trinitarian doctrine, Jesus' incarnation represents the boundless love of God for human beings, since God sent his only son, knowing that Jesus would be crucified as an atonement for the sins of humanity. Thus, the cross and Jesus' crucifixion are the most common representations of Jesus' passion. Although the crucifixion is described in all three gospels of the New Testament, it did not become represented in Christian art until four hundred years later because crucifixion was considered a horrific and degrading form of execution (Murray & Murray, 1996). This juxtaposition and conjunction of the glory of God with the abject suffering of human beings is itself a main theme of the passion of Jesus. The passion of Jesus is literally com-passion, divinity suffering with humanity, in order to deliver humanity from its failings and mortality.

Illustration 1.2

Mourning the Body of Jesus After Crucifixion: A Mexican Catholic Portrayal, Tzintzuntzan, Michoacan, Mexico.

(Photograph by Edward R. Canda)

Catholic, Eastern Orthodox, and some Protestant Christian traditions of iconography depict the passion of Jesus in many ways (Gieben, 1980; van Os, 1994; Weitzmann, 1978). In portrayals of the crucifixion, Jesus is often shown with explicit marks of pain and torture, such as starvation-exposed ribs, nails in hands and feet, and blood and water flowing from the sword wound in his side. But the divinity of Jesus is also portrayed, such as God looking on or weeping angels hovering above. Sometimes the cross is shown with a resplendent Jesus figure and sometimes with no figure at all, in order to emphasize the resurrection of Christ. When

Christians contemplate these symbols of the suffering Jesus, they may immerse themselves vicariously in his pain in order to work through to a catharsis in the mystery of Jesus' resurrection from the dead. During the season of Lent and Easter, Christian communities follow the various stages of Jesus' passion, death, and resurrection. This is both a commemoration of past events and a process of linking individuals' and communities' experiences of suffering and mortality into the redemptive model, so that hope and healing may be experienced. This refreshes Christians' understanding of the ritual of communion (or Eucharist), which commemorates the Passover meal that Jesus shared with his disciples shortly before his crucifixion. In the ritual of communion, the community shares bread and often wine, representing the body and blood of Jesus.

Jesus' torture and death was the culmination of many gospel stories about his compassion for people. Jesus defied social conventions to express care for the sick, the poor, and disrespected members of society, such as tax collectors and prostitutes. Jesus' compassion for the poor and oppressed has been the primary model for Christian-based medical and social services.

The Shaman as Wounded/Healed Healer

Shamanism is not a distinct religion, as Buddhism and Christianity are. Rather, *shamanism* is a name that anthropologists and religious studies scholars coined for a set of religious themes and practices found in many distinct cultures on all continents and in Oceania (Canda, 1983; Walsh, 1990). This will be explained further in Part II. For now, our focus is the shaman, a person who learns culturally prescribed ways of communicating with spiritual beings and forces in order to help heal his or her community of illnesses and maintain or restore social and cosmic harmony at times of crisis. A shaman uses intensified, ecstatic states of consciousness in order to communicate with these spiritual forces and to engage in healing with their guidance (Eliade, 1964).

In many cultures, a person becomes a shaman through a process of initiation in which the initiate is symbolically wounded, dismembered, or killed by envisioned spirits so that he or she can be reconstructed beyond the ordinary limits of social roles and conventions as a healer (Halifax, 1982). A period of spontaneous divine calling and disruption is followed by rituals of transformative death and rebirth, as well as training by master shamans, in order to help the initiate learn how to use trance and to communicate with spirits in a culturally prescribed and disciplined manner. In some cultures, people who eventually become shamans have often gone through severe experiences of illness, oppression, or mistreatment that fracture their psychosocial status quo and open them up to spirit influences. Thus, the shaman is able to use the learning from his or her own experiences of crisis and resolution as a pattern in the process of helping other people.

The Korean myth of Princess Pari illustrates this pattern (Canda, 1982, 1995a). In the version of the Seoul area, the princess was born as a seventh daughter in a royal family long ago. Given the patriarchal context, the king was angry that he had not yet had a son to inherit the throne, so he locked the princess in a box and cast her out to sea. Miraculously, she was discovered by a loving couple who adopted her. As a young woman, she learned of her true identity. But her royal parents were gravely ill. Despite their mistreatment of her, she decided to seek a magic cure for them that could be found only in the Western Paradise by a heroic journey through mountains full of dangerous monsters. With the help of spirit beings, she found the cure and returned, only to find her parents dead. Nonetheless, the medicine restored them to life. In the process, Princess Pari's suffering was resolved through reconciliation with her parents and fulfillment of the role of healer.

This theme of the wounded and healed healer may inspire potential shamans as well as general members of the community. For example, the sweat lodge purification ritual is one of the most widely shared spiritual practices among First Nations peoples of North America (Lyon, 1996). It is used to help people clarify and purify themselves, often in preparation for other ceremonies, to gain insight into one's life purpose and mission, or to gain wisdom and strength to deal with personal or community crises. The sweat lodge is usually constructed of saplings bowed over and tied to form a dome-shaped support structure. The frame is covered with hides or blankets so that the inside is completely dark, even during daylight. This lodge is the sacred womb of the earth to which people return, to be renewed and reborn. Red-hot rocks are brought from a sacred fire and placed in a pit in the middle of the lodge. Water and sometimes healing herbs are placed on the rocks to release their hot healing steam. The structure of the lodge and the sacred materials used in the ritual all reflect a prayerful recognition of the participants' connection with all things, and an invocation of healing and help from the spirit powers of earth and sky.

These stones share their hot, purifying energy as people pray and sing for the well-being of themselves, loved ones, the community, and all things. The hot steam may cause some suffering, but when the suffering is offered to help others, it becomes a sacrifice of compassion that also heals oneself. Literally, from the Latin roots, the word *sacrifice* means "to make sacred."

Black Elk, a Lakota shaman and Catholic catechist (De Mallie, 1984; Steltenkamp, 1993), shared this prayer from a sweat lodge (Brown, 1971, p. 40):

> O Wakan-Tanka, Grandfather, above all, it is thy will that we are doing here. Through that Power which comes from the place where the giant Waziah lives, we are now making ourselves as pure and as white as new snow. We know that we are now in darkness, but soon the Light will come. When we leave this lodge may we leave behind all impure thoughts, all ignorance. May we be as children newly born! May we live again, O Wakan-Tanka!

In the Lakota tradition, when people enter or leave the lodge, they say, "All my relatives." This is a prayer to honor all the beings and powers that support us and to share the benefit of the ritual for all.

A COMMON HEART OF COMPASSION

The religious views implied in these symbols might seem to be vastly different, even irreconcilable. Certainly, in the understanding of many adherents, this would be the case. But perhaps there is also a deep commonality. As social workers striving to develop a moral and ethical framework that honors diversity while finding common ground, we should consider whether there may be a common heart of compassion underlying the differences. This is not something that can be discerned scientifically, but it is a philosophical and moral question about which we need to take a clear position as a basis for formulating general ethical principles for spiritually sensitive social work. In order to do this, it is helpful to return to the study of social work scholars' diverse spiritual perspectives (Canda, 1990c).

Although there were significant contrasts in the content of beliefs among the participants, there was a surprising commonality of core values. Participants from atheist, humanist, Christian, Buddhist, existentialist, Jewish, and shamanistic perspectives agreed that each human being has inherent dignity and worth and deserves unconditional positive regard. They agreed that social workers should strive to complement both individual well-being and social justice. They also indicated that human beings should extend care and responsibility to the nonhuman world,

Illustration 1.3
Animistic Theme of Beings in Harmony: Anasazi Culture Petroglyphs (ca. 1000 C.E.), Petrified Forest National Park, Northern Arizona, United States.

(Photograph by Edward R. Canda)

because of our interdependence with it, or because it is seen as an expression of God's creativity, or because it is understood that all things are alive with their own personality and sacred power. All agreed that people should cultivate a moral perspective that goes beyond egoism, ethnocentrism, and human exploitation of the environment. Respondents of all perspectives felt a basic congruence between professional values and their personal values, but they also felt points of tension where professional ideals of justice and service to the poor and oppressed seemed to be eroding.

This commonality of core values among people of diverse spiritual perspectives is probably related to the fact that they are all social workers. It suggests that when social workers of diverse spiritual backgrounds enter into dialogue and share their deepest commitments and ideals, it may be possible to find our common heart of compassion. This humane heartedness can become a point of mutual respect and cooperation as we engage in dialogue and collaborate, even when dealing with very different and conflicting details of spiritual beliefs, values, and practices. But we believe this common humane heartedness cannot be found through empirical tests or rational arguments. It is found by looking deeply into each of our own hearts, and communicating deeply with each other heart to heart.

ETHICAL PRINCIPLES FOR SPIRITUALLY SENSITIVE SOCIAL WORK

By intention, this chapter has not proceeded in a linear, analytical way. We have introduced themes, stories, and symbols from various personal, professional, and religious perspectives associated with compassion and the call to service. Now, drawing on these moral and value reflections, we state formally a set of ethical principles for spiritually sensitive social work. These principles build on the professional mission and NASW Code of Ethics. We believe that they are consistent with the commonly held mission, values, and ethics of the social work profession, but they go beyond the way these are commonly understood and expressed when spirituality is not the focus. In Part III we consider more detailed ethical guidelines with regard to the application of spiritually or religiously based ideas and helping activities in social work. The values and ethical principles stated here shape the contents and perspective of the rest of this book.

In order to show how these ethical principles are consistent with the Code of Ethics, we describe them in direct relation to the six ethical principles set forth in the current NASW Code of Ethics (pp. 5–6). In the Code of Ethics, the six core values mentioned in the beginning of this chapter are matched with an explanatory ethical principle and a brief elaboration of the principle. In our presentation, we quote the core value and ethical principle from the code and then add our own elaboration that highlights how this principle could be expressed in the context of spiritually sensitive social work practice. *Original wording from the code is italicized.* (Used with permission of the publisher.)

We intend our statement of ethical principles to serve two purposes: (1) to clarify the values and ethical principles that guide us in our particular version of spiritually sensitive practice, and (2) to raise questions and controversies that stimulate readers to engage in their own formulation of ethical principles. Although the principles are stated as prescriptions, as in the NASW Code of Ethics, they are meant as encouragements and challenges for each of us to reflect morally on our hearts and open our hearts to learn from each other.

Actually, the real guide for day-to-day behavior is a social worker's personal code of ethics based on her or his core values, determined through experience and personal reflection as to which teachings and values one wishes to incorporate into one's personal worldview and to translate into one's behavior. Realistically, people do not accord a professional standardized code of ethics authority over their moral and ethical decisions unless it is incorporated into the personal code.

My students and I (LF) often get into discussions about the importance of having a personal code of ethics and that this is necessary before one can adopt a professional code of ethics. We discuss the influences on a personal code of ethics, such as teachings about right and wrong given by parents, clergy, teachers, and peers; professional standards such as the NASW Code of Ethics; as well as one's own moral standards developed through life experiences. Students must arrive at decisions about which of these teachings and experiences they truly believe and wish to incorporate into their own personal code of ethics and conduct. In this way, students can make well-informed decisions about whether they can assent to the professional code of ethics. The professional code is at a very general level. The details of a personal code integrate professional values and apply it to the specifics of life.

VALUE: *Service*

ETHICAL PRINCIPLE: *Social workers' primary goal is to help people in need and to address social problems.*

Spiritually sensitive *social workers elevate service to others above self-interest* whenever necessary and always seek mutually beneficial ways of service. They recognize and appreciate that serving others is itself a spiritual path that promotes the growth of both worker and client. Spiritually sensitive *social workers draw on their knowledge, values, and skills to help people in need,* including their material, biological, psychological, social relational, and spiritual needs, according to the priorities and aspirations of clients. They do not limit understanding of clients to needs, but support clients in clarifying and using their personal talents, strengths, and wisdom and their connections with the strengths and beauty available within their social relationships and relationships with the natural world.

Spiritually sensitive social workers also support clients who wish to clarify their understanding of life purpose, ultimate concerns, and the nature of reality. When clients identify religious or nonreligious forms of spiritual support, including religious communities or spiritual support groups and transcendent or sacred beings, these beliefs and related practices are respected by the worker and included in the approach to helping as relevant to clients' own preferences. Religious and nonreligious spiritual systems are recognized as potentially important sources of support for clients in working to change social problems. When religious and nonreligious spiritual systems and institutions are identified by clients as contributing to their personal or social problems, clients are assisted to challenge them or to change their relationship with them in a respectful manner.

Spiritually sensitive *social workers are encouraged to volunteer some portion of their professional skills with no expectation of significant financial return.* They are also encouraged to reexamine continually how the conduct of their professional roles is congruent with the virtue of compassion and their deepest sense of calling to a life of service.

VALUE: *Social Justice*

ETHICAL PRINCIPLE: *Social workers challenge social injustice.*

Spiritually sensitive *social workers pursue social change, particularly with and on behalf of vulnerable and oppressed individuals and groups of people.* Particular concern is given to advocacy on behalf of individuals and cultural or religious groups who are the target of oppressive, discriminatory, and prejudicial attitudes, practices, and policies because of their spiritual beliefs. Spiritually sensitive social workers' social change activities also address individuals and groups who are motivated by spiritual beliefs to perpetuate harm, especially regarding *issues of poverty, unemployment, discrimination, and other forms of social injustice. These activities seek to promote sensitivity to and knowledge about* the dynamics of *oppression* and empowerment in relation to all aspects of human diversity, especially *cultural and ethnic diversity.* Spiritually sensitive *social workers strive to ensure access to needed information, services, and resources,* especially from spiritual support systems relevant to clients; *equality of opportunity; and meaningful participation in decision making for all people.*

Spiritually sensitive social workers recognize that social justice and human well-being are closely interrelated with the well-being of nonhuman beings and the total planetary ecology. Therefore, they strive to overcome the challenges of environmental racism, international social injustice, oppression and war between cultures and nations, and human activities that are destructive to local and planet-wide ecological systems.

VALUE: *Dignity and Worth of the Person*

ETHICAL PRINCIPLE: *Social workers respect the inherent dignity and worth of the person.*

Spiritually sensitive *social workers treat each person in a caring and respectful fashion, mindful of individual differences and cultural and ethnic diversity, religious and spiritual diversity, and all other forms of human variation.* Spiritually sensitive social workers address clients as whole persons, applying professional roles, rules, and assessment labels in a flexible way that is responsive to the values of the client and his or her community. They also strive to make respectful connections across differences and to find common ground for cooperation. They honor the common and universal human needs for a sense of meaning, purpose, and morality.

Spiritually sensitive *social workers promote clients' socially responsible self-determination.* They assist clients to engage in clear moral and ethical decision making in a manner that respects the spiritual perspectives of clients, as well as the right of other people and communities to uphold their own self-determination. When there are conflicts of values between clients and social workers or clients and others in their environment, spiritually sensitive social workers engage in a process of dialogue that encourages mutual understanding and mutually beneficial solutions to problems.

Spiritually sensitive *social workers seek to enhance clients' capacity and opportunity to change and to address their own needs,* including the capacity to grow through crises and experiences of spiritual transformation.

Spiritually sensitive *social workers are cognizant of their dual responsibility to clients and to the broader society. They seek to resolve conflicts between clients' interests and the broader society's interests in a socially responsible, peaceful manner consistent with the values, ethical principles, and ethical standards of the profession.* Spiritually sensitive social workers reflect carefully on their own moral and ethical positions as they interact with those of clients and the broader society and engage in a process of continual moral discernment and growth.

VALUE: *Importance of Human Relationships*

ETHICAL PRINCIPLE: *Social workers recognize the central importance of human relationships.*

Spiritually sensitive *social workers understand that relationships between and among people are an important vehicle for change. Social workers engage people as partners in the helping process,* including collaboration with religious and non-religious spiritual support systems as relevant to clients. Spiritually sensitive *social workers seek to strengthen relationships among people in a purposeful effort to promote, restore, maintain, and enhance the well-being of individuals, families, social groups, organizations, and communities.*

Although the primary focus of social work is on human relationships, spiritually sensitive social workers understand that human relationships are closely related with and dependent on the rest of the world. Therefore, they grant respect to the natural world, and all the beings within it. They encourage relationships between people and the natural world that benefit both clients and the other beings and ecosystems with which clients relate.

Spiritually sensitive social workers understand that many people believe in and claim to experience relationship with sacred or supernatural aspects of reality or a transcendent, divine, or ultimate foundation of reality itself. Therefore, when such beliefs and experiences are important to clients, spiritually sensitive social workers explore how clients' relationships with these spiritual forces may influence their sense of well-being and the development of fulfilling relationships with other people and nature.

VALUE: *Integrity*

ETHICAL PRINCIPLE: *Social workers behave in a trustworthy manner.*

Spiritually sensitive *social workers are continually aware of the profession's mission, values, ethical principles, and ethical standards and practice in a manner consistent with them.* Spiritually sensitive *social workers act honestly and responsibly and promote ethical practices on the part of the organizations with which they are affiliated.*

In order to promote trust, spiritually sensitive social workers are open and honest about the moral, professional, religious, theoretical, ideological, political, cultural, and other assumptions of themselves and their organizations that are germane to the helping process. They provide this information to clients in a way that encourages informed consent and freedom of choice for the client to decide whether to maintain a professional relationship with the worker or the organization with which the worker is affiliated. Professional self-disclosure is done for the benefit of clients rather than for egocentric, judgmental, or discriminatory reasons.

VALUE: *Competence*

ETHICAL PRINCIPLE: *Social workers practice within their areas of competence and develop and enhance their professional expertise.*

Spiritually sensitive *social workers continually strive to increase their professional knowledge and skills and to apply them in practice.* Especially in regard to the explicit use of religious or nonreligious spiritual beliefs, symbols, rituals, therapeutic practices, or community support systems, spiritually sensitive social workers obtain relevant knowledge and skills. Social work practice across different spiritual traditions and communities is performed with respect for the values and preferences of clients and relevant members of those spiritual traditions and communities. Spiritually sensitive social workers learn how to cooperate and collaborate with community-based spiritual support systems, helpers, and healers in a culturally competent manner.

Spiritually sensitive *social workers should aspire to contribute to the knowledge base of the profession*, especially in relation to innovations in spiritually sensitive social work practice, theory, policy, research, and education.

SUMMARY

In this chapter we have reviewed core values in the history of the profession and in diverse spiritual perspectives of social workers. We have considered common themes and various symbolic expressions of compassion and the call to service. Finally, we offered a framework of values and ethical principles for spiritually sensitive practice by elaborating on the NASW Code of Ethics. These value themes and ethical principles pervade the remainder of the book. We will return explicitly to the NASW Code of Ethics and the value framework for spiritually sensitive practice as we consider various ethical dilemmas and questions in the following chapters.

EXERCISES

1.1 What Does Compassion Mean to You?

During the discussion of the virtue of compassion in social work history, we discussed some rival views. For example, compassion as unconditional love and care was contrasted with moralistic judgmentalism and condescending pity. Compassion as a commitment to social justice was contrasted with individualistic gratification. Compassion as an altruistic and generous way of service was contrasted with professional preoccupation with prestige, profit, and personal advantage. Consider how these different concepts of compassion play out in your personal and professional life. What kind of value conflicts and dilemmas occur when different motives for service come into conflict? Clarify your own understanding of compassion and how this is reflected in your professional work.

1.2 Writing a Vocational Autobiography

Return to the discussion of social work as a vocation, including the personal accounts of how social work scholars and practitioners, including us, understand the call to service. What is your reaction to these stories? Which can you identify with? What does your reaction tell you about your own core values, motives, and developmental experiences that guide you in the social work profession?

Whether you are a student, a seasoned practitioner, an agency administrator, or an educator, think back to why you became a social worker. Where did this motive to serve come from? What happened to you and within you that woke you up to this vocation? Were there any inspiring figures in your life? Were there any religious or moral teachings that influenced you? Did you have any experiences of struggle and resolution that pointed you in this direction? In case you have lost the original fresh sense of vocation, take this opportunity to recall it, to rest in it, and to restore it. By returning to our original inspiration, we are not only recalling, but we are being re-called. This gives us an opportunity to answer once again, perhaps by restoring an earlier sense of vitality, or by appreciating where we are now, or even by finding new ways to live according to our deepest life aspirations.

Now you are prepared to write an autobiography of your call to service. Organize your insights according to a time line, dividing the phases of your life in whatever way makes sense for you—for example, early childhood, school years, graduate education, beginning of professional practice, significant personal transitions or crises, your current situation. Write or tell stories to friends about important events and people. Discuss the key themes that run through your professional development. Consider how your current situation represents growth, stasis, or loss of original inspiration.

1.3 Symbols of Compassion

Take out three sheets of paper. Label one sheet "Early Childhood"; one sheet "Now"; and one sheet "My Ideal for the Future." On each sheet, use colorful markers or other decorations to draw or depict a representation of what compassion means to you. First think back to your earliest childhood memories of compassionate people or symbols of compassion from your cultural or religious heritage. Create a picture that represents your feelings, thoughts, or symbols about this. Next, do the same for your current understanding of compassion as you express it in your personal and professional life. Then imagine your ideal of compassion as you would like to achieve it in the future. Finally, compare the three pictures, and reflect on the changes and opportunities for further growth that they suggest. As an alternative to making pictures, write down key words or phrases that represent your symbols of compassion at each stage of life.

1.4 A Common Heart of Compassion

Think of occasions when you were involved with friendships or professional relationships that bridged significant cultural or religious differences. What qualities in yourself and the other person made this connection possible? If you discovered a sense of common purpose and common humanity together with the differences, explain what that involved. Consider how these qualities can be applied within social work practice to enhance empathy, respect, and cooperation with clients who come from spiritual backgrounds very different from your own.

1.5 Ethical Principles for Spiritually Sensitive Social Work: Personal Fit

Statements of core values and ethical principles are necessarily very broad and leave much room for interpretation. Each professional needs to consider the extent to which he or she feels a fit with these values and principles. What do they mean to you? Review each principle, including the original words from the NASW Code of Ethics and the additions for spiritually sensitive social work. Consider your agreement or disagreement with each principle, and explain why you have this reaction. Think of specific examples of how these principles might operate in practice.

Since the NASW Code of Ethics is binding for professional social workers, consider areas of tension or disagreement with it carefully. How do these disagreements affect your practice as a social worker? If you feel a basic disagreement with the NASW Code, consider whether it makes sense for you to continue to identify as a social worker or whether you should advocate for changes or clarifications in the Code of Ethics.

CHAPTER TWO

THE MEANING AND SIGNIFICANCE OF SPIRITUALITY

The Tao that can be told is not the eternal Tao.
Tao te Ching, Taoism
(trans. Feng & English, 1972).

INTRODUCTION

In Taoism, the term *Tao* means "way of life" or the natural flow of the universe. Taoist philosophy emphasizes that there is something mysterious about the Tao that cannot be captured in words. The nameless Tao gives rise to all things, but it cannot be reduced to them. Spirituality also has this quality. Its deepest meaning cannot be expressed, but its expressions and names are numerous. In this chapter, we provide definitions of *spirituality* and related terms, but we also recognize its mysterious quality.

Contemporary social work scholars usually distinguish between spirituality and religion (Canda, 1997b). Spirituality relates to a universal and fundamental aspect of what it is to be human—to search for a sense of meaning, purpose, and moral frameworks for relating with self, others, and the ultimate reality. In this sense, spirituality may express through religious forms, or it may be independent of them. Religion is an institutionalized pattern of beliefs, behaviors, and experiences, oriented toward spiritual concerns, and shared by a community and transmitted over time in traditions.

In order for us to develop a framework for spiritually sensitive practice that respects and appreciates diverse expressions, we need to refine these definitions. Sometimes disputes between colleagues or between social workers and clients result from lack of clear definition and unspo-

37

ken but contradictory assumptions about the nature of religion and spirituality. In order to communicate clearly to ourselves and others about spirituality, we need to form clear, explicit definitions. In order to conduct research about the impacts of religion and spirituality on human behavior, we need to apply clearly defined concepts in a consistent manner. In order for practitioners to do assessments of spiritual development or strengths and challenges posed by clients' participation in religious groups, we need to explain the key concepts underlying our standards for assessment.

But as soon as we try to reach clarity or consensus about the meanings of terms like religion, faith, and spirituality, we encounter many difficulties. This chapter identifies the difficulties inherent in trying to define *spirituality* and *religion* and our strategy for meeting the challenge. It reviews the current definitions of spirituality and related terms in the social work literature and the common themes among them. We also present a detailed working definition of spirituality, portrayed in two conceptual models, that encompasses insights from many disciplines. Finally, we respond to professional controversies and debates about spirituality.

THE CHALLENGES OF DEFINING SPIRITUALITY

A definition of spirituality that will be acceptable for the common base of the profession needs to be inclusive of diverse religious and nonreligious expressions. This poses challenges that can be summarized by two dichotomies that hold many people in tension around this topic: the particular versus the universal and the expressible versus the inexpressible.

Particular Versus Universal

There are three strategies for defining *spirituality*. One is to focus on spirituality in particular contexts, times, places, persons, and cultures. This means defining spirituality (or using the term at all) only in situation-specific ways. This is sometimes referred to as an *emic* approach, which means using the insider's or believer's perspective (Anderson, 1996). The advantage of this approach is that concepts and assumptions considered irrelevant or inappropriate by believers are not imposed and do not distort the meaning. Rich, detailed descriptions and accounts of particular beliefs, experiences, and patterns can be developed. As context-specific accounts for many different people and communities are collected or brought into dialogue, people can learn about each other on their own terms.

People who support the emic approach are highly suspicious of any general definitions or theories of religion and spirituality because they run the risk of oversimplification, stereotypes, and even imperialistic impositions of spiritual assumptions and agendas. In the postmodern world of tremendous cultural and spiritual diversity, competing value systems, and calls for the empowerment of disenfranchised individuals and groups, this emic approach is highly appealing (Griffin, 1988). For example, in clinical practice, it is the client's own beliefs, values, symbols, and rituals that should be paramount rather than any preconceptions on the part of the practitioner.

In contrast, the *etic* approach uses general concepts and theories that are thought to be applicable across various cultures and situations. We can use such general theories and concepts to describe, compare, and analyze the variety of spiritual perspectives. They also provide a common language for discussion among people coming from widely different spiritual perspectives. For example, if an atheistic social worker is assisting a charismatic Christian client, it would be useful to have a general framework for discussing spiritual matters that can bridge the differences and find common ground.

Some etic approaches are universalistic; they claim that the most important and fundamental level of spirituality is something that is universally shared by all religions, even if some believers do not recognize that. This view is suspicious of emic approaches because they are considered ethnocentric or idiosyncratic barriers to universal human understanding and cooperation. Some see this search for commonality as a balm for the postmodern situation of value relativism, moral confusion, and interreligious conflict (Cave, 1993; Rennie, 1996).

Our strategy in this book is a third option. We combine emic and etic approaches. We wish to appreciate diversity, remaining faithful to particular spiritual experiences and traditions while seeking common ground for understanding and communication. For this, we coin the term *transemic approach*. In other words, various particular (emic) perspectives are brought into interaction and dialogue with each other to affirm both the particular and the universal aspects of human experience. And even claims of universal truth or panhuman aspects of spirituality (given by others or ourselves) are themselves recognized as particular spiritual claims. We advocate for continuing self-reflection and dialogue among people of many spiritual perspectives, so that we can move toward even greater understanding and cooperation.

In a study of Buddhist mutual assistance associations among Southeast Asian refugees in the United States, Canda and Phaobtong (1992) used a generic (etic) social work classification of physical, mental, social, and spiritual supports to examine culture-specific community strengths and resources. Particular (emic) Theravada Buddhist terms and practices, based on field observation and interviews within refugee communities, were presented to illustrate this. Thus, a common base for mutual understanding and cooperation between Southeast Asian American Buddhists and others was established. Indeed, the search for strengths and resources in religious communities is itself a by-product of the strengths perspective, an etic approach to social work that values emic (client-based) perspectives (Saleebey, 1997).

This transemic approach retains an unavoidable challenge. Whenever general definitions of spirituality are developed that can be inclusive of all possible versions, such as theism, polytheism, atheism, animism, and nontheism, it may become vague (Canda, 1990b). When too much is included, a definition does not aid in making important distinctions. In order to address this concern, we develop a broad and inclusive conceptualization of spirituality and religion, while identifying many of their facets that aid in making more refined distinctions.

Expressible Versus Inexpressible

Many scholars say that religion and spirituality can be studied scientifically only if they can be expressed, observed, and even measured. How else could a practitioner know when a client is being religious or whether the client is exhibiting signs of a spiritual development crisis? But other scholars and mystics emphasize that the most distinctive features of religion and spirituality are beyond description, expression, or intellectual analysis. There are two major debates here: the ineffability of mystical experience and the irreducibility of the nature of religion or spirituality.

Mystical experiences are direct, personal encounters with aspects of reality that are beyond the limits of language and reason to express. They transcend human capacity for thinking and expression. They are described in various religious traditions as experiences of supernatural or paranormal powers and events (Hollenback, 1996), deep spiritual communion with God (Johnston, 1995), or ego-transcending expansions of consciousness (Wilber, 1995). Experiencers typically claim that mystical experiences are ineffable, meaning that they are so private and profound that they cannot be communicated to another (Dupre, 1987; James, 1982). They surpass rational understanding and the limits of words. Further, the sacred referents of religious devotion and belief are considered ineffable in many religious traditions because they are supernatural or inherently mysterious. For these reasons, the mystical aspects of spirituality and religion are considered to defy definition by many scholars of religion and the devout alike. This does not mean that mystical experiences or divine realities cannot be talked about, but it does mean that their reality will always be beyond whatever one says about them. It also means that much religious and spiritual language will be paradoxical, metaphorical, and allegorical.

Some scholars of comparative religions claim that the distinctive features of religion and spirituality cannot be reduced to any components or functions. As the eminent historian of religions, Mircea Eliade (1959), said, experience of the sacred is a sui generis reality, a fundamental experience, that can be understood only in religious terms. A sense of absoluteness, mysteriousness, awesomeness, and fundamental and ultimate priority is intrinsic to experience of the sacred in this view, so reduction of religious experience and belief to psychological or sociological functions and particular behaviors, for example, is considered unacceptable.

Although certain features of mystical or religious experience may be claimed to be beyond definition, measure, or reductive explanations, that does not mean that all features of spirituality are so. Some scholars object that the claim of ineffability or irreducibility is simply a strategy to avoid critical scrutiny of truth claims and to invest personal experiences or traditional doctrines with an aura of supreme unquestionable authority (Proudfoot, 1985).

Our own position is that key terms pertaining to spirituality and religion need to be defined carefully in order to encourage mutual understanding and consistency of usage, which are prerequisites for research and practice about spirituality. However, the definitions are for the sake of convenience. Concepts should never be mistaken for their referents. Referents can never be fully captured by labels and definitions in regard to any phenomenon, spiritual or otherwise. Indeed the definitions should take into account people's claims about ineffable, sacred, transcendent, or supernatural qualities.

AN OPEN CONCEPTUALIZATION OF SPIRITUALITY

We aim to be precise yet open in our definition of spirituality and related terms. For example, there are numerous competing definitions of religion in the field of religious studies. Debates have continued for decades about these definitions or whether there even should be any definitions. Exactitude and consensus remain elusive. We feel that this is not necessarily a problem. It is understandable that a complex, diverse phenomenon will evade capture by limited categories and definers. In this case, it is better to develop an open working definition that takes into account previous scholarly work and invites continued dialogue and debate. Thus, definition is a continuous process, not a final act. Open working definitions need to be clear but not rigid.

Cox (1996) and Hick (1990) have suggested that this can be accomplished by presenting a variety of definitions of religion and spirituality and then considering the family semblance among them. In other words, certain common patterns and themes emerge even with difference and disagreement. In the following discussion, we integrate insights from many disciplines in order to achieve this. We construct a comprehensive conceptualization of spirituality and related terms and compare it to findings from our national survey of social workers to consider how well it reflects actual usage in the field.

The Concept of Spirituality in Social Work Literature

Since professional social work developed partially out of religious movements for charity and community service, the early discussions of spirituality and religion hinged on particular theological terms and beliefs, mainly Christian and Jewish. However, it has been increasingly recognized that the tremendous increase of religious diversity, and the principles of church and state separation and client self-determination, require that spirituality be addressed in an inclusive manner (Canda, 1997b).

The earliest formal attempts to define spirituality inclusively were done by Christian social work scholars who felt that basic Christian values could be extended universally by presenting them in nonsectarian terms. For example, in 1945, Charlotte Towle (1965) said that a complete understanding of the person should involve material, psychological, social, and spiritual aspects. She highlighted spiritual needs as including use of church-based resources, developing a sense of life meaning and purpose, and formation of value frameworks and sense of social responsibility. Spencer (1956) felt that Christian values of freedom, love, and service are fully compatible with a nonsectarian approach to social work. Yet in their work, the distinctions between spirituality and religion were unclear, and Christian-specific language permeated their "nonsectarian" perspective.

During the 1970s and 1980s, the profession generally neglected education or research about religion or spirituality outside of religious settings for practice. But at the same time, prominent scholars advocated for a return of professional attention to spirituality. In addition to Christian and Jewish perspectives, existentialist, humanist, Zen Buddhist, and shamanistic perspectives were brought into the effort to define spirituality in an inclusive manner (Canda, 1988a, 1988b). For example, Max Siporin (1985) said that the spiritual is a moral aspect of the person, called the soul, that strives for relatedness with other people and supernatural powers, seeks knowledge of ultimate reality, and forms value frameworks. He emphasized that spirituality may be expressed inside or outside religious institutional frameworks. Later he clarified that the definition of spirituality should not be limited to ideas of God or the soul, since not all spiritual perspectives share these (Siporin, 1990). Faver (1986) called for social work to include multiple ways of knowing in research and practice in order to take into account the roles of religion and faith in human experience. She defined religion in terms of institutional cumulative traditions of faith. She used Fowler's definition of faith (see Chapter 7), which is more personal and, like Siporin's idea of spirituality, relates to a universal aspect of human beings, by which we orient ourselves to ourselves and the universe. Joseph (1987) similarly defined spirituality as "the underlying dimension of consciousness which strives for meaning, union with the universe, and with all things; it extends to the experience of the transcendent or a power beyond us" (p. 14).

In 1986, I (EC) completed a study of the diverse definitions of spirituality presented in American social work publications to that time (Canda, 1986, 1988b, 1988c, 1990b). In addition, I interviewed eighteen authors (the most prominent contributors who could be reached) to cull more detailed personal insights about spirituality and social work. These included participants who identified with atheist, Christian, existentialist, Jewish, shamanistic, and Zen Buddhist perspectives, some including more than one of these. The main purpose of this qualitative philosophical study was to develop a comprehensive and inclusive conceptualization of spirituality that built on all the work that had gone before. I summarized the conceptualization as follows (1990a):

> I conceptualize spirituality as the gestalt of the total process of human life and development, encompassing biological, mental, social, and spiritual aspects. It is not reducible to any of these components; rather, it is the wholeness of what it is to be human. This is the most broad meaning of the term. Of course, a person's spiri-

tuality is concerned significantly with the spiritual aspect of experience. In the narrow sense of the term spirituality, it relates to the spiritual component of an individual or group's experience. The *spiritual* relates to the person's search for a sense of meaning and morally fulfilling relationships between oneself, other people, the encompassing universe, and the ontological ground of existence, whether a person understands this in terms that are theistic, atheistic, nontheistic, or any combination of these.

In this definition, spirituality is distinguished from *religion*: "Religion involves the patterning of spiritual beliefs and practices into social institutions, with community support and traditions maintained over time" (Canda, 1997b, p. 173).

Similar definitions have been adapted commonly in recent writing. For example, Caroll (1998) reviewed the various definitions in social work literature and identified three common features. Spirituality is understood as an *essential or holistic quality* of the human being that cannot be reduced to any part of a person. It is understood also as an *aspect* of the person concerned with development of meaning and morality and relationship with a divine or ultimate reality. It is also understood to involve *transpersonal experiences,* in which consciousness transcends the ordinary limits of ego and body boundaries, such as in mystical experiences. Surveys suggest that the first two features of the definition are commonly held by practitioners who have an interest in spirituality and that they also distinguish between spirituality and religion (Derezotes & Evans, 1995; Sheridan & Bullis, 1991).

To summarize current definitions of spirituality in social work, we can identify six common attributes of the concept:

1. An essential or holistic quality of a person that is considered inherently valuable or sacred and irreducible.
2. An aspect of a person or group dealing with a search for meaning, moral frameworks, and relationships with others, including ultimate reality.
3. Particular experiences of a transpersonal nature.
4. A developmental process of moving toward a sense of wholeness in oneself and with others.
5. Participation in spiritual support groups that may or may not be formally religious.

6. Engagement in particular beliefs and behaviors, such as prayer or meditation, in a spiritual or religious context.

Definitions of Religion and Spirituality in Related Fields

Outside social work contexts, the term *spirituality* is not commonly used by scholars; when it is, it is usually given a much narrower definition. The term *spirituality* is most often used in the context of Christian theology, in which it refers to the way a person develops a personal relationship with God (Barry & Connolly, 1982; Jones, Wainwright & Yarnold, 1986; Van Kaam, 1983). So when religious studies scholars write about spirituality, it is often about particular Christian beliefs and practices, not about a general aspect of all people. In contrast, the term *religion* is often given a broad range of meanings, similar to the social work conception of spirituality (Capps, 1995; Padden, 1992, 1994; Pals, 1996).

Cox (1996) provided a helpful overview of types of definitions of religion in the broad sense of the term. *Theological definitions* focus on belief in a transcendent (and/or immanent) and usually personified divine being or beings and moral codes that relate to this. *Philosophical definitions* focus on concepts that a "believer interprets as ultimate or final in relation to the cosmic order and human existence" (p. 6). *Psychological definitions* focus on mental processes and states and behaviors that people relate to self-defined religious forces greater than themselves. *Anthropological and sociological definitions* focus on institutionalized patterns of symbols, beliefs, rituals, and stories that organize communities and relate to putative powers or forces greater than themselves, often considered supernatural. Except for theological studies, none of these academic disciplines makes a claim as to whether a sacred or supernatural realm exists. They simply observe, describe, and analyze the accounts of people who do hold such beliefs.

In the following two sections, we develop two conceptual models of spirituality. The first, a *holistic model of spirituality*, deals with spirituality in relation to the bio-psycho-social model of the person and environment. The second, an *operational model of spirituality*, deals with spirituality as an aspect of human experience, including categories of drives, experiences, functions, developmental processes, and contents of spiritual perspectives. These two models incorporate insights from social work and the other disciplines mentioned above in order to arrive at a comprehensive understanding. These models are heuristic devices—that is, simplifications

Figure 2.1
A Holistic Model of Spirituality

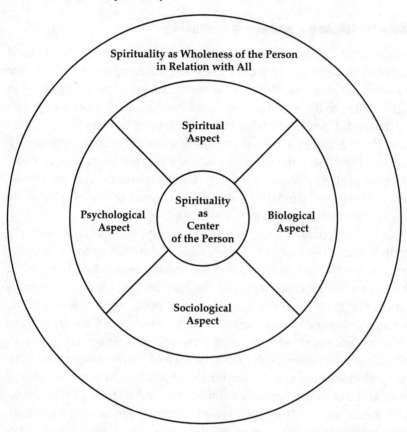

intended to aid understanding of a complex reality. They are not meant to be used rigidly.

A Holistic Model of Spirituality

As is common in social work parlance, spirituality can be considered an aspect of human experience and functioning, along with the biological, psychological, and sociological aspects. In addition, spirituality is often described as the wholeness or gestalt of the human being, irreducible to any part. Figure 2.1 depicts spirituality in relation to the bio-psycho-social model, using three metaphors: spirituality as the wholeness of the person, spirituality as the center of the person, and spirituality as the spiritual aspect of the person.

When spirituality is considered an *aspect* of the person, it completes a quaternity—the biological, psychological, sociological, and spiritual aspects, each with necessary functions (Robbins, Chatterjee, & Canda, 1998). Fields that study religion and spirituality assume that there is an aspect of the person that strives for a sense of meaning, purpose, and morality (Eliade, 1959; Fowler, 1996; James, 1982; Johnstone, 1992; Lessa & Vogt, 1972; Wilber, 1995). This "spiritual" aspect motivates experience and action to engage self with the world and symbolic reflection to interpret self and world. It orients the person and groups toward ultimacy, that is, things that are given ultimate value and priority, or the ultimate ground of reality itself. It is our position that this spiritual aspect is fundamental to human nature and infuses the other aspects. Indeed, the spiritual aspect impels us to give meaning and purpose to our bodies and biological functions, our thoughts and feelings, and our relationships with other people and the rest of the universe. This definition of spirituality is most commonly used and accepted.

But many scholars have also suggested that spirituality should refer to a quality of human being that is not reducible to any part. This is spirituality as the *wholeness* of what it is to be human. This wholeness is sometimes referred to as that which is sacred (Angel, 1994; Eliade, 1959; Imre, 1971). So each person is worthy of respect and care regardless of any of his or her particular qualities or conditions. This is the basis of the value of unconditional positive regard, common in humanistic psychology, pastoral theology, and social work. In religious contexts, this mysterious and holistic quality of the person may be described as a divine nature within humanity, "made in the image of God," the Buddha Nature of the person, or the true Self (Atman) which is one with Brahman in Vedantic Hinduism. Indeed, the root meanings of the words *whole* and *holy* are related. Even when these religious or metaphysical ideas are not accepted, as with atheistic existentialists, the notion of human wholeness and irreducibility is strongly valued.

Further, this wholeness is not limited to an individual because wholeness of self can be achieved only through meaningful and respectful relations with others. The quest for personal integration and wholeness brings individuals into a quest for mutually satisfying relations with other people, the rest of the world, and the ultimate ground of reality however a person understands that (Assagioli, 1965; Helminiak, 1996; Jung, 1938).

When individuals become aware of themselves as whole persons, with a creative integration of all aspects (bio-psycho-social-spiritual), there is a profound sense of personal integrity, which means literally the condition of being integrated. In fact, one important feature of the spiritual aspect of the person is the drive to achieve a sense of wholeness or personal integrity. The spiritual aspect helps weave together all the other aspects in the awareness and behavior of the individual.

As a person grows in personal integrity, the sense of responsibility for and connection with others also grows. The self is no longer defined in egocentric ways, but rather in relation to other people, other beings, and the ground of being itself. Further, a person may experience a sense of unity with the divine or all that exists. Then the whole self is experienced not only as a separate entity limited by body and ego but as a transpersonal self at one with all (Wilber, 1995). This transpersonal experience of wholeness is symbolized in Figure 2.1 by the outer circle that encompasses the person in relation with all things.

This irreducible, mysterious, or sacred quality of the person can also be described with the metaphor of "the center" of the person. This center is sometimes described as soul or consciousness, which is the connection and orientation point for all aspects of the person. This metaphor is used in the context of introspection—going inside oneself to find a center point of unity and integration. Even aside from particular religious beliefs, most people can relate to this metaphor as in the expression "to get centered." "Becoming centered" is to find a place of quiet within oneself that provides a sense of connection, integration, and clear awareness of self and world. Both the metaphors of the sacred center and sacred wholeness of the person seem to us to be different ways of experiencing the same thing. In theological language, this is like the dual aspects of relating to the divine: the divine as *transcendent* (wholeness) beyond yet encompassing all particular things and the divine as *immanent* (center) within each particular thing.

Whereas the notion of spirituality as an aspect of the person that seeks meaning is widely accepted in scholarly circles, the notion of spirituality as wholeness or center is not yet widely used, probably because these metaphors are difficult to state in operational terms for use in research and clinical assessment. However, these ways of experiencing and understanding spirituality are quite common both within and without religious contexts, so it is certainly appropriate to be aware of them and to be able to use them as metaphors with people for whom they make sense.

Although we wish to refrain from making any grand metaphysical claims, we do feel that these metaphors of spirituality as wholeness and as center are consistent with the social work professional perspective, which makes a commitment to honor all people with unconditional positive regard.

An Operational Model of Spirituality

The operational model of spirituality can support more precise and practical use of concepts in social work practice and research. In this model, spirituality as an aspect of human experience is depicted in terms of its various manifestations. Based on insights from social work and the other disciplines related to the study of religion and spirituality, we identify six interrelated categories of manifestations of spirituality: spiritual drives, spiritual experiences, functions of spirituality, spiritual development, contents of an individual's or group's spiritual perspective, and religious expressions in individuals and groups (see Figure 2.2).

Spiritual Drives

When we acknowledge that spirituality involves a search for meaning, purpose, and morally fulfilling relationships, we imply underlying drives toward attaining these qualities. We summarize this as the spiritual drives for profound experiences that enrich and vitalize life and for a sense of meaning and integrity. It is human nature to reach out and encounter the world, not only in banal ways but also in ways that have an intrinsic sense of authority, compellingness, ultimacy, and even sacredness (Davis, 1989; Eliade, 1959; Jung, 1938; Nielsen et al., 1993; Maslow, 1970). As we grow in empathic relationship with the world, our natural sense of compassion blossoms.

It is human nature to try to make sense of self and world. Who am I? Why do I exist? What is my purpose? What is the nature of reality? How did things get to be the way they are? How do I fit in the world? These are questions of meaning that everyone struggles with in various ways. Even if we accept religious or culturally prescribed answers to these questions, at certain points of life crisis, when our neat worlds are shattered, we ask again: Why?

We also need a sense of integration and wholeness within ourselves and in relation with the world. Do I know myself? Can I reach a place of clarity and calm within? Do I feel attuned within, or do I behave as if "the

Figure 2.2.
An Operational Model of Spirituality as an Aspect of Human Experience

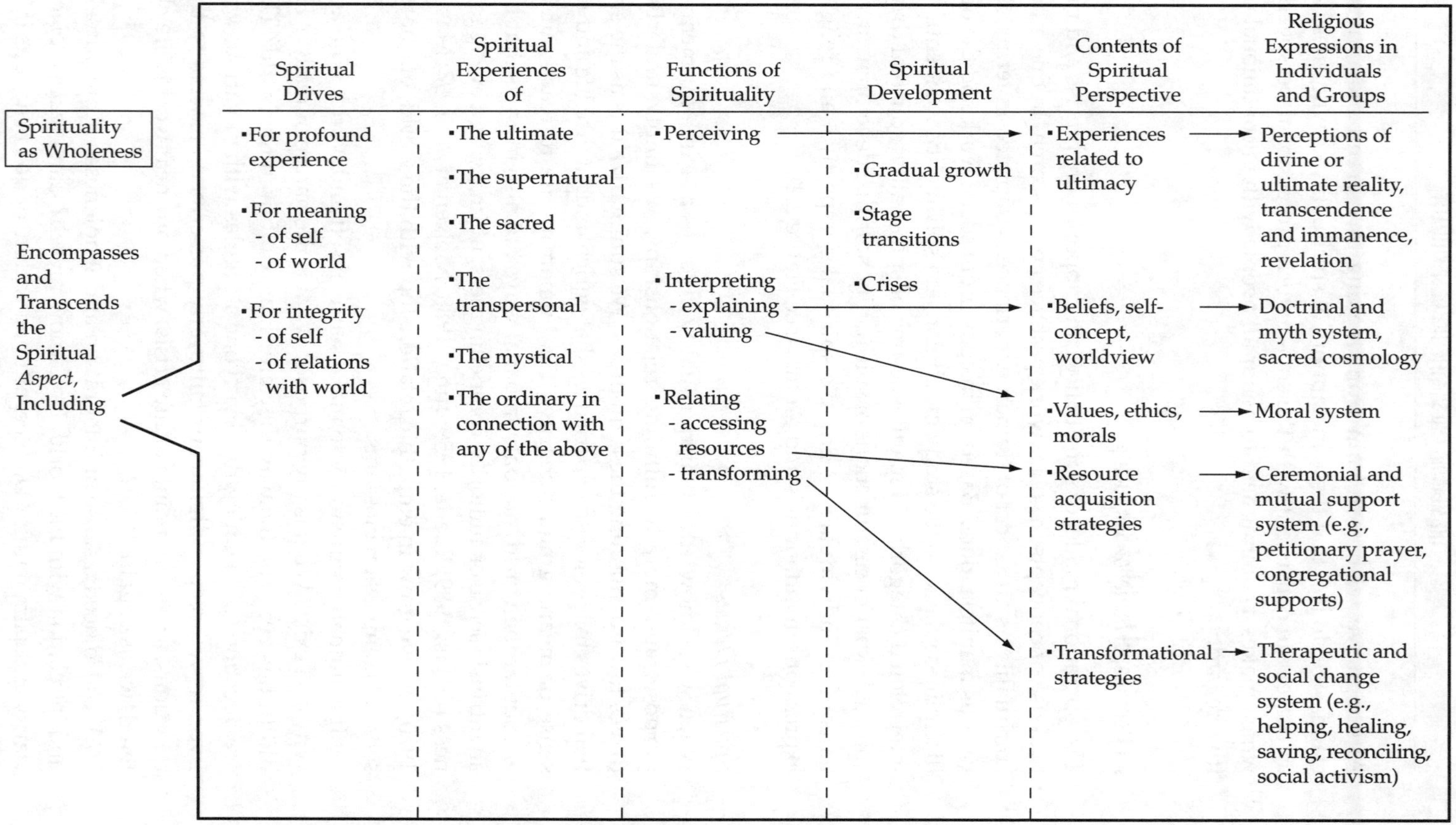

Spirituality as Wholeness

Encompasses and Transcends the Spiritual *Aspect*, Including

Spiritual Drives	Spiritual Experiences of	Functions of Spirituality	Spiritual Development	Contents of Spiritual Perspective	Religious Expressions in Individuals and Groups
▪For profound experience	▪The ultimate	▪Perceiving	▪Gradual growth	▪Experiences related to ultimacy	▪Perceptions of divine or ultimate reality, transcendence and immanence, revelation
▪For meaning - of self - of world	▪The supernatural	▪Interpreting - explaining - valuing	▪Stage transitions	▪Beliefs, self-concept, worldview	▪Doctrinal and myth system, sacred cosmology
▪For integrity - of self - of relations with world	▪The sacred	▪Relating - accessing resources - transforming	▪Crises	▪Values, ethics, morals	▪Moral system
	▪The transpersonal			▪Resource acquisition strategies	▪Ceremonial and mutual support system (e.g., petitionary prayer, congregational supports)
	▪The mystical			▪Transformational strategies	▪Therapeutic and social change system (e.g., helping, healing, saving, reconciling, social activism)
	▪The ordinary in connection with any of the above				

right hand doesn't know what the left hand is doing"? How do I relate with others? What is my place in the scheme of things? Am I loved? Whom and what things do I love? What is of greatest significance to me?

Spiritual Experiences

These drives motivate us to experience ourselves and the world in all ways, from the mundane to the profound. But usually people describe experiences as spiritual when they involve a sense of contact with powers and meanings of profound or ultimate significance. Experiences oriented around ultimacy are described in many ways, depending on the nature of the experience itself and the experiencer's interpretation. Spirituality and religion are often connected most intensely with people's experiences of the sacred, the supernatural, the transpersonal, and the mystical (Angel, 1994; Griffin, 1988; Grof, 1988; James, 1982; Johnston, 1995; Johnstone, 1992; Otto, 1950; Roberts, 1995; Wilber, 1995). Also, any event of an ordinary or extraordinary kind may be experienced as a reflection, manifestation, or reminder of ultimate concerns, values, and reality. For example, for the Zen practitioner, simply washing dishes with mindfulness can be an experience of beautiful clarity and appreciation for the extraordinariness of the mundane. There is a common Zen saying that Zen is nothing special, or Zen mind is ordinary mind. In other words, clarity also makes everything special. For agnostics and atheists, the experience of ultimacy is not put in terms of divinity or supernaturalism. Nonetheless, as we will see in the discussion of the existential spiritual perspective (see Chapter 5), there can be a sense of ultimate guiding principles, such as human freedom, responsibility, compassion, and justice, rooted in profound experiences of connection with humanity and the universe.

Functions of Spirituality

Perceiving. The drive for the experience of ultimacy engages all human faculties and capacities. For example, a biological imperative such as sexual craving can express through loving communion with another person. The faculties of the five senses can all be engaged in a way that opens awareness of extraordinariness or the immanent presence of the divine. Transpersonal theory and mystical traditions suggest also that there are other faculties of perception that enable people to experience a sacred or supernatural realm that transcends the limits of ego, physical boundary, space, and time (Grof, 1988; Wilber, 1995).

Interpreting. The drive for meaning engages people's symbolizing and story-making abilities in order to explain and grant value. We create representations for the phenomena of our inner experience and the world and create myths (sacred stories) for why things are this way (Anderson, 1996; Eliade, 1959, 1963; Fowler, 1995; Lehmann & Meyers, 1997; Morris, 1987; Nielsen et al., 1993; Pals, 1996; Proudfoot, 1985). We establish priorities, goals, and systems for moral decision making.

Relating. The drive for integrity engages us in relationship with ourselves, other beings, and the ultimate ground of reality, however a person understands it. We access resources to nourish our development as individuals and groups, including inner resources of wisdom and outer resources of social support and, for some, divine grace or revelation (Bellah, 1991; Jones, Wainwright & Yarnold, 1986; Lehmann & Meyers, 1997; Lessa & Vogt, 1972). As we relate with others and reflect on ourselves, we also engage in change, growth, and transformation. Natural compassion and ideals of justice shape our efforts to help others.

Spiritual Development
Our inherent creativity and efforts to adapt to changes in the environment and in ourselves take place through many kinds of developmental processes that challenge and expand our established frameworks of meaning (Barry & Connolly, 1982; Erikson, 1962, 1969; Fowler, 1996; Wilber, 1995). As we will discuss extensively in Part III, spiritual development flows through periods of gradual growth, life cycle stage transitions, and spiritual crises. Spiritual experiences can propel our development into peaks of insight and sometimes into pits of despair. And our ongoing developmental challenge is to integrate all our experiences into a sense of self as a whole person in fulfilling relations with others.

Contents of an Individual's or Group's Spiritual Perspective
Spiritual experiences, functions, and processes of development interact to form particular contents of an individual's or group's spiritual perspective. The function of perceiving yields specific experiences of ultimacy, the supernatural, the sacred, the transpersonal, the mystical, and the ordinary in relation with these. The interpretive function of explaining results in beliefs about self and world in an overall worldview. And the worldview changes in response to new insights into self and world. If this occurs in the context of religious language and institutions, doctrines are organized into a formalized sacred cosmology (Beane & Doty,

1975; Bellah, 1991; Hick, 1990; Johnstone, 1992; Nielsen et al., 1993; Paden, 1992, 1994).

The interpretive function of valuing leads to the formation of value systems, including priorities, life goals, ethical guidelines, and moral stances. If this occurs in a religious context, a sacred moral framework is established, vested by a community with a sense of ultimate moral authority coming from a transcendent source. This moral framework is sanctioned and supported by the religious community.

The relational function of accessing resources leads to strategies to acquire physical, mental, social, and spiritual resources that support coping and ongoing personal and community survival and growth. This may include intrapersonal strategies for self-reflection and meditation. This may also include interpersonal strategies for connecting with external supports, including family, friends, spiritual support groups, and communication with supernatural forces. In a religious context, the person learns ceremonies, mutual help, forms of worship, petitionary prayer and magic, and ways of examining conscience that have been formed by a religious community.

The relational function of transforming produces strategies for maintaining, restoring, and changing self and world over time as needed. The drive to connect with other beings and the ground of being brings constant challenges as our self-concepts and worldview are stretched by ordinary events, life crises, and feelings of sacred revelation or inspiration. Resources and strategies for helping, healing, and seeking justice are applied to strive toward ideals or to respond to physical, mental, social, or spiritual distress. In the religious context, the transforming function leads to community-sanctioned therapeutic and social service systems for religiously motivated helping, healing, saving, reconciliation, and social activism (Bellah, 1991; Carson, 1989; Dossey, 1993; Matthews, Larson & Barry, 1993; Niebuhr, 1932; Sobrino, 1988).

For the sake of simplicity, we have described how functions of spirituality lead to particular contents of a spiritual perspective. This is not only a one-way process, however. The expression of spiritual drives, the nature of spiritual experiences, spiritual functioning and development, and contents of a person's or group's spiritual perspective are all shaped by contact with established spiritual perspectives.

Spirituality and Religion of Groups

The drives, functions, experiences, developmental processes, and contents of spiritual perspectives occur in individuals as well as social systems, such as families, small groups, communities, cultures, and the global community. Meso and macro analysis has been developed well in religious studies, cultural anthropology, and sociology (Anderson, 1996; Bellah, 1991; Capps, 1995; Johnstone, 1992; Lessa & Vogt, 1972; Lehmann & Meyers, 1997; Morris, 1987; Pals, 1996; Roberts, 1995). We can define *religion* as an organized system of experiences, beliefs, values, and adaptational and transformational strategies that are shared by a community, with reference to concerns vested with a sense of ultimacy, sacredness, or supernatural status. However, it is possible for a group to interact for relatively brief amounts of time concerning spiritual matters without forming into a religion, so there are *spiritual support groups* that do not constitute religions. When interactions are sufficiently regular and enduring as to institutionalize patterns of belief, values, and behaviors, then a religion emerges from a spiritual support group. Similarly, members could depart from an organized religion and shift toward a private form of spirituality by retaining some religious symbols and practices but restricting them to idiosyncratic or private use, or by abandoning the religious modes altogether and creating some new spiritual beliefs, values, and practices (Brinkerhoff & Mackie, 1993; Dowdy, 1991).

Realistically, since every culture has some form of religious institutions and most people are exposed to them, the interaction and influence between individuals' nonreligious or nonsectarian spirituality and institutional religions will usually be reciprocal. For example, even those who adhere to small-scale New Age spiritual support groups, and borrow eclectically from diverse religious traditions to form new beliefs and practices, could not do so without interacting with those religious traditions, at least indirectly by appropriating and altering their symbols. And if a New Age spiritual support group begins to regularize and institutionalize its spiritual ways, it becomes a new alternative religious movement.

Mainstream religions are those that are predominant in a society because of their numbers of adherents and economic and political influence (Corbett, 1997). *Alternative religions* have smaller membership and marginal economic and political influence on a society. There is no absolute dividing line between these types, since this is partly a matter of perception and there is so much variation among religions. Some commonly cited identifying features of alternative religions are: charismatic lay leadership; less bureaucratic organization; relatively small size; emphasis on conversion and voluntary membership; spontaneous forms of worship; pervasive influence over members' daily lives; frequently an appeal to people who are marginalized, poor, or oppressed (Miller, 1995, pp. 3–4).

Sometimes alternative religions are called cults or new religious movements. The term *cult* has become pejorative and vague, so we will not use it. The term *new religious movement* is nonjudgmental, but not all alternative religions have originated recently.

Some sociologists also identify social patterns that resemble religion but are not limited to formal organized religion. Bellah (1991) called this civil religion. *Civil religion* involves fundamental values and beliefs about the relation between people and sacred powers that become pervasive through a society, even beyond the bounds of a particular religious institution. For example, American civil religion appropriates Judeo-Christian concepts of God and morals and applies them to political governance. The U.S. Constitution refers to God for its notion of human rights, and many political groups appeal to divine legitimation for their policies. To be consistent in our use of terms, we will refer to this as *civil spirituality*, since it is not limited to formal religious institutions.

There are also social systems built around meanings and values given ultimate significance that do not pertain to organized religions and may not use ideas of the sacred or supernatural. Smith (1994) called these *quasi-religions*. Quasi-religions provide elaborate structures of belief, ritualized behavior, and symbols. They may require supreme commitment from followers, even unto death. For example, Marxism gives ultimate priority to establishing utopian communism. Following Griffin (1988), in order to avoid confusion in our definition of religion, we will refer to a system of meaning (or a group) built around an ultimate concern but without reference to religious institutions as a *nonreligious spiritual perspective or group*. Chapter 5 will discuss two of these: existentialism and transpersonalism.

Can Spirituality be Measured?

Whether spirituality can be *operationalized*, that is, reduced to phenomena that can be directly observed and measured, depends on what one means by the term. By definition, spirituality as wholeness cannot be measured or reduced to any component for measurement without violating the very concept of spirituality as wholeness. As this chapter's opening quotation suggested, for those who uphold a holistic or mystical view of spirituality, there is something mysterious, and perhaps sacred, that cannot and should not be violated by empirical prying and intellectual analysis. However, even here, mystics would say that spirituality as wholeness not only can be experienced, but should be experienced. This is a kind of empiricism (knowledge by direct experience), but the means of knowing are claimed to go beyond the limits of the physical senses and ways of thinking or feeling that are bound by ego, space, and time. Yet when mystics talk about this realm of experience, they necessarily resort to metaphor, paradox, and parable, carefully pointing out that the reality of which they speak is beyond any words or concepts.

People whose own worldview rejects the possibility of sacredness, ego transcendence, and mystical experiences will view such claims as mere delusions, self-deceptions, or mistaken beliefs. For them, the claim of unmeasurability or inexpressibility is merely a hiding strategy; mysticism is seen as a mystification. This debate cannot be settled by argument. It rests on fundamentally different ways of apprehending and interpreting the world. It reflects two different spiritual perspectives (in the sense of worldviews and value systems).

In our operational model of spirituality as an aspect of the human being, the situation is much less murky. Although drives cannot be directly observed, we can observe the prevalence of human activities that strive for experience, meaning, and integrity that are found in all cultures. From this we can infer the existence of basic drives. We can also document people's description of their spiritual motivations and purposes. However, these drive-concepts are abstractions, not observable things in themselves.

Functions and contents of spirituality can be operationalized in terms of observable and measurable things and events. We can observe, describe, and analyze the way people perceive, interpret (explain and value), and relate (obtain resources and transform). We can also study developmental processes and relate them to ways of analyzing stages and crises of transformation. It is most easy to observe and measure the contents of a person's spirituality. For example, we can listen to people's accounts of transpersonal experiences and even use biofeedback equipment to measure physiological states and changes that correspond to subjective reports of alterations of consciousness and mystical experiences. This does not measure the subjective experience directly, but it does document its correlations with observable physical events.

We can also classify and rate spiritual and religious styles, such as religiosity, and examine correlations with other attitudes and behaviors (Benson, Donahue & Erickson, 1993; Brown, 1994; Shafranske, 1996; Watts & Williams, 1988; Wulff, 1991). *Religiosity* means the degree to which religious belief and practice are important to a person. This can be measured by rating such factors as *religious preference,* or sense of belonging to a particular religious group; *formal religious organizational affiliation; credal assent* to particular religious beliefs; *personal religious behavior,* or how often a person prays or engages in other religious activities privately; frequency of *attendance at places of religious practice;* religious *organizational activity* other than at places of religious practice; *amount of financial support* for religious groups; *sense of religious despair or hope;* and the extent of *growth seeking* through religious contexts.

For our purposes, we will use the term *religious propensity* to refer to religiosity. We will use the term *spiritual propensity* for the concept of intensity of spiritual concerns and activities in general, recognizing that spiritual experiences, beliefs, and behaviors may or may not occur within religious settings. The term *nonreligious spiritual propensity* specifies that a person does not use religion as a reference for his or her beliefs, attitudes, and behaviors. All features of spiritual propensity can take nonreligious forms. We will discuss this in more detail with regard to assessing clients' spiritual propensity in Chapter 8.

Concluding Thoughts on the Conceptualization of Spirituality for Practice

This conceptualization of spirituality both clarifies and complicates the meaning of the term. The term is used to refer to many different but related themes: spirituality as wholeness and spirituality in terms of drives, experiences, functions, developmental processes, and contents. Spirituality as a universal quality of human nature is not the property of any religion and need not express through any religious context. The drives, functions, processes, and contents of spirituality need not be discussed in religious terms. In fact, they need not be discussed by using the term *spirituality* either. But whenever these drives, experiences, beliefs, functions, developments, and behaviors are related to a sense of ultimacy, sacredness, or transcendence, it is useful to distinguish them with terms such as *spirituality* or *religion.*

Our usage of the term *spirituality* is not limited to beliefs in spirit, spirits, or a supernatural realm. These beliefs are often involved, but there are also atheistic worldviews and religious worldviews that do not require belief in spirits or the supernatural (e.g., Zen Buddhism). Nonetheless, they orient people around ultimate concerns and experiences. For some people, it may seem odd to separate spirituality from assumptions about spirit, so it may be helpful to recall that this is already common in English. Many terms derive from root words that originally meant "spirit" but are now used without a metaphysical implication. For example, sports fans can cheer for the home team and revel in the solidarity of "team spirit" without believing that they or their team are literally moved by spirits.

We can be inspired with creative ideas without experiencing that we are literally possessed by a spirit.

In the remainder of this book, we will remain consistent in our use of these terms. Our specific meaning should be clear from the context of usage or we will specify it. For example, the terms *spiritual* or *spirituality* used without qualification should be understood to include both religious and nonreligious expressions. If we say "spiritual and/or religious," this is a short form for saying "religious and/or nonreligious forms of" spirituality. Use of the term *religious* will always refer to an individual's or group's expressions of spirituality that are connected with institutionalized religions.

An important test of the usefulness of definitions is to examine their fit with actual use by social work practitioners. In the National Survey,

Table 2.1
National NASW Survey:
Social Workers' Definitions of Religion, Spirituality, and Faith

	Religion (%)	Spirituality (%)	Faith (%)
Meaning	37	85	44
Purpose	37	78	39
Belief	74	72	87
Ritual	77	22	10
Meditation	18	61	13
Organization	78	5	5
Community	64	20	7
Personal	31	82	53
Morality	51	47	15
Values	61	75	31
Ethics	49	64	23
Miracles	23	23	23
Prayer	66	47	33
Personal relationship with higher power	50	72	61
Sacred texts	59	12	9
Scripture	73	13	12

Note: Percents indicate percentage of respondents who selected a descriptor associated with a given term.

we explored the ways that social workers understand three common terms: *spirituality, religion,* and *faith.* We initially offered our own definitions of spirituality and religion so that respondents would have common meanings of the terms in mind when completing the survey. In addition, at the conclusion, we asked people to identify the descriptors (e.g., meaning, purpose, belief) that they relate to the terms *spirituality, religion,* and *faith* aside from our definitions. Respondents saw a close relationship between these terms, as nearly every descriptor had overlap for some people. However, a clear pattern of distinction between the terms emerges by comparing the top six descriptors for each. *Spirituality* was most often associated with the descriptors "meaning, personal, purpose, values, belief, and personal relationship with a higher power" (see Tables 2.1 and 2.2).

Faith was most often associated with the descriptors "belief and personal relationship with a higher power." These were the top two descriptors for *faith,* whereas they were the bottom two (though still frequent) descriptors for *spirituality.* This suggests that *faith* is more narrowly associated with beliefs and that *spirituality* is a much wider concept involving personal experience and a framework of meaning, purpose, values, and relationship with ultimacy, just as we have defined it. Interestingly, *faith*

Table 2.2
National NASW Survey:
Top Six Descriptors Selected in Each Category

Religion	%	Spirituality	%	Faith	%
Organization	78	Meaning	85	Belief	87
Ritual	77	Personal	82	Personal relationship with higher power	61
Belief	74	Purpose	78	Personal	53
Scripture	73	Values	75	Meaning	44
Prayer	66	Belief	72	Purpose	39
Community	64	Personal relationship with higher power	72	Prayer	33

Note: Percents indicate percentage of respondents who selected a descriptor associated with a given term.

was the least-often-checked term overall, indicating that practitioners in general found the term to be less relevant than *spirituality* and *religion.*

Religion was the mirror image of *spirituality*. The descriptors highly associated with *spirituality* ("meaning, personal, purpose, values, belief, and personal relationship with a higher power") were all associated with religion much less frequently. *Religion* was most frequently associated with "organization, ritual, belief, scripture, prayer, and community." This is consistent with our definition of religion as an institutionalized community pattern of beliefs, rituals, and values relating to spiritual concerns. Interestingly, the three terms are connected by the descriptor "belief." This was the only descriptor of the six most frequently selected that was used for each term.

These findings show that social work practitioners should find our definitions familiar and well fit with their own usage. We also hope that our expanded conceptualization of spirituality depicted in the holistic and operational models will assist with a more refined and precise application of these terms in social work practice.

RESPONDING TO THE SPIRITUALITY DEBATE

Although there is increasing support for dealing with spirituality in social work practice and education, this remains a controversial subject. Now that we have clarified what we mean by spirituality, it is important to consider how to respond to objections that may be raised. We do this by presenting arguments opposing the inclusion of spirituality in social work and then by showing how to respond effectively. As you progress through the presentation of opposing or supporting positions, you can reflect on your own misgivings or enthusiasm about the subject. For social workers who wish to advocate for the importance of the topic, or wish to defend against criticisms, or wish to work through uneasiness about the subject, it will be valuable for you to think carefully about each criticism and the response of supporters. In this way you can formulate your own rationale for addressing the topic in education or practice and can articulate it clearly to others.

Methodology and Purpose of the Literature Review

This discussion is based on an analysis of thirty articles, book chapters, or books published from 1988 through 1998 that focus on the topic of incorporating content of religion or spirituality into social work education.

These are cited in Table 2.3 by author and date, in chronological and alpha-betical order, classified according to whether the item was written primar-ily in opposition or support. Citations will be given in the text only as examples of key points. Items were selected if they were written by social workers, published in scholarly journals or books, and gave significant explicit attention to the educational preparation of social workers.

Each article, chapter, or book was examined for statements of opposi-tion or support for dealing with spirituality or religion in social work edu-cation. Three overarching themes, each with two subthemes, were

Table 2.3
Thirty Selected Publications Debating Inclusion of Spirituality and Religion in Social Work Education, 1988–1998

Opposing Positions	Supporting Positions
Clark, 1994	Canda, 1988b
Sullivan, 1994	Canda, 1988c
Weisman, 1997	Joseph, 1988
	Loewenberg, 1988
	Canda, 1989a
	Canda,1990a
	Constable, 1990
	Denton, 1990
	Dudley & Helfgott, 1990
	Krill, 1990
	Logan, 1990
	Netting, Thibault & Ellor, 1990
	Siporin, 1990
	Marshall, 1991
	Ortiz, 1991
	Sheridan & Bullis, 1991
	Sheridan et al., 1992
	Amato-von Hemert, 1994
	Canda & Chambers, 1994
	Cowley & Derezotes, 1994
	Furman, 1994
	Derezotes & Evans, 1995
	Krill, 1995
	Bullis, 1996
	Van Soest, 1996
	Canda, 1997a
	Russel, 1998

identified to organize and summarize the range of opinions expressed. The themes, subthemes, and content of the debate are presented in Table 2.4. For each of the three major themes, the opposing positions are presented first and then the supporting positions. These presentations are syntheses and expansions of the various ideas found in the literature review and incorporate ideas from all thirty items.

The opposing positions emphasize a problem-oriented perspective on spirituality and religion. They tend to assume that there are basic defects in the nature of religious institutions and individuals. They view connection of religion and spirituality to social work as inherently problematic. And they identify logistical and practical difficulties of dealing with spirituality and religion in practice or education as discouraging or insurmountable.

Supporting positions are often presented as a response to actual or hypothetical objections. The lists of opposing positions include those given in publications that were written from an opposing viewpoint, as well as those addressed by supporters. So, in part, supporting positions are reactions to controversies raised in formal surveys of practitioners and educators and in the professional experience of the various authors. But the supporting positions go beyond mere reaction to advocate for the significance of spirituality and religion on their own terms. They view difficulties as challenges and opportunities. They recognize the inherent strengths and resources that can be found through spirituality and religion. They recognize dilemmas and tensions, but these are seen as opportunities for clarification and dialogue. Supporters of spirituality also express enthusiasm about the growing momentum of work on this topic and the creative potential for innovation in practice and education.

There were only three articles or book chapters written primarily from an opposing standpoint (Clark, 1994; Sullivan, 1994; Weisman, 1997). These authors' essays were written by invitation to participate in a debate on the topic, so the context of the publication determined the fact that these opposing views were presented at all. And of these three authors, Sullivan (1992) has written elsewhere about the positive role of spirituality in the lives of people with severe mental illness, so he does not take a wholly negative view of the topic. The contrast between this lack of opposing publications and the plethora of supporting publications is quite remarkable. It belies the impression among many social workers that this topic is taboo. Or perhaps many naysayers are just silent in print.

Table 2.4
Resolving the Debate About Studying Religion and Spirituality in Social Work

Opposing Positions	Supporting Positions
Inherent Deficiencies of Religion/Spirituality	**Responding to Challenges and Strengths of Religion/Spirituality**
Institutional Defects	*Institutional Challenges and Strengths*
• Sectarian views are too limiting or biased for the profession • Rigidity, dogmatism, and judgmentalism of religions are worrisome • Religions are basically status quo maintaining • Spiritual concerns are overly focused on micro perspective rather than macro justice	• Use an inclusive view of spirituality • Engage diverse ideological and spiritual perspectives in dialogue; avoid negative stereotyping • Address the role of religions in both restricting and promoting justice • Identify both micro and macro implications of spiritual and religious perspectives
Personal Defects	*Personal Challenges and Strengths*
• Religion is an expression of psychopathology • Spirituality is inherently personal and idiosyncratic	• Identify the role of religions in both restricting and promoting mental health • Link micro and macro issues of spirituality
Religion and Spirituality Are Inconsistent with the Nature of the Profession	**Religion and Spirituality Express the Nature of the Profession**
Domain Concerns	*Domain Implications*
• Religion and social work are separate and mutually exclusive domains • Religion and spirituality are not very important for understanding clients • Addressing religion and spirituality would undermine the status of the profession	• Religion, spirituality, and social work are interrelated and complementary • Religion and spirituality are crucial for understanding clients • Addressing religion and spirituality competently would enhance the status of the profession

Table 2.4 (continued)
Resolving the Debate About Studying Religion and Spirituality in Social Work

Opposing Positions	Supporting Positions
Value Conflicts	*Value Dilemmas*
• Involving religion increases the danger of proselytization and violation of clients' self-determination	• Address spirituality in a manner consistent with professional values
• Addressing religion weakens church-state separation	• Support both church-state separation and respect for spiritual diversity
• Social work should be value free or objective	• Social work is inherently value based and spiritual
• Religion and spirituality are inconsistent with a scientific professional base for practice	• Addressing spirituality is consistent with the contemporary philosophy of science in social work
• Social workers tend to be irreligious or uninterested	• Social workers are often religious and always spiritual; ethical and moral reflection in practice are necessary
Logistical Problems	**Logistical Solutions**
Inadequate State of the Art	*Emerging State of the Art*
• Concept of spirituality is too vague for use	• Refine definitions
• Efforts to combine religion and social work are not adequately developed	• Utilize extensive available knowledge and skill for linking spirituality to service; continue development
• Workers are unprepared to address, so better to ignore or refer	• Enhance education of workers
Curriculum Concerns	*Curriculum Opportunities and Responsibilities*
• Curriculum is already too crowded	•Implement both infusion and specialization in curriculum
• Educators are unprepared to teach, so better to ignore	• Engage educators in continuing education and curriculum development

Response to Characteristics of Religion and Spirituality

Opponents often base their concerns on an assumption that there are basic defects inherent in institutional religions, spiritual perspectives, and individuals. Although Christian and Jewish theologies, moral precepts, and institutions supported the development of social service and professional social work at the foundation of this profession, both opponents and supporters of spirituality in social work have argued that the common base of the profession should not adopt sectarian frameworks for theory or practice (Canda, 1989a, 1997a; Sullivan, 1994; Weisman, 1997). Even when sectarian service is well intentioned, the particular religious beliefs cannot be imposed on all social workers or their clients. Sectarian beliefs and practices may need to be understood as relevant to clients and their sociopolitical contexts, but no one sectarian framework would be acceptable to the diverse range of religious and nonreligious workers and clients. In addition, some religious groups compete and conflict with each other. If this tendency were brought into the profession, it would fracture it.

There is also a worry that religious teachings may be used to blame or condemn clients rather than to help or empower them. Early in our professional history, religious precepts were used to distinguish between worthy and unworthy poor, to brand people with substance abuse disorders as moral reprobates, and to pass negative judgment on people with lifestyles different from the moral codes of the believers. Professional helpers who questioned these ideas could be ostracized by their religious community. There are many contemporary versions of this kind of moralistic judgmentalism and intolerance of diversity, ranging from blaming the victim in current so-called welfare reform to insulting portrayals of gay and lesbian people. Some religiously based missionary service organizations still require people who receive assistance to listen to evangelical preaching or attend religious services.

Religious institutions have also been criticized for protecting the status quo. By blaming victims for alleged immorality or pathology rather than criticizing oppressors and unjust social institutions, they turn people's attention away from social change. By teaching that the experience of suffering or injustice in this life is only a temporary (and perhaps even deserved) inconvenience, those who suffer are encouraged to keep quiet and wait for a better life beyond this one, in heaven or through reincarnation. Religious institutions that have large financial bases and memberships have to be especially cautious about challenging oppressive governments, or "biting the hand that feeds them."

The defects of spirituality go into the heart of the individual, in some opposing views. Following the assumptions of Freudian theory, Marxist analysis, or materialistic scientific rationalism, some opponents have argued that religion itself is built on the unrealistic fantasies, delusions, and hallucinations of misguided individuals (Canda, 1989a). At best, some say, religion is an individual or societal coping mechanism to deal with uncertainty, ignorance, fear of death, and the need to establish social controls over deviant behavior. In this view, as an individual becomes more mature, and a society becomes more progressed scientifically, the need for religion should disappear.

Some people also feel that spirituality in general, whether within institutional religions or not, is focused mainly on the private lives of individuals, such as personal salvation or individual fulfillment (Sullivan, 1994). In this view, spirituality skews our perspective to the micro psychosocial world of the individual and turns attention away from matters of social institutions and social policy.

Since the profession of social work has a purpose to promote individual well-being and social justice for all people, opponents argue it is not appropriate to use sectarian, judgmental, status-quo-maintaining, micro focused, fantasy-based frameworks to guide our profession. Put this way, who could argue with that?

From the supporting perspectives, the trouble is precisely that the opponents depict religion and spirituality in such a one-sided pejorative manner. This itself can be considered a display of unprofessional bias.

Supporters generally agree that there are legitimate concerns about using competitive and rigid ideological, judgmental, or oppression-maintaining frameworks to guide social work practice. But this applies to both religious and nonreligious forms of belief and behavior. Political ideologies, human behavior theories, practice models, and agency policies and procedures all can reflect rigid, punitive, judgmental, or oppressive assumptions. We need to face these biases and obstacles to human well-being and justice wherever they are found, in religious settings and elsewhere. Avoiding the topics of religion or spirituality because of these problems only allows them to continue without open examination.

Supporters of spirituality in social work (who are not taking an exclusively sectarian view) promote an understanding of spirituality that embraces all its diverse religious and nonreligious expressions (Canda, 1988b, 1988c, 1989; Denton, 1990; Dudley & Helfgott, 1990; Joseph, 1988; Sheridan et al., 1992; Siporin, 1990), as we have done in this chapter. Proponents often point out that such appreciation can develop only out of mutual knowledge, understanding, and cooperation. Therefore, diverse ideological and spiritual perspectives should be brought together in constructive dialogue. Simplistic and negative stereotypes should be avoided.

Institutional religions are not the opposite of spirituality. One is not all good or the other all bad. Institutional religion is one way that spirituality may be expressed. As with any other social institution, religious institutions will play various roles in promoting or restricting justice. For example, during the slavery period in the United States, various Christian denominations supported or opposed slavery, and there was dissension within denominations as well. Both sides used their theologies to support opposing views (Gravely, 1973). So it is important for social workers to understand the particular views and practices of particular religions as relevant to their clients. Obstacles can be identified as challenges to be addressed creatively, and strengths and resources can be honored and engaged in the helping process.

Similarly, religious and spiritual beliefs and practices may reflect individual mental disorders, or important insights, or both together. Rather than practice antireligious discrimination (which is illegal and unethical), social workers need to engage with the client in differential assessment to sort out these complexities (Bullis, 1996; Cowley & Derezotes, 1994; Derezotes & Evans, 1995; Sheridan & Bullis, 1991).

Proponents also emphasize that religious and nonreligious forms of spirituality have implications for all types and levels of social systems, from the micro to the macro. Many writings about spirituality and social work reflect an emphasis on micro practice, but this simply reflects the overemphasis on clinical practice among students and practitioners generally. Authors such as Netting, Thibault, and Ellor (1990) and Canda and Chambers (1994) have emphasized the importance of spirituality for macro practice and social policy.

Perceived Connection with the Nature of the Profession

Some opposition to addressing spirituality and religion is based on perceived inconsistencies between them and the nature of the social work profession. Again, this perception is usually based on a narrow definition of spirituality that limits it to formal religious beliefs and institutions (Clark, 1994; Sullivan, 1994; Weisman, 1997). Each is seen as having a separate domain, and the boundary between them should not be crossed. Some argue that religion deals mainly with ideas of the supernatural or private experiences that should not be brought into the public domain of social

welfare institutions and social work agencies. In this view, if clients identify an interest in religion or trace problems to a religious source, then
social workers should refer them to a religious specialist, such as clergy,
and stay out of the matter. It has also been claimed that religion and spirituality are not very important to most clients, or at least are not relevant
to issues they bring to social workers. A third concern is that social workers who become involved with spiritual matters in practice may be perceived as incompetent or unscientific by other professionals, thus
undermining the status of the profession.

Other domain concerns address value dilemmas. Social work is a profession committed to client self-determination, freedom of choice, objective professional judgment, and scientific rigor. These values all appear to
be jeopardized by bringing religion or spirituality into the social work
domain. It is feared that social workers may use their jobs to proselytize
clients. Especially in agencies supported by public funds, it is feared that
the constitutionally required separation between church and state will be
violated by zealous social workers.

Some social workers and educators promote a conception of practice
that is objective or value free, meaning that the worker's values do not distort or interfere with the helping process. This position sometimes reflects
a commitment to a neopositivist view of so-called empirically based practice, that is, a worldview that assumes there is an objective, independent
reality that can be known through traditional experimental or survey type
research. This type of research, in this view, should drive the decisions of
competent social workers. Consideration of unmeasurable faith claims,
invisible spiritual forces, or even a client's subjective reports of spiritual
experiences may be rejected as irrelevant or misleading sources of information. It has also been suggested that social workers tend to be irreligious
or uninterested in religion and spirituality, so it is natural and reasonable
that they avoid the topic.

Supporters argue quite the opposite. They believe that the domains of
social work and religion or spirituality are closely interrelated. First, given
the inclusive definition of *spirituality*, it follows that spirituality is involved
in some way with all situations of social work practice. The profession
advocates for a holistic person-in-environment way of understanding people. It is clear that religious institutions play an enormous role in society,
for better or worse. In fact, many social workers conduct practice in sec-
tarian-sponsored agencies and religiously supported programs, such as
Lutheran Social Services, Catholic Social Services, the Salvation Army,
Jewish Family Services, and mutual assistance programs for Buddhist

Asian Americans. To exclude them from our work would be to ignore major social institutions that impinge on many clients, in the realm of both mental health and social policy. Some social workers work in settings in which spiritual issues are routinely brought up by clients and require addressing spirituality as part of institutional accreditation, such as many substance abuse treatment programs, hospices, and hospitals. Likewise, as a basic aspect of human experience and development, it makes no more sense to cut off consideration of the spiritual than it would to ignore the biological, psychological, or social aspects. If we are committed to understand the whole person in the environment, then it is self-contradictory for social workers to exclude religion and spirituality.

The vast majority of Americans claim that religious beliefs and institutions are important to them, that they believe in a God, and that they have had personal religious or mystical experiences at some time (Amato-von Hemert, 1994; Bullis, 1996; Sheridan et al., 1992). Given the prevalence of religion and spirituality and the need to address related issues in mental health assessment and psychosocial history, it is clear to supporters that religion and spirituality are crucial for understanding clients. Supporters believe that the more social workers are able to address these issues competently, the status of the profession will be enhanced. When social workers are uninformed or commit errors of judgment, they do no one service.

Supporters recognize that value dilemmas arise and that these can be very complex. The solution is to address religion and spirituality in a manner consistent with professional values rather than to exclude them. Indeed, it is imperative that social workers start where the client is at concerning spirituality. This stance prohibits proselytization, but it supports respectful dialogue with the client about religion and spirituality as relevant to the particular situation. Church-state separation would be violated if a particular religion would be promoted for clients, but an inclusive approach that deals with the topic in terms that are meaningful to the client is not a violation. Indeed, if religion were excluded or derided in social work, this might be considered antireligious discrimination and violation of the constitutionally protected right to freedom of religious expression. When religious or spiritual beliefs are closely connected to a client's or community's basic culture, eliminating them from practice might also constitute a form of racial or ethnic discrimination. These ethical and legal issues are certainly complex, but only an honest attempt to sort them out has a hope of succeeding.

The profession of social work distinguishes itself by values embedded in the National Association of Social Workers Code of Ethics, the Council on

Social Work Education's accreditation policies, and statements of professional mission and purpose. We claim to support individual fulfillment and social justice. We are opposed to discrimination and oppression on the basis of gender, race, ethnicity, culture, religion, social class, sexual orientation, and differing abilities and disabilities. We promote a relationship of empathy between worker and client, which requires unconditional positive regard and a willingness to become proactively involved. Supporters would argue that it is nonsense to promote value-free or objective practice. Rather, practice should arise from deep reflection about the values, ethics, and morals involved in the helping situation. The client should not be seen as an object of study, but rather as a subject of respect and a collaborator in the helping process. According to supporters, these qualities are consistent with the nature of the profession and the ideal of spiritually sensitive practice.

Some supporters have suggested that an appreciation of the dynamic, creative, uncontrollable, and unpredictable aspects of human experience is indeed consistent with trends in contemporary philosophy of science, influenced by relativity physics, quantum theory, dynamic systems theory, chaos theory, hermeneutics, and transpersonal theory (Cowley & Derezotes, 1994). Postmodern philosophy of science in social work does not so much reject science as a basis for competent practice; rather it reenvisions scientific social work. Further, as Denton (1990) pointed out, metaphysical religious propositions may not be verifiable by scientific research, but one can study the consequences of religious belief on people.

Recent exploratory surveys of social work practitioners and educators indicate that it is not accurate to say that we are usually irreligious or uninterested in spiritual matters (Bullis, 1996; Canda, 1988b, 1988c; Derezotes & Evans, 1995; Dudley & Helfgott, 1990; Russel, 1998; Sheridan & Bullis, 1991; Sheridan et al., 1992). Although these surveys indicate that social workers on average may be less involved in formal religious activities than the general population, most are involved in religious practices currently or have been strongly influenced by them in the past. In addition, all social workers, like all other people, are dealing with spiritual matters in their personal lives, even if these are not put in religious terms. Many workers recognize this and wish they had more preparation for how to address these issues in practice.

Logistical Matters in Linking Religion and Spirituality to Social Work

There are two kinds of logistical barriers to addressing spirituality in social work, as expressed in opposing positions. The first pertains to limitations in the state of the art linking spirituality to social work. The second pertains to problems confronting social work education.

It is very difficult to define spirituality in a clear, unambiguous manner for use in practice and research. Opponents suggest that the term is currently too vague for use. Sectarian definitions are too limiting. Inclusive definitions are too broad (Sullivan, 1994). Another problem is that detractors believe that efforts to link religion and spirituality to social work are too new and untested to be reliable for practice (Weisman, 1997). It follows that if social workers are unprepared to address the subject with clients, it is best to ignore the subject or refer clients to religious specialists if necessary.

In debates about the social work curriculum, opponents to inclusion say that the social work curriculum is already too crowded with mandated content on various aspects of human behavior and diversity (Clark, 1994; Weisman, 1997). Therefore, it is not feasible to include more material on religion and spirituality. And even if this material were mandated, most social work educators are unprepared by training to teach on the topic. So again, in the realm of education, it would be better to avoid the topic or refer students to specialized courses in religious studies, if necessary.

Supporters see these logistical difficulties as opportunities for innovation and creativity (Canda, 1989a; Loewenberg, 1989; Russel, 1998). Although there is not yet a general consensus or even familiarity among social workers about how to define *spirituality* and *religion,* there is a consensus emerging in the literature about general issues of definition, such as using an inclusive definition that views spirituality as a basic aspect of human experience and distinguishes between religion and spirituality. The solution to this problem of ambiguity and disagreement is to continue work to refine the definition and clarify how this relates to practice and research, as we have done.

Proponents point out that religion and spirituality are not new topics for social work; they have been addressed to varying degrees throughout our history. Our experience can be reexamined for its relevance to contemporary practice. Further, there are tremendous resources of knowledge and skill pertaining to linkage between religion and helping in the fields of anthropology, academic religious studies, pastoral counseling, transpersonal psychology, and holistic health that social workers with proper education can use. There are already about five hundred articles, book chapters, or books related to social work on religion and spirituality, many of which draw on interdisciplinary study. Supporters see the current state of the art as a time of tremendous momentum that should be encouraged.

If practitioners feel unprepared to address spirituality and religion in practice, this does not justify ignoring the topic. Rather, it calls for more education on the topic within social work degree programs and continuing education. And if many educators do not feel prepared to teach about this, they need to engage in continuing education in order to learn how to address the topic. Surveys of social work educators indicate that many recognize the relevance of the topic but are not sure how to teach about it.

Educators need guidance for how to present such material. Supporters have proposed guidelines and strategies for addressing spirituality and religion in social work education, by both infusion of content throughout all aspects of the curriculum and developing specialized courses on the topic (Bullis, 1996; Canda, 1989a, 1997a; Dudley & Helfgott, 1990; Furman, 1994; Krill, 1990, 1995; Loewenberg, 1988; Ortiz, 1991; Russel, 1998). The Council on Social Work Education has also sponsored faculty development institutes at annual national meetings for several years. Russel (1998 and personal communication) has found that more than eighteen programs already have specialized courses on the topic and that the number is increasing quickly. During 1996–1997, she received more than seventy inquiries from around the country from educators who wanted to have information to assist with developing course content.

In summary, both opposing positions and supporting positions recognize difficulties for dealing with religion and spirituality in social work. Supporters view the difficulties as opportunities for innovation rather than as insurmountable obstacles. Opposing positions tend to frame religion and spirituality in terms of deficits and pathology. Supporting positions take a strengths perspective. They recognize that religion and spirituality, like any other aspect of human life, can play a role in troubles. But they are also a source of tremendous personal and community resources. The great opportunity is how we can use these resources to support individual and societal well-being.

The Council on Social Work Education now recognizes the importance of content on religious and spiritual diversity (Russel, 1998) in its accrediting guidelines. There is an explosion of interest among educators and practitioners, as indicated by national and international conferences and the rapid increase in the rate of publications on the topic in the past ten years. It is no longer a matter of whether the social work profession should address the topic. It is already happening. The question now is how we can address religion and spirituality in a manner consistent with professional values and purposes.

This contention is well supported by the National Survey findings. Most social workers in our study believed that it is appropriate to raise the topic of spirituality in a nonsectarian manner with clients on every issue we explored, but especially regarding terminal illness, bereavement, substance abuse, and suffering effects of a natural disaster. Most respondents also believed that it is appropriate to raise the topic of religion in cases of terminal illness, bereavement, difficulty in family relations, foster parenting, and suffering the effects of a natural disaster. But for every issue, fewer believed it was appropriate to raise the subject of religion than nonsectarian spirituality (see Table 2.5). These findings indicate that many social workers recognize the importance of spirituality and religion while also making a distinction in applying them to practice.

Unfortunately, as earlier studies also indicated, our National Survey showed that about 73 percent of respondents did not receive content on spirituality or religion in their social work education. As students, they had rarely received relevant content in the curriculum areas of human

Table 2.5
Appropriate to Raise Topic of Religion/Spirituality by Client Issue

Raise topic of religion/ spirituality with . . .	Religion			Spirituality		
	% agree	X	SD	% agree	X	SD
Terminal illness	73	3.90	1.11	90	4.30	.87
Substance abuse	43	3.19	1.20	74	3.90	1.03
Foster parent	62	3.58	1.15	66	3.75	1.04
Sexual abuse	46	3.23	1.20	69	3.79	1.04
Partner violence	44	3.20	1.17	64	3.69	1.05
Suffering effects of natural disaster	55	3.44	1.17	73	3.87	1.02
Bereaved	75	3.89	1.08	87	4.22	.89
Chronic mental disorder	36	3.05	1.17	52	3.47	1.10
Loss of job	36	3.08	1.15	57	3.55	1.08
Difficulty in family relations	47	3.27	1.14	64	3.68	1.03
Criminal justice	40	3.14	1.14	59	3.59	1.05

Note: A t-test of means showed a significant difference between religion and spirituality with clients presenting the same problem, with $p < .01$. Respondents were significantly more likely to believe it is appropriate to raise the topic of nonsectarian spirituality than religion.

behavior, research, and policy. Clinical practice and field practicum exposed somewhat more to the subject, but still a small minority (less than 12 percent of respondents). Even in courses dealing with human diversity, only about 13 percent had received content. Only about 17 percent agreed that social workers in general possess the knowledge to address religious or spiritual issues. Thirty-nine percent agreed that they do not have the skill to do so. It appears that many social work practitioners do not feel adequately prepared to address religion or spirituality, even though they recognize the importance.

SUMMARY

In this chapter we developed a detailed holistic and operational conceptualization of spirituality. Our conceptualization removes the charge that spirituality is too vague a concept to use in practice or research. As we saw in Chapter 1, if we are to remain consistent with professional values and a moral vision of compassion and justice, we need to address spirituality in social work. The only question is how to do so. In our response to opponents of spirituality in social work, we have set out a compelling intellectual rationale in support of a value-based commitment to practice in a spiritually sensitive manner. In the remainder of this book, we present a foundation of knowledge and skills for how to do this.

EXERCISES

2.1. What Does Spirituality Mean to You?

You are likely to have had some strong reactions to the various ideas about spirituality and religion presented in this chapter. Strong reactions often stem from feelings of congruence or conflict between one's own beliefs and others. In order to identify where these are coming from, try the following self-reflection exercise to determine your own definitions and issues related to the terms *spirituality* and *religion*. This exercise also makes clear that our definitions are affected by our life situation, sociocultural conditioning, and self-understandings. Since these change over time, our personal definitions of spirituality and religion may change as well.

Take out five blank sheets of paper. Label the top of each sheet with the headings that follow. Then, following the suggestions, record your reflections on each topic.

Understanding of Spirituality and Religion in Early Childhood

Take a moment to relax and be quiet. Think back to your earliest memories of hearing discussions or having experiences that relate to an understanding of aspects of reality that are ultimate, sacred, or supernatural. What words to label them did you learn to use at the time? Did parents teach you to believe or not believe in a God, spirits, or some other divine forces? Did you participate in a spiritual group or religious community? What kinds of stories did you learn to explain the nature of life and death? What rituals and symbols do you recall vividly? In association with these experiences and words, what mental pictures and feelings come to mind? What were the feelings of affirmation and strength related to this? What were feelings of confusion or distress related to this? Do not judge yourself about any of this. Simply be aware of these memories and accept them gently, without any discomfort.

Draw a picture or diagram or write down some key words that sum up your insights about this.

Understanding of Spirituality and Religion Now

Consider the same questions as above, but identify the terms that are meaningful to you now. What are the thoughts, images, and feelings that you now associate with the terms *religion, spirituality, faith,* or any others that are important to you? What are the strengths and struggles you now experience in regard to this?

Draw a picture or diagram or write down some key words that sum up your insights about this.

How Did You Get Here?

Be aware of the developmental process that you have gone through to move from your childhood experience of spirituality to your current experience. What were the key events that signaled change points? Who were inspirational or troubling figures in your life who have shaped your understanding of spirituality?

Again, depict your insights through a picture or key words.

Where Do You Want to Go?

Look over what you have written and drawn so far. Get a sense of the flow of your spiritual development to this point in time. Now imagine where you would like to go with your spiritual development. What are your overall life aspirations? How would you describe your images and feelings associated with your ideal of spiritual growth? How can you build on your spiritual strengths and resources? If you have identified limitations or conflicts, how could you address them to grow toward your aspirations? Draw a picture or diagram, or write down key words that depict your spiritual ideals and aspirations.

Reflection on the Reading

Now think back to your reactions to reading this chapter. If there were specific passages that provoked a strong response, consider whether there is any relation between what you have learned about yourself from this exercise and your reaction.

2.2. What is Your Position?

You may be reading this book for many different reasons. Perhaps you already have a strong interest in spirituality, and you want to learn more about applying this to practice. Perhaps you are unsure about the relevance of spirituality but are willing to consider it. Or you might believe that it is not appropriate to address spirituality in social work, but you are reading this book because of a class requirement or because you want to find out what your pro-spirituality colleagues are thinking. In any of these cases, it is important for you to clarify your position, in your own mind and in being able to articulate your views to people who disagree with you.

Look back to Table 2.4, which lists the rival positions. Review each position, con and pro, and consider the extent to which you agree. Think of an example and an explanation from your own personal and professional experience for each point that strikes you as especially important. Then write a short essay that articulates your position. If the position you had before you read this chapter remains the same, explain why. If it has changed, also explain why. Once your position is formulated, have a conversation about this with a trusted social work colleague who is likely to have a different position from yours. Try to reach mutual understanding, whether or not you end up agreeing.

PART II

EXPLORING SPIRITUAL DIVERSITY
for
SOCIAL WORK PRACTICE

CHAPTER THREE

HUMAN DIVERSITY, SPIRITUALITY, AND SOCIAL WORK PRACTICE

[I hope for a] Cathedral of Humanity
which should be capacious enough
to house a fellowship of common purpose.

> Jane Addams, *Humanism*, Settlement House
> Movement (cited in Oakley, 1995, p. 27).

INTRODUCTION

Human spirituality is like an intricate tapestry of all aspects of human diversity woven together with spiritual experiences, beliefs, and practices. In order to establish the context for this discussion of spiritual diversity, it will be helpful to use the metaphor of weaving to consider how the universal and particular aspects of spirituality relate to human experience.

Spirituality as *wholeness of the person-in-relation* is like the frame of a loom. The frame provides a structure and support to be filled by the interweaving of warp and woof fibers. Before weaving begins, the frame is empty; it represents a potential for form and beauty that is not yet actualized. This is like the universal potential for spiritual development of all people. The frame must be strong in order to hold taut the warp fibers, which are the necessary foundation for weaving a wonderful fabric. The frame (wholeness) can be thought of as the transpersonal or transcendent structure of human nature that provides for the possibility of particular spiritual experiences and expressions. It encompasses and holds all the fibers of particular spiritual experiences and expressions, but it also transcends them. Without this transcendent structure, the weaving of spirituality could not occur.

Before weaving on the loom frame can begin, a warp of parallel lengthwise fibers must be strung across the structure. This warp is the central threading that pervades the entire tapestry, but it is hidden within it. This is like the universal (panhuman) *spiritual drives* for profound experience, sense of meaning, and integrity that each person has. The warp fiber must be strong and durable. This dimension of spirituality is universal, like the frame, but it is immanent rather than transcendent. It pervades the tapestry, courses throughout it, and gives it shape. Also, the warp threads are connected to the frame, from which they derive the necessary tautness and support.

The woof consists of fibers woven through and around the warp. The woof can be composed of many colors and textures. These woof patterns are the outer aspects of the tapestry, which give it its particular appearance. The woof of spirituality results from the complex weaving together of many diverse strands deriving from *spiritual experiences* as shaped by such factors as gender, ethnicity, sexual orientation, age, religious or spiritual perspective, socioeconomic class, and various physical and mental abilities and disabilities.

The act of weaving is the spiritual creativity of the person-in-relation. We each weave a life tapestry by *functions of perceiving, interpreting, and relating* as they proceed through *developmental processes* of crisis and growth. As we weave our lives in relation with the world, we form particular *contents of spiritual perspectives,* such as experiences related to ultimacy and systems of beliefs, values, and strategies for resource acquisition and transformation of self and world.

Spiritual diversity is represented by the woof. The intricate patterns represent a person's way of life woven on the universal warp of spiritual drives, and the warp itself is connected to the transcendent frame. When the weaving is complete, the formerly empty frame of spiritual potential is filled with a particular and distinctive fabric associated with each person. Each individual weaves her or his spiritual tapestry in relation with other people and beings. Collectively we are all weaving a cosmic tapestry that connects all people and all things. This metaphor expresses the integral connectedness between differentness, distinctness, and diversity, as one aspect of spirituality, and commonality and universality, as another aspect.

In this chapter, we give an overview of spiritual expressions and forms in relation to human diversity. We discuss the history of religious diversity in American society and the social work profession. We consider links between ethnic diversity and the variety of religions. We also consider some concerns and controversial issues that arise from the intersection between religious diversity and other aspects of human diversity, in particular for women and for gay, lesbian, bisexual, and transgendered people. A pervasive theme of this chapter is that religious and spiritual diversity in the United States has always been characterized by a perplexing and challenging blend of religious freedom and religious persecution. Therefore, spiritually sensitive practice necessarily calls for a commitment to both personal well-being and social justice.

HISTORY OF SPIRITUAL DIVERSITY IN THE UNITED STATES

Historical Trends

For at least tens of thousands of years, hundreds of Indigenous cultures in North America have maintained distinct patterns of religious beliefs, rituals, and organizations influenced by relationship to the sacred earth. For example, peoples of the eastern woodlands, the southwestern deserts, the central plains, and the northwestern coastal rain forests developed distinctive spiritual ways in relation to the particular characteristics of the land, weather, and beings of the place. Europeans began to colonize North America in large numbers during the 1600s. The English pilgrims, other Puritans, and later, many other groups such as Quakers and Catholics came to North America seeking freedom from religious persecution (Chalfant, Beckley, & Palmer, 1987). Unfortunately, the Christian settlers often did not extend respect of religious freedom to members of rival Christian denominations and often engaged in denigration and persecution of First Nations peoples (Bullis, 1996; Canda, 1997b; Yellow Bird, 1995). Religious competition was compounded by nationalistic rivalries between French and Spanish territories (primarily Catholic) and English colonies (primarily Protestant). During the American Revolutionary War, many colonists in the Northeast sought freedom from both tyranny of the English government and the control of the Church of England. Christians both for and against the Revolution used religious justifications for their actions (Weber & Jones, 1994).

During this period, European American forms of Christianity predominated in the political and economic processes of the government and the general public. However, according to Melton (1993), many of the masses did not display strong church-based religiosity. In 1776, only about 5 percent of the colonial population were regular participating members of churches. In reaction to interreligious competition and the desire to free governmental control from any particular Christian denomination, formal church-state relations were cut at the time of the Revolution. This may also have been influenced by the First Great Awakening, beginning in 1734, which was a widespread Protestant evangelical movement that empha-sized salvation by personal relation with Christ and reliance on the Bible while deemphasizing the importance of religious affiliation (Chalfant, Beckley, & Palmer, 1987). But separation of church and state did not chal-lenge the predominance of Protestant Christianity. In the formerly English colonies, out of a population of about 3.5 million, about 20,000 were Roman Catholic and about 6,000 were Jewish. Limited religious pluralism was recognized, but Christianity was given privilege.

The nineteenth century involved forces that expanded significantly the religious diversity of the United States (Chalfant, Beckley & Palmer, 1987). Expansion of European settlers and colonialism westward to the Pacific coast brought contact with hundreds more Indigenous cultures and reli-gions. It also incorporated French and Spanish Catholic territories into the primarily Protestant nation. With the separation of church and state, Christian churches expanded private voluntary organizations and self-support systems while protecting their privileged position with the state. This opened more room to newer immigrant religious groups, such as the Moravians, Amish, Mennonites, and many more Catholics. In addition, theological disputes among longer-established Protestant groups increased the number of denominations.

The Civil War involved many splits between Christian abolitionists and proslavery Christians (Jones, 1991; Weber & Jones, 1994). Many Protestant denominations split into northern and southern branches. In the 1750s, slave owners began to allow proselytization among the slave laborers (Morris, 1991; Newsome, 1991). After the 1770s, voluntary par-ticipation of African Americans in Christianity increased, and they began to form separate congregations. Separate and independent African American Protestant denominations formed in the 1800s, such as the African Methodist Episcopal Church (established in 1816). Free African Americans, slaves, and emancipated African Americans formed religious movements that combined influences from traditional African religions, Christianity, and liberationism (Corbett, 1997; Logan, 1996; Logan, Freeman & McRoy, 1990). In the early 1800s, the Second Great Awakening movement led to the predominance of evangelical and revivalist Christian groups in the South and Southwest.

Between 1815 and 1920, about 5.5 million Irish (mainly Catholic) peo-ple emigrated to the United States. By 1850, there were 1.6 million Catholics (Takaki, 1993), and the Catholic church had become the largest single denomination. This rapid swelling of Catholics was met with oppo-sition by many Protestant groups.

The small percentage of the population who were Jewish in the 1700s were mostly of Spanish, Dutch, German, or Portuguese descent. In the 1880s, the first large Jewish emigration occurred from Germany and Russia. Many of these immigrants were secularized and urbanized, and some were political activists. Some of the German Jews established the more liberal humanistic branch of Reform Judaism. Others established the Conservative Judaism branch, which emphasizes Jewish traditions without strict orthodoxy. During the late nineteenth century, the more orthodox Eastern European Jews established Orthodox Judaism. Throughout this period, the Jewish emphasis on ethnic solidarity as well as constraints on Jews imposed by anti-Semitism served to maintain a distinct Jewish subculture, albeit with many religious and secular variations.

The 1800s also involved a period of religious innovation from Christians leading to major new denominations, such as the Church of Jesus Christ of Latter-Day Saints, Christian Science, and Jehovah's Witnesses. Each of these groups experienced organized opposition from established Christian groups and sometimes the U.S. government.

During the 1800s, there were three major areas of social justice–related religious debates in addition to the conflict between proslavery and abolitionist forces. The temperence movement (1860s–1933) involved intense opposition to alcohol, primarily by some Protestant groups, while many people of Catholic background supported alcohol consumption (Weber & Jones, 1994). The Social Gospel movement, from 1880 to 1910, arose primarily among liberal northern churches to link efforts for personal salvation with religiously based social justice advocacy. This movement led to the founding of the Federal Council of Churches, later named the National Council of Churches. The third debate related to the continuation and intensification of religious and cultural persecution of Indigenous peoples (Deloria, 1994). Westward expansion of European Americans brought territorial, military, economic, religious, and other forms of imperialistic destruction. By the time of the Allotment Act of 1887 (Dawes Act), which further destroyed the land base of Native peoples, virtually every form of traditional religion was banned on reservations. Although some Christians objected to this behavior, the majority actively supported this process through missionization and support of federal policies or else remained silent about it.

Trends of diversification continued to expand in the twentieth century. Antidiversity forces also rose in reaction. For example, by 1925 the anti-Catholic, anti-Jewish, and antiblack Ku Klux Klan was operating in all states and had a membership of about eight million. In contrast, ecumenical and interreligious movements also began to grow. For example, the National Council of Churches in Christ expanded formal cooperation between the more inclusive and liberal Protestant denominations in the 1950s and 1960s. Trends of unification increased within Lutheran, Methodist, and Presbyterian denominations. Interreligious dialogue between Protestants, Catholics, Jews, and members of other religions has increased since the Second Vatican Council of the Catholic Church (1962–1965).

Three major themes of religiously related social justice debate can be discerned in the twentieth century. First, during the two world wars, religious rationales for just war were elaborated, but religiously based pacifism and the antiwar movement also expanded. In the post–World War II period, religious debates concerning the civil rights movement and the Vietnam War increased the social activist agenda of many religious groups. Since the 1960s, there have also been countertrends of increased Christian conservatism and evangelicalism with highly organized political action on the one hand and, on the other hand, greater calls for ecumenical and interreligious cooperation, feminist approaches to spirituality, gay liberationism, and liberation theology among more politically and theologically liberal groups.

Contemporary Spiritual Diversity

According to Melton (1993), from 1800 to 1988, the number of Christian denominations grew from twenty to more than nine hundred. There are hundreds of Indigenous cultures, each with a variety of spiritual perspectives from culture-specific traditionalism to blending with Protestant and Catholic denominationalism, to completely new forms. Emigration from the Middle East and Asia, growth of the Nation of Islam among African Americans, and interest in Sufism by European Americans have resulted in many variations of Islam in the United States. Emigration from Asia, especially since the 1970s, has brought many ethnic-specific forms of Hinduism and Buddhism. In addition, many European Americans have become converts to offshoots of Hinduism (such as the Hare Krishna movement) and Buddhism (such as Tibetan Buddhism and East Asian forms of Zen and Pure Land Buddhism). The New Age movement of the 1970s and 1980s brought about many sectarian and nonsectarian blendings of humanism, new paradigm scientific thinking, and Eastern and Western mystical practices. At this point, most spiritual and religious perspectives in the world are represented in the United States to some degree (Canda, 1997b).

A sample of this variety of religious and spiritual perspectives is presented in Table 3.1. The figures are compiled from estimates provided by several sources (Chalfant, Beckley, & Palmer, 1987; Corbett, 1997; Famighetti, 1995; Lippy & Williams, 1988; Melton, 1993; Williamson, 1992). These researchers relied on surveys, reports of membership by religious organizations, and review of religious organization directories. They sometimes arrive at rather different demographic figures. This means that figures for groups without formal organizations or membership reporting procedures (e.g., the New Age movement or traditional Indigenous spiritualities) will not be represented or are based on inferences. Further, membership reports by religious organizations are not always accurate.

Table 3.1
Rough Estimates of Selected Religious Group Membership in the United States

Types of Religious Organization	Approximate Membership
Christian	
Roman Catholic church	60 million
Southern Baptist Convention	16 million
Other Baptist denominations	20 million
United Methodist church	9 million
African Methodist denominations	5 million
Lutheran denominations	8 million
Churches of God in Christ	6 million
Jesus Christ of Latter-day Saints denominations	5 million
Episcopal church	3 million
Jehovah's Witnesses	800,000
Church of Christ, Scientist	200,000
Jewish	
Conservative congregations	1.5 million
Reform congregations	1 million
Orthodox congregations	300,000
Other	
Islamic groups	1–6 million
Buddhist groups	1–5 million
Hindu groups	1–5 million
Wicca and neo-Pagan groups	10,000–50,000

This table therefore represents estimates only for the purpose of illustrating the tremendous diversity of religious and spiritual groups rather than definitive demographics.

In broad terms, one demographic fact is quite clear: the U.S. population remains predominantly Christian (Corbett, 1997). About 60 percent are Protestant, about 25 percent are Catholic, about 2 percent identify with Judaism, and about 4 percent indicate some other preference. About 9 percent do not identify with a religion.

This fact highlights three cautions for social workers. First, given the large number of Christian denominations, we need to avoid assuming any particular religious beliefs or practices when meeting a Christian client. We need to find out from the client what Christian affiliation means to her or him. Second, because most social workers are influenced by Christianity, we must be especially cautious not to impose religious assumptions or beliefs on non-Christian clients. Third, since those people falling in the "other" and "no religious preference" categories (e.g., atheists, Buddhists, Hindus, Muslims, and members of alternative religious groups) are most likely to experience negative social stigma and prejudice, we must be especially attentive to issues of religious freedom and social justice for these groups.

Contemporary Trends of Spiritual Belief and Practice

Corbett (1997) derived common features of religious and spiritual belief and practice for Americans in the 1990s from Gallup polls and other surveys. These features represent group trends, so they may not be true for any particular person. Andrew Greeley's (1989, 1995) survey studies show even more detailed patterns in relation to variables such as gender, religious affiliation, age, political affiliation, sexual attitudes, and religious images.

Spirituality in the United States involves great diversity, yet there is also a high level of consensus. Most Americans share the following beliefs: Christian (90 percent), there is a personal God (95 percent), there is a devil (66 percent), and there is an afterlife (heaven, 90 percent; hell, 75 percent). About 40 percent of the population attends a religious service in any given week. Religious organizations provide many formal and informal social supports for both members and nonmembers. For example, Sheridan et al. (1992) cited a 1989 Gallup poll finding that half of surveyed Americans who feel depressed utilize prayer, mediation, or Bible reading; 97 percent of these found these religious activities very or somewhat effective.

In American contemporary society, more people place first priority on private, personal, individualized faith rather than on institutional religious participation. Religious group membership often involves crossing boundaries set by expectations of family, ethnic group, and social class. In many congregations, there is a stronger focus on local issues and religious group particularism than on global issues and ecumenism. There is great interest in application of religion and spirituality to healing, alternative therapies, social action, and other practical "this-worldly" benefits. Emotional and experiential approaches to spirituality have grown more popular than intellectual approaches. Concern about women's issues among religious people has grown.

A more detailed survey of 1,599 baby boomers (born from 1946 to 1962) in California, Massachusetts, North Carolina, and Ohio suggested trends for this age cohort (Roof, 1993). Roof found that the term *spirituality* returned to popular use in the 1980s and 1990s. Boomers emphasize the importance of a spiritual quest for "a holistic, all encompassing vision of life" (p. 243). Interest in spirituality sweeps in many creative possibilities, often bringing together influences from diverse spiritual traditions and perspectives, including earth-centered and creation spiritualities, Indigenous spiritualities, Eastern (Asian) spiritualities, twelve-step programs, feminist spiritualities, and conventional Judeo-Christian traditions. Boomers also have a greater appreciation for religious pluralism and the importance of choosing one's religious affiliation rather than just being born into it. Boomers tend to emphasize that vital spirituality should stimulate personal growth and transformation, as well as social and political activism. Many boomers continue a rather traditional emphasis on religious institutional affiliation, but many also have little sense of commitment to a particular religious institution. They focus instead on personal faith and spiritual experience and exploration of spiritual alternatives. Although many boomers have a rather individualistic view of spirituality, many are also active in applying their personal spiritual quest to reforming and transforming religious communities. Some create small-scale spiritual support groups.

HISTORY OF CONNECTIONS BETWEEN SPIRITUALITY AND SOCIAL WORK

Three broad historical phases can be distinguished in the shifting trends of connection between spirituality and the social work profession (Canda, 1997b): *sectarian origins* (colonial period through early twentieth century), *professionalization and secularization* (1920s through 1970s), and *resurgence of interest in spirituality* (1980s through present) (See Table 3.2). In the first phase, voluntary social services and governmental social welfare–related policies were largely influenced, directly or indirectly, by Christian and Jewish conceptions of charity and community responsibility (Axinn & Levin, 1982; Brower, 1984; Bullis, 1996; Garland, 1992; Gelman & Schnall, 1997; Leiby, 1985; Loewenberg, 1988; Marty, 1980; Niebuhr, 1932; Reid & Popple, 1992; Van Hook, 1997). These involved rival applications of theological ideas to social life, such as emphasizing individual moral blame or merit (i.e., distinction between worthy and unworthy poor) versus social

Table 3.2
Historical Phases in Connection Between Spirituality and American Social Work

	Characteristics
Phase One: **To early** **twentieth century**	Primarily Christian and Jewish sectarian services Sectarian ideologies in governmental services Beginnings of nonsectarian humanistic spiritual ideologies for social services

Phase Two:
1920s to 1970s
	Professionalization and secularization of social
	    work ideologies and institutions
	Increased professional skepticism of religiously
	    based social work
	Separation of church and state more strictly
	    enforced in social service delivery
	Tacit religious ideologies continue in
	    governmental social services
	Social work education detaches from religion
	    and spirituality
	Sectarian private social service agencies and
	    educational institutions continue
	Beginnings of existential and new nonsectarian
	    approaches to social work

Phase Three:
 	
1980s to the
present
	Continuation of private sectarian social work
	Calls for inclusive approach to spirituality
	Increase of diverse religious and nonreligious
	    spiritual perspectives in social work
	Rapid increase of related research and publication
	Return of attention to religion and spirituality in
	    social work education

justice and communal responsibility (i.e., Jewish communal service and the Christian Social Gospel).

There were also social work pioneers who had strong spiritual motivations for service but did not focus on religious terminology or institutions to express them. For example, in 1888, Jane Addams, the Nobel Prize–winning pioneer of the settlement house movement and peace movement, used the metaphor of a "Cathedral of Humanity which should be capacious enough to house a Fellowship of common purpose, and which should be beautiful enough to persuade men to hold fast to the vision of human solidarity" (cited by Oakley, 1955, p. 27). An article in a Christian magazine in the 1930s, *The Churchman*, expressed it this way (Simkhovitch, 1950, p. 139): "The settlement, made up as America is made up, of various types of people with varying points of view, cannot fasten upon any one aspect of truth, political or religious, and, regarding it as the solely valid key to life, insist upon its acceptance by others."

During the second phase, as social work professionalized in competition with and along models of medicine and law, secular humanistic and scientific perspectives, such as socialism, social functionalism, Freudianism, and behaviorism, became more influential than theology. It was hoped that these scientific views would provide a more reliable base for practice. Increased involvement of federal and state governments in social work and social welfare brought greater concerns about separation of church and state within the arena of social services. In general, many social workers grew wary of the tendency of some religious providers of services to engage in moralistic judgmentalism, blaming the victim, proselytization, and exclusivism. During this period, the National Association of Social Workers and the Council on Social Work Education (CSWE) formed as inclusive, secular, professional organizations, in contrast to earlier sectarian social work organizations. CSWE's curriculum policy guidelines in the 1950s and 1960s referred to the spiritual needs of people in nonsectarian terms. But the CSWE guidelines of the 1970s and 1980s eliminated even these nonsectarian references to spirituality (Marshall, 1991; Russel, 1998).

Still, religious and nonreligious spiritual perspectives influenced social work throughout the second phase. Many religiously related agencies continued to provide social work services, such as through Catholic Social Services, Lutheran Social Services, Jewish Family Services, and the Salvation Army. Nonsectarian spiritual perspectives grew in influence, such as in twelve-step programs. Social workers brought their own personal spiritual views and values into practice, at least implicitly. And some social work scholars continued to call attention to spirituality in publications (Spencer, 1956; Towle, 1965).

The third phase, resurgence of interest in spirituality, expanded on the ecumenical, interreligious, and nonsectarian spiritual undercurrents that existed in the profession from its beginning. In the 1970s, there were some early calls for new spiritual approaches to social work, such as Zen (Brandon, 1976) and existentialism (Krill, 1978). During the 1980s, many publications called for a return to the profession's historic commitment to spirituality, but to address it in a way that includes and respects the diverse range of religious and nonreligious spiritual perspectives among clients (Borenzweig, 1984; Brower, 1984; Canda, 1988b, 1988c, 1989; Constable, 1983; Joseph, 1987, 1988; Loewenberg, 1988; Marty, 1980; Meystedt, 1984; Siporin, 1982, 1985).

During the 1990s, this trend continued to expand rapidly. As the References section of this book illustrates, numerous articles and books deal with spirituality and social work, including religious and nonsectarian approaches. I (EC) founded the Society for Spirituality and Social Work in 1990; since 1994, it has been directed by Robin Russel at the University of Nebraska-Omaha. It has more than six hundred members throughout the country and some in several other countries. It sponsors publications, conferences, and international networking. In addition, while many Christian and Jewish social service agencies, professional organizations, and social work education programs continue to function, newer social work and social action groups have developed, such as Buddhist and transpersonally oriented organizations. The 1995 version of CSWE's curriculum guidelines returned attention to belief systems, religion, and spirituality, especially with regard to client diversity (Russel, 1998). Two social work practice texts and a human behavior theory text focusing on spirituality were recently published (Bullis, 1996; Canda, 1998; Robbins, Chatterjee, & Canda, 1998). In general, recent social work textbooks now commonly refer, at least briefly, to spirituality and religion. The Society for Spirituality and Social Work has received at least seventy requests for advice on curriculum development on spirituality from social work educational programs around the country (Russel, personal communication).

Patterns of Spiritual Belief and Practice Among Social Workers

Surveys of social workers during the 1990s suggest some similarities and differences compared with the general population. Sheridan et al. (1992) conducted a survey of licensed counselors, social workers, and psychologists in

Virginia. Most social work respondents reported being raised with a religious affiliation: Protestant (60 percent), Catholic (25 percent), Jewish (11 percent), other (0.9 percent), or none (4 percent). Many reported changing religious affiliation, so that Christian and Jewish affiliations reduced while "other affiliation" (17 percent) and "no affiliation" (21 percent) increased significantly. Seventy-seven percent of social workers agreed that "spirituality is relevant to my personal life," while 75 percent disagreed with the statement that "participation in an organized religion is the primary source of my spirituality." The authors concluded, "As a whole, respondents were found to value the religious or spiritual dimension in their own lives, to respect the function it serves for people in general, and to address, to some extent, religious and spiritual issues in their practice with clients" (p. 200).

In a study of fifty-six social workers in Utah, nearly half of the respondents were Mormon, and one-fourth identified as Protestant (Derezotes & Evans, 1995). Eighty-nine percent felt that spirituality is an important part of social work practice; 91 percent said that clients bring up the subject. In a study of 142 social workers in North Dakota (Furman & Chandy, 1994), 94 percent belonged to a Christian church (45.8 percent Lutheran; 28.2 percent Catholic). Only 1.4 percent were atheist, and 5.6 percent indicated no church affiliation. Social workers indicated moderately high levels of religiosity—for example, 66.2 percent reported frequent private prayer, and 33 percent indicated that they frequently encountered issues of religion and spirituality in practice.

These findings suggest that types and degrees of religiosity and spirituality among social workers may vary by region of the country. As in the general population, most social workers in these studies were Christian. However, these studies indicated that more social workers report no religious affiliation and may explore different religions from their birth tradition. They also suggested that social workers believe that religion and spirituality are important to many clients, in keeping with general population survey results.

A more detailed picture of social workers' demographic and spiritual diversity can be derived from our National Survey of social workers. The sample was composed of 74.4 percent ($n = 1,539$) females and 24.7 percent ($n = 512$) males. The data for gender were missing on 0.9 percent ($n = 18$) of the surveys. The average age of the respondents was forty-eight (standard deviation of 10.5) with a range of twenty-four to eighty-six. There were twenty-seven questionnaires missing data pertaining to age. Most of the respondents were Caucasian/European American (90.3 percent; $n = 1,847$). The rest of the sample were African American 3.6 percent ($n = 73$),

Table 3.3
National NASW Survey:
Religious or Spiritual Orientations of Social Workers
(overlapping categories)

Orientation	Percentage	Number
Religious Orientations		
Buddhism	7.3	152
Christianity		
Protestantism	30.6	633
Catholicism	22.8	471
Nondenominational	5.7	118
Other	6.2	128
Unspecified	4.8	95
Latter-Day Saints	1.1	22
Eastern Orthodox	.7	15
Quaker	.4	8
Confucianism	.4	9
Goddess religion	2.6	55
Hinduism	1.4	30
Judaism		
Reform	4.7	97
Conservative	2.2	45
Unspecified	1.4	28
Orthodox	.2	5
Other	.2	5
Muslim	.1	3
Spiritism/shamanism	3.4	71
Traditional Native American (First Nations)	4.7	97
Unitarian Universalism	1.6	33
Wicca	1.1	23
Religious others	2.6	54
Nonreligious Spiritual Orientations		
Agnosticism	6.5	134
Atheism	2.9	59
Existentialism	5.4	111
Nonaffiliated Jews	3.9	80
None (no spiritual affiliation)	2.5	52
Other		
Missing	.5	11
Other unspecified	.3	7

Latino/Hispanic American 1.7 percent (n = 34), Asian American/Pacific Islander 1.1 percent (n = 23), Native American (First Nations) 0.7 percent (n = 15), mixed heritage/biracial 1.2 percent (n = 24), and other 1.7 percent (n = 34). Missing data accounted for 0.9 percent (n = 19).

The participants were also requested to indicate their current religious or spiritual orientation or multiple orientations (see Table 3.3). Not surprisingly, by far the largest percentage of the respondents related that they were Christian. Adherents to various forms of Judaism form a distant second largest religious category. There are also a wide variety of other religious orientation affiliations, most notably Buddhism, Goddess religion, spiritism or shamanism, traditional First Nations, and Unitarian (including some who separately identified as Unitarian and some as Christian/Unitarian). In addition, about 21 percent of participants indicated a nonreligious orientation, sometimes in combination with a religious orientation.

We allowed people to indicate more than one spiritual affiliation, so the figures in Table 3.3 are not mutually exclusive. In fact, one of the most interesting findings was that 9.9 percent of responding social workers chose more than one spiritual orientation involving at least one major religious category (e.g., Christian and any other orientation), and 9.1 percent chose more than one nonreligious spiritual orientation (see Table 3.4). Eighteen percent of all multiple affiliators chose two affiliations,

Table 3.4
National NASW Survey:
Multiple Spiritual Orientations of Social Workers (mutually exclusive categories)

	Percentage	Frequency
Religious multiple affiliations (combinations of at least one religion and any other orientation)	9.9	204
Nonreligious multiple affiliations (any combination of atheist, agnostic, existentialist, nonaffiliated Jewish, and none)	9.1	188
Total	19.0	392

Table 3.5
National NASW Survey:
Singular Spiritual Orientations of Social Workers
(mutually exclusive categories)

	Percentage	Frequency
Singular Religious Orientation Affiliations		
Buddhism	1.2	24
Christianity		
Protestantism	30.1	623
Catholicism	18.7	386
Nondenominational	3.6	75
Christian unspecified	3.1	65
Latter-Day Saints	1.1	22
Eastern Orthodox	.5	10
Quakers	.4	8
Subtotal Christian	57.5	1,189
Goddess religion	.3	6
Hinduism	.1	2
Judaism		
Reform	3.4	71
Conservative	1.7	36
Unspecified	.7	14
Other	.2	5
Orthodox	.1	2
Subtotal religious Jewish	6.1	128

the most frequent combinations being Christianity with Buddhism, Christianity with Traditional First Nations (Native American), and Christianity with Existentialism. Five percent of Christians affiliated with Buddhism, accounting for 48 percent of Buddhist respondents. Nearly 59 percent of those identified with Traditional First Nations spirituality also indicated they were Christian, accounting for 3.8 percent of Christians. Among existentialists, 46.8 percent also affiliated with Christianity, accounting for 3.6 percent for the Christian respondents. Seven percent of the sample selected more than two affiliations, mostly three or four. This finding reminds us not to assume that a religious or spiritual affiliation is singular for everyone. Also, religious orientations (such as Christian) may be combined with nonsectarian perspectives, such as existentialism. In

	Percentage	Frequency
Singular Religious Orientation Affiliations		
Muslim	.0	1
Spiritism/shamanism	.2	4
Traditional Native American (First Nations)	.3	6
Unitarian Universalism	1.6	33
Wicca	.1	3
Other singular religious[a]	2.6	54
Other unspecified religious[b]	.3	7
Total religious	70.6	1,459
Singular Nonreligious Orientation Affiliations		
Agnosticism	3.4	70
Jewish nonaffiliated	2.0	42
Atheism	1.5	32
Existentialism	.6	13
Total nonreligious	7.5	157
Total all singular affiliations	78.1	1,616
No spiritual affiliation	2.5	52
Missing	.5	11
Grand Total (multiple and singular affiliators, nones, and missing)	100%	2,069

[a]Marked "other" and wrote in a religion.
[b]Marked "other religion" but did not specify.

addition, some Christians identified with more than one Christian denomination. The complexity of spiritual views and practices of people who have multiple spiritual or religious affiliations has not been addressed so far in the social work literature.

Tables 3.4 and 3.5 show spiritual orientations as mutually exclusive categories. Table 3.4 indicates all those who marked more than one spiritual orientation (including religious and nonreligious). Table 3.5 indicates all those who selected only one spiritual orientation. Therefore, some of the numbers in Table 3.5 are lower than in Table 3.3 because multiple affiliators were subtracted from the total affiliators in each category. For example, the total number of Catholics is 471, compared to 386 who identified as Catholic only. This means that 85 Catholic participants affiliate with an additional non-Christian spiritual orientation. This is a striking contrast to Protestants, only five of whom affiliate with another non-Christian spiritual orientation.

Our study shows that while most NASW members in our study are Christian, the percentage (70 percent) is quite smaller than in the general population (about 85 percent). In addition, the percentage of Jewish, Buddhist, agnostic, atheist, existentialist, First Nations, and Unitarian social workers is considerably more than in the general population. This indicates that although most social workers affiliate with a religious tradition, there is considerably more variety than in the general population.

The picture becomes even more complex when we consider the ideological positions of social workers with regard to ethnicity and spiritual beliefs. Taken as a whole, a higher percentage of all ethnic groups selected the ideological position that there is a personal God than almost any other position. First Nations respondents also showed the highest response rate to the positions that there is a transcendent or divine aspect unique to self and a transcendent or divine aspect in nature. Transcendence in nature was also selected by a large percentage of Latino/Hispanic Americans and Caucasian/European Americans. However, chi-square tests showed no statistically significant differences between ethnic groups related to these ideological positions.

Christian respondents identified with the position that there is a personal God to a significantly higher degree than any other religious affiliation. This holds true for Christians with both single and multiple spiritual affiliations. The people least likely to take that position were nonreligious affiliators considered as a group. No Christians identified with the position at the other end of the ideological scale that notions of God are imaginary. Non-Judeo-Christian religious affiliators, considered as a group, selected the ideological position of transcendence found in nature significantly more often than religious Jews and Christians.

In general, as would be expected, those who claimed a religious affiliation were likely to have an average to high level of involvement in religious or spiritual activities, such as prayer and attendance at religious services. In contrast, atheists and agnostics were likely to have a low to average involvement in religious or spiritual activities.

ETHNIC DIVERSITY AND SPIRITUALITY

We have seen the interconnections between ethnicity and religious affiliations in the review of American history and social work. The spiritual diversity of the United States has been directly influenced by interactions between Indigenous peoples, people of African descent, and immigrants and refugees from all regions of the world. Even within a single religious tradition or a single religious congregation, ethnic diversity brings different modes of belief and practice. For example, very different patterns of language, worship styles, symbolism, and religiosity can be found among Catholics who are Hispanic residents in New Mexico for many generations, first-generation Catholic immigrants from Paraguay, third-generation Irish Catholics, and Vietnamese Catholics who came to the United States as refugees in the 1970s and 1980s.

In some cases, there are close associations between ethnicity and spiritual perspective, such as among the Amish, Jews, Eastern Orthodox Christians, Arab-American Muslims, Indian American Hindus, Asian American Buddhists, and traditional spiritual ways of Indigenous peoples (Corbett, 1997). This is not to say that any of the religious traditions are entirely ethnic exclusive; however, some religious communities maintain an intentionally close link between cultural identity and spiritual tradition and may seek to maintain a boundary between themselves and others. Often people in these groups view culture and religion as inseparable. They may discourage or limit participation in religious ceremonies by outsiders. Interreligious and interethnic marriage may be perceived as a dilution or threat to the continuance of the group. But this voluntary separatism is often complicated and reinforced by involuntary exclusion, ostracism, persecution, and prejudice directed at these groups by so-called mainstream European American Christians. For example, anti-Semitism, white racist practices of exclusion and segregation, anti-Arab and anti-Islamic rhetoric, and attack against Indigenous spiritual ways have all contributed to intergroup tensions.

Connections between cultural diversity and religious diversity increase the richness and complexity of patterns of spiritual diversity. In order to illustrate this, we introduce some characteristics of spirituality among the two largest ethnic minority groups as defined by the U.S. census: African Americans and Hispanic Americans. These discussions provide sources for more detailed explorations of these groups by the reader. They also provide a model for how to explore other groups not addressed here.

African American Spirituality

Within a single ethnic group, there are often many variations based on different religious and spiritual affiliations. For instance, among African

Americans, there are about 800,000 members of mainline Protestant denominations (e.g., Presbyterian, United Methodist) and another 800,000 members of the Roman Catholic church. Mainline Protestant and Catholic African Americans often belong to integrated congregations, and their religious worship style generally is not significantly different from their European American fellow congregants (Chalfant, Beckley, & Palmer, 1987). But most African American Christians belong to primarily black denominations, the largest of which are three National Baptist Conventions, two African Methodist Episcopal denominations, and the Christian Methodist Episcopal Church. These include more than 13 million members. Overall, about 80 percent of blacks are Protestant, less than 10 percent are Catholic, less than 1 percent are Jewish, and about 5 percent claim no religious preference or some other preference, including Black Muslims (Corbett, 1997). There are also about 3,000 to 5,000 Rastafarians, a religion with roots in Jamaica, and an unknown number of adherents to *vodoun,* a blending of African, Haitian, and Catholic religious elements (Payne, 1991).

The origin of the Black Muslims (which now includes several denominations) can be traced to slaves brought from Africa, among whom about 10 percent were Muslim. In 1934, Elijah Muhammad became the leader of the Nation of Islam. The 1960s and 1970s saw an increasing influence of Black Muslims in the African American community generally as well as the black power movement, one of the heroes of which was Malcolm X. Louis Farrakhan gained in national recognition recently with his organization of the Million Man March. For some African Americans, an advantage of the Black Muslim movement is that it is not associated with the history of slavery and racial oppression in the United States, as was Christianity. There are also African American members of Islamic groups that originate from the Middle East.

African American congregations have often provided a safe haven and source of community support for black people throughout their experience of Diaspora (Franklin, 1994; Leashore, 1995; Logan, 1996; White & Hampton, 1995). During the period of slavery, they provided a way to link traditional African patterns of culture and spirituality with the Christian religious practice mandated by white culture. They drew on Christian themes of perseverance and liberation to provide nurture, mutual support, assistance for escape, and support for the abolitionist movement. After the Civil War, churches became major sources for community support and leadership training. Hence, they have been active in promoting and organizing the civil rights movement since the 1950s.

Paris (1995) emphasized the continuity of heritage between African and African American spiritual perspectives and values. He stated that a fundamental principle of African and African American spirituality is the interdependency of God, community, family, and person in a holistic and sacramental view of life. Paris identified the following virtues as central to African American spirituality: beneficence to the community, forbearance through tragedy, applying wisdom to practical action, creative improvisation, forgiveness of wrongs and oppression, and social justice as the culmination of these other virtues.

According to Franklin (1994), worship style in many black Christian congregations is characterized by several common features. Times of intimate, cathartic "altar prayer" are encouraged in which members express pain and vulnerability and celebrate forgiveness and liberation in a public manner, thus joining individual feeling with communal care and support. Some congregations encourage cathartic shouting of praise and triumph, ecstatic dancing, and speaking in tongues. Choir singing and music often help stimulate collective feelings, growing in beat and intensity or calming as necessary. Religious education often has a strong political component, emphasizing civil rights, community support, and pride in African identity and culture. In regard to preaching, Franklin said, "Black people expect the sermon, as a word inspired by God and located within the community, to be spiritually profound, politically relevant, socially prophetic, artistically polished, and reverently delivered" (p. 265).

Kwanzaa is a nonsectarian Afrocentric spiritual celebration that was started in the 1960s by Maulana Karenga (1995), a civil rights activist and professor of black studies. He estimates that about 18 million African Americans and other African people throughout the world now celebrate it. Karenga was inspired by the Black Power movement's goals of individual and community self-determination, culturally grounded self-respect, and collective capacity to end and prevent oppression. In cooperation with others, Karenga drew on empowering principles, values, and symbols widely shared in traditional African cultures and adopted Swahili terms to create the format for Kwanzaa. The Kwanzaa celebration is intended to support and appreciate the strengths of African families, communities, and cultures within the larger context of re-Africanization and African American community empowerment. Seven principles (*Nguzo Saba*) represent core values to be encouraged in the African American community through Kwanzaa (p. 40); (used with permission of the publisher):

1. *Umoja* (Unity): To strive for and maintain unity in the family, community, nation and race.
2. *Kujichagulia* (Self-determination): To define ourselves, name ourselves, create for ourselves and speak for ourselves instead of being defined, named, created for and spoken for by others.
3. *Ujima* (Collective Work and Responsibility): To build and maintain our community together and make our sister's and brother's problems our problems and to solve them together.
4. *Ujamaa* (Cooperative Economics): To build and maintain our own stores, shops, and other businesses and to profit from them together.
5. *Nia* (Purpose): To make our collective vocation the building and developing of our community in order to restore our people to their traditional greatness.
6. *Kuumba* (Creativity): To do always as much as we can, in order to leave our community more beautiful and beneficial than we inherited it.
7. *Imani* (Faith): To believe with all our heart in our people, our parents, our teachers, our leaders and the righteousness and victory of our struggle.

Kwanzaa is a collective celebration of spiritual and cultural renovation, innovation, and liberation, but it is not sectarian. It is an opportunity for African and African American families and communities to come together across Muslim, Christian, Jewish, traditional African, and any other spiritual perspectives to reverence the Creator and give thanks for the gift of life, fruits of the earth, and the support of African heritage and community.

Social Work Implications

In order for social workers to provide culturally competent service with African Americans, it is crucial to engage the supportive and transformative aspects of African American spirituality, since this is so important for most black people (Logan, 1996; Logan, Freeman, & McCroy, 1990). This requires knowledge about and respect for the historical and contemporary roles of the wide variety of African American religious groups and practices. It requires familiarity with distinctive patterns of worship and values. And it requires practical ability to assess the particular spiritual style and practices of African American clients and to work collaboratively with their religious community, relatives, friends, and leaders.

For African American social workers working with black clients, there is an opportunity to build on common experiences and sense of solidarity. It is also important not to assume agreement or commonality on religious practices and beliefs because of the diversity within the African American population. For others working with African Americans, it is important to be able to deal honestly and comfortably with the context of racism as it may affect the current situation of the client and the client's relationship with and perception of the social worker. European American social workers must be especially cautious not to make ethnocentric evaluations of unfamiliar spiritual styles and beliefs.

Hispanic American Spirituality

The federal government designated the category "Hispanic" in the 1970s to refer to "a person of Mexican, Puerto Rican, Cuban, Central or South American, or other Spanish culture or origin, regardless of race" (cited in Castex, 1994, p. 189). This designation implies a cultural or linguistic commonality, which is rather misleading. The federal definition includes people originating from twenty-six countries with different languages, religions, other cultural patterns, and varied historical relations with the United States—people from countries in North, Central, and South America; from the West Indies; and from Spain. The three largest groups in the 1990 census were people from origins in Mexico (60.4 percent), Puerto Rico (12.2 percent), and Cuba (4.7 percent). In addition, there are Hispanic people whose ancestors have resided here since before the U.S. Revolutionary War. People classified as Hispanic under this definition may also commonly identify as white, African American, First Nations (Indigenous), Asian, or other.

The majority of Hispanics are Roman Catholic (about 72 percent) (Curiel, 1995). Since the Hispanic population is growing rapidly, by immigration, refugee flight, and birth, about 50 percent of all American Catholics may be Hispanic by the year 2000 (Corbett, 1997). However, there is also a large and growing number of Protestant Hispanics—about 23 percent (Castex, 1994). In addition, there are many religious beliefs and practices that are blendings of Christian and African and Indigenous spiritual traditions.

Even within a single denomination and ethnic group, there are further divisions. For example, about 70 to 90 percent of Mexican Americans identify as Roman Catholic (Curiel, 1995). Many regard the Catholic church as a source of significant social and spiritual support. However, there is also some ambivalence in the relationship between Mexican Americans and the Catholic church, rooted in the history of colonialism. Catholicism came to the Americas in cooperation with the Spanish campaign of military, economic, cultural, political, and religious conquest. Thus, many Indigenous peoples were forced to become Catholic. Many of their traditional spiritual places of worship, sacred texts, beliefs, and practices were destroyed, forced into hiding, or melded with Catholic forms of symbolism and ritual. The Catholic church was opposed to the Mexican War of Reform and the 1910 revolution, so after independence, the Mexican government formed an anticlerical policy. After Mexican territory was annexed by the United States, many Spanish-speaking clergy were replaced by Irish and Anglo clergy with a more austere doctrinal approach that was less sympathetic to syncretistic practices (Castex, 1994; Curiel, 1995).

In response to discontent, during the 1960s and 1970s, the American Catholic church instituted alternative liturgies that were culturally and linguistically relevant, appointed more Hispanic bishops, and established more active community-based programs to promote social and economic justice (Curiel, 1995). The American Catholic church has also been active in recent decades in opposing various human rights violations in Central and South America and in assisting refugees and undocumented entrants who fled war and persecution (Deck, 1989). Grass-roots Catholic communities and socially concerned clergy in Latin America have given rise to liberation theology, which has influenced social justice action among Hispanics and has also stimulated similar movements throughout the world (Garcia, 1987; Getz & Costa, 1991; Gutierrez, 1988; Sobrino, 1988).

Costas (1991) has suggested that Hispanic theology in North America is characterized by the cultural and historical factors of colonialism. It takes into account painful experiences of migration and refugee flight, and dilemmas and struggles pertaining to biculturality, isolation, or assimilation. Bishop Ramirez (1985) provided a summary of common features of Hispanic Christian spirituality. He said that God is often regarded as a compassionate and forgiving yet judging and punishing father and creator. Popular piety regards God with love and reverence, as well as fear and dread.

Popular spirituality focuses faith on Jesus as savior, king, and infant God through special titles and devotional practices (Ramirez, 1985). Mary is revered as the merciful, loving, and majestic mother of God. Saints are popular as models for behavior as well as miraculous benefactors. Blessed objects, such as depictions or relics of saints, are both symbols and conveyers of divine protection and care. Christian holy days, days of national celebration in the country of origin, and family life cycle transition times, such as baptisms and marriages and coming-of-age celebrations for girls, may be marked with religious ceremony and major family gatherings.

Hispanic spirituality often combines these more conventional Christian teachings with African and Indigenous spiritual traditions that vary considerably among and between particular Hispanic groups. In the social work literature, several types of spiritually based syncretistic Hispanic support systems have been identified (Delgado, 1977, 1988; Delgado & Humm-Delgado, 1982; De La Rosa, 1988; Paulino, 1995a, 1995b). *Curanderismo,* common among Mexican Americans, and *santiguando,* among Puerto Ricans, are forms of healing that combine herbalism and other physical interventions with Catholic beliefs and practices. Among Puerto Ricans and Caribbean immigrants, *espiritismo* (spiritism) is a folk healing practice involving mediumistic healers who employ group dynamics of role playing and catharsis, with the support of helping spirits. Mediumistic healing also occurs in *santeria,* a religion mainly among Cubans, and Dominican and Haitian forms of *vodoun* (voodoo), which formed from a syncretism between African traditions and Catholic beliefs.

Social Work Implications
The Hispanic population is large and fast growing. Given the many variations of culture, language, and spiritual beliefs and practices among Hispanic Americans, it is clear that social workers who work with Hispanic people need to learn the particular circumstances of their history, culture, and family experience in relation to particular spiritual beliefs and practices. Competent practice requires suspending assumptions and ethnocentric judgments while opening up to the stories of the clients. Clients and their religious or spiritual elders, leaders, healers, friends, and family are the best sources of information about their particular practices and beliefs. For example, De La Rosa (1988) and Delgado (1988) have given specific suggestions for tailoring social work practice style, setting, and beliefs to work with Puerto Rican clients influenced by spiritism.

The range of spiritual beliefs and practices can be quite startling to unfamiliar social workers. For example, social workers need to be open to learn about culture-specific beliefs addressing the spiritual causes and cures of physical, mental, and social problems. Some practices, such as possession trance among some healers or animal sacrifice in *vodoun* and *santeria,* may be uncomfortable to social workers who have opposing beliefs.

Indeed, in Hialeah, Florida, an entire community may be split over such practices. The city of Hialeah outlawed the practice of animal sacrifice among *santeria* practitioners. In 1993, the U.S. Supreme Court struck

down this law as a violation of the constitutional protection for free exercise of religion (Bullis, 1996). It is ironic that promoters of this law did not
think to question the massive killing of animals for secular business purposes, in the meat industry. Rather, it sought to impose a prohibition on a
relatively small religious group. Thus, support for the spiritual self-determination of clients is a social work issue in both clinical practice and community development practice and social policy.

WOMEN AND SPIRITUALITY

In the United States, women represent the majority of adherents in most
religious groups; however, their stories are usually subsumed (and
neglected) in conventional discussions of religion and spirituality because
of the androcentric assumptions of religious research and theology
(Braude, 1997). Most religious texts, theological discourses, and scholarly
studies of spirituality have been written by men. These authors have
tended to focus on formal religious doctrines and practices of religious
hierarchies (patriarchies), which themselves are usually dominated
numerically and politically by men. Since most adherents are women, this
male perspective presents an inaccurate picture of women's lives.
Feminist writing in social work has critiqued similar trends in the profession. But the topic of women and spirituality has rarely been addressed
explicitly in the social work literature. This section briefly introduces
some trends and issues concerning the junction of women, spirituality,
and gender justice in the United States. As in the case of ethnic diversity
and spirituality, women's spirituality raises many complex and controversial issues concerning both the liberating and oppressing functions of
religious traditions.

There is a great variety among women and their situations within and
between religions and spiritual perspectives. Women experience different
patterns of gendered symbolism, ritual, and leadership between different
religions (Holm & Bowker, 1994; Joy & Neumaier-Dargyay, 1995; King,
1987; Sharma, 1994). Generally women in the Judeo-Christian-Islamic
stream of monotheistic traditions operate with conceptions and symbols of
God that are usually masculine and have theological justifications for
restricting women from formal leadership positions. An interesting case in
point is the Catholic veneration of the Virgin Mary (Warner, 1976;
Zimdars-Swartz, 1991). Scholars have pointed out that Marian devotion
has served to imbue feminine symbols and attributes with sacred significance. It has also provided women (and men) opportunities to honor and

emulate these feminine qualities. On the other hand, Marian devotion has been contained within constraints developed by the all-male church hierarchy. Critics have contended that Marian devotion actually serves to support patriarchal gender stereotypes and male privilege.

Many nontheistic or polytheistic Asian religions, such as Buddhism, Hinduism, and Taoism, have positive feminine and androgynous representations of divinities and religious teachers. However, women have also commonly been restricted from leadership positions within these religious institutions. Many Indigenous tribal religions have positive feminine spiritual conceptions of women, the earth, and various spirit powers, and women have also been major leaders within many Indigenous spiritual traditions. However, under the impact of colonialism and Christian missionary influence, some of these women-affirming traditions have been eroded. So despite the wide variety of religious beliefs and spiritual experiences in the United States, it is all too common for women to experience constraints imposed by the very religious traditions to which they may faithfully adhere.

Most women in the United States belong to conventional Christian and Jewish denominations, and most appear generally satisfied with their affiliations (Corbett, 1997). Indeed, many belong to evangelistic, charismatic, and fundamentalist groups, which tend to be staunch supporters of traditional patriarchal religious and family arrangements for gender roles in family and religious group. Many others are movers for reform toward greater participation of women in their religious groups' patterns of ritual and leadership and advocate for gender-inclusive theological and scriptural language. Further, there are many women who call for radical restructuring of patriarchal religious institutions. Some have left them altogether for alternative spiritual paths or, as the feminist philosopher Mary Daly put it in the title of a famous book, to go "beyond god the father" (1973).

Women in Conventional Religions

Corbett (1997) has summarized various trends toward greater inclusion and leadership of women within the conventional Christian and Jewish denominations. Jewish and Christian feminist theologians have pointed out that some biblical passages use feminine images to refer to God. For example, a Hebrew word for spirit is *ruach* (a feminine word), which is translated as *pneuma* (a gender-neutral word) in the Greek-language Bible. God is sometimes described in images relating to bearing and suckling children. God (and Christ, in the New Testament) are sometimes referred to as wisdom, with the feminine Greek word *sophia*. Feminist theologians build on these biblical precedents to advocate for gender-inclusive language in Bible translations, hymns, and liturgy. Feminist scholars also suggest that biblical passages implying subordination of women should be understood within the historical and cultural context of their authors and should be reinterpreted in ways that support the liberation of women in contemporary society. Further, many biblical examples that directly affirm the worth of women can be found.

Many religious women are active in making their churches and synagogues more responsive to social issues, such as day care for children and elderly dependents, shelters for battered or homeless women and children, and support of or opposition to legal abortions (Corbett, 1997). Religious laywomen and nuns have also been active in the formation of major religiously based social movements, such as antislavery, temperance, religious missions, and Social Gospel–based activism (Braude, 1997).

In the past twenty years, many Christian churches and Jewish temples and synagogues have provided equal opportunities for women as lay leaders in worship. Some Christian and Jewish denominations allow women to become clergy. Others, such as the Catholic church, many conservative Protestant denominations, and Orthodox Jewish synagogues, do not allow women to become clergy. Some Christian women have developed their own organizations, such as Church Women United, an ecumenical group with fifteen hundred local groups.

Alternative Women's Spiritualities

Some women have decided that the traditional patriarchal religions are not viable spiritual support systems for women and have created alternatives. Some women become secularists, such as atheists, or form nonsectarian informal spiritual support groups. Some are exploring religions imported from Asia, such as Buddhism, and transforming them by focusing on their traditional feminine or androgynous religious images and expanding their potential for women to become leaders and teachers (Gross, 1994).

Wicca is a small but important movement for growing numbers of women and men (Corbett, 1997; Starhawk, 1979). *Wicca* means the tradition of "the wise one"; it is also known as witchcraft, or the Craft. Since there are no formal, centralized Wiccan organizations or membership lists and many members are cautious about identifying their belief out of fear of ostracism, it is difficult to identify numbers of practitioners. The number of Wiccans in the United States is probably under 50,000. They are usually organized in local, informal small spiritual support groups, often called covens.

Some trace contemporary Wicca to pre-Christian indigenous European spiritual traditions, with animistic, magical, and earth-honoring characteristics. Witchcraft was maligned and persecuted during the medieval Inquisition. Some accounts suggest that millions of people were killed in Europe under accusations of witchcraft and heresy, most of whom were women, homosexuals, people with disabilities, and others defined as deviant by political and church authorities. Wicca continues to be portrayed with negative stereotypes and hostility in conventional religious groups and popular American movies and news media.

Wiccan beliefs emphasize harmony with the earth and balance of female and male spiritual powers. Special attention is given to feminine aspects of life and the spiritual realm, since these have been often neglected in conventional society. Female characteristics are viewed as good and powerful. Women's experience of biological cycles is related in a positive way to the cycles of the earth, seasonal changes, and the phases of the moon. Women's roles as maiden, mother, and wise elder are honored. These roles are reflected in the worship of the Goddess in her three forms as Maiden, Mother, and Crone. All living beings and the earth are regarded as holy. Therefore, people are enjoined to live respectfully with the planet. Contrary to popular misconceptions, Wiccans do not worship Satan (which is a Christian concept) or put evil spells on people. Rituals are often geared toward seasonal celebrations and emotional and physical healing for individuals.

Social Work Implications

Social workers should consider the impact of gender and gender roles on the spirituality of women and men. Our experiences, perceptions, needs, and goals are likely to vary by our vantage point as men and women because of our different experiences of spirituality in relation to our embodiedness and in relation to gender role definitions, empowerments, and restrictions placed on us by social and religious contexts. But we need to avoid assuming or imposing standards of gender-based views on clients. As we have seen, there is a great variety among women with regard to their attitudes toward and participation in conventional religions. Yet, especially in practice with women, whatever her own position regarding patriarchy and feminism, the importance of the distinctness of being a woman is inextricably related with spirituality. Randour (1987) suggested that women in both conventional and alternative spiritual groups tend to share an ideal of healthy connectedness between people and between people and the divine, such that women's roles and traits are respected.

In clinical practice, women may be trying to work out a sense of resolution between their loyalty to a faith tradition that is patriarchal and their personal aspirations for affirmation of their experience. In extreme cases, women who are victims of familial abuse may be told by religious leaders to be patient and stay within the relationship, even under risk of serious injury and death. If a woman feels that her affiliation with a religious group is no longer tenable, she may need assistance exploring alternative spiritual support systems and working through feelings of guilt.

Kahn (1995) pointed out how innovations in ritual within conventional religions can affirm and empower women. She discussed the adult bat mitzvah as a Jewish life cycle ritual for women that simultaneously helps to clarify identity and commitment as a Jew and as a woman. As Laird (1984) pointed out, social workers can help clients use existing rituals or invent new rituals in order to support transition through life crises and to celebrate life cycle transitions. Feminist spiritual innovations, both within and outside conventional religions, highlight many possibilities for developing symbolism and ritual that affirm women's experience and honor female aspects of the earth and the divine.

Social workers also need to be alert to issues of gender justice in spirituality. If clients experience ostracism or discrimination because they question patriarchal constraints and oppression within religious groups or because they adhere to alternative religious groups such as Wicca, social workers may be called on to help them respond.

HOMOSEXUALITY, SEXUAL ORIENTATION DIVERSITY, AND SPIRITUALITY

Estimates of the homosexual population in all cultures range from 2 to 10 percent, so every large religious and spiritual tradition is likely to have some gay or lesbian members. There are distinct issues related to sexual orientation in each tradition (Dynes & Donaldson, 1992; Swidler, 1993). It is difficult to research the prevalence of and teachings about homosexuality in most religions. Contemporary distinctions between sexual orientation and sexual acts are often not made in traditional teachings. The very concepts of gender and sexual orientation vary across cultures and religions. Formal religious texts rarely address the question explicitly. There are major disagreements about the proper interpretation and significance of religious texts among theologians, academic scholars, and activists. In most cultures, the realm of sexuality is considered very private, and so it is difficult to gather reliable information about it. Contradictions occur between official religious pronouncements on the subject and actual life experience and attitudes of religious adherents.

According to Duran (1993), in some religious cultures, such as Islamic ones, same-gender sexual contacts are sometimes tacitly accepted in the context of temporary or alternative relationships, as long as the person forms a heterosexual marriage. At the same time, homosexuality is formally labeled as an immoral crime. According to Duran, in most Islamic cultures, homosexuality, when restricted to privacy and secrecy, is rarely punished under Islamic law because conviction would require formal confession or public witnesses.

Ethnographers and others have documented various forms of male and female homosexuality in 113 Indigenous nations of North America (Baum, 1993). In some cases, adolescents explore homosexual liaisons in the context of friendship prior to or in addition to heterosexual marriage. Many Indigenous cultures honor transgendered people (*berdache*, French; *winkte*, Lakota) because they display skill in both male and female roles, may be called to serve the community as spiritual helpers, and are often given a sacred status. In this context, the transgendered person is not regarded as homosexual in the European American sense, but rather fulfills a third gender possibility (transgendered) beyond male or female. The influence of Christian missionaries seems to have made antihomosexual attitudes more prevalent among some Native peoples recently; however, in many communities, affirming spiritual perspectives on gay and lesbian people and transgendered people continue.

The link between sexual orientation and spirituality is one of the most controversial aspects of contemporary American society. Conventional social mores concerning sexuality, sexual identity, and sexual orientation have been strongly shaped by the Judeo-Christian tradition, which has generally maintained heterosexuality as the taken-for-granted standard for normality and morality. Among those who have been raised in Jewish or Christian traditions, there is a wide range of responses to homosexuality that can be summarized by four alternative views placed on a continuum. The first three views operate within the Judeo-Christian framework, and the fourth rejects it. They vary in interpretation of and adherence to biblical passages and denominational doctrine regarding homosexuality

Table 3.6
Four Christian Ideological Responses to Homosexuality

Condemnation

Patriarchy and heterosexism accepted as divine mandate

Biblical texts interpreted as punitive toward gay and lesbian people

Homosexuals labeled as deviant, immoral, criminal

Homosexuals in congregation ostracized, defined as sinners; forced to leave congregation or subjected to "changing" or hiding

Accept the Person, Condemn the Behavior

Patriarchy may be questioned while heterosexism accepted as divine mandate

Biblical texts interpreted to condemn homosexual acts, but affirm dignity and care for all people

Homosexuals granted acceptance with inherent dignity and worth

Homosexual expression of sexual intimacy labeled as sinful

Homosexuals in congregation subjected to ambivalence and restricted from leadership

Affirmation

Patriarchy and heterosexism criticized as oppressive social constructs

Biblical texts interpreted to support affirmation and liberation of oppressed

Homosexuals affirmed as whole persons, including sexual orientation and sexual intimacy

Homosexuals in congregation openly accepted and included in leadership

Congregations advocate for social justice regarding gay and lesbian issues

Departure from Christianity

Patriarchy and heterosexism criticized as oppressive social constructs

Christianity viewed as inherently oppressive religious institution

Biblical texts on homosexuality criticized and rejected

Homosexuals and advocates depart from Christian congregations

New spiritual support groups and religious organizations are formed

(Coleman, 1980; Comstock, 1993; Cromey, 1991; Mickey, 1991; Seow, 1996). It should be noted that many denominations have issued formal policies and teachings about homosexuality, and they are being revised quickly as these issues are debated (Melton, 1991). These should be consulted for more detail. Also, attitudes and behavior about homosexuality vary within each religious congregation and each individual beyond the official denominational policies.

The four major alternative ideological responses move from strident support of traditional Judeo-Christian heterosexist assumptions to complete rejection of them. By *heterosexism,* we mean a worldview and moral framework that privileges patriarchy and heterosexual people while denigrating gay, lesbian, bisexual and transgendered people. We will focus on the Christian context.

The first type of response is *outright condemnation.* This comes from a perspective that posits patriarchy and heterosexuality as divinely ordained aspects of human nature and society. Gay and lesbian people are viewed as deviant criminals or immoral sinners. Biblical passages that refer to homosexuality are interpreted in the most literal and punitive manner. In such communities, homosexual people may be driven out, punished, or pressured to confess as sinners or to "change" into heterosexuals. In such a religious context, a person who is just beginning to realize that he or she is gay will have to contend with guilt-inducing and shaming messages from the social environment and internal homophobic feelings learned from religious upbringing. In extreme cases, antihomosexual Christian militants make a public mission out of harassing gay, lesbian, bisexual and transgendered people.

The second type of response is *accept the person, condemn the behavior.* This perspective also accepts heterosexuality as divinely ordained. However, it advocates for acceptance of all people, of all sexual orientations, on the basis of respect and dignity. Biblical passages referring to homosexuality are interpreted as opposing same-gender sexual relations in a larger context of affirming God's love for all people. This position separates homosexual orientation from same-gender sexual activity. It leaves open the question of how people become homosexual and acknowledges that this may be a matter of identity, not only a lifestyle or choice. However, while homosexual people are welcomed (often with ambivalence) in such Christian communities, either they are enjoined not to engage in same-gender sexual activity or the issue is politely avoided. Openly gay, lesbian, bisexual, and transgendered people are also prevented from holding leadership positions.

This is the official position of the Catholic church. In 1997, the American Catholic bishops released a public statement of apology for the church's frequent mistreatment and rejection of gay and lesbian people. However, the bishops maintained the official teaching against homosexual sexual activity which opposes "unjust discrimination" toward homosexual persons while claiming that they "are called to chastity" (U.S. Catholic Conference, 1994, p. 566). Some Catholic parishes have religious support groups for gay and lesbian members, such as the organization named Dignity.

In denominations that maintain this "accept the person, condemn the behavior" position, it seems inevitable that gay, lesbian, bisexual, and transgendered people will be subject to ambivalence. They will also be forced to make a rather artificial split between their experience of who they are (which is granted dignity) and how they express intimacy with loved ones (which is defined as sinful).

The third option is to *critique and transform Christian tradition* in order to move out of a patriarchal, heterosexist viewpoint. In this case, biblical passages referring to homosexuality are critiqued or dismissed. Common errors or skewing of conventional translations to support antigay and antilesbian doctrines are critiqued through biblical and historical exegesis. Even where there are unambiguous biblical attacks against same-gender behavior, they are interpreted as an expression of an overall divine ethic of compassion that was distorted through human heterosexism. In other words, homosexual acts of exploitation or violence are condemned in the Bible, just as are heterosexual exploitive acts and other actions that have nothing to do with sexuality. This position sees the Christian message as one of affirmation and empowerment of all people, especially those who have experienced social discrimination and persecution, such as homosexuals. In this context, gay, lesbian, bisexual, and transgendered people may be openly accepted, full members of a congregation. Christian marriage ceremonies may be performed for gay or lesbian couples. In some denominations, openly gay and lesbian people are eligible as clergy. Also, Christian denominations with primarily homosexual membership have developed, such as the Metropolitan Community church.

The fourth response is to *reject the Judeo-Christian tradition* as entirely unacceptable for homosexual people. In this view, the Christian religion has demonstrated a long history of persecution and discrimination of gay, lesbian, bisexual, and transgendered people. Persecution has varied in intensity, from murder during the Inquisition to contemporary ostracism. The antigay theme is judged to be so deeply entrenched in scripture, theology, and congregational social behavior that Christianity is not considered a viable spiritual environment. In this case, people may reject the Christian tradition of their upbringing in favor of atheism, agnosticism, exploration of other religious traditions that are more congenial, or creation of new patterns of spiritual belief and support groups. For some people, this could be a comfortable and liberating option. Yet the process of breaking from one's religious heritage and community could also be painful. Lingering feelings of internalized homophobia may still have to be dealt with.

Social Work Implications

The NASW Code of Ethics takes a clear stance with regard to diversity of sexual orientation, as with other aspects of human diversity. Social workers are required to obtain knowledge and understanding about diversity and oppression, including sexual orientation (Standard 1.05). They are also prohibited from directly or indirectly practicing any form of discrimination on the basis of diversity, including sexual orientation (Standard 4.02). These same standards also take a proactive stance on religious diversity. Since many spiritual traditions and groups take a negative stance toward homosexuality, the two ethical principles of supporting religious diversity and sexual orientation diversity may conflict. Therefore, the most basic social work implication is that we need to be able to deal openly and honestly with different and conflicting spiritual positions on homosexuality in such a way that constructive dialogue for mutual understanding is created in direct practice settings, professional education, and social advocacy. We believe this dialogue should take place with the full inclusion of gay, lesbian, bisexual, and transgendered people, who themselves reflect a variety of religious and nonreligious spiritual beliefs. Social workers on all sides of the issue should be able to communicate on the basis of respect and dignity.

It needs to be emphasized, though, that the overall ethical stance of the social work profession is to oppose any form of discrimination or oppression and to support self-determination and empowerment for all people. Therefore, it seems to us that there are certain limits on what spiritual perspectives on homosexuality could be promoted in professional capacities by social workers. The first option, which is directly antigay and antilesbian and takes a degrading outlook, is clearly inconsistent with social work ethics. If a social worker holds such a view, we believe it is incumbent on the worker to do some serious thinking about whether he or she can in good conscience affiliate with and practice in the social work profession. It does not seem honest to claim to be a social worker while holding a position that demeans people. The same can be said about any value position, religiously based or otherwise, that demeans and oppresses any person or group of people.

Indeed, Keith-Lucas, a prominent writer on Christian social work, identified four patterns of Christian belief in relation to social work ethics (Ressler, 1992). He named one extreme Christianity of Morality, which is judgmental and punitive, and as such, is least compatible with social work. He promoted Christianity of Grace, which views all things created by God as perfect, to be the ideal orientation for social work. This view is most consistent with the second and third types of Christian responses to homosexuality we have described.

Social workers who hold the second perspective, "accept the person, condemn the behavior," should also consider whether it is possible for them to do competent practice with gay, lesbian, bisexual, and transgendered clients. Studies of gay and lesbian sexual identity development and the coming-out process highlight common developmental challenges that relate to clarification of self-identity and long-term relationships in relation to the heterosexist and homophobic social context (Robbins, Chatterjee, & Canda, 1998). If a social worker promoted the second theological position, it would likely compound identity and relationship confusions for gay clients by creating a split between self-awareness of sexual orientation, feelings of affinity for others, and restriction or denigration of honest expressions of intimacy with others. If a social worker is unable to provide an unambiguous relationship of empathy and respect, then the worker needs to refer the client elsewhere. Furthermore, the worker needs to engage in a process of self-examination and professional development in order to move toward an empathic and respectful understanding. Whatever the social worker's position, he or she cannot impose it on clients, if one remains true to the principle of client self-determination.

For gay, lesbian, bisexual, and transgendered people, relating within spiritual groups that hold each of the four stances will present different kinds of challenges or opportunities. When religious affiliation and spiritual development are issues in practice with gay, lesbian, bisexual, and transgendered people, these issues will need to be addressed.

Different and conflicting positions on homosexuality obviously exist among social workers, often related to rival spiritual beliefs. As a result, tension is evident in current controversies in social work education (Cain, 1996; Parr & Jones, 1996; Van Soest, 1996). Some social work education programs exist within theologically conservative Christian and Jewish colleges and universities that have explicit policies of discrimination against gay, lesbian, bisexual, and transgendered people in selection and retention of students, staff, and faculty. CSWE accreditation standards, based on similar principles to the NASW Code of Ethics, require that social work programs provide requisite knowledge and values for understanding people of all sexual orientations and for opposing discrimination and oppression. Even if social work departments affirm this (and they must to attain accreditation), they may be forced to comply with discriminatory policies by the host institution. CSWE has been attempting to formulate policy that will balance the right of free exercise of religion with an affirmative stance toward diversity of sexual orientation, thus allowing these social work programs to exist. But this raises a major question as to whether it is possible for the educational objectives to be met if a double standard is modeled within the program and there is a lack of opportunity for constructive interaction between people of different sexual orientations.

A further implication of this debate is that social work education needs to prepare social workers for a more astute analysis of the religious and spiritual issues involved in attitudes about homosexuality and the diverse spiritual opportunities available for gay, lesbian, bisexual, and transgendered people. For example, many students and faculty seem to accept the mistaken idea that Christianity uniformly opposes gay, lesbian, bisexual, and transgendered people. As we have seen, there is much variety and debate within and between Christian denominations on this issue. A social work student who is trying to work through these dilemmas on a personal and professional level could be guided to the literature on Christian theology and sexual orientation in order to engage in careful discernment.

SUMMARY

In this chapter, we have summarized the history of spiritual diversity in the United States and the American social work profession. We have also introduced varieties of spiritual traditions, styles, and controversial issues pertaining to ethnic diversity, women's experience, and homosexuality. We have discussed many ways in which spiritual perspectives can be used to enhance human well-being or contribute to discrimination and oppression. Genuine compassion moves us to empathize and join together with people who experience suffering and injustice. It stretches us beyond our egocentric, ethnocentric, and religiocentric assumptions in order to meet the other. In doing so, we grow to the point at which no one is "the other" in the sense of a person who seems remote or estranged. Indeed, the encounter with diversity inevitably challenges us to broaden and deepen our spirituality, so that we can appreciate both difference and commonality. If we succeed in doing this, then the potential of spirituality to bring about personal healing and social justice will surely express in both our personal and professional lives.

EXERCISES

3.1. Writing a History of Spiritual Diversity in Your Community

Use the historical overview in this chapter as a model to study the historical development and contemporary situation of spiritual diversity in your community. A history of local spiritual diversity can be useful to acquaint practitioners and policymakers with the cultural and religious backgrounds of client populations and constituencies. Source materials can include library materials such as regional religious historical studies, survey and census data, and directories of religious organizations, such as those compiled by J. Gordon Melton (1991). Examine local newspapers (especially the religion sections), telephone directories, and social service directories for listings of religious organizations and religiously affiliated social service organizations. Some religious groups that have a strong ethnic orientation, such as the African Methodist Episcopal church, can also be identified from these listings. Social service agencies that provide specialized services for ethnically diverse groups (such as refugee resettlement programs, ethnic mutual assistance associations, and universities or colleges with geographical area studies and international studies programs) can also be identified. Any of these organizations can be contacted for further information, including identification of denominational policies, programs, and spiritually oriented support systems regarding women, gay and lesbian people, and other special populations we have not discussed.

3.2. Self-Assessment of Your Own Spiritually Based Attitudes About Homosexuality

One of the most contentious issues in many religious communities, and in the general public, is the standpoint toward gay, lesbian, bisexual, and transgendered people. Given the social work profession's ethical stance of nondiscrimination, this is a good starting point for self-reflection about your own openness, empathy, and support regarding human diversity.

Use Table 3.6, on the four major Christian ideological positions toward homosexuality, to reflect on where you stand. Even if you have not been raised as a Christian, there are analogous positions possible within other religious and secular spiritual perspectives.

The first step in this exercise is to identify which ideological position is closest to your own and to state your position in your own words. If none of these positions is an accurate depiction of your own view, then articulate your view. Be aware of feelings that arise in response to this self-questioning. What are areas of comfort and discomfort? What particular beliefs do you have about homosexuality that rationalize your position? What sources of religious authority, if any, do you use to support your position, such as sacred texts, traditional doctrines, or spiritual leaders' teachings? How does this position affect your behavior in your private life, within your religious or spiritual community, and in your professional social work practice?

Now consider the degree of fit between your position and the NASW ethical standards cited in this chapter. Do you feel comfortable affirming these ethical standards? Do you feel tension between professional values and ethics and your own personal beliefs?

Once this is clear, engage in direct respectful dialogue with someone who holds a different ideological position from you on this issue. It is important to emphasize that this dialogue is for the purpose of understanding another's perspective, not to try to convince someone else of the rightness of your own position. For example, if you hold the position, "accept the person; condemn the behavior," it would be valuable to identify a fellow student, colleague, or community member who holds one of the other positions. An appropriate person would be someone who is comfortable and willing to discuss this topic openly. In the conversation, each person should take turns sharing his or her own position and explaining the rationale. Each person should also express honestly his or her feelings about the other's position.

It is essential that the conversation take place in a setting that feels safe and private for both parties. Ideally, the conversation could be facilitated among students in a class, with faculty support and guidance, or in some other professional setting. The conversation needs to be based on an explicit expression of mutual respect, willingness to learn, and agreement to disagree.

After the conversation, write a self-reflective essay about your ideological position, its ethical implications for you, and the subsequent conversation. Then identify areas for your own growth.

3.3. Self-Assessment of Your Own Spiritually Based Attitudes About Other Forms of Diversity

A similar procedure to the previous one could be used for any other topic related to spirituality and human diversity. For example, you could explore your spiritually based attitudes and beliefs regarding the role of women, people with disabilities, or particular racial and cultural groups. Identify the degree of your own acceptance of a particular group that is significantly different from your own. Reflect on the religious or nonreligious spiritual sources of your attitude. Have a respectful conversation with a person from the selected group about issues of discrimination. Strive to understand the other person's perspective. Then write a self-reflective essay, including implications for your growth.

CHAPTER FOUR

RELIGIOUS PERSPECTIVES ON SOCIAL SERVICE AND THEIR INSIGHTS FOR SOCIAL WORK PRACTICE

Woe to those who pray
but are heedless in their prayer;
who make a show of piety
and give no alms to the destitute.

The Koran (Islamic)
(trans. Dawood, 1974, p. 28).

INTRODUCTION

In this chapter we provide an introductory overview of various religious traditions that are currently influencing American social work. Our purpose is to increase knowledge about diverse approaches to social work that have an explicit connection to religious traditions and communities. The information in this chapter can provide a foundation for further exploration of traditions that are of particular personal interest or relevance to professional development. Each religious tradition yields insights for social work practice, both for working with clients who share the tradition and also for general innovation in social work practice. Therefore, we are focusing this presentation on ideals, beliefs, values, and helping activities of the religious traditions that have particular relevance to social service in general and professional social work in particular.

Each of these religious perspectives influences a spiritual community sharing core beliefs, values, and social service approaches. We examine five worldwide religious systems that have highly organized and elaborate religious institutions, doctrines, moral frameworks, and social service programs:

119

Buddhism, Christianity, Hinduism, Islam, and Judaism. We also address common features of the religious style of healing named shamanism. Unlike the other perspectives presented, shamanism is not a single religious tradition. Rather, scholars of religion coined the term to encompass similar themes of worldview and religious healing practices found throughout the world. Although many hundreds of culturally distinct religious systems go under this term, they share certain common traits that we summarize here, especially as these are represented in social work literature. The next chapter provides examples of nonsectarian spiritual perspectives on service. Portions of these two chapters are significantly revised and expanded from Canda (1988 b and c). (Used with permission of the publisher.)

Each religious or nonsectarian spiritual perspective is presented according to the following topics: historical origin and contemporary varieties, basic beliefs underlying the approach to service, basic values motivating service, and social work practice implications. There is tremendous variety within each spiritual perspective, so we wish to emphasize that the summaries in this chapter are oversimplifications. We present core beliefs, values, and orientations toward service for each perspective, but keep in mind that there are many different (and sometimes conflicting) interpretations and applications of these basic ideas within variations of each tradition. We do not wish to reduce rich and complex traditions to simplistic stereotypes.

In order to keep the focus on social work, this discussion is based primarily on writings that link the spiritual perspectives to the American context of social work and social service. There are many other writings that deal with each of these traditions in relation to psychology and psychotherapy, which are not included here. Also, writings that focus on these traditions in other national contexts and those that discuss the traditions without reference to social service are used sparingly in order to provide background information not available in the social service literature.

Christian approaches to social work receive the most attention in the literature. There are many articles about Jewish social service, most of them in the *Journal of Jewish Communal Service*, but there are few publications about each of the other religious perspectives.

BUDDHISM AND SOCIAL SERVICE
Origin and Contemporary Varieties of Buddhism

Buddhism originated around 500 years B.C.E. (before the common era) in what is today Nepal and northeastern India (Nielsen et al., 1993;

Schuhmacher & Woerner, 1994). Its founder, Siddhartha Gautama, was a prince who left the luxury and confines of his royal life to seek understanding of human suffering and how people can become free from suffering. After several years of spiritual discipline and meditation, he achieved enlightenment, which means "awakening into the true nature of self and reality." Thus, Siddhartha is called a Buddha, which means "awakened one." The Buddha spread his teachings for forty-five more years until his death. Because Buddhism emerged from a Hindu context, many Hindu religious terms, symbols, and practices are shared and given different nuances by Buddhism.

During the next five centuries, Buddhism spread throughout India and South Asia, formalized its doctrines, established orders of monks and nuns, and separated into various schools. The Theravada branch (Way of the Elders) traces to this original form of Buddhism. Theravada is most common today in South and Southeast Asia. Buddhism spread into Central and East Asia around two thousand years ago. The Mahayana (Great Vehicle) school developed from interaction between Indian Buddhism and philosophical and religious systems of Central and East Asia. From China, Buddhism spread to Korea, Japan, and Vietnam. Currently these are the countries in which the Mahayana branch is most common. Vajrayana (Diamond Vehicle) Buddhism is a Mahayana form common in Tibet and Mongolia. Theravada and Mahayana branches of Buddhism have many variations, shaped by different schools of philosophy and practice, as well as the cultural environments in which they have taken root.

Many forms of Buddhism are present in the United States, with many ethnic-specific forms of Buddhism brought by Asian immigrants and refugees (Canda & Phaobtong, 1992; Furuto et al., 1992; Timberlake & Cook, 1984). For example, Japanese immigrants brought Pure Land and Zen, sects within the Mahayana branch. Pure Land Buddhism is promulgated by Buddhist Churches of America, which has about 100,000 members in the United States (Corbett, 1997). Zen philosophy and meditation practice was promulgated by Japanese scholars and missionary monks. It started to become popular among American intellectuals, such as artists and poets, in the 1950s. Now there are many different Zen-oriented centers in the United States, founded by Japanese, Korean, Chinese, Vietnamese and American Zen Masters. Since 1975, many Southeast Asian refugee communities have established Buddhist temples and mutual assistance associations. Also, some European Americans trained by Southeast Asian teachers have spread Theravadan forms of spiritual practice, such as

Vipassana meditation. Tibetan Buddhism, headed by the Dalai Lama, has become widely known recently due to publicity generated by such movies as *Kundun* and *Seven Years in Tibet*. Many Tibetan clergy and laypeople fled Tibet to escape the Chinese occupation. Some have become teachers in the United States.

The form of Buddhism that has been discussed in social work literature most often is Zen, the name of a Japanese school that emphasizes the priority of attaining enlightenment through direct personal experience and disciplined effort. Zen actually originated in China under Indian influence, incorporating elements of Taoism and Confucianism, and spread to Korea, Japan, and Vietnam and on to the West. In the social work literature, the Zen perspective usually is presented without adherence to any specific religious affiliation; rather, it is portrayed as a way of life and a nonsectarian spiritual approach to social work practice (Brandon, 1976, p.2).

Basic Beliefs

All forms of Buddhism accept the original teaching of Siddhartha, summarized in the Four Noble Truths. The first truth is that human existence is characterized by *suffering,* that is, a sense of unsatisfactoriness due to experiences of pain, injustice, and lack of fulfillment. The second truth is that this suffering arises from *desire*. In desire, we cling to what we have and reject what we do not wish to have. However, nothing is permanent, all conditions change, and all things we have, including the body itself, pass away. Further, we inevitably have things and conditions we do not like, such as illnesses. The third truth is that *suffering can be stopped* by eliminating inappropriate desire. Ironically, in living a life based on desire, we become glued by our attachments to the situation of suffering. The most basic attachment to be stopped is the attachment to the illusion of a separate self. Since all things are interdependent and coproducing (as in systems theories), the idea of a separate self is faulty. Belief in a separate self is not only an intellectual error; it is also an emotional trap. Egocentrism and desire-based clinging or rejecting all hinge on the illusion of a separate self. The fourth truth is that egoistic desire can be stopped by practicing a *disciplined way of life* (the Eightfold Path) to develop wise understanding and motivation, behave morally and compassionately in relations with self and others, and practice meditation to become clearly aware of reality at every moment.

In social work, Keefe (1975, 1996) recommended Zen-inspired meditation techniques for the psychological benefit of clients and the training of workers in empathy, relaxation, and concentration skills—without maintaining the cultural or religious set of beliefs that are traditionally associated with it. As Brandon (1979) asserted, Zen-oriented social work cannot be restricted by a set of beliefs or attitudes. Rather, it should be "a way of actually walking the mountains, a method of training, the basis of which is a gradual opening out into love, by emptying the mind" (p. 35).

The Zen approach rests on a fundamental conviction that reality can be known only by transcending the limitations of human thinking, beliefs, and desires. In Buddhist terms, human suffering can be overcome only by liberation from desires as manifest in personal beliefs and cravings. Enlightenment involves awakening from the illusion (*samsara*, Sanskrit) that we exist as autonomous egos that must possess objects separate from ourselves in order to be satisfied (Brandon, 1976). Paradoxically, then, the most fundamental Zen belief is that all beliefs and desires must be transcended. At that point, our experience is rooted in reality clearly.

Basic Values

With enlightenment, one realizes the essential oneness of oneself with all other beings. From this experience of oneness arises a sense of compassion (*karuna*, Sanskrit) to help other beings become enlightened and overcome suffering (Blofeld, 1988; Brandon, 1976; Eppsteiner, 1988). In Mahayana Buddhism, the supreme ideal is the Bodhisattva, a person who attains enlightenment and vows to help all other beings do the same (Canda, 1995a; Keefe, 1975). Thus, the Zen-oriented social worker upholds a profound commitment to empathic relations with clients, undistorted by countertransference (Keefe, 1996). Yet this compassion extends to all beings, not just one's clients and not just human beings.

The central virtues of Buddhism are called *paramitas* (Sanskrit). *Paramita* literally means "to reach the other shore" of enlightenment. Practicing these virtues is a process of simultaneously helping oneself and others to become enlightened and, hence, saved from suffering. Canda, Shi, and Canda (1993, p. 91) summarized, "The *paramitas* are generous giving, ethical conduct, patient endurance, zealous effort, concentration of the mind, realizing wisdom, and integration of all the virtues in service to others." Thus, compassion flows through them all.

Social Work Implications

Many Asian Americans have been influenced directly or indirectly by Buddhism, especially first- or second-generation immigrants or refugees from East and Southeast Asia. For Asian American Buddhist clients, it is important to identify the particular form of Buddhism they practice and the significance it has for them. Many Southeast Asian refugee communities establish temple-based mutual assistance associations that provide a wide variety of physical, mental, social, and spiritual supports (Canda & Phaobtong, 1992; Timberlake & Cook, 1984). These can be important environmental resources for collaboration. In addition, many Buddhists of all ethnic backgrounds practice personal, family, and community-based rituals and meditation techniques that can assist with stress management, personal insight, and conflict resolution. For example, Nakashima (1995), a Japanese American social worker, wrote that her upbringing and practice as a Buddhist has helped her to deal with issues pertaining to her own mortality and has provided her with a nonsectarian framework for helping clients in hospices deal with their own issues around dying and death.

Some social workers have promoted insights from Zen that can guide spiritually sensitive practice in a nonsectarian manner, without using explicit Buddhist language. According to Brandon (1976), Zen-oriented practice is wary of conceptual constructs, a priori treatment plans, and diagnostic categories because these tend to obstruct direct and spontaneous interactions with the client. Rather than impose professionally designed interventions that arise from the worker's own desires and conceptual constructs, the Zen-oriented worker strives to merge harmoniously with the spontaneous, ongoing process of mutual interaction with the client. Indeed, the Zen approach assumes that the client truly knows the way to resolve his or her suffering, but is unaware of it or is not implementing it. As Brandon put it, social work is a process of attempting to widen and illuminate people's choices and their costs in order to extend autonomy rather than restrict it (p. 30).

Zen-inspired practice can make use of meditation training for both the worker and the client (Keefe, 1996). Zen meditation combines relaxation of the body with focusing of the mind. The meditator learns to be aware of the stream of consciousness without being attached to the thoughts and feelings that pass through. The meditator then becomes able to perceive the world directly, without the distortion of desires and illusions. When interested clients are taught this type of meditation, benefits may include stress management, enhanced self-awareness, and clear insight into one's situation and how to deal authentically with it. The social worker can benefit from meditation by increasing her or his skills of concentration, attentiveness, accurate listening, empathy, and stress management.

A broad implication of Buddhism for social work is to expand the conception of the person and environment. In Buddhist thought, as in dynamic systems theory, the person does not exist independently of the environment (Macy, 1991; Robbins, Chatterjee, & Canda, 1998). Helping oneself and helping others must be interrelated. Human rights of individuals must be linked with collective responsibility (De Silva, 1995; Abe, 1995; Thurman, 1996). Understanding and action must necessarily address both micro and macro systems, because all are woven together. Achieving human aspirations for peace and justice is inextricable from supporting the well-being of the entire planetary ecology and all beings within it (Eppsteiner, 1988). Thus, Buddhist philosophy can inspire social workers to weave together micro and macro practice and local and global issues and to seek creative solutions to problems that provide maximum mutual benefit to all human and nonhuman beings involved.

CHRISTIANITY AND SOCIAL SERVICE
Origin and Contemporary Varieties of Christianity

Christianity traces its origin to Jesus of Nazareth, who was born in Israel in about the year 4 B.C.E. (before the common era) (Crim, 1981; Nielsen et al., 1993). Jesus was a Jewish teacher whom Christians consider the Messiah, born as the incarnation of God to save humanity from sin. The title of Jesus, Christ, is derived from a Greek word meaning "Messiah." Early in the first century, Christian communities were established in Israel and then spread to Gentiles throughout Asia Minor and parts of Europe. Gentile Christians came to outnumber Jewish Christians as missionary efforts expanded. During this period, Christians were a persecuted minority in the Roman Empire. However, the Roman emperor Constantine converted to Christianity and in 380 C.E. Christianity was made an official religion of the empire.

This alliance between the Roman Empire and Christianity eventually changed the status of the religion from persecuted minority to the politically and numerically predominant majority. This pattern of alliance between church and state continued in Europe throughout the Middle Ages. Christianity became referred to as Catholic, in order to indicate its universal scope, under the authority of the Roman pope. In 1054, Christianity underwent a major division between Western Catholic Christianity (centered in Rome) and Eastern Orthodox Christianity.

The 1500s began a period of theological and political challenges to reform the Western Catholic church under such Protestant leaders as Martin Luther (German), John Huss (Czech), and John Wycliffe (English). Many Protestant denominations of Christianity have been established since that time. They tend to hold in common a denial of the authority of the pope and an emphasis on salvation by divine grace rather than human effort. The various denominations of Christianity have engaged in extensive missionary activities, leading to its predominance in the United States and in many other parts of the world.

Most Americans identify as Christians. There are more than nine hundred denominations, including Catholic, Orthodox, and Protestant denominations that originated elsewhere, and also denominations that have originated in the United States, such as the Church of Jesus Christ of Latter-day Saints, Church of Christ, Scientist, Seventh-day Adventists, and the Watchtower Bible and Tract Society (Jehovah's Witnesses).

Christianity has been extremely influential in the formation of professional social work. Many professional and volunteer social services are provided under Christian church auspices (Garland, 1992; Loewenberg, 1988; Van Hook, 1997). Three of the largest Christian organizational providers of social services are Catholic Charities, USA, Lutheran Social Services, and the Salvation Army. The North American Association of Christian Social Workers sponsors conferences, a newsletter and journal, and book publications. Most of its membership is Protestant, from evangelically oriented denominations. The National Catholic School of Social Services of Catholic University of America for many years has sponsored the journal *Social Thought* as a forum for Christian (especially Catholic) and other theological and philosophical approaches to social work. This journal was formerly published under the auspices of Catholic Charities. It is now published by Haworth Press and has a nonsectarian orientation to spirituality.

Basic Beliefs

Although there are many variations in doctrine and practice among Protestant, Catholic, and Orthodox denominations, Christian authors in social work tend to present viewpoints that are commonly shared in Christianity. Therefore, this presentation will emphasize beliefs and values that are widely shared by Christian social work authors (Biestek, 1956; Consiglio, 1987; Corbett, 1997; Garland, 1992; Keith-Lucas, 1985 & 1994; Ressler, 1992; Van Hook, 1997).

Christian theology forms through the interaction of several sources: scholarly exegesis of the Old and New Testaments, regarded as the inspired word of God; the traditions and doctrines of various denominations; and personal inspiration of Christian individuals and communities.

Christians believe that the universe was created by a personal supreme God who loves the world. Humankind was created with the capacity for moral choice. Unfortunately, people often choose sin, asserting their own prideful desires in disobedience to God's will. Jesus Christ became incarnate as both God and human being in order to save humanity from sin through his crucifixion and resurrection from the dead. Christ will come again to usher in the fullness of the Kingdom of God on earth. The Holy Spirit continues to guide and strengthen Christians. These three divine persons—God the Creator, Christ, and Holy Spirit—are One God. People who turn away from their sinfulness and align their wills with the will of God are promised salvation and eternal reward after death.

The central message of Christianity is that God is love (King, 1965). Human beings achieve fulfillment through personal and loving relationship with God (McCabe, 1965). God's love is given in a pure act of grace. When people are open to the grace of God, they discover a sense of meaning; reconciliation between self, the world, and God; and strength and hope in the face of suffering. This reconciliation is expressed and experienced through loving relationships between people and between God and people. As Hess (1980, p. 63) stated it, Christianity sees human nature as being-in-situation-with-others-for-a-purpose. Moral, loving relationships with God, self, and others are necessary for personal fulfillment and social well-being. In the tradition of the Social Gospel and liberation theology, some Christians emphasize that loving service should extend beyond helping individuals or Christian communities in order to work for liberation and social justice of all peoples, especially those who experience discrimination and oppression.

Basic Values

Perhaps the most central value commitment of Christians is to live a life of charity (love). Since this word has become distorted in popular usage to mean condescending help, it is important to return to the theological meaning. Charity (*caritas* in Latin; *agape* in Greek) is recognized in the New Testament as the most important virtue (Benton, 1981; see 1 Corinthians 13, New Testament). Charity does not expect gratitude or reward. Charity is a spiritual impulse of love, arising from union with God. As Christ is recognized to be present in all people, the Christian shows love of God in service to the needs of people. Charity involves recognizing the essential communion of all people, in both their shared suffering of the human condition and their unity with God. As Tillich (1962) explained, relating to another person in charity involves both unconditional acceptance of the person's worth and caring expression of constructive criticism. As the National Conference of Catholic Charities (1983) asserted, four related primary values are love (as charity), truth, justice, and freedom. The Christian upholds the truth of God's reconciling work in the world and works toward the just ordering of social relationships, respecting the needs of all people. The Christian supports freedom of opportunity for all people to live in a fully human and loving manner. This may involve active opposition to corrupt social policies and social institutions (Scharper, 1975).

Biestek (1956) gave a Christian interpretation to the meaning of some basic social work values. First, *acceptance* of the client means that the worker perceives the client accurately, both his or her strengths and weaknesses, while maintaining a sense of the client's innate dignity and worth. Second, *self-determination* means respecting the client's right to free choice within the context of the client's capacity for constructive decision making, moral reflection, and social responsibility. Finally, *nonjudgmentalism* means that the worker carefully evaluates whether the behavior of the client is helpful or harmful to self and others, without judging guilt or innocence.

Social Work Implications

For the social worker who practices from a Christian perspective, there is an integral connection between life in Christ and professional activity (Keith-Lucas, 1985, 1994; Ressler, 1994; Van Hook, 1997). For example, Smith (1961) suggested that helping the client to be healed of emotional wounds requires a constant expression of love in the helping relationship, as well as in the ongoing daily interactions of agency staff. This modeling and sharing of love involves the personal spiritual growth of the worker as well as the healing of the client. Indeed, for Keith-Lucas (1994), the empathic helping relationship is a human reflection of the divine love shown by God to people through the incarnation of Christ and the grace of the Holy Spirit. For these reasons, according to Keith-Lucas (1985), the Christian social worker should use practice methods that affirm the distinctiveness, worth, and capacity for choice of the client.

Tillich (1962) identified four main aims of this love expression in social work. First, the worker helps the client promptly satisfy immediate needs.

Second, the worker guides the client toward independence and withdraws from the dependency relationship. Third, the worker communicates to the client a sense of being a necessary and significant person. This provides a perspective of cosmic meaning in which each person has "a necessary, incomparable, and unique place in the whole of being" (p. 16). Finally, the worker helps to fulfill the ultimate goal of humanity and the world, which is to integrate each individual aim into the universal aim of being itself. Thus, Christian social work deals with practical material needs in the context of spiritual needs; the two kinds of needs are inextricable (Canda, 1988c).

Essentially the Christian view explains the fact of human suffering in terms of sin. When sin is understood as alienation from one's authentic self, from others, and from God (King, 1965), it becomes clear that the primary goal of Christian social work is personal and community reconciliation. Keith-Lucas (1985, p. 14) described the helping process in Christian terms as including four main elements: repentance, which requires that a person recognize a problem needing help; confession, which requires telling someone about the problem; submission, which requires giving up familiar old but unproductive behaviors; and faith in the positive outcome of the change efforts.

One controversial practice method some Christian social workers employ is witnessing their faith to the client. Keith-Lucas (1985) suggested four situations in which witnessing might be appropriate: (1) when a client is a Christian, would like to become one, or wishes to have companionship in prayer; (2) when a client inquires about the worker's motivation for providing caring and helping; (3) when the client's view of Christian faith needs enlargement or theological reflection; and (4) when the client is explicitly asking questions about the purpose of life and suffering. He added that the most effective Christian witness is not talking about religion "but treating people in a Christian way oneself" (p. 29). In this context, witnessing should be done only according to the need and interest of the client.

Another Christian helping method is seeking help from God for specific situations through prayer in a professional context (Canda, 1990a; Gatza, 1979). Prayer may involve petition for help, quiet meditation, prayerful scripture reading, ritual and community celebration, and relating to each moment of life prayerfully. According to Gatza, healing prayer involves an openness to God's grace that goes beyond ordinary human ability to heal. Gatza recommended that healing prayer be used to complement ordinary professional knowledge and skill. Sneck and Bonica

(1980) pointed out that one need never overtly and explicitly pray with a client in order to help prayerfully. According to them, the Christian worker should trust in the power of God to heal through the therapeutic relationship itself. Their contraindications to praying with clients are when the counselor is inexperienced, when the client is potentially hostile or in danger of being exposed to needless additional pain, or when an act of prayer is a substitute for a more genuine and imaginative intervention. Canda (1990a) offered ethical guidelines for use of prayer in social work. These are presented in Part III.

DiBlasio (1993) summarized research findings indicating that religious ideas and rituals concerning forgiveness can help religious families and individuals to resolve problems and conflicts and to strengthen relationships. His own study of social workers' religiosity and attitude toward forgiveness indicated that many are not aware of or comfortable with forgiveness theory and practice. He recommended development of more research and clinical applications on the appropriate and effective uses of forgiveness.

All social workers can cooperate with Christian clergy and church communities insofar as these are sources of support for Christian clients (Bigham, 1956; Furman & Chandy, 1994; Furman, Fry & Fontaine, 1996 & 1997; Garland, 1992; Joseph, 1975; Loewenberg, 1988; Pepper, 1956). When social workers and pastoral workers understand each other and share basic aspects of worldview, their work can complement each other. Thus, clients can deal with problems in both psychosocial and spiritual terms. However, significant issues of logistics and trust need to be addressed in clergy–social worker collaboration. This is addressed in Part III.

Christian volunteers and professional social workers may also engage in community service, social policy advocacy, and social justice activism through Christian church auspices (Breton, 1989; Netting, 1982a, 1982b, 1984). In fact, many Christian private agencies, such as Lutheran Social Services and Catholic Social Services, hire staff primarily based on professional qualification. Staff do not necessarily belong to the same Christian denomination, and some may not be Christian. Therefore, services may be provided in a nonsectarian manner, although consistent with basic Christian social ethics. This is particularly likely when the program is funded by federal or state money, due to the separation of church and state (Ressler, 1998). Weber and Jones (1994) identified several Christian religious social issue interest groups with more than a $15 million annual budget, such as Church World Service, National Council of Churches of Christ, the U.S. Catholic Conference, and Women's Division of the United

Methodist Church. Christians vary and conflict in their concepts and goals for social justice, so numerous lobbying and social action groups vie to influence public policy and behavior on such issues as abortion, church-state relations, civil rights, education, poverty relief, foreign policy, pornography, world peace, and gay rights.

Some social work scholars have raised concerns about the role of fundamentalist Christian groups in promoting judgmental, exclusivistic, patriarchal, and sometimes militant conservative approaches to individual, family, and social issues (Denton, 1990; Loewenberg, 1988; Midgely, 1990; Midgely & Sanzenbach, 1989; Sanzenbach, 1989). By Christian fundamentalism, we mean a movement primarily among Protestant and newer Christian denominations that has the following characteristics: conviction of personal salvation by faith in Jesus; commitment to evangelize others; faith in the inerrancy of the Bible as the literal, authoritative word of God; special interest in the imminent apocalyptic second coming of Christ; practice of exclusion of "unbelievers"; and active opposition to liberalism and secularism (Marty & Appleby, 1991). Denton (1990) distinguished between fundamentalists with a polemical, exclusivist style and those with a faith-nurturing style. Particularly in the polemical groups, rigid standards of patriarchy and authoritarian discipline may pose risks to women and children in families. On the macro level, militant fundamentalists may actively oppose social work values and agendas and spread distrust of social workers and mental health professionals. On the other hand, fundamentalist religious communities can provide families with positive experiences of social support, forgiveness, reconciliation, and spiritual guidance. Canda (1989b) and Joseph (1989) cautioned against negative stereotyping of fundamentalists. Denton (1990) suggested that fundamentalist families be addressed as culturally distinct. Culturally sensitive practice should encourage growth and mutual satisfaction among family members by working respectfully and knowledgeably within their religious communities and belief systems, whenever possible.

HINDUISM AND SOCIAL SERVICE

Origin and Contemporary Varieties of Hinduism

Hinduism is the common name for the predominant religion of India and Indian Americans. The term, which originated from Persian, literally means "the belief of the people of India" (Nielsen et al., 1993). Since there are other religions in India, such as Jainism, Buddhism, Sikhism, Islam, and Christianity, sometimes the term *Brahmanism* is used to distinguish it. This term refers to the important status given to the priestly class that presides over ritual and scriptural study. Hinduism is an extremely diverse tradition. Common scriptures are highly regarded, such as the Vedas and Upanishads, but there are many different schools of philosophical orientation and types of religious groups and practices. Hinduism is not organized with a central overarching institution, and there is little attempt to regulate conformity of beliefs. Rather, a common Hindu viewpoint is that there are many legitimate spiritual paths, just as there are many paths to the top of a mountain. Thus, Hindus may embrace many varieties of monotheism, polytheism, animism, nontheistic philosophy, or combinations of these. There are also many variations based on caste, region, language, and ethnicity. Variations in these aspects of diversity, and various stances toward cross-cultural experience, can have significant influences on the particular spiritual forms of Hindu Indian Americans (Banerjee, 1997a, 1997b).

Early Hinduism emerged from the Indus Valley agricultural cultures, which were well established by 2400 B.C.E. (Corbett, 1997; Crim, 1981; Nielsen et al., 1993). By about 1600 B.C.E., Indo-European people, called the Aryas, had colonized the Indus Valley region. Mingling between traditions of the original Indus civilization and the Aryas gave rise to historical Hinduism. Between 1200 and 800 B.C.E., the priestly class compiled the Vedas from a long tradition of oral literature. By around 200 B.C.E., the main core of the Upanishads ("secret teachings") was written. These teachings gave rise to the worldview of Vedanta ("Veda's End"), which is widely considered to be a culmination and refinement of earlier Vedic teachings. The classical language of Hinduism is Sanskrit.

In the United States, there are many varieties of Hindu-originated religious systems and practices. For example, Swami Vivekananda was a major proponent of karma yoga as an approach to social work in India (Patel, 1987). In 1894, the first Hindu organization, the Vedanta Society, was founded in the United States by Swami Vivekananda (Corbett, 1997; Melton, 1992). In the United States, the Vedanta Society promotes intellectual study of Vedantic philosophy. In 1965, the International Society for Krishna Consciousness was founded in the United States by Swami Prabhupada. This organization (also called the Hare Krishna movement) promotes a devotional approach to worship for Indian Americans and many European Americans. This group gives special devotion to Krishna, an incarnation or manifestation of God featured in one of the most important Hindu scriptures, the *Bhagavad Gita*. There are also many kinds of yoga centers and yoga practice groups throughout the United States. Perhaps the most widely known form of yoga in the United States is hatha yoga, which employs spiritual disciplines combining physical movements and postures, controlled breathing, and meditation. Aside from formal Hindu-related organizations, the primary locus of Hindu practice is the home, with many varieties based on the family tradition. There are also regional support groups for Indian Americans that may sponsor community rituals.

In the social work literature, two forms of Hindu-oriented views are most often addressed. One is karma yoga, based largely on the teaching of Swami Vivekananda and other yogic traditions (Bhattacharya, 1965; Patel, 1987; Seplowin, 1992; Singh, 1992). The other is a Gandhian approach to social work (Cappozi, 1992; Dasgupta, 1986; Sharma, 1987; Walz, Sharma & Birnbaum, 1990). Although Mahatma Gandhi (1869–1948) has been well known throughout the world for his spiritually based social activism in India and South Africa for decades, his ideas were not systematically applied to American social work until the mid-1980s. Here we focus on karma yoga and Gandhian social work. Social work writers advocate these ideas in order to promote nonviolent, spiritually based practice for all social workers in a nonsectarian manner. Patel (1987) suggested that there are many similarities between Gandhian social work and karma yoga. However, she suggested that the Gandhian perspective is more focused on social action goals, while karma yoga has *moksha,* or spiritual liberation and union with the divine, as its explicit goal.

Basic Beliefs

In general, the Vedantic worldview emphasizes a universal, ultimate, non-dualistic reality that underlies all things, called Brahman. It also emphasizes the importance of transcending suffering and rebirth (*samsara*) through the attainment of *moksha* (liberation), which involves realizing the unity of one's true self (*atman*) with Brahman. *Moksha* also implies liberation from the bondage of *karma. Karma,* which literally means "action," implies that all actions generate reactions. Moral and helpful actions generate beneficial reactions for oneself and others. Immoral or irresponsible actions generate harmful results for self and others. Karma binds the person to the cycle of death and rebirth until the person attains liberation through moral action and religious practices.

Singh (1992) defined karma yoga as "the realization of the divinity through complete selfless dedication to work and duty" (p. 9). Vivekananda elaborated principles of karma yoga by building on the foundation of Vedantic philosophy (Patel, 1987). Karma yoga is a spiritual discipline of selfless service that leads to the liberation of the social worker from karmic suffering at the same time as helping to relieve others' suffering. Karma yoga involves cultivating an awareness of the divine (Brahman) as the absolute ultimate reality that envelops everything, including the social worker's true self (*atman*) and the true selves of clients. Patel (1987) explained that karma yoga means helping others, even to the point of death, without being attached to any outcome.

Gandhian social work rests on similar principles. Although Gandhi was a Hindu, he did not promote sectarianism. He believed that ultimate truth is beyond the comprehension of any one person or any one religion. He believed that all people should seek the truth through their various religious and cultural frameworks. This is called self-realization (Pandey, 1996; Walz, Sharma & Birnbaum, 1990). Gandhi's approach to social action was based on *satyagraha,* meaning "truth force." *Satyagraha* means living life as a nonviolent pursuit of truth, while honoring everyone else's pursuit of truth, even in the midst of conflict.

Basic Values

Since all beings are regarded as manifestations of the divine truth, every being should be treated with respect. Vedantic beliefs lead directly to three fundamental values to guide practice. First, social workers should maintain clear benevolent purpose toward clients. Second, social workers should not be attached to the fruits of their actions. This does not mean being careless. Rather, it means not having an egoistic attachment to one's own goals for clients. It also means altruistic motivation; service is its own reward. One does not serve in order to reap rewards.

The third value principle is nonviolence (*ahimsa*). In nonviolence, all people are granted unconditional respect and compassion, including people who are one's opponents and oppressors. Nonviolence is not passivity, however. Nonviolence involves dedicated and persevering search for truth and assisting others to live with dignity and freedom so they too can pursue truth. Oppression and dehumanization are to be resisted actively, but in a way that does not oppress or dehumanize others. In Gandhian thought, nonviolence actively promotes individual and social peace such that even one's opponents are assisted in their own search for truth. *Ahimsa* and *satyagraha* are inseparable.

These three values imply the value of seeking mutual benefit in social work. It is not sufficient to benefit only an identified client. Since all people and beings are interconnected by *karma,* the results of helping actions on clients and others need to be discerned. Harming some to help others is not nonviolent. Further, the process of helping is itself a natural karmic benefit for the social worker. Thus, helping others naturally helps oneself work toward *moksha* or realization of truth.

There is a paradox inherent in these values. Karma yoga and Gandhian social work both advocate that the social worker should seek the benefit of others without seeking personal benefit. However, it is also understood that engaging in this selfless action results in spiritual benefits for the social worker. Yet if one's motivation is solely to accrue material or spiritual benefits, then even apparently good action does not help the social worker toward the spiritual goal of liberation.

Social Work Implications

The helping relationship should be established according to these values of respect, selflessness, and nonviolence. As the traditional Hindu greeting, *namaste,* means "the God within me greets the God within you," the social worker should relate to clients with this sense of their inherent worth and divinity.

On a practical level, karma yoga practitioners in India have established many educational and social service programs, medical institutions, cultural activities, rural and tribal development programs, and youth training for social service (Patel, 1987). Such formal service organizations based on karma yoga have not been described in the American social work literature. However, the principles of karma yoga could be applied in American social work contexts. Nor have Gandhian principles been applied widely in American social work. But advocates suggest that American social work could move toward a more holistic, spiritually attuned, and nonviolent approach by considering Gandhian principles.

Singh (1992) suggested that the Vedantic perspective and traditional helping techniques, such as yoga systems, could provide a culturally familiar framework for many Hindus (and other Asian Americans) in the United States. He identified four types of yoga: karma yoga (as already described), bhakti yoga, devotional dedication to a personal God; raja yoga, opening awareness of the divinity within oneself through mental and physical exercises; and jnana yoga, realizing one's own divine nature through intellectual disciplines. The yogas provide a holistic approach to individuals by using different means suited to particular talents, personalities, and beliefs, in "application to stress management, mental clarification from confusions, self-unification, emancipation from suffering and enhancement of self-image" (p. 9). Singh also identified some helping techniques that have similarity to yogic disciplines, such as biofeedback and healing visualization.

Seplowin (1992) recommended meditation in conjunction with group therapy. Logan (1997) gave a personal example of how her practice of an Indian-originated meditation practice (*siddha yoga*) simultaneously helps her achieve clarity while relating in a clear and open-minded way with social work students.

Gandhian principles highlight the importance of spiritually explicit, compassionate approaches to macro action. The practical techniques of Gandhian community organizing and development could be applied to American social work. This would require reenvisioning the nature of social work (Walz, Sharma & Birnbaum, 1990). For example, the personal lifestyle of the worker, the consumption patterns of the agency, and efforts for larger social change should all foster material simplicity, "a means of reducing violence by performing work simply, limiting demands on the environment, and taking no more than necessary" (p. 25). Helping strategies should seek the welfare of all (*sarvodaya*) by taking a holistic and systemic understanding of situations and applying a value of compassion for everyone affected by change. Social work should also embody the principle of *swadeshi*, which means focusing help for those most needy in the local environment. But *swadeshi* also means rippling out local benefits to the wider social systems, including the global context, so local and global dimensions of justice are linked.

In general, the Vedantic-inspired approaches to social work suggest innovative possibilities for working with Indian American clients in a culturally appropriate way. In addition, when the principles are extended beyond specific traditional Hindu terminology and religious beliefs, they provide guidelines for developing holistic models of social work in general.

ISLAM AND SOCIAL SERVICE

Origin and Contemporary Varieties of Islam

Islam originated among Arab bedouins in the sixth century (Esposito, 1991; Nielsen et al., 1993; Peters, 1982). The word *Islam* is derived from an Arabic term meaning "surrender." Islam is a faith based on the person's and community's submission to the will of God, Allah, in all spheres of life. Islam developed in the monotheistic stream of traditions that includes Judaism and Christianity. Each shares a respect for the biblical books of Moses (the Torah). Islamic monotheism was in part a reaction against the polytheistic beliefs, preoccupation with striving for wealth and power, and feuding among Arab tribes prevalent at the time of Islam's founder, the Prophet Muhammad (c. 570–632).

Muhammad was born into a wealthy clan of Mecca. As a young man, he spent much time in reflection on problems of social corruption (Nielsen et al., 1993; Haynes et al., 1997). At around the age of forty, while in solitary meditation in a cave, he had a series of revelations. Tradition has it that the angel Gabriel delivered God's messages to Muhammad, which were set down in the Quran, the Islamic scripture. After 613, Muhammad spread his message to his family and community, especially focusing on disadvantaged groups, such as women, slaves, poor people, and children. Muhammad soon moved to Medina, which accepted him as the prophet of Allah and agreed to fight on his behalf. With support of people from Medina, Muhammad established authority in Medina by 630.

From the time of the prophet's death in 632 to 661, his successors led campaigns of conquest and proselytization that extended from North Africa to the Indian frontier (Crim, 1981). Early in this period, a major division occurred between Sunni Islam, the largest group, and the Shiite Muslims. The Shiite Muslims claimed Ali, Muhammad's cousin and son-in-law, to be his successor. Ali and many of his family were murdered by opponents. Since that time, Islam has spread throughout the world, with large numbers of adherents in the Middle East, Africa, Europe, India, and East and Southeast Asia. In most countries except Iran, the Sunni Muslims are the majority.

In the United States there are now three major groupings of Muslims: Muslim immigrants and their descendants (mostly Sunni), converts to these traditional forms of Islam, and primarily African American new Islamic groups, such as the Nation of Islam. The primary immigrant Muslim national organization is the Islamic Society of North America (Corbett, 1997; Melton, 1992). The American Muslim Mission is the largest organization of American-born Muslims. Sufism, a mystical form of Islam, was brought to the United States in 1910 by Pir Hazrat Inayat Khan. The Sufi Order sponsors many spiritual groups, meditation and ecstatic rituals, and educational programs.

Muslim mosques and student organizations in the United States presumably provide social support for members, but details have not been described in the social work literature. So far, the social work writing on

Islam has focused on Islam in other countries, or it has advocated for greater understanding of the Islamic social justice perspective among social workers generally (Al-Krenawi, 1996; Graham & Al-Krenawi, 1996; Haynes et al., 1997; Jain, 1965).

Basic Beliefs

Muslims believe that Muhammad was the last and final prophet, culminating the earlier Jewish and Christian prophetic revelations (Corbett, 1997; Haynes et al., 1997). Islam is strictly monotheistic. The central tenet is that there is no God other then Allah, the supreme, incomparable, inconceivable, personal creator deity. Muslims declare their submission to and reliance on Allah in all things. Since Allah cannot be conceived of in terms of any created thing, it is strictly prohibited to produce images of the deity.

Muslims regard the Quran as the culmination of the scriptures of Allah. Jewish and Christian scriptures are respected, but insofar as there is disagreement with the Quran, the Quran takes precedence. Respect is also given to people considered to be previous prophets, such as Abraham, Moses, David, John the Baptist, and Jesus. According to Islam, divine scriptural revelation was completed with Muhammad. None of these people are considered divine themselves, for divinity is a quality of God alone.

Muslims also believe in angels who serve Allah and may be messengers from Allah to humanity. They also believe in Paradise and Hell. Allah rewards good deeds and punishes evildoers.

The Five Pillars of Islam are the core of belief and practice. The first pillar is faith in Allah. Faith is proclaimed in daily repetition: "There is no God but Allah, and Muhammad is the Prophet of Allah." The second pillar is prayer, which takes place five times daily and, if possible, at a mosque on midday Friday. The third pillar is the giving of alms to the needy (*zakat*). The fourth pillar is fasting, from sunrise to sunset, during the month of Ramadan that celebrates the revelation to Muhammad. The fifth pillar is the pilgrimage to Mecca, which should be done at least once in a lifetime if a person is able. These pillars of practice assist the person in striving toward self-improvement and community welfare in all aspects of life.

Muslims also have beliefs related to distinctive cultural traditions. For example, Graham and Al-Krenawi (1996) and Al-Krenawi (1996) identified bedouin belief in the influence of God's will on human life as a fate that should be accepted with courage and patience. Also, the spirit of a deceased husband may appear in dreams, as though to attack, thus requiring a preventative ritual.

Basic Values

Since the person and community should be wholly oriented toward the will of Allah, there is no separation between religious and secular spheres of life. Individual fulfillment, family life, and community well-being are all related to following the precepts of Islamic law (*shari'a*). As Muhammad originally advocated for social reforms on behalf of women, children, and disadvantaged groups, there is a strong social justice value framework in Islam. Ideally, there should be a reciprocal relationship between individual freedom and community obligations and responsibilities. People should be persistent in their efforts toward self-improvement, not only in actions but also in inner feelings. Family roles involve patriarchal gender roles, but women and men are to respect each other. Islamic social norms reflect these basic values.

The Islamic community of believers (*umma*) is regarded as having a special mission from Allah to create a just society for its members and to be a model for others (Esposito, 1991). The Quran recognizes differences in social status, wealth, and tribal origin, but it promotes a unity and equality of all believers under Allah. The Quran condemns exploitation of the poor, widows, other women, orphans, and slaves. It denounces economic abuse, such as false contracts, bribery, hoarding of wealth, and usury.

Social Work Implications

Since Islam is predicated on the idea that all of life should be oriented toward Allah, social work practice with Muslim clients should respectfully incorporate the clients' beliefs and practices. Its community orientation provides an opportunity for social workers to collaborate with Islamic social support networks, Islamic teachers, and friendship support groups. Sometimes problems may be defined in relation to Islamic law. In these cases, familiarity with relevant passages in the Quran, as well as family and ethnic customs, would be helpful.

The third pillar, almsgiving, has significant social welfare implications. All Muslims are expected to share in the support of the community and the relief of those with special needs. Almsgiving is both an act of worship to God and a service to the community. Adult Muslims who are able are expected to tithe about 2½ percent of their assets (Esposito, 1991; Jain,

1965). This payment is owed because people receive their wealth from the bounty of God. Almsgiving reflects the broader concern for social justice ideals of equality, mutual respect, and relief of the disadvantaged.

The Islamic view of social service emphasizes a complementary relation between individual well-being and social welfare. The helping process itself is seen as a spiritually significant action and relationship, not only between worker and clients, but also with the divine.

JUDAISM AND SOCIAL SERVICE
Origin and Contemporary Varieties of Judaism

Judaism originated from the agrarian nomadic Hebrew tribes of Israel around 2000–1000 B.C.E. (Crim, 1981; Neusner, 1979; Nielsen et al., 1993). During this period, the tribal God Yahweh came to be regarded as the one true God, creator transcendent over creation. According to tradition, the patriarch of Israel, Abraham, migrated from Mesopotamia to Canaan to leave the polytheistic past and dedicate himself and his descendants to God. Later, Jacob and his people went to Egypt during a time of famine. The people of Israel became oppressed by the pharaoh. Finally, Moses led his people across the wilderness to freedom. Moses received revelation of the Torah from God, confirming the covenant of God's care for the Jews and the Jewish people's commitment to God. The first five books of the Bible are attributed to Moses, though they were probably not completed in their present form until the fifth century B.C.E. Key themes of Judaism were established during this time: monotheism, a covenant between God and God's chosen people, and endurance of suffering, exile, and liberation.

In 586 B.C.E., the temple of Jerusalem was destroyed, and the Hebrews were exiled to Babylonia. The tradition of the synagogue developed as a place for study and worship without sacrifice. Many Jews returned to Israel around 500 B.C.E. and reestablished the temple in Jerusalem. During this period, priests took responsibility for sacrifice at the temple; scribes studied and interpreted the scriptures; and messianic Zealots struggled against foreign rulers. The core of Hebrew scriptures (*tanakh*) was formed, including the Torah (Pentateuch) prophetic writings, and other writings.

The Second Temple was destroyed in 70 C.E. by the Romans. After the destruction of the Second Temple, the rabbis (learned teachers) gradually emerged from and supplanted the priests and scribes. The classical or rabbinical period continued to the nineteenth century, along with dispersion of the Jews to many parts of the world. Jews in the Diaspora struggled with various means of retaining cultural distinctiveness and faithfulness to the Torah, often enduring discrimination and oppression.

During the nineteenth and twentieth centuries, various forms of Zionism emerged that emphasized the importance of Jews' returning to Israel to establish a state and fulfill their religious and cultural aspirations. The Holocaust amplified this growing Zionist movement, as the need for state protection and political autonomy became a matter of survival. The Holocaust also accelerated the immigration of Jews to the United States.

In 1654, the first twenty-three Jews arrived in the United States. Currently, there are about 5.8 million Jews in the United States (Gelman & Schnall, 1997). There are three major groups of religious Jews: Orthodox, Conservative, and Reform. There are also many Jews who are not affiliated with a religious group. Since the late 1800s, there have been many forms of Jewish agencies and social services in the United States.

Basic Beliefs

According to Neusner (1979), a Jewish scholar of religion, Judaism is a tradition built on the scriptures (*tanakh*), ethical commandments governing daily conduct (*mitzvot*), Talmudic commentaries, faith in God, and membership in the Jewish community. For religious Jews, Jewish law (*halakhah*) dictates living in accord with the covenant between God and the Jewish community. Therefore, it follows that a Jewish perspective for social work would emphasize its intimate connection with and relevance for the Jewish community. Given the challenges of Diaspora and Holocaust, and more recently the high rates of intermarriage and secularism, many Jewish communal service workers view the heightening of Jewish identity and preservation of the Jewish community as the key issues in Jewish social welfare (Bubis, 1981; Gelman & Schnall, 1997; Sprafkin, 1970).

Judaism is a way of life, not just a religious or philosophical system. However, there is a great deal of variety of lifestyle and belief within the Jewish community pertaining to cultural backgrounds, degree of religiosity, and sectarian orientation (e.g., Orthodox, Conservative, Reform, Reconstructionist, nonreligious).

In the Judaic religious view, there is an inextricable connection between faith in God and service, because the *tanakh* requires Jews to imitate God through partnership in the ongoing process of creation, including social welfare activities (Eskenazi, 1983; Schecter, 1971). According to Eskenazi, the God of Israel has no identifiable appearance or a name that Jews may speak. Yet God sanctifies diverse and authentic emotions as well as falli-bility. God transcends human images but also sanctifies the uniqueness of human experience.

The details of this relationship are prescribed by the Torah and its com-mentaries pertaining to diet, Sabbath, morality, civil law, and Torah study (Ostrov, 1976). There are also communal commemorations of annual holy days (e.g., Yom Kippur), life events (e.g., bar and bat mitzvah), and his-torical events (e.g., the Six-Day War). Religious observance is most strict among Orthodox Jews.

According to Ansel (1973), Judaic thought views human nature as essentially good, having been created in the image of God, including an innate need for growth. However, this growth may be blocked by misun-derstandings of self or external conditions. When this growth runs con-trary to God's purpose and moral relationships, one must practice *t'shuva* (repentance), involving self-awareness and change of heart, to return to God's will. This process may involve a healthy feeling of guilt and recon-ciliation. Accordingly, Judaic thought includes an understanding of human behavior in terms of sin. Yet the relationship between sin and men-tal illness is a complex one in the Torah. Identification of a person who has mental health problems as a sinner, in the pejorative sense, is not appro-priate (Wikler, 1977). However, Wikler (1986) pointed out that some Orthodox Jews may attach a sense of stigma and community sanction (such as damage to family reputation or reduced marriage prospects) to people with mental illness.

Basic Values

In Judaism, since all people are believed to be created in the image of God, each person has intrinsic worth. The Torah injunction to love one's neigh-bor is expressed through commitment to standards of righteousness, compassion, and truth with regard to all people (Schecter, 1971). In par-ticular, this value has been expressed through systematic means of pro-viding help to members of the Jewish community in need. Ideally, the unconditional love and acceptance shown by God to humanity serves as a model for all relationships between people. Buber (1957) called this an I-Thou relationship.

The devout Jew performs acts of loving kindness (*hesed*) and righ-teousness or justice (*tsedekah*) out of a sense of compassion modeled on the compassion of God (Linzer, 1979). Therefore, according to Linzer, the Jewish social worker should extend compassionate help to clients while restraining his or her own self-needs that may interfere with the client's benefit. Yet Bubis (1980) asserted that within the context of Jewish communal service, workers who are sanctioned to uphold the Jewish community must advocate community values to the Jewish client when those values are demonstrably essential to the continuity and prosperity of that community (p. 233).

According to Nussbaum (1983), the core value of *tsedakah* (righteousness) has promoted organized and private efforts toward social welfare. Traditionally it was focused on the Jewish community and has supported class inequalities. Nussbaum suggested that the concept of *tsedekah* can be reevaluated in more universal and egalitarian terms to support a broad concern with social justice. Gelman and Schall (1997) translated *tsedakah* as "justice." This value implies that no one who requests service should be denied and that the benefactor should follow "in the paths of righteousness and sanctity that characterize the Lord" (p. 169). In general, acts of charity and philanthropy are regarded as social obligations required by Jewish law.

Social Work Implications

Biblical and Talmudic injunctions have supported community-based welfare since ancient times. For example, provisions were made for the benefit of the poor, fair treatment of workers, fair credit, and for care of widows, orphans, strangers, and refugees (Gelman & Schall, 1997). The value of justice has led American Jews to establish many formal social service programs, most of them independent of synagogues. Since at least the late 1800s, Jewish communal service agencies have provided services to indigent people, resettled refugees and helped immigrants adjust to American life, responded to international crises, and fought anti-Semitism.

Since the 1960s, according to Gelman and Schall (1997), communal services have increased funding by public monies, adopted more rational planning and business approaches, and expanded professionalized services in the fields of mental health, rehabilitation, drug addiction, and poverty. There are also many Jewish community centers, family service agencies, hospitals, services for the elderly, and vocational services. Recent trends have broadened the outreach of these programs to non-Jewish communities and shifted many services to a nonsectarian approach. There are eleven educational programs in North America that train people for professional work in Jewish communal service, several of them connected with social work graduate schools.

When the focus of service involves issues specific to the Jewish community, it is often helpful for Jewish workers to assist Jewish clients. The Jewish worker who works with Jewish clients affirms Jewish identity, values, and experiences (Berl, 1979). Therefore, the Jewish worker needs to understand Jewish history, ideologies, geography, sociology, religious customs and teachings, and calendar (Bubis, 1980). According to Eskenazi (1983), in order to be a good role model for other Jews, the Jewish worker needs to uphold Jewish values in his or her own life. This applies not only to adherence to Jewish regulations, but also to the inner cultivation of compassion, kindness, and restraint of egoism as personal attributes (Linzer, 1979). In essence, the committed Jewish worker needs to combine professional knowledge and skill with personal Jewish commitment (Miller, 1980).

It should be emphasized, however, that diversity among Jews, including degrees and types of religiosity, needs to be respected by the Jewish worker. Wikler (1986) found that some Orthodox Jews may prefer to see Orthodox workers or non-Orthodox Jewish workers. Matching should be a matter of client preference rather than presumption. Wikler also found that many Orthodox rabbis may not refer people who could benefit from mental health services to agencies. His study suggested that careful work needs to be done to establish good ties of respect, mutual understanding, and cooperation between agencies and Orthodox rabbis and communities.

While the Jewish helping professional needs to be knowledgeable about and sensitive to the religious dimension of clients' needs, he or she must also be able to discern between functional and dysfunctional uses of religiosity (Ostrov, 1976; Spero, 1981, 1987). In order to avoid nonconstructive overidentification or collusion between the worker and the client's religious resistances, Spero (1981) recommended that therapy begin with the following recognitions: that shared religious beliefs may involve shared distortions of religious expectations, that shared religious belief is not a legitimate motive for positive or negative regard, and that both therapist's and client's religious beliefs will be subject to examination. Ostrov (1976) urged caution in challenging dysfunctional religious practices and beliefs. One approach is to attempt to deal with the underlying psychopathology itself in order to free the client to develop more constructive religious expression. If the religious issue is too great an obstacle to effective treatment, then consultation with a religious authority who is sensitive to psychological dynamics is advisable.

The increasingly nonsectarian nature of Jewish communal service demonstrates that the Jewish ethos for service can be effectively extended to non-Jewish people. In this case, particular religious language and regulations would not be applied. However, the spirit of *tsedekah* is relevant to all people.

When social workers who are not Jewish work with Jewish clients, it would be useful to assess the meaning of Jewish identity for the client and the implications of religious or secular orientation. If the client considers this relevant, aspects of Jewish history, customs, community support systems, and religion could be affirmed as strengths and resources.

SHAMANISM AND SOCIAL SERVICE
Origin and Contemporary Varieties of Shamanism

The term *shamanism* is used here to cover a diverse range of religious traditions found on every continent and among Pacific Islanders. It does not refer to a particular religion, but rather to certain common underlying features of many religions associated with diverse cultures and American ethnic groups (Canda, 1983). These include aspects of many traditional Indigenous religions centering around the healing practices of spirit-guided people; components of many Hispanic and African American syncretistic religious healing systems, such as *santiguando, santeria, espiritismo, curanderismo,* and *vodoun;* and traditional healing practices of Asian Americans, such as the Cambodian *krou kmer,* the Hmong spirit medium, and the Korean *mudang* (Canda, 1988b; Canda, Shin & Canda, 1993).

This cultural and ethnic diversity must be recognized as the context of the generalizations portrayed here. In social work practice, it is most appropriate to learn about the particular cultural forms of shamanism as understood and named by clients rather than to rely on these overly broad generalizations. We should also clarify that we will be using a broad definition of the term *shamanism.* Drawing on anthropology and religious studies, shamanism can be defined as "a religious style which centers on the helping ministrations of a sacred specialist, the shaman, who utilizes a technique of ecstatic trance in order to communicate with spirits and other powerful forces, natural and supernatural. The shaman obtains sacred power from the spiritual realm to heal and edify the human community in harmony with the nonhuman environment" (Canda, 1983, p. 15).

It is common for anthropologists to distinguish between shamanism (which is dedicated to healing) and harmful magic. However, in some traditions, shamanistic practitioners may coexist with and oppose harmful magic practitioners or apply harm magic themselves.

We are also including in shamanism the wider animistic worldview usually associated with shamanism (Anderson, 1996; Eliade, 1972; Lehmann & Myers, 1997). By *animism* we mean the belief that all things are animated with soul or spirit; the root word for *animated* (*anima* or *animus*, Latin) means "soul."

Frey and Edinburg (1978) and Canda (1983) pointed out that shamanistic healing is the historical precursor of social work and other helping professions. Shamanism probably originated within Paleolithic-period gathering and hunting bands and tribes. It is the oldest documented religious approach to healing and service in the world. There are currently many hundreds or thousands of forms of shamanism in the world, given the great number of cultures in which it appears. In addition, in many cultures, missionary religions, such as Christianity and Buddhism, have been converged with older indigenous shamanistic traditions to form new varieties of shamanism. Unfortunately, shamanism has often been persecuted by missionaries and colonizers throughout the world.

There is also a recently developed religious movement in many countries that adapts general cross-cultural themes of shamanism to contemporary urban life by removing them from traditional culture-specific contexts and formulating generic shamanistic spiritual beliefs and practices. This movement is sometimes referred to as *neoshamanism* to indicate both its origins from and revision of traditional forms of shamanism (Doore, 1988). Neoshamanism began to emerge in the late 1960s with the writings of Carlos Castenada (1968) and other countercultural writers. In the 1980s, centers for (neo)shamanistic study expanded, including the Dance of the Deer Foundation (by Brant Secunda), the Foundation for Shamanic Studies (by Michael Harner), the Cross-Cultural Shamanism Network (by Timothy White), and the Sun Bear Medicine Society (by Sun Bear, now deceased).

Neoshamanism involves loose networks of people, mostly European Americans, who are interested in exploring diverse spiritual practices to support personal growth and healing, as well as ways of living in harmony with the earth (Townshend, 1988). Two related trends of neoshamanism in the United States can be identified. The first has grown directly from the teachings, workshops, and rituals of traditional shamans who have decided to share their spiritual way with people of cultures different from their own. The second trend has grown mainly from European Americans who have studied shamanism from traditional teachers and academic research.

Some Indigenous people are opposed to neoshamanism. Opponents view it as an inappropriate use of Native spirituality by non-Natives and self-seeking Native teachers, which furthers the process of colonialism and cultural destruction for Native peoples (Canda & Yellow Bird, 1996). Other traditional teachers from many regions of the world believe it is time to share these teachings in order to change the course of industrial and postindustrial ways of life that are destroying the earth. This is a topic full of controversy (Buhner, 1997).

In social work literature, there are two main approaches to shamanism. The first addresses culture-specific forms of shamanism and similar practices and beliefs, such as Puerto Rican spiritism (Delgado, 1977), Native Hawaiian helping (Mokuau, 1990), spiritual aspects of First Nations worldviews and healing (Nabigon & Mawhiney, 1996; Yellow Bird, 1995), and Korean shamanism (Canda & Canda, 1996; Canda, Shin & Canda, 1993). The second addresses the cross-cultural features of shamanism (Bullis, 1996; Canda, 1983; Cataldo, 1979; Frey & Edinburg, 1978; Laird, 1984).

Basic Beliefs

Shamanism typically describes the universe as consisting of three cosmic zones—heaven, earth, and underworld (under earth and water)—each populated by spirit powers. Spirit powers relate to the spirits or souls associated with physical beings (such as plants, animals, mountains, stones, thunder), the souls of human beings (living and deceased people, with special regard for ancestors and culture-founding heroes), spirits with no origin in the physical realm (such as deities), and sometimes a supreme being or spiritual force that presides over all. Some shamanistic traditions also deal with spiritual energies, such as *chi* (Chinese) or *mana* (Polynesian).

The shaman is a religious specialist of healing who uses trance and ritual to communicate spiritually between these three realms in order to maintain or restore harmonious relations among them. The shamanistic worldview is holistic. It posits the intimate interdependence of the person (body, spirit, and mind) and the environment (social, physical, and spiritual). Therefore, shamanistic assessment seeks to discern whether human problems and illnesses may be related to attack of harmful spirit forces or conditions of disharmony within the person, society, and cosmos as a whole.

The natural (nonhuman) world is seen to be a source of beauty and inspiration. The earth and sky are often described as mother and father, with all creatures our relatives, since our lives are sustained by the natural environment. Therefore, shamanistic lifestyle and healing typically include sharpening awareness of human connections and harmony with the natural world (Cataldo, 1979). The shamanistic view of human development recognizes that life crises offer opportunities for major leaps of growth. Since crises are dangerous, causing feelings of disorientation and personal disintegration, shamanistic techniques are directed toward helping an afflicted person pass through a crisis successfully, at least with restored harmony, and hopefully with enhanced well-being (Canda, 1983). In fact, the shaman has usually been called to the profession by inspiring spirits, announced through visions and dreams. The initiatory period usually includes rigorous training under a master shaman and personal resolution of the initiate's own spiritual crisis.

Basic Values

Although there are forms of shamanism that involve the practice of magical attack, shamanic healers are primarily committed to compassionate service for the human community (Canda, 1983; Canda, Shin & Canda, 1993). This compassionate stance is mandated by the spirit guides of the shamans. Therefore, shamans intercede with harmful and helpful spirits on behalf of human welfare. Shamans also value the personal cultivation of spiritual wisdom as well as practical competence, since both are considered necessary to perform healing effectively. Shamans are committed to uphold the harmony of relationships among all things. Shamanism views insights derived from a wide range of consciousness states as valuable, including dreams and visions.

Social Work Implications

When clients have a shamanistic perspective, the specific form of worldview needs to be identified in ways that are comfortable to the client. For some people, shamanistic beliefs and practices are very private, either because the teachings are considered secret or because of concern about misunderstanding and ostracism.

Many forms of community support and traditional healing may be available. For example, Nabigon and Mawhiney (1996) gave a detailed description of Cree medicine wheel symbolism and teachings that provide a holistic and culturally familiar framework for understanding human development and social work practice. Coggins (1990), an Ojibwa and Ottowa social worker, developed a Recovery Medicine Wheel as a sixteen-step approach to addiction recovery and spiritual maturity in relationships with oneself and the world. Bullis (1996) discussed healing ritual and symbolism of the Native American Church, which combines influences from Indigenous Mexican sacramental use of peyote with Indigenous Plains cultures' spirituality and Christian elements. Yellow Bird (1995) described the power of traditional storytelling for preserving community life and culture, honoring elders, and transmitting important spiritual insights.

In general, shamanistically oriented social work would deal with the person-environment constellation in a holistic manner, incorporating the whole person, important social networks, and the physical environment (Canda, 1983; Chenault, 1990). Indeed, the I-Thou quality of relationship advocated for people and God in Jewish and Christian traditions would be extended to the natural world. As Canda stated, healing in shamanism involves restoring or creating anew balanced I-Thou relationships between all beings and Being itself. Shamanistic healing addresses the client, relatives, friends, ancestors, animals, plants, and beneficent and malign noncorporeal entities.

Social work in general can benefit by learning from shamanistic traditions of helping and healing. The concept of person-in-environment can be given a more profound significance through the shamanistic ideal of harmony between all beings. Of course, not all social workers believe in spirits, but we could all strengthen our relationship with the world by regarding all beings, human and nonhuman, as sacred and significant. Therapeutic practice would also help the client to pay attention to the quality of relationship with the natural environment, not only in terms of physical resource acquisition but also in terms of the client's openness to the inspiration and beauty of the earth, sky, and all the beings of this universe (Cataldo, 1979).

Shamanistically oriented social work could use a wide range of consciousness states for both the practitioner and the client, such as meditation and trance to heighten empathy and stimulate creativity of insights. The kind and quality of ritual celebrations of life transitions employed by the client would be examined and improved where found lacking or dysfunctional (Laird, 1984). The shamanistically oriented social worker would also practice personal disciplines that encourage constant personal growth and resolution of fundamental existential issues and crises, so that he or she is prepared to offer assistance for the clients' spiritual quests from a standpoint of personal experience (Canda, 1983). Finally, the social worker who is respectful of shamanism would be willing to collaborate professionally with religious support systems of the client that offer spiritual comfort and spiritual strategies for helping the client (Canda, 1983).

Canda and Yellow Bird (1996) indicated some cautions about non-Native social workers' borrowing shamanistic or other spiritual practices from Indigenous spiritual traditions. In general, given professional commitment to social justice, social workers need to be mindful of the history of colonial occupation and religious persecution directed against First Nations peoples by Europeans. Until recently, Indigenous spiritual ways were actively persecuted by governmental and Christian religious authorities as a matter of policy. This continues in various ways, as indicated by the Supreme Court's upholding of restrictions on certain Native religious practices (such as ritual peyote use) when states have laws against them. Therefore, suspicion on the part of First Nations people is common regarding the borrowing of their traditions. For a social worker to employ professionally shamanistic practices raises further issues, such as how and whether permission from traditional communities can be (or should be) obtained, how the social worker can be properly trained, and how powerful transformative practices can be used safely in a social work setting. We discuss this further in Chapter 8.

Bullis (1996) offered some guidelines for referral to and collaboration with shamanistic healers. First, he suggested that the social worker should identify the shaman's type of expertise, specific beliefs, healing practices, and possible impacts on the client. Second, the social worker should ascertain the reputation of the shaman within his or her own community. Third, the expectations of the social worker within the shaman's and client's culture should be clarified to enhance cooperation and culturally appropriate behavior. The social worker should make clear his or her own professional expertise and sense of respect for the client's culture. Fourth, the social worker should seek to establish an ongoing knowledgeable and respectful relationship with the shamanistic culture by approaching it as a learner. Fifth, the social worker should assess the consistency between the shaman's assessments and planned helping strategies for the client.

Table 4.1
Comparison of Religious Perspectives on Service

	Beliefs	Values	Service
Buddhism (Zen)	(1) Nontheistic Buddha Nature. (2) Beliefs from traditions, sutras, direct spiritual experience; nonattachment to beliefs. (3) Existence is suffering, caused by desire; suffering ends through disciplined lifestyle, meditation, and enlightenment.	(1) Primary life task is to seek enlightenment. (2) Commitment to compassionate help toward all beings. (3) Transcendence of self/other dichotomy in virtuous living.	(1) Mutuality and harmony in helping relationship. (2) Aim to help client clarify awareness, act realistically; ultimately attain enlightenment. (3) May use meditation for client and worker.
Christianity	(1) Theistic and trinitarian. (2) Beliefs from Old and New Testaments, church traditions, faith experience. (3) People are prone to sin; relation with loving God yields reconciliation, meaning, and purpose.	(1) Primary life task to love God and people. (2) Commitment to charity and justice. (3) Moral relation between individual needs, social welfare, God's will.	(1) I-Thou helping relationship. (2) Aim to help client meet physical and spiritual needs, reconcile with others and God. (3) May use witnessing, prayer, sacrament, clergy as appropriate.
Hinduism (Vedantic)	(1) Nondualistic, with theistic and other forms. (2) Beliefs from Upanishads and Vedas, religious teachers, and local traditions. (3) Karmic bonds to suffering and rebirth can be released through spiritual disciplines (e.g., yogas); liberation comes through union with divinity (Brahman).	(1) Primary life task to achieve liberation (*moksha*). (2) Commitment to respectful nonattached service. (3) Nonviolent means and ends for everyone's attainment of truth and spiritual liberation.	(1) Helping relationship honors the divine in all. (2) Aim to achieve welfare of all. (3) May use various yogas, rituals, and cooperative nonviolent community action.

Table 4.1 (continued)
Comparison of Religious Perspectives on Service

	Beliefs	Values	Service
Islam	(1) Monotheistic. (2) Beliefs from Quran, community (*umma*) traditions and teachers, and body of law (*shari'a*). (3) There is no God but Allah and Muhammad is Allah's prophet; personal and social well-being comes from submission to Allah in all things.	(1) Primary life task is to live in accord with will of Allah and the Islamic community. (2) Commitment to life of prayer and justice. (3) Community responsibility of almsgiving and protection of disadvantaged.	(1) Helping relationship honors God and supports client in community context. (2) Aim to help client meet basic needs, as bases for living in accord with God and community. (3) May use almsgiving (*zakat*), mutual support in community, reflection on Quran, daily prayer, and religious practice.
Judaism	(1) Theistic. (2) Beliefs from *tanakh, halakhah,* Jewish community. (3) People created in God's image but may be distorted by experience; sinful behavior requires reconciliation.	(1) Primary life task to love God and people, uphold Jewish community. (2) Commitment to loving kindness and justice. (3) Compassion both inner personal quality and behavior.	(1) I-Thou and communally concerned helping. (2) Aim to help client problem solving in context of Jewish community. (3) May use Jewish role modeling, religious reflection.
Shamanism	(1) Theistic/animistic. (2) Beliefs from cultural traditions and spiritual visions. (3) Human well-being requires harmony with nature and spirits.	(1) Primary life task to uphold harmony in universe and well-being of people. (2) Commitment to help people and honor earth and sky powers. (3) Cultivation of skill, wisdom, and compassion.	(1) Caring and often directive helping relationship. (2) Aim to help client toward wholeness and harmony with world, including spirits. (3) May use meditation, ritual, and nature retreats.

Source: Revised and expanded from Canda (1988b); used with permission of publisher.

Sixth, the social worker should ascertain what protective and supportive strategies will be used to ensure the well-being of the client.

SUMMARY

The religious perspectives we reviewed have significant contrasts in the content of beliefs, but they also have a remarkable similarity in the core of their values with regard to service. The commonalities imply possibilities for finding common ground. The differences provide many insights for various helping strategies in social work. Comparisons and connections between spiritual perspectives will be examined further at the end of Chapter 6. Next, we turn to nonreligious spiritual perspectives on service.

EXERCISES

4.1. Exploring Religious Perspectives on Service

These descriptions of religious perspectives on service only touch the surface. It is important to explore them in more detail, especially those religions that are relevant to clients with whom you are likely to work. It is helpful to include both cognitive and experiential learning in order to increase both "head" knowledge and "heart" understanding.

The first step is to choose a religious tradition mentioned here that has special personal or professional relevance. It would be most productive for you to choose a tradition with which you are unfamiliar, uncomfortable, or have a desire to deepen or refresh familiarity. Then go to the sources on this tradition cited in the chapter for further reading. In addition, identify the key religious texts for this tradition, and read some of them, looking especially for passages relating to themes of compassion, justice, and service. You may be able to find indexes to these texts. For example, many translations of the Bible have a detailed index, called a concordance, to assist searching for key terms.

Next, follow the recommendations in the previous chapter's exercises for contacting a representative of the religious group for personal discussion. If permissible, participate in a religious ceremony, or visit a religiously significant place, and learn from your contact person about proper conduct for a visitor and the meaning of the symbols and actions.

The third step is to think through ways in which you might use this information to enhance your practice with clients who share the tradition and for your general social work practice. Clients and people they respect as religious authorities are the best experts on this. Take a respectful and appreciative learner stance in discussing possibilities with the client. You might also establish a focus group of people familiar with the relevant religion and related client population to brainstorm with you and agency staff on possible innovations.

CHAPTER FIVE

NONSECTARIAN SPIRITUAL PERSPECTIVES, COMPARISONS, AND IMPLICATIONS FOR AN INCLUSIVE APPROACH

Life is—or has—meaning and meaninglessness.
I cherish the anxious hope
that meaning will preponderate
and win the battle.

Carl Jung, Transpersonal, Analytical Psychology
(1965, p. 359)

INTRODUCTION

In this chapter, we examine two major nonsectarian spiritual perspectives that have emerged in the past hundred years, existentialism and transpersonal theory. Both perspectives, which grew out of humanistic intellectual developments in Europe and the United States, reflect the concerns of industrialized and postmodern societies, especially regarding reaction to dehumanizing aspects of twentieth-century social conditions and the threats of global catastrophes, such as war and environmental degradation. In postmodern life, all peoples in the global community have become interdependent economically, politically, militarily, and spiritually—for better or for worse. Disenchantment with ethnocentrism, patriarchy, colonialism, religious rivalry and exclusivism, and positivistic science have led to alternative ways of understanding the spiritual purpose and developmental possibilities of human beings. Thus, existentialism and transpersonal theory attempt to deal with basic spiritual issues of meaning, purpose, and response to suffering by drawing on many religious and philosophical views.

These perspectives are not sectarian or allied exclusively with any religion, although they integrate many insights from religious traditions. Some of their adherents belong to religious or nonreligious spiritual groups or are atheists or agnostics. They tend to be multicultural and transreligious in orientation. They see the global interdependence of all peoples as an opportunity for creative spiritual transformation of individuals and societies through mutual learning and cooperation. But they also recognize the all-too-common happenings of exploitation, oppression, and chauvinism.

The current trend in social work toward developing inclusive and holistic understandings of spirituality can be seen as one manifestation of postmodern spiritual trends. In fact, social work innovators often draw explicitly on these two nonsectarian spiritual perspectives (Cowley, 1996). It is possible to connect their insights to many religious perspectives and to use them as a basis for working with clients of diverse religious and nonreligious backgrounds. In fact, many people who advocate these nonreligious spiritual perspectives in social work are also adherents to particular religions.

We present these two perspectives in historical order, since one builds on themes established by the other. Again, we focus on their presentation in social work and social service literature, but we draw on other writing to clarify or amplify as necessary.

After considering these nonsectarian spiritual perspectives, we compare all the spiritual perspectives on service presented in Chapters 4 and 5. We describe similarities and differences and consider some general personal and professional issues pertaining to mutual understanding and cooperation among people of diverse perspectives within an inclusive approach to spirituality in social work.

EXISTENTIALISM AND SOCIAL SERVICE

Origin and Contemporary Varieties of Existentialism

Existentialism developed as a social critical school of philosophy in Europe (Bradford, 1969; Kauffman, 1956; Robbins, Chatterjee & Canda, 1998). Between the late 1800s and the middle of the twentieth century, many intellectuals began to react negatively to dehumanizing aspects of urban, industrial life. The close, familiar ties of agriculture and small town life were rapidly becoming supplanted by more formal, task-oriented, anonymous modes of living in large industrial cities. Workers became reduced to commodities—labor to sell to produce mass quantities of goods on assembly lines, or to work in health-threatening conditions in coal mines and oil fields to fuel the industrial lifestyle. The two world wars and the rise of Nazism displayed with horrifying intensity how the efficiency and power of science and technology could be applied to mass production of weapons and mass destruction of people.

Some existentialists developed their thought primarily in the context of political resistance to tyranny, as did the French atheist philosophers Camus and Sartre. Some focused on critique of religious establishments and social convention while remaining strongly religious, as did the Russian Orthodox novelist Dostoevsky, the Danish Lutheran Soren Kierkegaard, and the Jewish theologian Martin Buber. Some philosophers, such as Edmund Husserl, reacted against the reductionism and mechanistic view of positivistic science by emphasizing the importance of human subjectivity and consciousness. Some psychologists and psychotherapists developed humanistic approaches to therapy, focusing on the human search for meaning and creativity in the midst of suffering, as have Rollo May and Victor Frankl.

The major writing on existentialism in social work has been done by Donald Krill (1978, 1979, 1988, 1990, 1995, 1996). Lantz (1993) has applied Frankl's logotherapy approach to family therapy and social work. Although existentialism has been discussed in the social work literature for more than twenty years, it seems to have affected the field mainly as an intellectual approach and value orientation to practice. Existentialism is a spiritual perspective that can relate to many different religious and nonreligious traditions. For example, social work scholars who espouse an existential perspective have also drawn on Christian, Jewish, and Zen traditions (Krill, 1995; Canda, 1988b, 1988c).

Basic Beliefs

Existentialists focus on the immediacy of human experience and how people deal with the human condition of impermanence, suffering, death, and the inhumanity of human beings. They are not concerned about ultimate reality or metaphysics so much as immediate reality and how we make meaning of it. In particular, many existentialists are interested in how people respond to situations that challenge our systems of meaning, such as natural catastrophe and warfare, or, on a more personal level, crises of loss, confusion, and death. At such times, the socially constructed nature of our meaning systems may become apparent. The hand-me-down truths of social convention and religious tradition are put to trial by fire: how can we make sense when it seems nothing makes sense anymore? Humanly constructed meaning is "shown to be *absurd*, that is, without absolute, essential, or ultimate meaning or divine sanction" (Robbins, Chatterjee & Canda, 1998).

Existentialists claim that individuals are responsible to determine the meaning of their own lives. When social norms or religious teachings stand in the way of human freedom to experience life fully and to discover and create meaning, then they are to be challenged. *Authentic meaning* derives from clear awareness of one's identity in relations with others in the constant process of moment-to-moment change (Krill, 1978). The qualities of freedom and individual dignity arise from the distinctive subjectivity of each person. This subjectivity of the individual is not a matter of isolation, however. The human condition involves inextricable intersubjective transactions between the self and other people (Bradford, 1969; Krill, 1996).

Yet a person's subjective sense of potential for satisfaction and meaning encounters inescapable human limits and finitude, most intensely with regard to the fact of death and conditions of social injustice. This contradiction results in suffering. Existential suffering is inevitable because there is a creative force for growth at the core of the person that brings one into experience of the conflict between desire and limit, life and death (Krill, 1979). Existential suffering, often manifested in feelings of dread, shame, and guilt, is rooted in the problem of alienation within the self, between self and others, and between self and the totality of being. Paradoxically, the human being is impelled to create and discover meaning in the knowledge that all systems of meaning are finite and flawed approximations of a mysterious and often painful reality. This awareness invokes a sense of dread in the face of the absurd. Nonetheless, each person must make choices, create meaning, and learn to survive through his or her own mistakes and the assaults of social pressures toward conformity.

Being human involves self-responsibility for one's choices in discovering and inventing arbitrary rules and authorities. To be a free person means never allowing oneself to be controlled by the illusion that one's meaning is determined by an agent beyond one's awareness (Edwards, 1982). In the view of Christian and religious Jewish existentialists, authentic meaning becomes possible when the individual is able to transcend limitations and anxiety through spontaneous and immediate experience of others and God. Yet in the existentialist view, God is beyond the limits of human concepts. Therefore, the spiritual emphasis is on experience rather than adherence to doctrines (Imre, 1971). Relying on the convenience of beliefs asserted by religious or other authorities constitutes a rejection of freedom and responsibility.

However, even in a nontheistic view, authentic faith is a crucial element in the successful creation of meaning. Edwards (1982) stated that authentic faith is not belief in illusions or fantasies. Rather, it is an empathic expression of self toward others. It is the moment-to-moment manifestation of a spiritual communion that encompasses the be-ing of individuals in interaction.

Basic Values

The existential perspective opposes the influence of depersonalization and conformity in contemporary industrial society (Imre, 1971). In contrast to the pressures of society toward conformity and to the awesomeness of human suffering, the existentialist asserts human freedom and dignity (Krill, 1978). Each person must take responsibility for his or her own freely chosen views of self and the world and their consequences in action (Krill, 1979). Existentialism also asserts that merely rational means of knowing are inadequate, particularly in that they tend to reduce understanding of human relationships to relations between things as mere objects. Truth must be known through intimate personal experiences (Bradford, 1969). In fact, individual determination of meaning should occur through responsible and loving relations with others.

Krill (1979) said that human love is the effort to understand, share, and participate in the uniqueness of others. Existentially authentic relationship involves acceptance of a person's intrinsic dignity and worth, expressed through caring and helping. In the terms of Buber's Jewish theological existentialism, this type of relationship is called I-Thou—one subjectivity relating lovingly with another subjectivity. This human relationship is rooted in humanity's relationship with the eternal Thou, the divine source of being. The solidarity of caring people helps them to hold the courage required to affirm meaning and creativity in the face of doubt, suffering, absurdity, and oppression (Imre, 1971; Krill, 1979, 1996; Lantz, 1993).

Social Work Implications

The existential social worker helps the client to overcome both social institutional forms of oppression and psychological barriers that limit the expression of freedom and dignity. Through the solidarity of a therapeutic I-Thou relationship, the client is supported to actualize potential and meaning through clear self-awareness and responsible relations with others (Imre, 1971; Krill, 1979; 1996). The helping relationship is intense, open, and intersubjective, genuinely sharing the selfhood of the worker with the client. The therapeutic encounter helps the client to develop keen awareness of self and to tap creative possibilities for attaining meaning and satisfying relationships (Bradford, 1969). Given the concern about constraints on human freedom and dignity, existential social work favors more effective service for poor and minorities; an attitude toward the client of caring, empathy, and affirmation; present-focused, experiential, short-term therapies; and eclectic use of treatment techniques within the spontaneous therapeutic relationship (Krill 1978, 1996). It discourages rigid diagnostic categorizations, stereotyped treatment plans, and dogmatic uses of theory that strip clients of their distinctiveness and freedom (Krill, 1986, 1990).

The existential therapeutic approach can be summarized as client centered, experiential, focused on rapid change, and sensitive to issues of values and philosophical or religious perspectives (Krill, 1978, 1979, 1996). According to Edwards (1982), some specific treatment approaches that are consistent with an existentialist view are brief and paradoxical therapy, family systems therapy, reality therapy, rational emotive therapy, psychodrama, holistic therapies integrating body and mind, relaxation and meditation methods, client-centered therapy, and existential group therapy. Krill (1978) emphasized the importance of phenomenological, humanistic, reality-oriented, interpersonal, and unselfish social action types of helping approaches. He also incorporated insights and techniques from Eastern and Western religious traditions. Krill (1990) developed many exercises for social workers to help them deepen in self-reflection and self-understanding as preparation for authentic, spiritually sensitive relating with clients. These include systematic introspection about our systems of meaning, identification of our highest ideals and aspirations, distinguishing between realistic and unrealistic guilt, and examination of religious images and their change over the life span.

Lantz (1993) pointed out that the family is the primary locus for persons to encounter each other intimately, to experience both the tragic and joyful possibilities of life, and to receive and reconstruct meaning. He discussed several family therapy techniques that can assist family members to learn to know each other more genuinely and to construct mutually fulfilling patterns of meaning and relationships. For example, paradoxical intention encourages the client to do something that is perceived to be anxiety provoking or problem causing, so that by confronting it with explicit awareness and reflection, the problematic behavior can be resolved and the anxiety can be relieved. Paradoxical intention can break a rigid pattern of meaning and behavior and open up a new possibility. In Socratic dialogue, or "self-discovery discourse," the family therapist asks clients questions that probe the deeper meanings of their spirituality and aspirations, helping them to discover meaning in the midst of suffering. He also emphasized the importance of helping clients to link with sources of strength and revitalization in their environment, such as spiritual support groups, religious communities, and natural places of beauty. Although some of Lantz's techniques involve a directive approach by the therapist, all techniques should be done within the context of a therapeutic relationship of trust, openness, honesty, permission, and sense of camaraderie in the process of making meaning out of suffering.

TRANSPERSONAL THEORY AND SOCIAL SERVICE
Origin and Contemporary Varieties of Transpersonalism

Transpersonal theory is a perspective on human experience, development, and therapy that focuses on our highest potentials for creativity, love, and spiritual awareness. It spans many disciplines, such as philosophy, mental health professions, religious studies, medicine, and social work, and draws on ancient insights from diverse Eastern and Western spiritual traditions as well as contemporary scientific research (Canda, 1991; Cowley, 1996; Robbins, Chatterjee & Canda, 1998). Like existentialism, it is a spiritual orientation rather than a religious institution. Also like existentialism, transpersonal theory promotes a nonsectarian, spiritually sensitive approach to social work. Transpersonal theorists and their humanistic precursors share with existentialists a critique of personal and social structural conditions that lead to a sense of alienation, oppression, and meaninglessness (Cowley, 1996; McGee, 1984). Transpersonalists believe that the solution to this malaise can be found in experiences that carry the person into a sense of profound communion with other people, the universe, and the ground of being itself.

Transpersonal theory is often called the "fourth force" of psychology, because it arose in response to limitations of the previous three intellectual forces that had a major impact on the field: Freudianism, behaviorism, and humanistic psychology. In 1969, Abraham Maslow announced the arrival of the fourth force, which would be dedicated to understanding what he called the farther reaches of human nature. In his view, Freudian theory reduced human beings to neurotic psychological defense mechanisms, desire-based instincts, and unconscious psychodynamics. Freud viewed religion as a social institution based on neurotic reality-denying fantasies and normative controls. In contrast, behaviorism reduced human beings to machine-like or ratlike things at the mercy of inborn response patterns and environmental conditions. For strict behaviorists, religion was considered irrelevant or unscientific and misleading fantasy. Neither Freudianism nor behaviorism distinguished between religion and spirituality.

Humanistic psychology emerged in the 1950s and 1960s in order to focus on positive and distinctive aspects of human experience, such as creativity and loving relationships. Humanistic theory was strongly influenced by existentialism. As Maslow and others continued humanistic research and therapy, they identified that many people who reported high levels of life satisfaction also reported important transformative events that moved them to explicit spiritual interests. As Robbins, Chatterjee, and Canda (1998) put it, "They discovered that many highly self-actualized people reported experiences of self-transcendence that were, paradoxically, crucial to their sense of self-fulfillment. These experiences are termed *transpersonal* because they transcend the limits of the 'persona,' ego-bounded self-identity" (p. 360). Transpersonal theory focuses on understanding these experiences, related varieties of altered states of consciousness, the spiritual development process, and therapeutic techniques that facilitate transpersonal awareness.

Contemporary American transpersonalism has several major influences. Many theorists have refined or revised the work of the Swiss psychologist Carl Jung, who developed the theory of the collective unconscious through study of clinical reports by clients and cross-cultural study of mythology and religious symbolism (Jung, 1959). Since the 1960s and 1970s, many researchers have investigated the therapeutic aspects of altered states of consciousness related to drugs, meditation, biofeedback, and hypnosis. Stanislav Grof's transpersonal approach to psychiatry, called *holotropic* (wholeness-seeking) *theory*, arose from this (Grof, 1988; Grof & Halifax, 1977). One of the most influential transpersonal writers is Ken Wilber, who draws on many intellectual and religious traditions but has been most influenced by the work of structural cognitive developmentalists (such as Jean Piaget), systems theorists, postmodern philosophers, and religious concepts and practices of Buddhism (Wilber, 1995, 1996). Several authors have introduced these ideas to social work (Borenzweig, 1984; Canda, 1991; Cowley, 1993, 1996; Cowley & Derezotes, 1994; McGee, 1984; Robbins, Chatterjee & Canda, 1998; Smith, 1995; Smith & Gray, 1995).

Although there are no religious institutions built around transpersonal theory, it has had a strong influence on the so-called New Age movement, despite the fact that many transpersonalists, such as Wilber, criticize the popularized and commercialized versions of New Age thought. The New Age movement refers to a loosely connected set of informal spiritual groups and intellectual innovations, begun in the 1960s. It incorporates ideas from many different religions, philosophies, and contemporary science to form holistic ways of understanding the world and encouraging global harmony (Corbett, 1997). In addition, there are many graduate educational institutions that provide training in Jungian and transpersonal approaches to mental health and social work (Simpkinson, Wengell & Casavant, 1994). The Association for Transpersonal Psychology publishes the *Journal of Transpersonal Psychology* and sponsors an annual conference. In social work, the Society for Spirituality and Social Work includes many members interested in transpersonal theory. It sponsors national conferences, publications, and advocacy for spiritually sensitive social work theory, practice, education, research, and policy. (See "Further Information" on page 351.)

Basic Beliefs

Transpersonalists share an optimistic view of human nature and believe that people are intrinsically growth oriented. As long as adequate environmental supports exist, people have a natural tendency to strive toward more comprehensive ways of understanding the world, more loving and responsible ways of relating with others, and more creative ways of living (Grof, 1988; Jung, 1938; Maslow, 1968, 1970; Robbins, Chatterjee & Canda, 1998). There are two directions of growth for people: *inward*, toward a sense of integration, balance, and wholeness within oneself, and *outward*, toward a sense of mutual fulfillment, coresponsibility, and communion between self and others. These two trajectories of growth can be thought of as arcs that curve around to meet each other in a full circle. The complete or true self is attained when one's awareness and actions encompass this full arc of inward and outward growth.

Transpersonal theories criticize most conventional theories of human behavior and social ideals because they do not honor the full potential of human beings. They generally claim that the formation of an autonomous, personal, separate self (ego), bounded by body and social roles, is the epitome of development. But transpersonalists advocate for further transpersonal developmental possibilities (Canda, 1991; Cowley, 1996). They generally recognize three major phases of development: pre-egoic (infancy through early childhood), in which the young child has not yet developed a clear sense of ego, distinct from caretakers and the environment; egoic (usually older childhood and beyond), in which a person establishes a clear sense of ego autonomy and capacity for rational thought along with mature social relationships; and trans-egoic (most likely in adulthood if at all), in which a person realizes his or her fundamental connectedness and unity with all others. The trans-egoic or transpersonal self is able to use the egoic modes of thought, feeling, and action but it is not limited to them.

The transpersonal self recognizes that true self-actualization is insepa-rable from other-actualization. The transpersonal self develops enhanced skills of intuition, empathy, holistic thinking, and ultimately a sense of complete unity with all that is. Depending on the spiritual perspective of the person, the ultimate level of development may be described as union with God, unity of true self (atman) with the true nature of the universe (Brahman), enlightenment, or cosmic consciousness. Some transpersonal-ists view all these descriptions as different religious or philosophical ter-minologies for the same mystical experience.

Basic Values

Transpersonalists believe that human development is purposeful and goal oriented (toward integration, wholeness, and self-transcendence). How-ever, they also claim that few people ever achieve transpersonal levels of development. This is largely due to restrictions imposed by lack of physi-cal, emotional, and social supports; social pressures toward egoism and conformism; and a contemporary, materialistic, scientific worldview that tries to convince people that spiritual and transpersonal experiences are mere fantasies. Therefore, transpersonalists advocate for spiritual empow-erment on several levels. They advocate for individuals to demonstrate self-initiative, exploration, creative nonconformity, and effort for growth. They also advocate for social structures that provide full access and oppor-tunity for all people to resources that support development. For example, Maslow (1970) criticized religious institutions when they inhibit or punish their members for spiritual experiences that challenge formal teachings. Wilber (1995) decried "dominator hierarchies," which are social structures that impose exploitive conditions and restricting beliefs on people.

Cowley (1996) provided a summary of key transpersonal values per-taining to the ideal of optimal health or well-being: seeking self-transcen-dence, working toward personal balance and integration of self, and establishing harmony between oneself and others. As a person experiences profound connection with others, the value of compassion naturally arises (Dass & Gorman, 1985). Transpersonal compassion goes beyond the ordinary ideas of selfishness or altruism. True self-actualization needs to be reciprocal with others' actualization, and the true self is not limited to or owned by any one person or culture. The true self is one with all beings. Therefore, according to transpersonalism, compassion is to be extended actively toward all beings, not just human beings.

Social Work Implications

The transpersonal helping relationship is modeled on the principles of unconditional love and mutual compassion (Cowley, 1996). All clients are viewed as having unconditional worth and unlimited possibilities for growth, regardless of their difficulties. The social work value of self-determination is extended to mean that each client's self-defined spiritual strengths, resources, and aspirations should be the focus of attention in practice. In this process, starting wherever the client's goals and needs are, the potential for growth is encouraged. This is a mutual process, because the social worker as well grows through this relationship. "From a transpersonal perspective then, the helping situation is an opportunity for both client and worker to deepen their spiritual insight and to grow toward their highest potential, including transpersonal awareness if that is relevant to the client's needs and aspirations" (Robbins, Chatterjee & Canda, 1998, p. 383).

Transpersonal social work helps people to address situations of suffering and existential confusion, first by establishing a clear sense of self-esteem and identity, and second, by helping people to go beyond the limits of the ego-bounded self identity. Therefore, crises are seen as opportunities for growth, because crises fracture the person's ordinary psychosocial status quo and open up new possibilities (Canda, 1988a; Reese & Brown, 1997; Smith, 1995; Smith & Gray, 1995). Certain kinds of crises are directly related to spiritual development, such as a crisis of faith, questioning of religious affiliation, or confusion resulting from experience of new states of consciousness through practice of meditation or ritual. Transpersonal social work is especially interested in helping clients to optimize the possibility for transformation to an enhanced transpersonal awareness and creative relations with others.

Transpersonal theory challenges social work to broaden its conception of the person-and-environment (Canda, 1988c; Robbins, Chatterjee & Canda, 1998). According to transpersonalism, a person is not just an ego-limited self. The environment is not just the small range of the relationships a client has with significant others, which is usually the focus in practice. Rather, the person and environment are viewed as systemically interrelated and fundamentally one. Social work's commitment to assist personal fulfillment is thereby extended to self-transcendence. And social work's commitment to environmental supports and justice is extended to global justice and harmony for the entire life web of the planet. Further, personal strengths are recognized to include intuition, beyond egoistic emotion and thinking (Luoma, 1998). Environmental resources are recognized to include the beauty and inspiration of nature, as well as the client's experiences of spiritual beings and the ground of being itself.

Cowley (1996) suggested that transpersonalists can use any theories or techniques for social work practice that fit the developmental level and interests of the client. But theories that are particularly well suited to address the trans-egoic levels of development are Jungian archetypal theory (Jung, 1959), Assagioli's (1965) psychosynthesis, Grof's (1988) holotropic theory, and Wilber's (1995) spectrum model of development. Nonsectarian clinical skills and techniques could include any of those previously listed under existential social work, as well as meditation, yoga, disciplined breathing techniques, guided visualization and healing imagery, holistic body therapies, therapeutic use of symbolism and ritual, biofeedback, self-reflective journaling, art and music therapies, and deep relaxation exercises (Robbins, Chatterjee & Canda, 1998). In addition, transpersonal social workers should assess whether clients use any particular religious beliefs, practices, and support systems. If so, religion-specific symbols, rituals, healing practices, and means of seeking reconciliation or support in community can be used by either collaboration and referral with relevant religious helpers or direct use by a qualified social worker (Derezotes, 1995; Derezotes & Evans, 1995).

COMPARISON OF SPIRITUAL PERSPECTIVES ON SERVICE

Tables 4.1 and 5.1 summarized and compared key ideas of the eight spiritual perspectives on social service reviewed in Chapters 4 and 5. The tables can be used to assist in the following comparisons.

Comparison of Basic Beliefs

The Beliefs column of Tables 4.1 and 5.1 has been organized according to issues and themes found in all spiritual traditions: (1) the nature of the

Table 5.1
Comparison of Nonsectarian Spiritual Perspectives on Service

	Beliefs	Values	Service
Existentialism	(1) Theistic/atheistic/ nontheistic varieties. (2) Beliefs from direct moment-to-moment experience. (3) People are free; experience is intersubjective; people must cope with suffering by authentically making meaning.	(1) Primary life task to take responsibility for making/discovering meaning. (2) Commitment to uphold freedom and dignity of person. (3) Mutual caring and support between people.	(1) I-Thou and freedom promoting helping relationship. (2) Aim to help client overcome inner and outer barriers to free and responsible action. (3) Uses humanistic, eclectic, change-promoting, client-centered, and experiential techniques.
Transpersonalism	(1) Theistic/atheistic/animistic/ nontheistic varieties. (2) Beliefs from many cultural contexts: philosophical, scientific, and spiritual inquiry; personal and transpersonal experiences. (3) Human nature is oriented toward growth to establish ego and transcend it, integrating whole self, others, and cosmos.	(1) Primary life task is to attain self integration, ego transcendence, and harmony with all. (2) Commitment to help individuals achieve full potential within just society and balanced world ecology. (3) Mutual benefit between self-actualization and other actualization.	(1) Client centeredness and mutuality in helping relationship. (2) Aim to help client actualize and transcend self in fulfilling relations with all others. (3) May use diverse religious and nonreligious helping practices as client wishes, including meditation, ritual, body therapies, healing imagery, dream work, collaboration with spiritual support systems.

Source: Revised and expanded from Canda (1988b); used with permission of the publisher.

divine or ultimate reality, (2) major authoritative sources for beliefs, and (3) propositions about the nature of human existence, suffering, and ways to resolve suffering. A broad contrast is between spiritual perspectives that invest primary authority for truth in divine revelation and scriptures (Christianity, Islam, Judaism, and some forms of Hinduism) and those that rely more on direct personal experience, guidance by living spiritual teachers, and unwritten community tradition (Zen Buddhism, some forms of Hinduism, existentialism, transpersonal theory, and shamanism). Even though there are mystical traditions within Judaism, Christianity, and Islam that give great importance to personal mystical experiences and guidance by spiritual teachers, they still uphold scriptures and formal doctrines as crucial in religious formation of people.

Some of the perspectives are theistic (Christianity, Judaism, and Islam; some existentialists and transpersonalists; and some forms of shamanism and Hinduism). Zen Buddhism, particularly as portrayed in the social work literature, neither affirms nor denies theistic concepts. It may be described as nontheistic. Existentialism and transpersonalism encompass theistic, atheistic, agnostic, and other variations. Like Zen, they emphasize the primacy of direct experience. The shamanistic perspective often encompasses theism as well as belief in spirit powers in the natural world.

Regarding human nature, all perspectives recognize suffering and alienation as basic to the human condition. Despite contrasting beliefs about whether people are innately good, sinful, or undetermined, each perspective sees that human beings have an innate desire to stop suffering by developing a sense of meaning, purpose, and fulfilling relationships. For Zen, this involves seeking enlightenment through direct experience. For Christianity, Judaism, and Islam, it involves alignment with the will of God in all aspects of life. In shamanism, it involves recognizing and honoring the sacredness and harmony among all beings. For existentialism, authentic meaning arises from courageous confrontation with absurdity and crises. For transcendentalism, ultimate meaning is discovered when the individual realizes one's true nature in union with all others.

All perspectives agree that human existence is intrinsically relational. Individual fulfillment is possible only through moral relations between self, society, the nonhuman world, and ultimate reality. Christian, Jewish, Islamic, Hindu, traditional Buddhist, and shamanistic perspectives tend to define standards of moral relationship in terms that are specific to cultural or religious institutional doctrines and customs. American Zen, existentialism, and transpersonal theory, in contrast, emphasize that moral standards naturally arise from authentic moment-to-moment interactions rather than from norms or regulations.

Comparison of Basic Values

The Values column in Tables 4.1 and 5.1 is organized according to the following themes: (1) the primary purpose or task of human life, (2) commitments to principles of service, and (3) basic moral orientation toward compassion. Although there is great diversity of beliefs, there is a striking similarity of fundamental values among these perspectives. Each perspective upholds the inherent dignity of people. While some perspectives emphasize individual autonomy (American Zen, existentialism, and transpersonalism) more than others, every perspective advocates for loving and just relations between people, the nonhuman world, and ultimate reality. Indeed, each perspective asserts that compassion toward others is the natural outcome of authentic communion in relationships.

The monotheistic traditions tend to emphasize compassion toward fellow human beings. All of creation is to be respected as God's creation, but human beings typically are seen as stewards of this creation, set above it. Shamanism emphasizes that compassion and a standard of harmony should be extended to all beings in the environment, including plants, animals, and spirit powers. Buddhism, Hinduism, and some forms of transpersonal theory go furthest in extending compassion to all beings in the universe.

In each of these perspectives, the concomitant of compassion toward others is transcendence of one's own selfish desires. In essence, one's own fulfillment requires a life of communion between self, society, the nonhuman world, and ultimate reality. This means that compassion must be joined with justice. The specific meanings of compassion and justice vary tremendously by traditions, spiritual community, and situational applications.

Comparison of Basic Approaches to Service and Social Work

In Tables 4.1 and 5.1, the Service column addresses three themes: (1) the ideal quality of the helping relationship, (2) the basic aim of helping, and (3) particular helping strategies and techniques. Given the common value commitment to compassionate, just, and moral relationships, each perspective approaches the helping relationship as one of mutual growth and benefit. Each perspective is also holistic and ecological in addressing the connection of bio-psycho-social and spiritual aspects of the client and community. Each perspective sees the primary aim of helping as enabling the client to overcome suffering and alienation in terms of both subsistence and fulfillment needs. Therefore, the client is helped to heighten awareness of self and environment in order to establish mutually beneficial relationships.

Each perspective uses various techniques of prayer, meditation, ritual, and social supports to assist both client and social worker in this task. Each perspective asserts that the professional helper must engage in his or her own process of coming to terms with suffering and alienation in order to help clients effectively and to model the process successfully for the client. Each perspective is also open to cooperation between social workers and religious specialists. However, some adherents of all religious traditions may be suspicious of social workers who come from different religious or cultural backgrounds. Trust must be earned in order to enjoin religious beliefs and practices and to cooperate with religious specialists of helping and healing.

ENGAGING IN DIALOGUE AND COOPERATION ACROSS SPIRITUAL PERSPECTIVES

We advocate an inclusive approach to spirituality in social work that respects diverse religious and nonreligious forms of spirituality and demonstrates this respect through spiritually sensitive and culturally competent practice, in accord with professional ethical principles that support client self-determination and social justice. Inclusion does not mean ignoring differences and disagreements or forcing others into artificial or self-serving spiritual assumptions. Rather, it means inviting others into dialogue and cooperation, as whole people.

This is a tall order. There are numerous variations of spiritual perspectives and associated practice issues and controversies—far too many for any one social worker to master. But each social worker can adopt an inclusive attitude and respectful behavior to be applied in each practice situation as needed. The spiritually sensitive social worker also can pursue the development of knowledge and skills specific to the spiritual perspectives of particular clients by following the leads and suggestions we have given in this book.

To do this requires the social worker to have a personal framework of spiritual beliefs, values, and practices that encourage an inclusive approach. An inclusive approach could be established on the basis of any of the spiritual perspectives that we have reviewed and on numerous others. Each perspective contains implications and insights that can be applied in service to adherents by social workers who share the perspective and by others who wish to cooperate with it. Further, social work writings on each perspective have identified underlying principles and practices, based on compassion and justice, that can be applied to innovative conceptions and practices of social work in general, without restriction to sectarian settings or particular religious language.

Of course, there are people within each perspective, especially those identified with particularistic religions and cultures, who hold exclusivist and domineering approaches as well. While social workers also need to find ways to include and accommodate such clients, it is neither feasible nor ethical for us to promote exclusivist and domineering versions of spiritual perspectives in our professional work. It would be very difficult to practice in accord with professional values and ethics this way. The best that could be done would be to suspend our exclusivist spiritual perspective in practice, hide it from clients and colleagues, and fake our way through. But as existentialists would put it, that would hardly be authentic. Neither would the charade likely succeed for long.

A spiritually inclusive approach to social work must be practical. This takes more than lip-service. We must *be* and *act* in a genuinely inclusive manner. Two ways this can manifest in practice are in dialogue and cooperative action.

Steps for Dialogue Across Spiritual Perspectives

Raimon Panikkar, an influential figure in the field of interreligious dialogue, offered valuable insights about the prerequisites for genuine dialogue between people of different spiritual perspectives. His methodology for dialogue can be summarized in seven steps, which we will adapt (Krieger, 1996). We add an eighth step, bringing the dialogue into cooperative social service action.

Step 1: Understanding One's Own Perspective
Spiritual sensitivity to others starts with spiritual sensitivity to oneself. We must know ourselves well at a deep level. We need to be aware and clear about our spiritual beliefs, values, and implications for our practice as a social worker. We need to understand how this is derived from and illuminated by the spiritual tradition or traditions to which we are committed.

This requires introspective insight as well as serious study of our inherited or chosen traditions.

Step 2: Learning About Another's Spiritual Perspective
Dialogue presupposes more than one person and more than one perspective. In order to prepare, we need to engage in serious study of another's spiritual perspective and its implications for social work. The exercises of the previous two chapters would be helpful here.

Step 3: Transforming Ourselves
Deep encounter with a new spiritual perspective necessarily engenders self-transformation. If one takes seriously the worldview, rituals, and helping practices of another tradition and to some extent enters this perspective, one cannot avoid being transformed. This is genuine communication—"communing with." Who we are becomes inclusive of the other spiritual perspective.

Step 4: Engaging in Spiritual Dialogue with Ourselves
As we continue to engage our own tradition, we engage with another. As we reflect internally on the transformation happening within us, we need to engage in dialogue within ourselves between the two perspectives, to bring them into communion with each other within our own hearts.

Step 5: Engaging in Spiritual Dialogue with Others
Genuine encounter with others brings into sharp relief the distinctiveness and disagreements between our positions and opens the possibility for finding common ground and empathy. Going beyond just reading and thinking about different spiritual perspectives to dialogue with others makes the encounter real and practical. This is what happens in social work practice. We must find practical ways to honor the client's spiritual path, to help him or her along it, or to change course according to her or his own terms. That stretches our minds, hearts, and actions and broadens our spiritual vantage. And it opens the possibility for mutual growth and transformation throughout the helping encounter.

Step 6: All Partners in Dialogue Engaging the Previous Five Steps
If we extend ourselves in dialogue across spiritual perspectives in the general community and with professional colleagues, all partners in the process need to engage the previous steps. Otherwise, we have monologue or diatribe designed to control rather than to grow.

This step is different in relation to clients. It is not reasonable (or often relevant) to expect clients to transform their spiritual perspective in relation to ours. That is not usually what they are seeking. But a genuine I-Thou helping relationship is naturally mutually transforming. In some cases, a client is in fact seeking help to address questions, dilemmas, or new possibilities related to her or his spiritual perspective. These steps of dialogue could enhance the therapeutic process.

Step 7: Checking Understandings with the Partner in Dialogue

As we weave through these steps of dialogue, our understanding of the other spiritual perspective will change. We will form interpretations of formerly alien ideas to make them understandable to ourselves. We will try to find areas of agreement, common purpose, or common language. But as we do this, it is necessary to check the understandings with the client or other representatives of the other spiritual perspective. If they do not confirm our understandings, we need to reexamine our views. The purpose of dialogue is not to impose our own understandings on others. We also need to give feedback to the partners in dialogue about their understandings of our own spiritual perspective.

Step 8: Engaging in Active Cooperation for Service

For social work purposes, the reason to engage in dialogue is to enhance service. Enhanced understanding, including empathy, knowledge, and skill for connecting with others, should be applied to effective action. Dialogue becomes the basis for cooperation with the spiritual strengths and resources of clients and their communities. Part III explains how to do this.

Personal and Professional Issues Regarding Cross-Perspective Cooperation

We are advocating respectful cooperation within and across spiritual perspectives in social work. We have discussed many innovations and benefits that can result from this, and we have also indicated some dangers in superficial, condescending, coercive, or unskillful attempts to connect across spiritual perspectives. The steps for dialogue just described can help avoid these dangers. I (EC) would like to take this further now by considering more deeply the cultural and political contexts of cross-perspective dialogue and cooperation based on my own experience with this. I do not mean to suggest that others should follow my spiritual path. But since my experience involves interreligious dialogue and practice to a major degree, it offers an example of possible benefits and concerns.

A Light of Many Colors

I have been richly blessed as the student, friend, and colleague of teachers and healers from many different spiritual perspectives. I have already mentioned the importance to me of my Roman Catholic heritage. The teaching and guidance of my extended family, Catholic religious teachers, and spiritual directors provided my spiritual foundation. By facing both the positive and negative aspects of Catholic tradition and history, I have learned to become more realistic. Particularly the mystical, activist, and interreligious aspects of the Catholic tradition, as represented by the monk Thomas Merton (1968; Burtonin, Laughlin & Chakravarty, 1975), have been most important to me.

I have also been fortunate to be taught, guided, mentored, and helped along my way by wise friends and elders of other Christian denominations, Confucianism, Buddhism, Korean shamanistic traditions, Indigenous spiritual ways, and earth-centered spiritualities. They have nurtured, encouraged, challenged, and helped me. They opened my mind to new ways of experiencing and living and my heart to a greater sense of compassion for all. And they gave me skills of prayer, meditation, and ritual for my own replenishment and for the help of others.

I met my wife, Hwi-Ja, in Seoul, Korea, when I was a graduate fellow of East Asian philosophy at Sung Kyun Kwan University from 1976 to 1977. In our personal lives, we have brought insights and practices together from our European American and East Asian spiritual traditions. She grew up in a rather traditional family that drew on Confucianism, Buddhism, and shamanism while encouraging exploration of Christianity, without any sense of tension. Now, I am a member of the Kwan Um School of Zen. My wife (who became a Catholic) and I have a close association with the Forest of Peace Catholic House of Prayer in Kansas, which is an inclusive center for retreat and contemplation.

My personal life, relationships with family and friends, and professional work have grown from this spiritual diversity. To me, all the insights and helping approaches of these spiritual perspectives are wonderful and precious. Living in harmony with them all feels very natural and ordinary. But that is certainly not the case for everyone I meet along the way. Many people expect me to fit into a particular religious box. Often if someone asks about my spiritual perspective, they frame the question like a multiple-choice test: You must select one and only one answer from the options given, and if you don't pick the "right" one, you are wrong. Sometimes this comes from a rigid, authoritarian way of thinking that views all spiritual ways other than one's own as wrong. But this may also come from people who have a sincere and admirable commitment to their own tradition while respecting others. They may feel that to draw on multiple spiritual perspectives can lead only to confusion or dilution.

On one visit to a Lao Buddhist temple in the Midwest, a monk asked me about my practice of Buddhist meditation. I had stayed overnight with the monks and participated in their religious practices, so he wanted to know more about my spiritual orientation. I used the metaphor of sunlight. I said that sunlight appears to be one color, which we call white. But this is misleading. When we hold a prism to the light, we see it displayed as a brilliant array of colors, all finely blended from one to another, even going beyond our ability to see. I said that I see spiritual truth that way. There is one light of truth that encompasses all, but it can be perceived according to many different colors, each one in its distinctness brilliant and beautiful and yet inseparable from the complete white light. Some people choose to live within one band of spiritual color. Others perceive truth in multiple bands and may even be able to move between them. I explained that this is the spiritual way to which I am committed.

The monk said that unless I followed only one spiritual way, I would never get very far. In a friendly manner, he urged me to dedicate my life to the supreme Buddha Way if I had any hope of attaining enlightenment. His comment was a valuable warning against superficial eclecticism, wishy-washy spirituality, or undisciplined wavering between this, that, and the other thing. I have heard similar admonitions from teachers in many other religious traditions. However, his comment also missed my point. For me at least, this way of commitment to spiritual diversity, even in my personal life, is itself a particular discipline. In any case, to be authentic, I cannot be any other way.

Although I do not recommend my personal spiritual style to others, I do feel that there are very practical reasons that social workers must be able at least to appreciate the many colors of spiritual insight shining through their clients. Just as practice across different cultural contexts requires a bicultural, multicultural, or even transcultural approach (while remaining faithful to one's own cultural identity and way of life), so practice across different spiritual perspectives requires an inclusive spiritual approach.

Interreligious Tension and Cooperation: The Example of Refugee Resettlement
Refugee resettlement serves as an excellent illustration of the practical ramifications of cooperation across spiritual perspectives. Throughout

most of the 1980s, one of my (EC) major areas of service was practice, training, and research in regard to Southeast Asian refugees. In resettlement and postresettlement services, a complex set of international, national, state, and local organizations must cooperate. The United Nations, International Red Cross, the U.S. Immigration and Naturalization Service, Lutheran Immigration and Refugee Services, Catholic Migration and Refugee Services, local Christian congregations, local Buddhist temples, mental health centers, and state human service departments are just a few of those involved. Each organization represents various nonsectarian and sectarian humanitarian values and perspectives that must link for all this to work.

The principle of separation of church and state complicates this. Much refugee resettlement is channeled through cooperation with religious organizations. When they receive federal funds, they cannot proselytize or impose religious beliefs on the refugee clients. However, the religious ethos of service pervades the entire process of sponsorship and helping. On a practical level, many congregations and family sponsors for refugee families have a personal agenda to welcome the refugee into the religious community to offer fellowship. Yet most Southeast Asian refugees come from non-Christian traditions and practices, such as Buddhism, Confucianism, and shamanistic animism.

In order to explore this complexity, in 1990 I informally interviewed twenty active participants in refugee resettlement about their experience with interreligious and sectarian and nonsectarian connections. They represented many vantage points: public refugee program administrators in two states, voluntary religious agency staff, church-based volunteer refugee sponsors, private nationally known consultants, federal Office of Refugee Resettlement administrators, refugee ethnic mutual assistance association leaders, and shamans and monks in Southeast Asian refugee communities. The following discussion is based on these informal interviews, as well as my observations during nine years of involvement with Southeast Asian refugee services.

I have observed three areas of possible tension in interreligious cooperation. First, some representatives of refugee communities have told me that they feel torn between loyalty to their original religious beliefs and the expectation of their local Christian sponsor that they convert to or participate in the sponsor's religious group. Commonly, refugees told me that they felt comfortable combining Christian and non-Christian beliefs and practices, on the grounds that they all have aspects of truth, caring, and helpfulness. But if their Christian sponsor had an exclusive view of spirituality, then the refugee was put in a bind. Respondents typically said that they felt gratitude and indebtedness to their Christian sponsors, so they did not want to disappoint or alienate them. But neither did they want to abandon the religious traditions that were precious to them. So refugee respondents often said, "Please don't tell my sponsor about my continued practice of my traditional religion. I don't want to cause trouble."

Second, some professional refugee resettlement staff have told me that they believe some religious voluntary agencies do not want the federal government to know about the religious pressures exerted on refugees because that might jeopardize their public funding, so the topic is rarely discussed openly. It should be noted, however, that the official policies of religiously based refugee services, such as Lutheran and Catholic, prohibit imposing religious beliefs on clients. According to interviewees, the difficulty usually comes at the local congregation and family sponsor level.

Third, some staff at refugee service programs, health and mental health organizations, and church volunteers exhibited the belief that Asian religions and traditional healing practices are primitive, superstitious, or even demonic. Therefore, staff may neglect to engage them in cooperative helping or may encourage proselytization and acculturation to European American social conventions. In one case, a Hmong couple brought their sick infant to a hospital. The physicians diagnosed a cancer in the eyes that would require surgical treatment and result in the child's blindness. The parents were shocked and sought traditional shamanistic healing as an alternative.

Child welfare workers and physicians became upset about the parents' delay in obtaining conventional treatment. They also regarded the traditional healing as bizarre. They obtained custody of the child by court order. According to newspaper investigators, the judge said that the parents' religious beliefs (Hmong shamanism) were not common in America and so did not deserve protection. The primary pediatrician said to me, "They are in our country now, so they better do things our way." The infant was put in the hospital for mandated treatment. By now, the parents felt alienated and persecuted, much as they had under conditions of war and refugee flight in Laos. The professional helpers became the enemy. So the parents "stole" their child from the hospital and fled to a Hmong community in another state, thus becoming "kidnappers"!

When refugee advocates became involved, they discovered that the professional helpers had not used translators and had not collaborated with refugee sponsors or Hmong community leaders. The parents did not fully understand what was happening to them and their baby, except for the obvious threat. This cultural and spiritual arrogance on the part of the helpers only served to destroy the helping relationship. Fortunately, the parents found a set of professional helpers in the new community who engaged a multicultural and spiritually sensitive approach. The child received necessary treatment, and the family also benefited from the Hmong community supports and traditional religious practices.

Despite these three areas of tension, it has been inspiring to see the generally high level of cooperation across spiritual perspectives and religious institutions that is common in refugee resettlement. Many Southeast Asian refugees are comfortable combining beliefs and religious practices from different traditions in their personal lives. Sometimes this is based on a philosophical principle, such as the view of many Buddhists that all spiritual paths can lead to truth. Sometimes this is a matter of doing whatever works, as when an ill Cambodian refugee consults a shaman, a Buddhist monk, a Christian minister, and a Western-style physician in order to find a cure for an intractable problem.

Spiritual diversity calls for creative responses within refugee families as well. For example, a Cambodian community leader told me that Buddhism is very important to him as an integral part of cultural heritage and as a source of spiritual guidance. Yet, he explained, his children, who have grown up in the United States, have become more comfortable practicing within a Christian context, because most of their peers and friends are Christian and Christianity is a major aspect of the American cultural milieu. This father encouraged his children to attend the local Methodist church and often accompanies them. In addition, he educated them about Cambodian traditional culture and religion. He encouraged them to attend the Buddhist temple for special religious festivals and for learning Cambodian language and traditional arts. He viewed the Christian message of love and the Buddhist message of compassion as compatible. So the family has learned to combine both spiritual ways.

Some health and mental heath centers have traditional Asian medicine practitioners on staff and refer clients to shamans and monks as needed. Many Christian sponsors feel that the best way they can witness to their faith is to help the client on her or his own terms rather than to impose their own religious agenda. For example, one of my Lao Buddhist clients was having severe cross-cultural adjustment stress. He participated in the sponsor's church services comfortably, but he felt that the local Buddhist temple could help him through his crisis. The Christian sponsor, after conferring with the state resettlement program, arranged for him to live for a time at the temple. There, the monks counseled the Lao client, guided his practice of meditation, and performed healing rituals for him.

SUMMARY

Part I established fundamental values and concepts for spiritually sensitive social work practice. Part II has presented a more detailed base of knowledge regarding spiritual diversity and implications for practice. Part III builds on this material to present suggestions for incorporating a spiritually sensitive approach within social work practice.

EXERCISES

5.1 Exploring Nonsectarian Spiritual Perspectives on Service

Return to the exercise at the end of Chapter 4 on exploring religious perspectives on service. You could apply this exercise to learn more about the nonsectarian existential or transpersonal perspectives on social work.

5.2 Engaging in Dialogue Across Spiritual Perspectives

Think through the eight steps for dialogue across spiritual perspectives to help you refine your exploration begun in the previous exercise. Reexamine how you have begun to explore one of the perspectives in the light of these steps for dialogue. Engage in a dialogue process with a person or group, completing as many of the steps as possible.

PART III

SPIRITUALLY SENSITIVE SOCIAL WORK
in
ACTION

CHAPTER SIX

CREATING A SPIRITUALLY SENSITIVE CONTEXT FOR PRACTICE

> You shall love your neighbor as yourself.
>> Leviticus 19:18, Judaism and Christianity
>> (Holy Bible, Revised Standard Version).

INTRODUCTION

The purpose of Part III is to develop a generic and inclusive framework for spiritually sensitive practice that is applicable to a wide range of religious and nonreligious clients. This generic framework can then be tailored to the particular spiritual perspective of a given client.

Mencius, the Confucian sage, said that if an archer shoots an arrow at a target and misses, the archer should not blame others but rather look to oneself for the mistake (Lau, 1970). Spiritually sensitive practice stems from the social worker's close examination of self, the helping relationship, and the human service organization as the context for helping. If the context for helping is not spiritually sensitive, then success in supporting the client's spiritual growth can only come despite it. A shaky arm shooting an arrow at a target is a dangerous thing! In this chapter we describe a spiritually sensitive approach to the helping relationship and process and their organizational and environmental context.

The Third National Conference of the Society for Spirituality and Social Work (June 1997, St. Paul, Minnesota) opened with a panel of presentations about ways that we can nurture the soul of social work. A common theme was that we need to cultivate and support the spiritual development of ourselves, colleagues, students, and clients in all aspects of the helping experience. We introduce this chapter with the remarks of Michael Sheridan (1997, p. 3) who succinctly presented the challenges and promises we face in creating a spiritually sensitive context for practice in a prose poem. Her remarks are heartfelt and provocative. We hope that they put you in touch with your own feelings and aspirations about the best of what social work is and what it can be.

IF WE NURTURED THE SOUL OF SOCIAL WORK

(used with permission of the publisher)

If we nurtured the soul of social work,
our students would feel stimulated and supported, instead of stressed-out, pushed through, used, and abused.

If we nurtured the soul of social work,
our faculty members would act like colleagues and friends, instead of like competitors and adversaries.

If we nurtured the soul of social work,
our administrators would spend their time being creative leaders, instead of finding themselves being harried arbitrators of warring factions.

If we nurtured the soul of social work,
our educational programs would be more committed to creative and transformative learning, instead of to being in the top 20 list of *US News and World Report.*

If we nurtured the soul of social work,
our scholarship would focus on pressing human needs, instead of counts of faculty productivity and debates about competing paradigms.

If we nurtured the soul of social work,
our agencies and organizations would be concerned with improving the human condition and eradicating oppression, instead of maintaining the status quo and defending their "turf."

If we nurtured the soul of social work,
our practitioners would rejoice in the life paths they've taken, instead of becoming burnt-out, cynical and marking time until retirement.

If we nurtured the soul of social work,
our clients would experience themselves as respected partners in the journey, instead of faceless, nameless "others" on some census of agency effort.

If we nurtured the soul of social work,
our society would benefit from our passion and commitment to social justice, instead of suffering from our actions as hand-servants of harmful, outdated policies or as misguided meddlers in human affairs.

If we nurtured the soul of social work,
our earth would know us as dedicated, stewards of her wonders, instead of just another group of indifferent consumers of her bounty and spoilers of her beauty.

If we nurtured the soul of social work,
the spiritual would be recognized as an essential part of what we're about and would be reflected in all that we do—and the mystery would smile and be glad.

Many people already nurture the soul of social work, and the profession-wide momentum for this is growing. So in order to emphasize the actuality and promise of Sheridan's prose poem, we suggest that you reread it with a slight change of wording. For each sentence, change "If we nurtured" to "When we nurture." Then change the result to the present tense, as an affirmation of the best of what social work is. For example, the first sentence would become:

When we nurture the soul of social work,
our students feel stimulated and supported, instead of stressed-out, pushed through, used, and abused.

THE HELPING RELATIONSHIP AND PROCESS

All the spiritual perspectives on service that we have reviewed emphasize that the helping relationship is the foundation of spiritually sensitive service. The full humanity of both client and worker should be honored in the nature of the relationship itself. Talk about spiritual ideals is empty without embodying those ideals in action and relationship. Principle and practicality need to be joined. We begin our discussion of spiritually sensitive practice with five guiding principles for all aspects of the helping relationship and context. These principles draw on the values and ethical guidelines established in Part I, as well as the common themes of the spiritual perspectives presented in Part II. We offer suggestions and examples for putting each principle into action. These illustrations make clear that spiritually sensitive practice is not merely a matter of discussing religion or spirituality with clients. It is a way of being and relating throughout the entire helping process.

Value Clarity

The spiritually sensitive helping relationship is characterized by value clarity. The worker needs to be clear about his or her feelings, opinions, beliefs, and moral commitments that shape the approach to practice. One's own strengths and resources, including those based in spiritual and religious perspectives, need to be identified and linked to social work in a way that is congruent with the NASW Code of Ethics (see Chapter 1). One's own limitations, biases, prejudices, and negative attitudes also need to be identified, so that one can grow beyond them. Major value commitments of the worker and agency that have an impact on clients should be disclosed so that the client can exercise informed consent or refusal of service.

For example, some social workers identify their mode of practice primarily in religious terms, such as a "Christian social worker in a private group practice." In such a case, the name of the group practice, informational materials, and the worker's business card should identify this clearly so that clients can decide whether this social work approach is appropriate for her or him. But "Christian social worker" can mean many different things, so the specific meaning and implications for service should be explained in a brochure and initial meeting with the client.

Value clarity should pervade the entire helping process. Self-reflection by the worker and the client and ongoing dialogue about the process of helping should enhance each other. Value clarity requires openness to explore and refine one's values and moral and ethical understandings of oneself, the client, and the helping process in an ongoing manner. This is the basis of what existentialists call authentic faith.

Value clarity and ongoing self-reflectivity can be enhanced by regular activities of introspection. Traditional process recording can be very helpful (Wilson, 1980). We suggest that reflections on the interplay of the values, feelings, thoughts, and actions of the worker and client include explicit attention to religious, moral, and spiritual concerns and dynamics.

Also, the format for journaling that we explained in the exercises for the Introduction can be adapted to the practice setting. For example, the social worker can identify a particular interaction with a client as a topic for reflection rather than a reading. Then the worker can go through each step of identifying:

1. What predisposes me to this reaction?
2. What does this suggest about my strengths and limitations in general and in relation to this particular helping situation?
3. What are specific implications for personal and professional growth?
4. What are the steps I will take to accomplish this growth?
5. How will I use this self-understanding and growth to help this person and future clients?
6. What is my time line for working on this?

Respect

Spiritual perspectives have many ways of describing a respectful helping relationship: affirming inherent dignity and worth, recognizing the divinity or sacredness of each person, upholding an I-Thou relationship, being mindful of the essential unity between worker and client. In each case, the client is not to be perceived merely as an object or thing. In spiritually sensitive social work, no client or client system is reduced to a label, diagnosis, number on a chart, or demographic stereotype. Each person, group, or community is given unconditional positive regard.

This may not be easy. Partly as a matter of convenience or because of pressures from funders, insurance companies, and governmental and agency policies, clients tend to be processed in terms of fixed categories, with predetermined expectations, eligibility options, and services attached. The danger is that the client becomes subjugated by this categorization. In such a case, the clinical social worker learns that her or his new client has a diagnosis of borderline personality disorder. Based on previous experience and stereotypes, she or he might feel anxiety at anticipated frustration and mentally write off the client as hopeless—and all this without even meeting the client. Respect means encountering the client with a fresh mind, unhindered by presumptions, and open to the mystery and possibility of the person.

One way to encourage this fresh mind is to treat the first meeting with a client as a precious opportunity not to be wasted. This first encounter is characterized by mutual uncertainty and testing, which means many possibilities are open. In order to keep the possibilities as open as possible, avoid reading any assessment or diagnostic material about the client beforehand because this information tends to create a mental foreclosure. Do not use standardized intake or assessment forms. Rather, invite the client to tell his or her story in an open-ended way. Once rapport and a basic understanding of the client's world is established, more specific assessment tools can be used as relevant. If there is previous assessment or diagnostic information available, look at it after the first session. We will say more about assessment in the next chapter.

At all times, avoid being carried away by inner mental chatter (Krill, 1990). Our inner chatter labels, analyzes, categorizes, and judges ourselves and our clients, and misses what is really happening. In Chapter 9, we examine basic relaxation and meditation techniques that can help you to avoid the distraction of inner chatter. For now, whenever you notice your mind waver, become drowsy, or full of chatter, return awareness to the flow of your breath. Then pay special attention to the sound of the client's voice, the color of his or her clothes, the nuances of body posture and motion, and the emotional tone of his or her words. Perceive these details as you would smell a freshly cut flower or taste a new kind of food. This simple activity can quickly cut through the mental fog and open us up to the here-and-now experience of ourselves in relation with the client.

Client Centeredness

Spiritually sensitive social work gives the value of client centeredness special nuances. If we truly respect the client, we honor her or his aspirations, self-understandings, beliefs, and values. We recognize, as Gandhi put it, that we are all on a search for truth. Professional education prepares social workers to assist clients in achieving their aspirations, but it does not make us experts about what is best for the client. Nor does it make us authorities about the nature of reality who can judge the validity of spiritual beliefs and practices. Client centeredness means taking the client's worldview and spiritual experiences seriously. When we have disagreements, detect signs of delusion or deception, or feel a responsibility to intervene to protect the client or others, we still need to relate in a way that respects the client. Proselytization or moralistic judging of clients based on religious, political, theoretical, or other ideological positions is not an appropriate activity for a professional social worker.

Social workers in mental health settings often encounter clients who report visionary experiences with religious imagery and meaning. As we discuss in Chapter 7, assessment of such reports needs to be done in the context of the client's own spiritual and cultural context, just as the guidelines in the *Diagnostic and Statistical Manual of Mental Disorders*, fourth edition (DSM-IV) (APA, 1994), indicate. Suppose that a person reports that she has recently had an important conversation with her grandmother, who has been deceased for several years. The significance of this experience can be ascertained only by careful, open-minded dialogue with the client. Even if the worker believes that such an experience must be a hallucination, the worker's belief is irrelevant to the actual significance for the client. It may well be that the conversation with the spirit of her grandmother has yielded an important insight and sense of spiritual support for the client. Indeed, within her religious community, such experiences may be considered quite ordinary and commonplace.

Inclusivity

Spiritually sensitive practice goes beyond tolerance of spiritual diversity among clients. It moves us to appreciation and advocacy for clients' religious freedoms and spiritual self-determination and the many variations of spiritual expression. We have discussed in previous chapters the importance of this value and have suggested guidelines for cross-perspective dialogue. For example, inclusivity was demonstrated when Southeast Asian refugee resettlement took place through interreligious cooperation and collaboration, bringing together governmental and nongovernmental agencies and staff, local religious communities, and refugees of various religious and cultural backgrounds.

One of the most difficult challenges is to be able to include *exclusive* spiritual perspectives in practice. Some people believe that their way is the only right way. They may reject dialogue and cooperation and operate in a coercive or punishing manner toward people who do not conform to their beliefs. Some clients use religious rationales to justify child abuse, ethnocentrism, racism, homophobia, or violence against women. Some religious communities, such as the Amish, wish to live separate from others in order to maintain a unique lifestyle and moral commitments. In any of these situations, there will be additional challenges for the social worker in establishing trust, mutual understanding, and cooperation.

There is hope for this connection only if the social worker truly values inclusion and connection. We need to have a broad enough sense of respect and compassion that we can genuinely engage with clients and their spiritual communities, even when aspects of them are contrary to our own beliefs and values. Even if we do not agree, we need to create a relationship that encompasses agreement to disagree. If we advocate for change of spiritual beliefs and values, change needs to occur in the context of a dialogue in which we also are open to learning and change as the interaction continues.

In a class on spirituality and social work, one of my (EC) students was a charismatic and theologically conservative Christian. When she introduced herself and explained her beliefs, my gut reaction was to become cautious, expecting that she might try to proselytize or inhibit free discussion and experiential exercises. There was a practitioner of Wicca in the class, and I expected a conflict between them to develop. That was my presumption, and I was not alone in the feeling. Fortunately, we were able to let go of this presumption and just relate to each other person to person. As we all got to know each other better, those of us who did not share the charismatic student's religious experiences became impressed by the depth of her inner spiritual life, her deep sense of intuition and inspiration, her vivid experience of personal relationship with God, and her resources of support in her religious community. She also came to appreciate us and saw us not as lost souls but rather as fellow seekers, each sincerely dedicated to our own spiritual paths. Polarization and suspicion were replaced by mutual understanding, appreciation, and support. The charismatic Christian and the Wiccan did indeed exhibit suspicion toward each other at first, but by the end of the course, they had literally embraced each other in a spirit of mutual acceptance.

Whenever I (EC) facilitate courses, intensive workshops, or dialogue groups on spiritual diversity, I begin with an explicit statement of the ground rules and explain that we need to hold them in order to have a fruitful experience. The following explanation could be adapted in the formation phase of a course, intensive workshop, dialogue group, family therapy, or group work.

> The subjects of religion and spirituality can be very controversial. We each have beliefs, values, and traditions that we hold dear. As we get to know each other, we will discover common ground as well as areas of difference and disagreement. In this course [or workshop, group, etc.], we need to create a climate in which each person's spir-

itual commitments are honored. Therefore, I am asking that all of us make an explicit agreement to relate in a manner that encourages open dialogue and mutual learning. This means that we demonstrate appreciation for religious and spiritual diversity among us. On occasions when we may disagree, we need to agree to disagree, while still respecting each other. In this course [or workshop, group, etc.], we will not engage in proselytization. We may well challenge each other to pursue new understandings of truth, but we may not coerce or denigrate each other on the basis of our own versions of truth. [Group discussion follows until a sense of closure and agreement is reached.] Now that we have agreed on this mutual respect, let's applaud ourselves to celebrate our beginning of this time together that promises to be very rich and enjoyable.

Creativity

The spiritually sensitive helping relationship is creative. Possibilities for growth, problem solving, crisis resolution, and solution finding are encouraged. All spiritual traditions identify that human suffering is only one aspect of our condition. There is also the aspect of healing, reconciliation, salvation, and enlightenment. As we will see in Chapter 8, even in crises, breakdown of the person's sense of security, safety, and meaning opens an opportunity for transformation toward an enhanced way of being (Canda, 1988a). This is not a notion of seeing the world with rose-colored glasses or naive optimism. It is a recognition that every person has a mysterious capacity for resilience and that there are creative possibilities in every situation. To achieve transformation may well require great pain and sacrifice. But, to use a religious notion, the term *sacrifice* comes from the Latin root words meaning "to make sacred." By going through the hazardous tunnel of ego dis-integration, we may be able to come through to ego transcendence (Smith, 1995; Smith & Gray, 1995).

Creative possibilities need to be nurtured. The creative social worker encourages creativity in the client. The spiritually sensitive social worker is like a midwife who provides a supportive and caring environment, helpful skills and knowledge, and positive enthusiastic energy to help the client to give birth to a new self and situation. The creative social worker needs to be flexible and spontaneous, clearly present in the moment with the client. The creative social worker may feel inspired, as if "breathing in" wisdom and energy from a sacred or transpersonal source and then sharing that in empathic flow of being with the client.

In fact, following one's breath is one of the simplest ways to keep the mind clear, to stay focused with the client, and to encourage a creative process. I (EC) once was called by a refugee resettlement agency to consult on a case of potentially violent conflict between two Lao men who were roommates. One man had allegedly threatened the other with a knife during an argument. Fortunately, I also had the excellent assistance of a multilingual and multicultural Thai international student, Thitiya Phaobtong (see Canda & Phaobtong, 1992). Thitiya and I went to the apartment of the Lao clients to meet them and their church sponsor. We were apprehensive, given the volatile nature of the situation.

Conversation proceeded through Thitiya's interpretation. Disagreements were aired, the knife incident was recounted, and more threats were made. As the heat of anger and frustration mounted, I felt my stomach tightening and became hyperalert, and checked the closest exit. My palms were sweating. Thitiya ably relayed messages among us all, but the complexity of conversation among five people and the growing tension also strained her. Still, I sensed the possibility for a resolution behind the overt conflict. The roommates had shared goals and good times. The church sponsor was supportive and open to any possibility to help. As soon as I realized that I was feeling carried away into the tension of the conflict, I was able to return awareness to my breathing. While Thitiya interpreted, I focused on drawing deep and gentle breaths, releasing all tension, taking in the feelings and possibilities of the situation with clarity. The obvious suddenly hit me: everyone involved was spiraling out of control into tension, magnifying each other's anxiety. So I asked for a glass of water. I knew that customary politeness would require the roommates to pause while one of them left the room to fill the glass. That gave us all a moment of quiet. I followed my breath, feeling as though the room itself settled down to a gentler quality of energy.

Those simple acts—following my breath and asking for water—made a shift in the interactions. Afterward we were able to reflect on the goals and aspirations of the roommates, reaffirm their friendship, and discover a solution that would meet their goals. After the session, Thitiya and I reflected on our feelings. We had shared an unspoken connection in the process of mounting tension and release. We felt that the pause, quiet, and breathing had averted a disaster and felt quite grateful for the small miracle of transformation that happened. Often creativity, intuition, and transformation arise from just such simple things as breath, awareness, and a glass of water.

The creative social worker attends also to the aesthetics of helping. We can fill the place of helping with colors, sounds, and images with which the client resonates. The helping relationship can put the client in touch with the aspects of the human and nonhuman environments that feel like a boon or blessing. The beauty and inspiring qualities of art and nature can be engaged.

A nurse for the Navajo (Diné) Nation once told me (EC) about the reaction of many traditional Navajo people to a hospital there when it was first opened twenty-some years ago. The hospital was built in a conventional manner with the usual standards of efficiency, cleanliness, and technological proficiency. Many traditional people did not want to go there. The building was made of squares and rectangles, with barren and cold rooms. Patients were expected to divest themselves of clothing and daily items that lend a sense of identity, community connectedness, and sacred support. Inside those square, barren rooms, people felt cut off from the healing powers of earth and sky. The natural beauty way moves in circles and cycles: the curve of earth, the roundness of moon and sun, the rotations of day, night, and seasons. Hence, traditional homes (hogans) and healing places are circular. Traditional lifeways are intimately connected with the beauty and harmony of all around us and within us. The sacred spirit beings are invited into the healing ceremonies and places. The hospital was just the opposite of all that: cut off from beauty, circularity, community, the sacred. In order to avoid this problem, many current leaders in the health, mental health, and social service systems of the Diné Nation advocate strongly for cooperative connection between spirituality and programs for treatment and prevention.

The boxed-in hospital is a great metaphor for the way helping in general, and social work in particular, is often done. And the Diné spiritual perspective reminds us to welcome back all the places, powers, beauties, relationships, colors, sights, sounds, smells, tastes, dances, songs, and memories that can have an inspiring, healing, and helping significance for our clients.

A HOLISTIC APPROACH TO SOCIAL WORK PRACTICE

If we take together all the implications of these five principles for spiritually sensitive practice, we can see many challenges to innovate holistic ways of understanding and doing social work. The words *heal*, *whole*, and *holy* all have the same root meaning. Holistic helping is healing—making and restoring wholeness and holiness, not only with clients, but in ourselves and in our agencies and educational institutions. In order to clarify some of these possibilities, we will suggest models for holistic understanding of the person and environment and for a holistic approach to social work activity.

Holistic Understanding of the Person and Environment

We often say in social work that we want to address the whole person in the environment. But usually in practice what we really mean by that is to pay attention to some small parts of the person and his or her immediate social environment that are relevant to our specialization or agency function. Spiritually sensitive practice means reconsidering what is the whole person and what is the whole environment.

Spirituality encompasses and transcends the biological, psychological, sociological, and spiritual aspects of a person. It engages the relationships between an individual and his or her family, community, nation, the global community, the planetary ecology, the cosmos, and ultimate reality. Systems theories can be used to help us think about these various types and levels of systems and to map them with genograms and ecomaps. We can be alert to draw creatively on insights from many human behavior theories and practice models that address various aspects of the whole person and environment. For example, Robbins, Chatterjee, and Canda (1998) developed guidelines for comparison and critical reflection on a wide range of theories for practice. Their book provides detailed discussion of these theories and how to engage in critical reflection about them. In order to open up the possibilities for holistic approaches to theory in practice, we include here their two mandala diagrams (Figures 6.1 and 6.2) that identify human behavior theories with special relevance to various aspects of the person and environment.

Robbins, Chatterjee, and Canda (1998) emphasized that application of theories to social work practice should be based on careful critical reflection on theories and their implications for practice. Holistic practice can gain many insights by integrating useful aspects from many theories. No one theory can encompass all aspects of human experience adequately. Each has various advantages and disadvantages and reveals important features of human life and ways to enhance it. But each obscures or omits important features as well. As these authors put it:

> The critically reflective approach [to theory] involves cultivating clear awareness of one's own values, goals, practice commitments, strengths, and limitations. It also involves developing a thorough knowledge of a wide range of theories that deal with the whole per-

Figure 6.1
The Mandala of Person-Focused Human Behavior Theories

Social Environmental Context
Systems
Conflict
Empowerment
Cultural
Life span
Moral and cognitive development
Symbolic interaction
Exchange
Transpersonal

Planetary Ecological Context
Dynamic systems
Deep ecology
Contemporary transpersonal

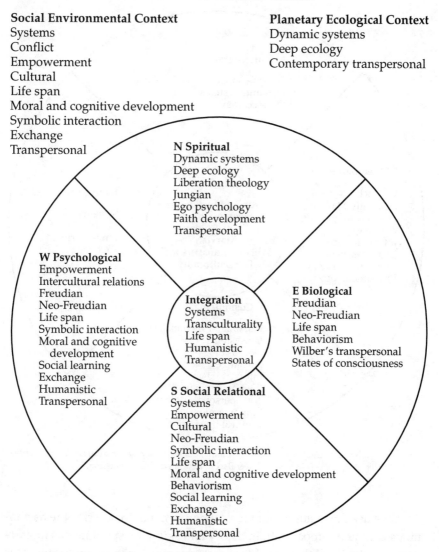

N Spiritual
Dynamic systems
Deep ecology
Liberation theology
Jungian
Ego psychology
Faith development
Transpersonal

W Psychological
Empowerment
Intercultural relations
Freudian
Neo-Freudian
Life span
Symbolic interaction
Moral and cognitive
    development
Social learning
Exchange
Humanistic
Transpersonal

Integration
Systems
Transculturality
Life span
Humanistic
Transpersonal

E Biological
Freudian
Neo-Freudian
Life span
Behaviorism
Wilber's transpersonal
States of consciousness

S Social Relational
Systems
Empowerment
Cultural
Neo-Freudian
Symbolic interaction
Life span
Moral and cognitive development
Behaviorism
Social learning
Exchange
Humanistic
Transpersonal

(From S. P. Robbins, P. Chatterjee, and E. R. Canda, *Contemporary human behavior theory: A critical perspective for social work.* © 1998 by Allyn & Bacon. Reprinted with permission.)

son and the environment. It requires making informed evaluations about the strengths and shortcomings of each theory. And it requires careful professional discernment about the relevancy of theories to a particular situation in collaboration with the client. (p. 396)

Figure 6.2
The Mandala of Environment-Focused Human Behavior Theories

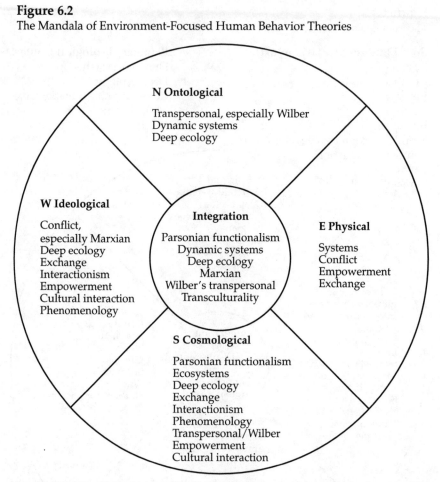

(From S. P. Robbins, P. Chatterjee, and E. R. Canda, *Contemporary human behavior theory: A critical perspective for social work.* © 1998 by Allyn & Bacon. Reprinted with permission.)

They use the metaphor of musical performance to describe the harmonious joining of preparation in theory and skill with spontaneous interaction with the client that should characterize good practice—what we refer to as spiritually sensitive practice:

Indeed, in that moment of inspired performance, the theory and skill are, in a sense, forgotten at the same time that they give form to the beauty and spontaneity of the music. In order to achieve such a harmonious expression of theory, skill, and spontaneity, the performer must engage in a continuous process of training, self-reflection, and performance. In social work, this quality of rapport, harmony, and spontaneous insight during helping is often called practice wisdom. (p. 395)

In addition to drawing on theories that address all aspects of the person and environment, the spiritually sensitive practitioner needs to be familiar with theories that give more specialized knowledge about the religious and spiritual aspects of clients' experience and development. These are theories that have been developed through the conventions of academic scholarship and science. It should be added that there is a wealth of insight available in the eight spiritual perspectives that we introduced in Part II. Religious views of human behavior and development often have been developing for hundreds or thousands of years. They join religion and culture-specific understandings together with particular therapeutic techniques and social support systems. Existentialism and transpersonal theory demonstrate that many transcultural understandings of people can be developed by examining these religious perspectives for their relevance to common human needs and aspirations.

Holistic Activity in Social Work

Imbrogno and Canda (1988) developed a conceptual model for viewing social work activity as a holistic system. Many times we get bogged down in dichotomistic thinking and debates: cause versus function, process versus outcomes, logic versus feeling, objective versus subjective, strengths versus pathologies, qualitative research versus quantitative research, and so on. By drawing on insights from Chinese philosophy in the Book of Changes (Wilhelm & Baynes, 1967) and principles of general systems theory, they developed a model of social work activity that shows the connections of all stages of the helping process, as well as complementary aspects within each stage. Koenig and Spano (1998) discussed similar ideas related to Taoism and the strengths perspective. With some modifications, we expand Imbrogno and Canda's model here as an overall orientation to how we can approach social work practice in a holistic manner.

The stages in this model are understanding the situation, designing and planning action, implementing service, evaluating the process and results, and integrating all these activities within a coherent system of activity. Each stage can be conceived as involving two complementary and contrasting aspects that need to be converged (see Figure 6.3). All stages are interconnected. Although we may emphasize stage-related activities at certain times in practice, actually each stage and its related activities influence each other and may repeat recursively throughout the helping process. Each individual social worker needs to integrate each stage and activity in her or his work, and each human service organization needs to integrate the stages and activities of helping among all its staff. Therefore, this model should be understood as cyclical rather than linear. The vertical and horizontal cross lines show the interconnection among all stages. The encompassing circle shows the essential unity of all the stages in the flow of helpful change. Each direction is labeled with the appropriate stage and two complementary and contrasting aspects of activity relevant to that stage. One aspect of each stage is commonly addressed in social work education, so we will not focus on it. We will pay special attention to the aspect that is typically neglected, so that both aspects can be brought together.

Stage 1: Understanding

Usually in social work education, we are taught to seek *knowledge* by establishing facts through empirical observations, logical reasoning, and learning of facts and theories from established experts and scholars. This type of knowing is necessary but not sufficient. We also need to pay attention to nonlinear, nonrational, and spontaneous modes of awareness. We need to have an intuitive grasp of the client and his or her situation. Intuition in this context refers to a holistic way of knowing that derives from rapport with the client as a whole person in his or her situation. To achieve this, we need to become a participant in the client's world, listen to her stories, and relate to his feelings with empathy. When rapport is established, we can experience the world from his or her perspective and realistically anticipate reactions. Intuitive awareness can give rise to unexpected insights for what to do at just the right time. This is what Thitiya and I felt in our meeting with the conflicting roommates. Koenig and Spano (1998) described *intuition* as "all-at-once knowing" that comes from immersion in the moment and the perspective of the client. Luoma (1998) discussed intuition as a process of direct knowing derived from a sense of merging between the subject (the knower) and the object (the known). Intuition arises before analytical thinking, which splits subject and object and operates in linear terms.

One simple technique that can encourage intuitive, creative insight into a client situation is to ask for a dream or daydream about it: Before taking a nap, going to sleep for the night, or just resting, become aware of your breath, and settle into a relaxed feeling. If you enjoy drawing, painting, or writing poetry, try this before beginning your artwork. Then call to mind

Figure 6.3
Social Work as a Holistic System of Activity

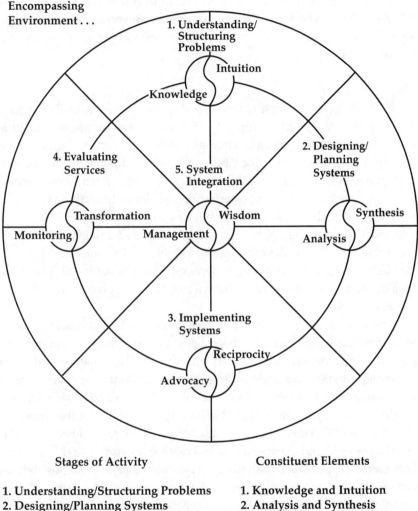

Encompassing
Environment . . .

Stages of Activity	Constituent Elements
1. Understanding/Structuring Problems	1. Knowledge and Intuition
2. Designing/Planning Systems	2. Analysis and Synthesis
3. Implementing Decisions	3. Advocacy and Reciprocity
4. Evaluating Outcomes and Performance	4. Monitoring and Transformation
5. Integrating System Activities	5. Management and Wisdom

(by Imbrogno & Canda, 1988; used with permission of the publisher)

the practice situation about which you feel a question or blockage. Recall vividly your sense of sincere caring and connection with the client. According to your own belief system, ask your deep self, your unconscious, inspiring spirit, or God for a dream or symbol that relates to it. Be sure to do this in a way that feels safe and comfortable. Do not try to make it happen or to grab at it. Just prime yourself for the possibility. Then let go of it. It may well be that something will occur to you at that time or maybe when you least expect it—in sleep, in a daytime reverie, or while taking a shower. Most often, these insights spontaneously arise when we are relaxed and receptive.

Stage 2: Designing

Understanding opens possibilities for action. When we creatively design a helping plan, we need to apply both analysis and synthesis. *Analysis* involves rational evaluation of alternative results of actions, based on the best information available. The situation is broken down into components and characteristics, such as assessment categories, system levels, action steps, professional roles, and alternative outcomes. In analytic thinking, we link empirical observations and information about the actual situation with starting assumptions, values, and theoretical and policy models that seem relevant. This is the conventional mode of planning taught in academia. Analytic understanding is necessary but not sufficient. When we break a picture into its parts, we have a puzzle to be solved, but no longer the actual picture.

Analysis needs to be converged with synthesis. In this context, *synthesis* means that we use our immersion in the helping situation and our rapport with the people involved to link together alternative and even opposing perspectives and feelings. We do not limit ourselves to neat roles, categories, theories, and rational plans. Like a child having fun in a sandbox, we get into the messiness and unpredictability of the situation. We seek possibilities of synergy, that is, creative interaction between contrasting people and perspectives, so creative outcomes that cannot be anticipated are possible. Analytically derived information and possibilities can be brought into the dialogue and action, to be synthesized with the spontaneous and messy realities of everyone involved.

Brainstorming is a helpful approach to this. In brainstorming, no idea is rejected and no possibility is impossible. Every sincere idea is given expression and considered by the participants. For example, in a family therapy session, each member could be asked to imagine her or his ideal family. How would each member of the family be the same or different compared to how they are now? What are the goals, aspirations, hopes, and dreams that color this picture of the ideal family? Each member of the family could be asked to present her or his ideal, with a rule that no one interrupts, except for asking for clarification or examples. Then the social worker could help everyone consider the points of each person's ideal that are similar or different. The family can brainstorm about how to create a collective ideal that incorporates the hopes and dreams of each member.

Stage 3: Implementing

Designing opens up possibilities and various roads we can travel. But we have to travel down a particular road to get somewhere, so change requires implementing the plans that have been designed. Often implementation of social work plans is called *intervention*, a word that implies that an external force intrudes on some client system and directs it. The same term is used in military strikes against enemies. To us, a term more consistent with spiritually sensitive practice is *cultivation*. The difference between these two approaches to implementation is well illustrated by the analogy of gardening.

The intervention mode of social work is like the common American practice of lawn care. Suppose a homeowner has a patch of earth to take care of. He or she "owns" this earth, so it is his or her job to control it, to make it look like the neighbors expect it should. Cultural convention dictates that this patch of earth be covered with green grass, ideally to look like a miniature golf course. If the grass is too long or too weedy, neighbors may complain or even ask the city government to order the grass to be cut. Heaven forbid that lovely yellow dandelions should sprout up, lest they turn to seed. Wind or fun-loving children might blow those seeds around to contaminate other people's lawns. For some reason, it does not occur to anyone that dandelions are lovely or can be used to make salads or wine. Instead, grass is planted for the desired texture and color. Since the grass often is not particularly well suited to the local growing conditions, the homeowner has to give the lawn frequent water and fertilizer. If anything "undesirable" appears, like weeds, grubs, or moles, out come the herbicides and pesticides. So in the process of keeping a cosmetic lawn, that which grows well is killed and that which does not grow well is maintained by willpower, hard effort, and time. Toxic runoff from lawns joins the toxic runoff from farms, and then we drink the poisons from our tapwater.

Too often we view clients like this. They and their situations are weedy with problems. We think we know what they should look, think, and act like in order to be "normal," "functional," "reality based," "healthy," and "adaptive." We try to make clients fit into the artificial socially constructed standards of normality within our mental health, social welfare, and criminal justice systems. We weed, prune, pull, and poison the behaviors, thoughts, and attitudes that do not meet our standards. This is the social-worker-as-expert model of intervention.

But social workers can also operate more like organic gardeners. In this case, we identify the strengths, aspirations, and resources of clients. We help them to discern how these relate to their loved ones, the workplace, the larger social environment, and the natural environment. We help them to cultivate the natural growth potential already inherent within them and their situation. We may not know what the end product will look like, but we can experience directly that the process of getting there is affirming to everyone involved. This kind of helping action has been called *Taoistic change* (Brandon, 1976; Maslow, 1968), meaning that help flows along with the natural course and potential of the client system in their situation. This is not passivity. It is creative, harmonious action.

When the Confucian sage Mencius encouraged help and support between people, he warned against two common mistakes (Lau, 1970). He said that a rice farmer must be caring and attentive in cultivating rice. So one mistake is to do nothing. But the other mistake is to be impatient, to force growth in a direction the farmer desires. This is like the farmer who feels that the rice seedling is growing too slowly, so he reaches into the water of the paddy and tugs on the seedling, to stretch it and encourage it. Of course, he uproots the seedling and destroys it.

Taoistic change means that the social worker joins with the client system and situation, understands it with empathy and rapport, and encourages the growth potential already there or helps the client to discover it. This is consistent with the strengths perspective (Saleebey, 1997). "Harmony with" does not mean avoiding conflict, however. It means relating authentically and realistically with situations as they are, conflict or not, and flowing with the creative process.

There was an American student who had learned the Japanese martial art of aikido (Dass & Gorman, 1985). His teacher had always told him that aikido was for spiritual discipline, not for picking fights, but still he longed to encounter a situation of threat when he would be justified to try out his skills in actual combat. One day he was riding a train in Japan. A drunken, angry man became belligerent and intimidating to passengers. The student became alert, ready for a fight in which he could rescue everyone. While the student was poised to strike, an elderly gentleman called out to the drunken man: "Come over here. What are you drinking?" "Sake," answered the man. This caught his attention, and he lumbered over to the elderly gentleman. The old man said, "Ah, I love to sit with my wife and sip a cup of sake." Then the drunken man began to cry. He said that his wife had died and that he was deeply sad. His anger and threat disappeared. He sat and commiserated with the elderly gentleman, who had subdued him without flexing a muscle. The elderly man, not the brash student, was the real master of martial arts.

This does not deny that there are occasions that call for forceful action to protect someone's safety. In a crisis, the client may feel overwhelmed, confused, disoriented, perhaps a danger to self or others, so temporary protection, restraint, and support may be necessary. This is a naturally compassionate response. But compassion also means that we help the client to become empowered, reoriented, and proficient again, so that her or his aspirations can be achieved in relationship with others.

We can summarize this by referring to two complementary aspects of helping: *advocacy* and *reciprocity.* As an advocate, we identify a client or client system and assist the accomplishment of the client's goals. In this process, we often identify problems, barriers, opponents, and enemies that block the client's goal achievement. While commitment to the client and zeal for justice are important and necessary, these qualities become dangerous when they are pursued in a one-sided manner. One danger is that we do not pay attention to harmful impacts on other people or the natural environment that result from our advocacy. To use a Christian expression, this is a *sin of omission*—harming others by not paying attention or caring. Another danger is that we act from an enemy mentality. We identify some persons or situations as enemies to be combated. This is the militaristic implication of "intervention" taken to an extreme. We might even feel glee at our victory over the opponent. In this enemy mentality, we perceive the other only as enemy. He or she is no longer precious or even important. Ironically, if we exploit, damage, or diminish others in our efforts for victory on behalf of the client, we become exactly what we opposed. This is a *sin of commission*—committing acts of violence or dehumanization. We despised the opponent for the indignities and harm caused for the client. And in returning indignity and harm to that opponent, we become just like the enemy. This approach does not afford any possibility of reconciliation or mutual benefit.

Jesus said that we should love our enemy; we should do unto others as we would have them do unto us. Confucius said we should not do to others what we would not have them do to us. All spiritual traditions proclaim their highest aspirations as love and compassion for all. If we take this seriously, there are major implications for spiritually sensitive practice. In order to avoid falling into an enemy mentality, it is helpful to complement advocacy with reciprocity. In *reciprocity,* we seek mutual growth and benefit through creative solutions. We respect all parties, even when we disagree or are in conflict. When conflict is unresolvable, we find ways to continue the conflict in a humane manner, or to forgive and move on. Mahatma Gandhi and Rev. Martin Luther King, Jr., were excellent examples of social activists who strove to put this ideal into action.

Of course, this is easier said than done. In 1997, I (EC) presented at a symposium on spirituality and social work at the Inter-University Centre in Dubrovnik, Croatia. Another presenter was Arun Gandhi, grandson of Mahatma Gandhi and director of the M. K. Gandhi Institute for Nonviolence in Memphis. Many of the presentations addressed the ideals of compassion, forgiveness, reconciliation, service, and nonviolence. The fact that our building had only recently been rebuilt since prolonged bombings on the city added an intensity and urgency to our discussions. Croatian participants struggled with how to act on these ideals while recovering from emotional trauma and the physical destruction of many of their homes, loved ones, and social infrastructure. But at the same time that the difficulty of this was shown, the importance was equally clear. Somehow we must all keep going on the way of peace in order to get out of the cycles of violence and victimization that all too often characterize human life.

A related trend in contemporary conflict mediation is called *win-win problem solving* or *solution making* (McLaughlin & Davidson, 1994). In win-win strategies, victory is not at the expense of others. It is intended for the mutual benefit of both sides in the disagreement or conflict. Table 6.1 summarizes the major principles and steps of the win-win approach.

Chapters 7 through 9 give many more practical suggestions for implementing spiritually sensitive practice.

Stage 4: Evaluating

Spiritually sensitive evaluation is an ongoing process of discernment. We reflect gently yet consistently on ourselves and clients in their situations so that we recognize the impacts of our activity in both the process and outcomes of helping. But this is not an egocentric type of reflection. To borrow an insight from karma yoga, spiritually sensitive evaluation cares about results but is not egoistically attached to them. Evaluation is not for the purpose of guaranteeing that clients conform to the expectations of social workers or their agencies. It is for the purpose of helping the client to be aware of and encouraged by beneficial change and to avoid the pitfalls of mistakes or ineffective helping strategies.

The conventional aspect of evaluation is *monitoring*. We keep track of continuities or changes in the client's functioning in relation to our help-

Table 6.1
Principles and Steps for Win-Win Solution Making

1. Bring all parties into a dialogue based on mutual respect and willingness to understand each other.

2. Do not reduce people to problems or enemies. Get to know each other as fellow people.

3. Identify the positions of all parties and the most important principles and aspirations underlying them.

4. Identify what each party feels will result in success from his or her point of view.

5. Identify the common interests and different standards for success.

6. Brainstorm to discover alternative solutions in which all parties would feel they have won, based on their various aspirations and standards.

7. Select solutions acceptable to all parties.

8. Develop an action plan and roles, involving cooperative teamwork by representatives of all parties.

9. Follow up implementation of the plan, evaluating success in terms of common interests and different standards.

10. Examine collaboratively the long-term impacts of the change, and revise activity as necessary.

ing activities. We adjust the help as needed to seek the most effective help-ing approach. We learn many professional mechanisms for monitoring, such as clinical dialogue, helping contracts, psychological measuring instruments, single-subject research designs, and consumer satisfaction surveys. We may have standards of progress dictated by agency pro-grams or funding sources. This is all useful. But if that is all we do, there are dangers. We may simply be measuring client conformity rather than genuine growth. As Imbrogno and Canda (1988) put it, "All too often it happens that assessment of service delivery leads to a quantitative increase of clients served or income earned (i.e. as an indicator of change) with a decrease in the quality of service and client satisfaction" (p. 26).

Monitoring needs to be complemented by a process of *transformation*, in which the client system and help provider system mutually shape each other. Evaluation, then, is not just for imposing change on clients; it is for mutual reflection on the partnership of helping in which both client and worker change each other. The social worker and the agency are open to self-transformation of goals, strategies, technologies, rules, and policies based on learning from the clients.

I (EC) have often seen the ineffectual result in agencies when this is not the case. I have done many trainings for cultural competence in mental health and social service agencies. One aspect of the training is a self-study of the cultural competence of the social workers and the agency. We may do surveys of clients, workers and administrators, field observation of agency operations, brainstorming sessions, and cultural awareness exercises. Enthusiasm rises as new possibilities for providing services are identified, but too often, once this monitoring has finished, the process of innovation fizzles out. Genuine transformation may entail long-term discussions between workers and administrators about difficult issues such as racism, prejudice, and factionalism in the workplace. It may call for greater efforts for recruitment, retention, and promotion of staff who are well qualified to work with a wide range of diverse clients. It may require creating new multicultural teams and community networks. These are changes that challenge the status quo of the organization and the daily patterns of the service providers. It may not be easy to engage in such transformation, especially if the agency is struggling for survival in the face of threatened funding cuts or some other organizational crisis. But without self-transformation, evaluation can hardly be authentic or fruitful. Inauthentic evaluation may create the illusion of change, for public relations purposes, but it serves only to maintain a helping system more dedicated to the benefit of the agency than to the clients.

Holistic evaluation relies on modes of inquiry and research methods that can tap into the many different ways of knowing and the wide variety of spiritual perspectives and worldviews, consistent with the heuristic approach to research (Tyson, 1995). The heuristic approach recognizes that there are many ways of knowing that draw on human capacities for thinking, feeling, sensing, and intuiting. There are many techniques for gaining knowledge, each with advantages and disadvantages, such as qualitative and quantitative methods. And there are many different worldviews that shape assumptions about what can be known and how it is best to know it. The most common debates in social work research pertain to positivistic versus naturalistic or constructivist paradigms (for summaries, see Lincoln & Guba, 1985; Tyson, 1995). The heuristic approach recognizes that each way and method of knowing can lead to insights, and each has limitations. None can give a whole picture. Indeed, holistic understanding requires bringing together (synergizing) many different ways and methods of knowing.

Conventional social scientific research has long been rooted in the philosophical tradition of *positivism*, which asserts that reliable knowledge must be based on sensory experience subjected to logical analysis. Research methods most often associated with positivism are controlled experiments, quantitative surveys, highly structured detached observations, and statistical analysis. This is valuable as an advance over prejudice, untested assumptions, or sloppy thinking. But the shortcoming of positivistic research is that it does not use the full range of ways of knowing, and it also presents an overly simplified, reduced understanding of the world. Figure 6.4 illustrates that the positivist domain of inquiry addresses only one quadrant of possibilities for ways of knowing.

Spiritually sensitive research and research that is likely to provide useful insights into the many facets of spirituality need to be holistic, encompassing the full circle of ways of knowing. Depending on the nature of the research question and the aspects of spirituality studied, experiments and statistical studies could be useful, but we also need detailed case studies, narratives, field research, ethnography, historical and hermeneutic studies, phenomenological research, and qualitative analysis.

Even if a social worker is not doing formal research, the evaluation of practice always involves some kind of systematic questions, information gathering, and interpretation. We also believe that spiritually sensitive evaluation should emphasize the active involvement of clients and other research participants in the formation, conduct, and interpretation of the research design. The process and outcomes of research should directly and indirectly benefit participants and other people who have similar issues. This approach to research is often called *empowerment* or *participatory action research* (Chesler, 1991; Lincoln, 1995; Rapp, Shera & Kisthardt, 1993).

Stage 5: Integrating

All stages and aspects of the helping process need to be integrated. Imbrogno and Canda (1988) placed system integrating at the center of the holistic helping model in order to symbolize that it must pervade and connect the other four functions: understanding, designing, implementing, and evaluating. Management and wisdom are the complementary aspects of integrating holistic social work activity. The integrating function is most closely connected with the administrative and executive levels within human service organizations.

In conventional bureaucratic models of administration, the administrative function is located at the top of a pyramidal-shaped organizational structure. There are fewer people at the top of the agency hierarchy, but they

Figure 6.4
Synergizing Ways of Knowing

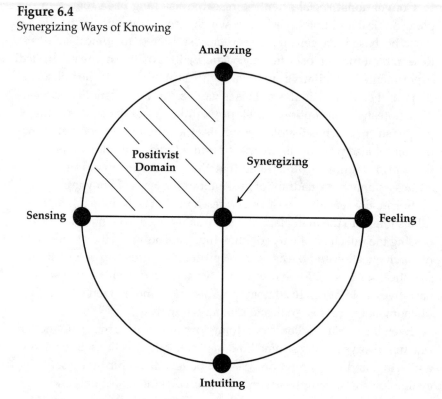

wield greater power in forming policy, making decisions, governing staff behavior, and distributing resources (Netting, Kettner & McMurty, 1998). The executive administrator oversees all the operations of the organization in order to maintain order and integration of activities. If there is input from direct service staff and clients, the executive and administrators have predominant power and authority to decide what to do with this input.

This *bureaucratic management model* is designed to maximize efficiency by rational determination of goals and control of staff behavior to be in conformance with achievement of the goals. The danger of this model is that the power hierarchy may engender administrative exploitation of workers, remoteness of administrators from clients and direct service staff, and inflexibility of rules and roles. It does not emphasize the importance of I-Thou relations between all staff, clients, and the community. It neglects creativity in favor of conformity.

Spiritually sensitive practice is more likely to flourish in an organizational culture and structure that actively support creativity, flexibility, person-to-person respect, input from all stakeholders in decisions, and human development goals as well as organizational goal attainment needs. Such an approach requires administrators to complement management with *wisdom*. As Imbrogno and Canda explained:

> In an holistic professional system, an executive has a central rather than top position. The executive maintains the integrity of the service providing system as a whole, appraises and links the performance of professionals at all phases of activity, and encourages the constant creative development of the service system in interaction with its environment. (p. 27)

More participatory, human relations–oriented models of administration are gaining in acceptance, even within business. Aldridge, Macy and Walz (n.d.) developed a model of human service organizational administration that is very consistent with spiritually sensitive practice. They drew on humanistic administrative models such as human relations, theory Z, and insights from Asian philosophy. In order to show a contrast with the bureaucratic model and to emphasize the prime importance of humane administration, they named their model *humanocracy*. Their model focuses on the human relations component of organizational life. We will adapt their model and expand it with consideration of the transpersonal and nonhuman aspects of organizational life.

The spiritually sensitive human service organization (HSO) should be designed to serve social and spiritual aspirations as well as economic needs. In keeping with the NASW Code of Ethics, the mission of HSOs should be to support individual well-being and social justice. All economic considerations should be in service of this mission. Policies, rules, and roles should not foster alienation or dissatisfaction among workers and clients. For example, if third-party payers require use of DSM-IV diagnoses in a mental health setting, the diagnostic process should include client input and full consideration of the cultural and spiritual beliefs and experiences of the client. The organizational environment, including the values, goals, communication patterns, and physical design of the agency, should actively support the self-actualization and fulfillment of workers and clients. Agency statements of goals and objectives should include staff needs for personal development and enhancement of family relations. Relevant programs could be instituted, such as flex time, provision of on-site child care, job rotation, continuing education subsidies, recreational and stress management activities, designation of a quiet space for meditation, and staff-

and client-originated artistic decoration of offices. Impact of service delivery on the nonhuman environment should be carefully studied.

Procedures that minimize harmful impact on the natural world and maximize healthful human-nature interactions could be instituted. For example, agency vehicles used for home visits should be fuel efficient. Carpooling for staff could be encouraged. All disposable materials should be minimized and recycled whenever possible. All recyclable materials should be recycled. Lighting can be done with energy-efficient bulbs. Toxic wastes, such as refrigerants, hazardous medical materials, and computer equipment, should be disposed of in a safe and environmentally friendly manner. Staff and clients could participate in organic gardening projects around the agency and neighborhood in order to enhance the beauty of the place, build camaraderie, generate food, and create livable habitat for birds and other local animals and plants. Staff could share wilderness retreats to enhance group solidarity and replenish their spirits.

Possibilities for creative revisioning of social work administration are vast when we consider the spiritual aspects of social service delivery. Innovation should be the shared responsibility of all staff, with meaningful involvement of clients. Administrators are in a special position to be aware of all the facets of the organization. Therefore, they can be especially valuable as facilitators of this innovation process. Table 6.2 lists eleven principles for spiritually sensitive administration with brief examples of innovations that would support them.

SUMMARY

In this chapter, we have presented an overall revisioning of the helping relationship and its organizational context. We drew freely from insights of many spiritual perspectives as well as humanistic and transpersonal approaches to human service and organizational behavior. We made the point that spiritually sensitive practice is not solely a matter of including religious or spiritual topics in social work activity. We envision spiritually sensitive practice as a whole way of being and relating within all aspects, stages, and environments of helping. Our suggestions here open many possibilities for innovation, but they are a small beginning. We hope that they encourage you to examine yourself and your service setting in order to find creative ways of enhancing your practice. In the following chapter, we consider spiritually sensitive ways to understand and support human development through clinical practice.

Table 6.2
Principles and Activities for Spiritually Sensitive Administration

1. *Human scale.* The size and complexity of HSOs should be limited to a scale in which all personnel can be familiar with each other personally and professionally. In large organizations, such as state human service systems, area offices and departments should reflect human scale.

2. *Personal communication.* All personnel should be able to communicate with each other directly and personally on a regular basis. If memos or e-mail modes of communication are used, they should supplement personal communication rather than replace it.

3. *Satisfaction of aspirations.* Aspirations for personal growth of staff should be ascertained so that programs can be designed to support them. Satisfaction of growth aspirations should be a formal organizational goal. Examples of activities are flex time, on-site day care, stress management activities, subsidies for continuing education, and places for meditation.

4. *Participatory decision making.* All people who will be affected by a change of policy or program, including staff and clients, should be meaningfully included in the decision-making process. Examples of activities are brainstorming, surveys, inclusion of representatives from all levels of staff and clients on advisory boards, and staff retreats for reflection on possible innovations.

5. *Functional flexibility and integration.* Staff should be prepared to be competent in multiple organizational tasks, so that they can meaningfully cooperate and shift roles across specializations as needed. Responsibility for organizational goals should be shared between all administrative levels. Examples of activities are cross-training, job sharing, interdisciplinary teamwork, and shared worker-administrator ownership of the organization.

6. *Meritorious leadership.* Formal leadership positions should be filled by people who have the respect of staff, and staff should be meaningfully involved in selection of leaders. Staff could rotate through various leadership positions. Informal leadership, based on qualities of innovation, collaboration, and communication skills, should be recognized and rewarded officially. Examples are rotating directorships, rotating team leadership, and egalitarian or cooperative patterns of team leadership.

Table 6.2 (continued)
Principles and Activities for Spiritually Sensitive Administration

7. *Work environment aesthetics.* The physical work environment should be designed in a way that promotes health and well-being. Staff and clients should be consulted to assess and design the work environment. Examples are ergonomic work stations, artwork, live plants, aquariums, personalized decoration of work spaces, and photos of places and events fond to clients and staff.

8. *Rule flexibility.* Agency policies, procedures, rules, and roles should be clear yet flexible. They exist to serve people; people do not exist to serve them. Staff and clients are involved in the ongoing assessment and revision of all rules. Rules are adapted to fit unusual staff and client circumstances. Examples are procedures for revision and appeal of rules, client-centered procedures for assessment of their challenges and strengths, and periodic reviews of agency manuals.

9. *Convivial technology.* Technologies that support the HSO should be simple to operate and repair for most staff or conveniently accessible consultants. They should be used to increase staff and client comfort and goal achievement. Technologies should be periodically evaluated with staff and client input. Examples are worker safety protocols for technology use and user-friendly copy machines and computers.

10. *Social and cultural environmental rapport.* The community environment of the HSO should be enhanced by all aspects of organizational activity. Community leaders and support systems should be involved in program design and evaluation. Interagency and community-based networks and teams should be established through formal interagency agreements, task forces, and informal cooperative arrangements. Religious and spiritual leaders, helpers, and healers should be included in service collaboration as relevant to clients.

11. *Natural environmental rapport.* The natural environment of the HSO should be enhanced by all aspects of organizational activity. Damaging impacts should be identified and minimized. Inspiring places of natural beauty should be included in programs for staff and clients as desired. Examples are energy-efficient vehicles and lighting, carpooling and recycling programs, use of biodegradable materials for cleaning, safe disposal of toxic materials, developing neighborhood organic gardens, landscaping the grounds around the organization with organic methods, and arranging staff or client visits to natural parks.

EXERCISES

6.1. Linking Self-Understanding to Practice with Clients

This chapter includes many exercises in the body of the text designed to help you link self-understanding to practice with clients. We suggest that you choose one to carry out:

A. Journaling about a practice situation (p. 187)
B. Experiencing the client with a fresh mind (p. 188)
C. Dissolving inner chatter (p. 188)
D. Developing an introduction on inclusivity for groupwork (p. 189)
E. Asking for an intuitive insight (p.198)
F. Brainstorming (p. 200)

Return to the text for an explanation about how to do the exercises.

6.2. Planning for Innovation in the Context of Practice

Each table and figure in this chapter depicts ideals, principles, guidelines, or suggestions for creating a spiritually sensitive context for practice. We suggest that you review each table and figure and reread the relevant section of text. Make a commitment to one significant innovation:

A. Identifying theories for holistic practice (Figures 6.1 and 6.2)
B. Organizing social work activity in a holistic system (Figure 6.3)
C. Synergizing different ways of knowing (Figure 6.4)
D. Making win-win solutions (Table 6.1)
E. Administering in a spiritually sensitive manner (Table 6.2)

Write out a plan for how you can accomplish it in your practice. The plan should include your objective for enhancing practice, a specific course of action, and a time line for implementing the activity.

CHAPTER SEVEN

UNDERSTANDING AND ASSESSING SPIRITUAL DEVELOPMENT

Wake up! It is time to wake up!
The Dhammapada, Buddhism
(trans. Lal, 1967, p. 134).

INTRODUCTION

The conceptual models of spirituality formed in Chapter 2 suggest two major ways of thinking about human development. First, when we think of spirituality as an aspect of the person that strives for a sense of meaning and purpose, our attention focuses on the way people develop meaning through immersion in spiritual groups and belief systems and through questioning of meaning systems due to personal doubts and life challenges, such as crises. Second, when we think of spirituality as the wholeness of what it is to be human, our attention focuses on how people develop toward a sense of integration and integrity between all aspects of themselves (bio-psycho-social-spiritual) and in relation with other beings and the universe. For people who believe in a transcendent or divine ultimate reality, this actualization of wholeness is seen as an accomplishment of communion between oneself, others, and the divine.

These two ways of thinking about human development are closely related. The existential quest for meaning can motivate a person toward actualization of wholeness and communion. Thus, the existential quest can lead us into the transpersonal realm. Among those who believe in a divine plan or transcendent goal for human existence, some would say that transhuman spiritual powers, or our true self, of which the ego is yet latently aware, can reach out to us and call us onward toward integrity and wholeness.

214

These two developmental metaphors have been discussed widely by humanistic and transpersonal developmentalists, such as Maslow (Robbins, Chatterjee & Canda, 1998). The first is the metaphor of innate human potential. In this metaphor, the potential for spiritual unfoldment is like a seed with which we are born. When environmental conditions are sufficiently supportive and nurturing, the seed of spirituality sprouts and grows. Our innate drives for profound experience, integrity of self, and relationships express as we grow throughout the life span. Eventually we form a clearly integrated individual self and move beyond it into transpersonal awareness.

The second developmental metaphor is that of striving toward perfection or an ideal of wholeness. The person is like a green plant that naturally orients itself toward light and grows to reach it. As the plant encounters light, it receives energy from above that sustains and replenishes it. In this metaphor, the ideal of wholeness, encompassing personal integrity and universal communion, is like the sun to which we are drawn. People who believe in divine beings, a cosmic order, or a supreme being may feel that they are called toward perfection and wholeness to rise up out of their ego-limited self into transpersonal awareness. In theistic and animistic belief systems, this spiritual calling (vocation) may be initiated by sacred powers, including nonhuman or nonphysical beings, such as spirits, angels, deities, or a supreme being.

Both of these metaphors are related. The earth nurtures the seed of our spiritual potential, allowing it to sprout and grow, but rain and light from the sky are also necessary to feed and draw forth that growth. The first metaphor emphasizes that innate and immanent qualities of spirituality require nurturance by a supportive environment. The second metaphor emphasizes ideals and transcendent qualities of spirituality that draw forth human potential. It emphasizes the importance of the environment not only as a support, but also as a catalyst and even initiator of developmental breakthroughs.

This chapter explores these themes of individual human development. First, we consider how spiritual development relates to everyday life. Second, we discuss types of developmental phases and events, including gradual growth and sudden transformational breakthroughs. Third, we relate these to life span developmental theories. Then we offer suggestions for how we can help clients to discern the difference and relationship between growthful spiritual experiences and psychopathology. Throughout, we link theoretical insights into development with the practice of assessment.

SPIRITUAL DEVELOPMENT AND EVERYDAY LIFE

In Canda's (1988b, 1988c, 1990c) study of social work educators' views of spirituality, participants often emphasized that spirituality should be understood in relation to everyday life, including the ordinary events and circumstances of our personal lives and our professional work with clients. Of course, there may be occasions of powerful insights, spiritual crises, and breakthroughs and experiences of trances, visions, and revelations. People may feel powerfully moved by sacred powers and divine beings. But these extraordinary events and realities must be related to our ordinary everyday life, or our experience of them is merely a flash in the pan.

As social workers, we have a mandate for practical action. We recognize that spiritual development is an ongoing process, day to day, night to night. The nitty-gritty tasks of obtaining food and shelter, washing the dishes, and raising children are the spiritual ground on which we walk during our spiritual journeys. To borrow Maslow's (1968, 1969) concept of the hierarchy of needs, the satisfaction of subsistence, security, and self-esteem needs is the basis for the emergence of loving connections with others, creativity, and transpersonal experience.

But Maslow's idea is too often used superficially to imply that spiritual development starts only *after* all these so-called lower needs are satisfied. Maslow's point was that when a person's energy and attention are preoccupied with survival needs and fending off dangers or threats, it is natural that there will be less energy and time available for artistic and mystical pursuits. So when a homeless client states that her goal is to find a shelter from the winter cold, that is the appropriate point to help. By starting where the client is and joining with the client's present concern, we are already being spiritually sensitive. We are acknowledging the significance of her priorities and the preciousness of who she is just at this moment. Indeed, by relating with her in terms of her own aspirations, we create an opportunity for a profound connection and reflection. And in pursing shelter, the client is already on the path of spiritual development. When the shelter for homeless people reflects a humane, caring, and uplifting physical appearance and social climate, the provision of the shelter service nurtures the spiritual potential of the resident.

Also, it is often the times of greatest deprivation and oppression that call forth a response of creativity, discovery of meaning, and sense of divine support. As Victor Frankl, the founder of logotherapy (therapy of meaning) pointed out, when people get in touch with an inner source of spiritual support and hold dear the sense of their own and others' integrity, they may find surprising sustenance and resilience in the face of tragedy (Frankl, 1969; Lantz, 1993). For example, during the period of slavery, African American slaves and antiabolitionists drew on Christian hymns, both to glorify God and to proclaim their secret hopes and strategies for winning freedom (Harding, 1990). The underground railroad was made not of rails but of prayer, song, risk, courage, mutual support, and tremendous effort, day and night.

When we realize that spirituality encompasses the wholeness of what it is to be human, we become aware of the precious and wonderful nature of every moment and interaction. There is a common Zen expression that Zen mind is simply, "When hungry, eat; when sleepy, sleep." This does not mean that habitual, mindless routines and actions promote spiritual growth. Rather, the simplest act, when done with mindful awareness, is an occasion for realizing the amazing and mysterious quality of the moment (Welwood, 1992). Every day, as we work, play, love, become sick, heal, flame in anger, speak words of forgiveness, or go through the process of dying, we can be moving on a spiritual journey toward meaning and wholeness if we realize it and grow from it.

Spiritual development is not one aspect of life. Rather, spiritual development *is* everyday life. By calling human development *spiritual,* we are calling attention to the potential for deep meaning and realization of wholeness inherent in human life. When we become aware of this potential and dedicate ourselves to actualizing it, then our lives become explicitly spiritual in orientation.

In 1976, while I (EC) waded in gentle waves lapping on the shore of the East Sea of South Korea, I had an experience that made this point unforgettable. Suddenly a tall wave came rushing in. It knocked me down into the water, and an undertow pulled me out to the deep. I am not a good swimmer, and I strove to keep my head above water. Each time I surfaced, another wave washed me under. I could not find my way to the shore. This bobbing and submerging continued for what seemed an endless time. I felt that I was being swallowed into a pitiless void to die before my proper time.

Finally my cries for help brought a friend to my aid. He tried to take my arms around his neck and swim us both back to shore, but the crushing waves overcame us, so he had to release me back into the water to save himself. My hopeless bobbing continued. To my amazement, my mind and body had shifted into a state of strength and endurance that seemed impossible. Everything in the universe collapsed into each moment—no hope for the future, no help from the past. There was only the up and down, up and down. Finally, a Korean soldier stationed on the beach made his way to me with an inflated inner tube. He swam me back to the beach, pushed the water out of my lungs and stomach, and put me to rest in his encampment.

As I lay on a cot, I became acutely aware of the miracle of my survival. All my senses were heightened. The sounds of the soldiers talking about me, the radio music playing in the background, the shining sunlight—all struck me as absolutely amazing, precious, and wonderful. In contrast to the pitiless void from which I had been rescued, each simple moment of life was brilliant and fantastic. A soldier asked me, with a humorous tone of voice, "How does it feel to come back from hell?" I said, "Wonderful!"

About a week later, I was rushed to a hospital in Seoul with an attack of acute pancreatitis, an excruciating abdominal disorder that may have been triggered by the physical trauma of my drowning and lifesaving efforts. When I came out of the hospital about a week later, again I was amazed at the glory of life.

In the long run, what this experience showed me was how each moment—whether dramatic or boring, intense or gentle—is amazing and precious. The gentle lapping of the waves was amazing, the drowning and rescue were amazing, the feeling of pitiless void was amazing, the medical crisis in the hospital was amazing, the care and love I received from friends and strangers were amazing, and the recovery and return to ordinary life were amazing.

I recount this experience to remind you of any experiences you may have had that woke you up to the wonder of the ordinary. And if you have not had such an experience, let us hope that you can realize how wonderful each moment is without going through some catastrophe.

SPIRITUAL EMERGENCE AND EMERGENCIES

Stanislav Grof and Christina Grof coined the term *spiritual emergence* to refer to the developmental process in which people learn to orient themselves to their daily lives with clarity and appreciation, work out a sense of authentic meaning and purpose and relationship with other people and the world, and open up to transpersonal awareness (Bragdon, 1990; Grof & Grof, 1989; Watson, 1994). As Robbins, Chatterjee, and Canda (1998, p. 372) summarized, "*Spiritual emergence* is an experience of relatively gradual, but progressive expansion of a sense of wellness, freedom, responsibility, and connection with the cosmos. The related experiences and insights are rather easy to integrate into ordinary life." Of course, there are many twists and turns, steps forward and back, and leaps and falls on this journey of spiritual emergence, but the overall trend is toward meaning, wholeness, and communion.

Although spiritual emergence is usually a relatively gradual process, there are variations of intensity during developmental phases and transpersonal experiences. Spiritual awakenings sometimes occur to us in the most mundane and ordinary circumstances and through gradual unfolding of spiritual potential. Maslow (1970) described the *plateau experience* as a sense of profound yet gentle happiness and enjoyment that elevates our awareness of the moment beyond the taken-for-granted. He gave the example of a mother who watches her baby playing and marvels at the preciousness and loveliness of this young life.

Sometimes we experience startling breakthroughs that are exhilarating and enjoyable, as in periods of unusually fluid creativity, especially profound loving connections with other people, or meditative experiences of expanded consciousness. When we are able to integrate these experiences relatively easily, then our spiritual growth is accelerated without any sense of crisis. But sometimes the intensity is overwhelming. Our sense of psychosocial status quo may be severely disrupted. We may feel lost, disoriented, panicked. When spiritual development becomes a crisis, the Grofs refer to it as a *spiritual emergency* (Grof & Grof, 1990). They explain:

> When spiritual emergence is very rapid and dramatic, however, this natural process can become a crisis, and spiritual emergence becomes spiritual emergency. People who are in such a crisis are bombarded with inner experiences that abruptly challenge their old beliefs and ways of existing, and their relationship with reality shifts very rapidly. Suddenly they feel uncomfortable in the formerly familiar world and may find it difficult to meet the demands of everyday life. They can have great problems distinguishing their inner visionary world from the external world of daily reality. Physically, they may experience forceful energies streaming through their bodies and causing uncontrollable tremors (p. 35)

Like any other crisis, a spiritual emergency is fraught with both danger and opportunity. The danger is that the person may feel destroyed; the opportunity is that the person's destructuring can open the possibility of reconstructing a new, more fulfilling way of living. Ego shattering opens the way to ego transcendence. Spiritual emergency, when successfully resolved, propels us rather suddenly into transpersonal realms of experience.

Grof (1988) contrasted two modes of consciousness that help to clarify this process. The first mode is called *hylotropic,* literally "moving toward matter." It characterizes typical ordinary waking states of consciousness in which awareness of reality is limited to input through physical senses, physical boundaries of the environment and body, and the dimensions of time and space. This mode characterizes the typical mental orientation of egoic development.

The second mode of consciousness is called *holotropic,* literally "moving toward wholeness." This mode involves trans-egoic experiences that become more common and typical as a person's spiritual emergence moves into the transpersonal levels. We will discuss the transpersonal levels of development in more detail later in this chapter. For now, it is important to note that spiritual emergencies involve sudden openings to transpersonal experiences that can be a shock to the ego. The person's sense of identity and reality and usual strategies for living and relating may be thrown into doubt and confusion. Gradual emergence of transpersonal awareness allows for a smoother transition to new ways of experiencing and relating with the world, but spiritual emergencies may temporarily overwhelm us with a flood of mind-blowing insights, visions, sensations, and feelings. Table 7.1 lists examples of various transpersonal experiences.

Maslow (1968, 1970) made a useful distinction between two types of spiritual breakthrough events: the peak experience and the nadir experience. The *peak experience* is an intense life-changing event that propels a person into a profound sense of communion with self, other people, the universe, or divinity. A peak experience loosens or dissolves the limiting ego boundary, opening the person to transpersonal awareness and experiences. It is as if the person has suddenly flown to the top of a mountain and is able to look out at a vast, fantastic vista. For example, a mountain hiker may suddenly come out from a forest onto a precipice, looking out to an expansive plain far below. Standing poised between heaven and earth, looking out to the vastness, the hiker may feel swept away with awe at the beauty and magnitude all around. He or she may feel suddenly at one and at peace with the universe. After such an experience, his or her perspective on life can never be the same.

A peak experience is a sudden developmental breakthrough, but it does not necessarily lead to a sense of emergency. Although the emotional valence of the peak experience is positive, it may be so intense and con-

Table 7.1
Examples of Transpersonal Experiences

Identification or merging with other people

Identification or merging with plants, animals, and other beings of nature

Communication with spirits of ancestors, deceased loved ones, and spirit powers associated with nature

Communication with angels and spirit guides

Communication with God

Oneness with the universe or ultimate reality

Remembrance of past incarnations

Remembrance of past planetary or cosmic evolution

Awareness of subtle energies, such as *ch'i*[1] or *kundalini*[2]

Distress caused by magical attack or harmful spirit possession

Out-of-body travel

Insight into universal symbolic meanings (archetypes)

Extrasensory perceptions such as precognition, telepathy, and telekinesis

Near-death experiences

---

[1]In Taoism and Neo-Confucianism, *ch'i* (Chinese) refers to vital energy or life force that flows through the cosmos and, in the body, can be influenced by special breathing practices and acupuncture.

[2]In Tantra Yoga or Kundalini Yoga, *kundalini* (Sanskrit) refers to a spiritual energy coiled like a snake at the base of the spine. Meditation with special breathing and postures can stimulate the energy to rise up through the energy centers (*chakras*) of the body (Schuhmacher & Woerner, 1994).

trary to expectations that one's sense of self and reality is shattered. Then it becomes a spiritual emergency.

There is also the spiritual breakthrough event that Maslow called the *nadir experience,* an intense life-changing event that plunges one into a pit of confusion, despair, or grief. If a loved one has died, one's very sense of self, formerly closely connected with this person, is shattered. The bereaved may feel lost and hopeless. He or she may feel bewildered that a supposedly loving God could allow such a thing to happen. Like Job in the Bible story, one's sense of reality and rightness may be dashed in a way that seems incomprehensible and unjustifiable. But when a person is able to work out of this pit, one becomes able to reorient self and relationships, understand the meaning of life, and connect to the sacred in a more realistic, resilient, and profound manner. This is the existentialist path of con-

fronting the absurdity of life in order to come to an authentic and more fulfilling sense of meaning.

This is the kind of pivotal experience that I (LF) experienced when my
husband, Phil, was dying of cancer. It was inconceivable that my husband,
an ENT (ears, nose and throat) specialist who had surgically removed can-
cers from others, now had inoperable cancer himself. What happens when
the silver bullet of modern medical technology no longer provides the
cure? But it was Phil's own response to his illness and impending death
and my faith that helped me find the strength and answers I needed.

For Phil, it was not his renaissance intelligence that gave him courage
or his material estate that consoled him. What sustained him was his
unwillingness to give up hope that a cure would be found at the same time
as he accepted the inevitability of his death. The operant factor in this dual
perspective was his discovery of a profound faith in a very personal God
who could empower him in his own physical and spiritual vulnerability.
Often when I entered his hospital room, his medical colleagues would be
standing around his bedside, listening to him ask for forgiveness for somehow coming short and they would ask for his. Phil's deep faith through
this experience was a personal gift to all of us, especially to me.

Death or the threat of death has been called the decisive teacher
because it goads us into appreciating what we have or what we can do. We
can create our own opportunities from the same raw materials from which
other people create their defeats.

Initially I felt that I could not face the inevitable. I remember one
evening I was sitting eating Widman's homemade chocolate-covered
potato chips (a Grand Forks, North Dakota, specialty) and was feeling
angry that I had been given this bitter slice of life. Why was this happening to me? Why was my husband dying, and how could I possibly live
without him? I did not have the strength to face the future—the terrifying
short term or the lonely long term. That moment of utter despair was the
definitive moment in my life. The reality of death was present there in our
home, in our very bedroom. But somehow, looking at Phil and seeing his
incredible calmness, I was able to rise above my own narcissistic self-cen-
teredness and enter into his dying experience with him. In a certain way,
his cancer and his response reached into my psyche and my soul and stimulated them to growth.

I realized that what I needed was to return to the foundations of my
youth, my religious and spiritual heritage. I needed to seek guidance in the
Christian Holy Scriptures and to find empowerment in personal and communal prayer. But most of all, I knew that what I needed was the support

of other human beings. Phil and I would go through this experience together, but we needed guidance, and so we sought pastoral counseling. I realized that grief issues would be most important for us to process. I would be saying goodbye to a marriage of twenty-five years and preparing to be without him. Phil was saying goodbye to his family he loved so well and to his medical practice. We both needed help in the transition from the known to the unknown and what Phil's meeting Christ would mean to both of us.

Phil's illness had a profound impact on our marriage. Before his diagnosis, our marriage and love for each other was like most other long-term marriages—anything but perfect. There were times when we misunderstood each other, were insensitive to each other's needs, or demanded too much of each other. During our first twenty-three years together, I realized that I did not know Phil very well. He was busy with his career and I with mine and the raising of our sons. Marital quid pro quo (you do for me, and I'll do for you) was also prevalent in our marriage, as it is in most other marriages. During the last years of Phil's life, this type of thinking totally stopped. Through Phil's spiritual journey, he began to open up to me and share his innermost feelings—his greatest joys and his deepest fears. I really got to know him, and I fell in love with this wonderful, brilliant man all over again.

During those last years, our marriage had no visible quid pro quo. I was the primary caregiver for Phil because I loved him, expecting nothing in return. But what Phil and his illness gave me was psychological and emotional maturity. I experienced a total acceptance of my husband, including the breakdown of his body and all of its functions. In most relationships, it is easier to live in a fantasy of how we wish the other person to be or how we think she or he is. These images may be more positive or more negative than the person really is. They do not identify the person in reality. As Phil lay dying, there was no room for an inaccurate image of him. I saw the plain truth of his deteriorating body, the shutdown of his intellectual mind, and his inevitable death.

On the day of Phil's funeral, Mr. Widman came to my door with a huge tray of his homemade chocolate-covered potato chips for our family and friends. As I looked at those confections, I remembered how far I had come up out of the pit of confusion and despair. But it was Phil's example, his courage, honest intimacy of his death, and my religious faith that had worked a profound change in me. This crisis tapped a source of spiritual support within me and revealed the integrity of Phil's life and his most dignified death.

It is never really possible to predict how we will react in a crisis. As in combat, it is often unknown who will have the courage to stay and fight. I am thankful that I chose to stay and fight because Phil's illness and his courageous response to his inevitable death presented me with enduring gifts. I have no feelings of guilt for not doing enough; I did all I could. I am not only no longer afraid of death; I am no longer afraid of life. I have a fearlessness to tackle almost anything.

The unconditional acceptance of my husband as he lay dying carried over into other areas of my life. As I examined what was most important in my own particular beliefs and spiritual practices and as I began to put them to work through the events of my husband's illness and death, I was allowed to get out of my own frame of reference and learn to see other people from their own perspectives. This has resulted in taking a less critical stance toward those whose worldviews are considerably different from mine. I have learned to be less judgmental and am cultivating more empathy and understanding. Most important, I have moved away from being dependent on what others think and being concerned with conformity toward an independence of spirit and a recognition of my own individuality. The myth of my not being strong enough was peeled away by this experience. However, as much as I value my independence and solitude now, I still recognize a need for others in my life. Without interpersonal connections, I would not have been able to grow throughout this life crisis nor would I be able to continue to discover more about myself, deepen my personal experience with God, and find ways to be of service within my community. For me, spirituality has become an intimate communication with God and others.

Yet Maslow emphasized that the peak and nadir types of experiences do not necessarily result in an enhancement of life. We could try to deny the revelation or forget the insight. Insofar as we are dramatically changed by these experiences, our customary patterns of relationships with other people will be challenged as well. In order to fit back into our psychosocial status quo, we may try to deny and hide our profound experiences and insights. Our loved ones and helping professionals may brand our spiritual emergency as a form of pathology to be squelched by therapy and medications. Sometimes even our spiritual or religious support groups oppose us for daring to have insights, revelations, visions, or communications with the divine that go outside the constraints of their regulated beliefs, so integration of our transpersonal experiences into our ordinary lives may pose a challenge to our social environment.

On the other hand, some people become spiritual thrill seekers. They become so enamored of the intense highs or lows of peak and pit experiences that they seek to repeat them on demand. In this case, ordinary life and relationships may be discarded in order to chase after the next transpersonal thrill. In some cases, this leads to abuse of drugs and self-damaging extremes of spiritual disciplines. This approach can eventually lead to addiction or burnout. If the spiritual insights are not integrated into ordinary life, they are merely fireworks displays at night that wink out and leave only the darkness.

But even if a person is conscientious in the pursuit of spiritual growth or does not seek it at all, sometimes a spiritual emergency comes with such suddenness and overwhelming force that it is impossible to cope with it or integrate it personally or socially. Spiritual emergency in the form of a debilitating crisis imposes a serious risk for physical illness, psychopathology, and social disruption. According to some belief systems, such as shamanism, nonphysical entities may disrupt our bodies and minds for the purpose of calling us into a new way of life. Although this presents a great opportunity for growth, it can also be a frightening and dangerous process.

When we are able to integrate transpersonal insights into our ongoing daily life, we grow to an enhanced level of functioning and fulfillment. Maslow (1970) referred to this as another kind of plateau experience—a way of being that is oriented toward compassion, beauty, wisdom, responsibility, creativity, and profundity. This is a developmental ideal and a major goal of spiritually sensitive practice. In other words, we can not only support people to recover from crises (restore the status quo); we can also support them to learn and grow through the process. In Chapter 8, we offer suggestions for how this can be done in practice.

SPIRITUAL EMERGENCE THROUGHOUT THE LIFE CYCLE

Spiritual emergence occurs in the context of our growth through the life cycle, from birth to death, and possibly beyond. In this section we draw on three life cycle theories that shed light on the relation between spiritual emergence and stages of the life cycle: Erik Erikson's (1962, 1963, 1968, 1969, 1982) psychosocial development theory, James Fowler's (1981, 1984, 1996) cognitive-structural faith development theory, and Ken Wilber's (1995, 1996) transpersonal spectrum model of development. Table 7.2 summarizes the names, stages, and major themes for each of these theorists

Table 7.2
Qualities of Spiritual Development Emerging Through the Life Cycle in Three-Stage Theories

Usual Age of Emergence	Erikson: Ego Challenge Stage and Virtue	Fowler: Faith Stage and Quality	Wilber: Consciousness Stage and Quality
Older adulthood	Ego Integrity versus Despair: *Wisdom*	Universalizing Faith: *Nonjudgmental, Transcendent, Inclusive View*	Nondual: *Union of Ultimate and Ordinary*
			Causal: *Formlessness, No Separation*
			Subtle: *Communion with Divinity*
Middle adulthood	Generativity versus Stagnation: *Care*	Conjunctive Faith: *Complex and Pluralistic View*	Psychic: *Communion with World*
Early adulthood	Intimacy versus Isolation: *Love*	Individuative-Reflective Faith: *Critical Reflection*	Vision Logic: *Holistic Inclusivity*
Adolescence	Ego Identity versus Role Confusion: *Fidelity*	Synthetic-Conventional Faith: *Personalized Peer Referenced Beliefs*	Formal Operational: *Sophisticated Rationality*
Older childhood	Industry versus Inferiority: *Competence*	Mythic-Literal Faith: *Loyalty to Community Representational Beliefs*	Concrete Operational: *Autonomous but Conformist Perspective*
Middle childhood	Initiative versus Guilt: *Purpose*	Intuitive-Projective Faith: *Creative Fantasy*	Late Preoperational: *Symbolic Representational Thinking*
Early childhood	Autonomy versus Shame, Doubt: *Will Power*		Preoperational: *Fantasy-Emotional Centeredness*
Infancy	Trust versus Mistrust: *Hope*	Primal Faith: *Trust in the Universe, Divinity*	Sensori-physical: *Body-Oriented Awareness*

by drawing on these sources. (For further information, see Robbins, Chatterjee & Canda, 1998.)

Erikson's View of Spiritual Development

Erikson's psychosocial development theory is based on an *epigenetic perspective*, which sees development as a process of psychosocial responses to age-related changes in the body (e.g., physical maturation) and socially defined transitions (e.g., marriage or retirement) that occur in sequential stages. Epigenesis means that each stage presents particular tasks, opportunities, and challenges. Development at each stage builds on the accomplishments of the prior stages. As the person responds to these challenges successfully, he or she accrues coping skills, ego strengths, and social resources. But when these challenges are not met successfully, due to inadequate coping or lack of support from the social environment, the person fails to learn effective coping patterns and carries the burden of unresolved issues.

Erikson's theory reminds us to be aware of relatively predictable age-related challenges that may affect spiritual emergence, as determined by physical changes and socially programmed transitions. For example, the adolescent, according to Erikson, typically is dealing with the challenge of forming a clear sense of personal identity in relation to socially available roles, increasing emotional ties to peers outside the family of origin, and exploring budding sexuality. Therefore it is expected that many adolescents will be dealing with spiritual challenges pertaining to reevaluation of family-based religious beliefs and practices. Also, insofar as a society demarcates significant life cycle transition points, such as birth, marriage, childbirth, retirement, and death, it is expected that people will have a heightened sense of preoccupation with existential issues of meaning and purpose, as well as practical behavioral responses determined by spiritual and religious reference groups, such as rituals. When a person experiences a lack of guidance from spiritual support systems at important life cycle transition points, the person will have greater difficulty meeting the challenge. However, when a person has accrued a wide repertoire of internal strengths (which Erikson called virtues) and skills in using external spiritual support systems, then we can expect greater creativity, sense of positive self-esteem, and resilience in confronting crises, including spiritual emergencies.

Erikson suggested that people in latest adulthood (after age fifty) often review their lives with increased interest and concern as the fact of mortality and physical decline becomes more evident. He believed that most people have a heightened sense of spiritual concern at this stage, because there is greater urgency to establish a sense that one's life has been meaningful and worthwhile. Questions about the nature of death and the possibility of an after-death existence naturally increase.

Erikson also suggested that some people have a precocious and unusually strong interest in spiritual matters throughout life. Even in childhood, such a person may focus on questions about the meaning and purpose of human life. He discussed Martin Luther and Mahatma Gandhi as examples of such extraordinary people, and referred to them with the Latin term *homo religiosus,* which means "the religious person" (Erikson, 1962, 1969). In adulthood, the *homo religiosus* extends the sense of responsibility to connection with people beyond family and one's own society to all humanity and even the entire cosmos. Such personalities are more likely to experience peak and pit experiences at early ages and throughout the life cycle. Their approach to life overall is to integrate these insights into ever-increasing levels of spiritual plateaus. They are more likely to try to build on unfolding psychosocial virtues to develop an overall way of living committed to joining personal edification with benefit for others. Therefore, they often have an unusually high degree of facility, with both inner self-reflection (wisdom) and humane relations with others (compassion) leading to effective action (service).

James Fowler's Faith Development Theory

Fowler is a Christian theologian and developmental theorist who built on the structural-cognitive perspective of Piaget and Kohlberg in addition to psychosocial theory. In the cognitive-structural perspective, development reflects the process of learning increasingly sophisticated and comprehensive ways of mentally comprehending the world. Stages of development represent levels of cognitive complexity achieved rather than age-determined tasks.

Fowler's theory focuses on the formation and transformation of faith throughout the life cycle. By *faith,* Fowler meant "the pattern of our relatedness to self, others, and our world in light of our relatedness to ultimacy" (1996, p. 21). *Ultimacy* refers to that which a person gives a sense of first importance and greatest profundity in orienting his or her life with fundamental values, beliefs, and meanings. Just as we have defined spirituality, faith may take religious or nonreligious forms. Fowler depicted faith as a universal aspect of human nature that gives coherence and meaning to life, connects individuals together in shared concerns, relates people to a larger cosmic frame of reference, and enables us to deal with suffering and mortality.

Ideal faith development is portrayed as a progression from childhood conformity to expectations of belief and behavior set by family and society with relatively simplistic and concrete images of God or other spiritual realities; through adolescent questioning and formation of a more personally tailored faith; to critically reflective, flexible, and even inclusive forms of faith. Fowler described a mature faith stance as one that upholds one's own particular beliefs and practices at the same time as being able to empathize and cooperate with people who have other faith commitments.

Fowler provided a helpful set of categories to understand various contents of a person's developing faith: (1) the things or qualities with greatest value to us, (2) the "master stories" that we use to guide and explain our lives, (3) the images of sacredness or power that sustain us, and (4) our locus of authority for what we consider moral and right (Robbins, Chatterjee & Canda, 1998). Over time, people refine and change their contents of faith, both within stages (at the same level of complexity and sophistication) and by moving to a more advanced stage of faith. The latter case is called *conversion,* which is sometimes rather sudden (Fowler, 1981). Sudden conversions can involve what transpersonalists call peak or pit experiences, including spiritual emergencies. Given Fowler's Christian perspective, he suggested that conversion may sometimes result from an unpredictable revelation of God's grace and intentions for us to reform our lives (Fowler, 1981, 1996).

Ken Wilber's Spectrum Model of Development

Like Fowler, Wilber draws heavily on the cognitive-structural theories of development. But unlike Fowler, his spiritual assumptions are more influenced by Vedantic Hinduism and Buddhism than Christianity. Wilber (1980, 1993, 1995, 1996) based his theory on the belief that human development is a process of evolution with the goal that each person, and eventually the human species as a whole, should attain unitary consciousness. Each level of consciousness includes yet transcends the capacities and strategies of the lower levels. As we develop increasingly complex, comprehensive, and inclusive modes of spirituality, we move from a pre-egoic orientation (early childhood) to an egoic orientation (typically established firmly in adolescence). Wilber is most interested in the trans-egoic levels of development, which some people achieve in a stable manner during adulthood. He does not separate adulthood into age-linked stages of spiritual development.

Wilber refers to his model as a *holarchy,* that is, an ordering of increasingly comprehensive wholes. Although the model is often portrayed as a linear sequence of stages, that is a simplification. One might better portray each stage as a circle that encompasses the earlier stages as smaller circles. In other words, at each stage, the person's consciousness is able to incorporate more aspects of reality and more modes of functioning. At the stage of transition from egoic to trans-egoic consciousness (vision-logic), the person learns to perceive the world holistically. In the early trans-egoic stages (psychic, subtle, and causal), the person realizes that the self is not limited to ordinary space-time limits or ego boundary. The transpersonal experiences categorized by Grof, such as extrasensory perceptions and mystical experiences, become more common and consistent. Ultimately the person's identity may grow beyond the confines of the self bounded by ego, body, and social roles until it becomes unified with the totality of the universe.

This ultimate stage of development, called the *nondual,* is characterized by a consciousness beyond all separations and distinctions. It is really a nonstage, because it is experience of pure consciousness—the source, process, and goal of all development. In the nondual stage, a person realizes that every moment is already complete. Every particular thing, including oneself, is fundamentally one with all. Ordinary life becomes infused with awareness of the sacredness of every experience. Wilber (1995, p. 301) proclaimed that the nondual is "the Ground or Suchness or Isness of *all* stages, at all times, in all dimensions: the Being of all beings, the Condition of all conditions, the Nature of all natures."

Wilber recognized that peak and pit experiences can temporarily propel one into the trans-egoic levels of consciousness, even while one is operating regularly at an egoic or pre-egoic level. However, it takes time, effort, and practice to develop proficiency and regularity of functioning at the trans-egoic levels. In Maslow's terms, temporary peak experiences can catalyze trans-egoic development, but it takes dedicated and consistent work to stabilize at a transpersonal plateau of functioning.

Critique of the Stage Theories of Spiritual Development

The stage theories provide useful concepts and insights, and in the next section on assessment, we make use of them. However, there are many weaknesses and controversies about them that limit their usefulness for a client-centered, spiritually sensitive approach to assessment in social work. One of the limitations is that they overemphasize the emergence of spiritual issues in adulthood. Coles's (1990) narrative interview studies with children from many cultural backgrounds show a great richness and profundity of spirituality that needs to be explored further. Sometimes adult views of religion and spirituality may become jaded and routinized, as compared with childhood open-mindedness and spontaneity. The importance of childhood as a key formative period for development of spiritual propensity was demonstrated in our National Survey. According to scatter plot analyses, the more a social worker participated in religious (e.g., church) services and felt positive about religious and spiritual experiences in childhood and adolescence, the more likely the person would continue to participate and feel positive in adulthood.

All of the stage theories present an oversimplified picture of development. Since they are standardized, they cannot accommodate the tremendous individual and cultural diversity of developmental experiences and paths. Although Erikson, Fowler, and Wilber have all addressed concerns about diversity to some extent, there continue to be many problems when trying to take into account diversity of gender, culture, religion, sexual orientation, and cognitive abilities (Robbins, Chatterjee & Canda, 1998). All of the stage theories are based on a great deal of theoretical and philosophical speculation but insufficient empirical evidence.

On a practical level, if we take a stage theory too seriously, there is the risk that we will not be open to the unique developmental story of each client. We may assume that at a certain age, a person *should* act and think in such and such way, and then impose our prejudice on the nonconforming client. Instead of listening carefully for the particular themes, plots, sequences of events, and interpretations within the client's life story, we may be listening to our internal dialogue based on our own ideal version of a life story.

In addition, many people recount unexpected and complicated twists, turns, detours, reversals, revelations, and breakthroughs that do not fit any preconceived notion of how development should proceed. The following discussion of assessment will draw on stage theory concepts to augment an individualized and contextualized approach to understanding a client's spiritual journey.

ASSESSMENT OVER THE LIFE SPAN

Social workers may encounter spiritually concerned clients in any of these situations: simply working through the gradual unfolding of spiritual awareness, recounting important peak or pit experiences in the context of understanding one's life story, or being overwhelmed in a state of crisis. It is therefore very important that we be prepared to identify characteristics of spiritual emergence so that we can lend our support. It is important that we be able to distinguish spiritual emergencies from psychopathology, so that we can assist the person toward successful resolution of the crisis rather than try to suppress it. And we must also be able to help clients who do have mental disorders to deal with spiritual emergence and spiritual emergencies.

In keeping with the guidelines for a spiritually sensitive helping relationship described in Chapter 6, we suggest that assessment be done in a collaborative manner with clients. When clients describe transpersonal experiences or experiences unique to particular religious beliefs and practices, social workers must be wary of imposing irrelevant, ethnocentric, or religiously biased assumptions and judgments. The social work dictum, "start where the client is," means that we need to take seriously the client's current reality, even if it seems quite alien to our own. Jung (1938, 1959, 1965) said that each person lives in a world of mental experiences that are vivid and real to him or her, although they may appear strange and bizarre to another. He referred to this as a person's *psychic reality* (the reality of the psyche). For example, if a client says that he is being punished by God for some behavior he believes to be sinful, this is the reality that must be the starting point for help. It does not matter if the social worker does not believe in God, or thinks guilt is an inappropriate feeling, or objects to the idea of a punishing God. To work with this client's psychic reality means that the social worker can help him explore the helpful and harmful implications of his concepts of God, morality, and punishment.

Suppose that the client is an estranged Methodist and has not gone to church for many years. In the course of therapeutic dialogue, it is possible that the client will seek rapprochement with the church as part of the process of dealing with the burden of sin and guilt. The social worker could help the client to find a faith community that would be supportive and comfortable.

In the context of the strengths perspective, Saleebey (1997) said that the social worker needs to suspend disbelief in order to connect with the reality of the client. If a client feels she is supported by a guardian angel, then this sense of support can be enlisted at times of spiritual crisis. If a client believes he is under attack from a demon, then collaboration with an exorcist in that client's tradition may be useful if this is not merely a case of delusion. The important thing is to enable clients to tell their stories unhindered and to help them discover the themes, plots, characters, and developments within these stories.

Starting where the client is does not mean staying stuck there. It may well be that the client will change the story or reinterpret it as the process of self-reflection and discernment continues. Except in the case of clear and present dangers to the client and others, the prerogative of making meaning in the life story should stay with the client rather than the social worker. And even in the case of people who do have severe mental disorders, the prerogative for existential and spiritual understanding of personal meaning of the disorder also should be with the person.

We can visualize these patterns of spiritual development as variations in our life journey that may or may not move to transpersonal awareness. Spiritual emergence is a process of growth, including ups and downs and variations of intensity. It may include climbing to peaks and descending into pits and efforts to incorporate these experiences into our ongoing daily lives. Sometimes these peak and pit experiences are so sudden, drastic, and overwhelming that we cannot cope. We need assistance from loved ones, healers, and helpers. But with assistance and our own effort, we can progress on our travel toward even higher plateaus.

It is useful to think of spiritual emergence as the total process of development of meaning, morality, relationships, and orientation toward ultimacy throughout the life span. Peaks, pits, and plateaus can be considered phases and punctuations along this path of emergence.

This typology provides a basis for helping clients to assess their spiritual development in the present and over the life span. The first distinction we can make is between gradual phases of spiritual growth; rapid transformational periods (peak and pit experiences), including their expression as spiritual emergencies; and plateaus of relatively stable functioning at enhanced levels. In order to depict this development, we expand on the concept of a spiritual development time line (Bullis, 1996).

Figure 7.1 depicts a graph of a segment of a person's life, from the age of ten to thirty years. We will name the fictional person Alice. The graph indicates that Alice shifted from pre-egoic to trans-egoic plateaus of consciousness during this time.

Ages ten through nineteen show a period of increasing growth. In mid- to late childhood, Alice incorporated the beliefs and values of her parents and religious community into her sense of identity and worldview. As an adolescent and young adult, Alice began to question her Presbyterian religious upbringing. Although the master stories and guiding images of childhood had provided a sense of security during childhood, she had

Figure 7.1

Example and Suggestions for Constructing a Spiritual Development Time Line

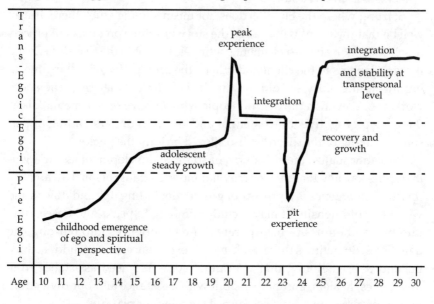

Alice's Spiritual Development Time Line

At each developmental phase and transition, identify the person's significant:

- personal spiritual practices, such as prayer, meditation, inspirational reading
- qualities of spiritual emergence insights, emergencies, peak and pit experiences
- quantity and quality of participation in spiritual and religious support systems
- spiritual exemplars, mentors, friends, and supporters
- key beliefs, symbols, rituals that support transformation

Explore how all this relates to the person's overall life narrative and guiding story of spiritual transformation.

come to feel that they were too narrow to address her interests in extrasensory perception, mystical experiences, and religious diversity. She felt that her family's way of understanding religious doctrines and rituals did not help her to experience directly the sacred realities to which they referred. Her locus of spiritual authority was shifting away from family, church, and Bible toward her own inner experience and a few trusted friends.

At the age of eighteen, Alice joined a Zen meditation group that one of her close friends recommended. She began practicing meditation on a regular basis. As she became more adept at the technique, she felt herself becoming more centered and calmer. When challenging events occurred, she was better able to deal with them and could let go of any distress quickly. She felt herself changing in subtle but important ways. She felt more empathetic in her relationships with loved ones, and she was able to enjoy the beauty of nature during morning walks more deeply. During this time, she found a job as an office receptionist that supplied her with necessary income but also left time for her to pursue her spiritual interests.

Her values began to emphasize caring and compassion for all people and beings. She became a vegetarian and an active volunteer in a hospice program. The life story of the Buddha, Siddhartha Gautama, became her master story, encouraging her to keep up consistent effort to attain enlightenment. She appreciated the Zen emphasis on coming to conclusions about the nature of self and reality through direct personal experience rather than unquestioning acceptance of beliefs.

This phase ended rather abruptly after two years, at the age of twenty, when she went on an intensive meditation retreat. This meditation retreat precipitated a peak experience. For three days, she and a group of retreatants practiced meditation for fifteen hours each day, punctuated by brief meals and periods of silent work. The first two days were very difficult to endure, as they caused a dramatic break from customary patterns of sleep, eating, and communicating. The prolonged periods of meditation and silence intensified her awareness of her mental chatter. As she learned to let go of it, she experienced times of profound peace and clarity. On the third day, Alice had a breakthrough in her meditation. She suddenly realized that the person she had believed herself to be was not substantial and had no lasting existence. The self she defined in terms of physical appearance, social roles and expectations, social status, and various possessions no longer seemed very real. Alice became acutely aware that all this would disappear with death and maybe even sooner.

This was a somewhat frightening realization. Neither her Christian upbringing nor her Buddhist learning had prepared her for the intense and perplexing quality of her experience. She suddenly experienced a tremendous doubt about the validity of all values, beliefs, and religious images from any source. But she also experienced a deeper, truer sense of self beneath all this transitory surface. She came to call this her true self. She had heard such an expression in Zen teaching, but until this time it was just a fascinating concept. Her realization was exhilarating. Although she did not understand exactly what this would mean, she committed herself to change her life to be more in accord with this true self. After the retreat, she returned to her job as a receptionist. Although she was not able to keep the same vivid awareness of her true self as during the retreat, she was able to retain the insight and begin changing her life.

Until the age of twenty-three, Alice continued her meditation practice. She made moderate changes in her daily life to reflect her new insights. Overall, she felt a greater sense of well-being than before the peak experience. Her friendships became more satisfying. She decided to go to college and major in social work so that she could obtain a job that matched her growing interest in human service. Thus, she had arrived at a plateau of beginning transpersonal awareness in daily life (Wilber's Vision Logic to Psychic stages).

A pit experience began with a tragic precipitating event when Alice was twenty-three years old: a car accident that caused a severe spinal injury. It took several months of intense effort, medical care, and physical therapy for Alice to regain health and mobility. This accident shocked her. Up to the point of the accident, she was feeling quite content with her life. She felt that she had a meaning and purpose that she was able to express through her work and friendships. She began to feel protected and nourished by the universe. But the accident reminded her of her earlier peak experience insight with great starkness: all this could pass at any moment, and unpredictably. The universe no longer felt safe. She questioned her sense of meaning and purpose. Overwhelmed with physical pain and emotional turmoil, she gave up on her meditation practice. She felt at a very low point in life.

Alice never forgot about her meditation and transpersonal experiences. This gave her a feeling of positive possibility, although it took about six months for this to come to the forefront of her awareness as she began to work her way out of this pit experience. Alice dedicated herself to physical therapy and also met with a social worker for counseling. The social worker recognized that Alice viewed her life as a spiritual journey and that Alice was working hard to make sure that this crisis would not be a dead end. The social worker helped Alice to recall the benefits that she had received from meditation practice and connection with her Zen meditation group. Alice decided to begin her meditation practice again and to seek the comradeship and support of her friends in the meditation group. This supported her physical and emotional resiliency. Gradually, she healed to the point of being able to return to school at the age of twenty-four.

Alice reestablished her precrisis range of activities and relationships. However, as she continued to reflect on the implications of her accidental injury, she decided to begin an even more concerted effort to transform her lifestyle, relationships, and meditation practice so that there would be greater congruence with her transpersonal insights. She was on guard against complacency or taking anything for granted. Life seemed both more precious and more vulnerable. But she felt that there was a new strength emerging as she shifted her sense of identity and reality more consistently in accord with her true self. This process of recovery and growth took three years. During this period, Alice completed her B.S.W. degree. She found a social work job as a case manger for people with disabilities. She felt good that she could use insights from her own experience with a temporary disability to enhance her rapport with clients.

By the age of twenty-six, Alice felt that she had stabilized, with an even deeper understanding about her true self through all of this. She learned to be comfortable with the unpredictability of life and to sense a mysterious yet significant purpose behind all of it. Now she is thirty years old. For the past four years, she has been rather consistent in her spiritual practice and daily lifestyle. This does not mean she has been stagnant. On the contrary, she has felt highly creative and energetic. But she did not feel adrift or chaotic. She feels confident that she will be able to deal with any unforeseen challenges with even greater resiliency than she ever had before.

Alice's values of compassion and respect for diverse peoples helped her blossom as a social worker. She felt a high level of congruence between her personal values and the social work profession's commitment to individual well-being and social justice. She also developed a more comprehensive master story of life that encompassed her Presbyterian upbringing and more recent Zen practice. She found ways to connect these two traditions in her daily life. Alice started a local nonsectarian spiritual support group for people who wanted to discuss the challenges around linking various spiritual perspectives and practices. Recently Alice arranged for a Presbyterian minister who was also an authorized Zen teacher to lead a meditation retreat for her support group.

This fictional example illustrates how the concept of spiritual emergence can be used for assessment of self and clients. We can write our own spiritual autobiography or invite a client to tell his or her story. Starting with whatever event is the current focus of attention, the spiritual growth time line can put it into perspective of overall life development. We can recall the learning from past experience and apply it to the present, therefore enhancing our confidence in the future.

There are infinite possible variations on this time line. Periods of gradual growth, gradual decline, sudden peaks and pits, and steady plateaus can all alternate in any order and duration. By using the spiritual time line as a basis for life review, we can form an assessment of spiritual development in a way that is entirely congruent with the person's own spiritual orientation, cultural background, and personality. We do not need to start with any particular theoretical assumptions or religious beliefs about how development should occur. We can discover the person's own self-understanding.

Assessment of Spiritual Emergencies and Psychopathology

Spiritual Emergency as Crisis

A person in an acute state of crisis will likely be cognitively disoriented, extremely anxious, overwhelmed by real or imagined events, and incapable of making rational decisions and engaging in effective action (Dixon, 1979; Golan, 1981; Simos, 1979). The person may even experience delusions and hallucinations, characteristics shared with mental disorders. However, in contrast to most types of mental disorders, crises usually are characterized by a combination of sudden onset, limited duration, and intense temporary distress. Also, crises are responses to actual events that pose a temporarily overwhelming challenge. Usually the person in crisis returns to a precrisis level of functioning or grows through the experience within several months of onset. Although crisis resolution sometimes requires assistance from social workers or other professional helpers, people's established coping patterns, resilience, and creativity are the primary forces in healing. The helper works with these natural healing capacities. When directive techniques or medications are used, they are temporary measures designed to enable the client to restore self-sufficiency.

If the temporary symptoms of crisis are mistaken for mental disorder, antipsychotic medications could be mistakenly employed that cause more harm than good. Indeed, the symptoms of crisis are indicators of dramatic change and potential for growth. If these symptoms are suppressed or pejoratively labeled by the actions of professionals, the person's growth potential and capacity to learn from the experience may be jeopardized.

Professional helpers who are unfamiliar with the special issues and symptoms of spiritual emergencies are more likely to misunderstand them as expressions of a mental disorder. As is well known, for example, schizophrenia, bipolar disorder, and severe depression often involve delusions, hallucinations, and preoccupations with religious themes or images similar to transpersonal experiences. Many forms of mental disorder and personality disorders involve a sense of confused identity, impairment of reality testing, and loosening of the boundary between ego and others. So when clients in crisis talk about peak or pit experiences that entail ego transcendence, questioning the nature of reality, and visions, alarm bells may go off in the mind of the social worker. Contrarily, if a client does have a chronic and persistent mental disorder, mental health professionals may be prone to dismiss all of her or his ideas and feelings about religion and spirituality as nothing more than symptoms of the illness. Ironically, a study of mental health service consumers' views about the strengths and resources that were most helpful to them in dealing with a mental disability showed that many people felt their spiritual and religious insights and support systems were very important (Sullivan, 1992). Unfortunately, the respondents in this study indicated that the spiritual and religious experiences and supports were often ignored or dismissed by professional helpers. In our National Survey, more respondents indicated it is appropriate to raise the topic of spirituality (52 percent) than religion (36 percent) with a client who has a chronic mental disorder. This indicates that a large percentage of mental health social workers may not be assessing clients' spirituality, and most may not be assessing their religious involvement.

Assessment Guidelines Related to DSM-IV

The DSM-IV includes some useful information to help mental health professionals differentiate between mental disorders and spiritual emergencies. Our National Survey shows that 79 percent of responders use DSM-IV in practice, yet only 47 percent consider clients' religious or spiritual beliefs in determining a diagnosis, despite the instructions of the manual that they should do so. This indicates that mental health practitioners need to become better informed about this issue.

Through the past few editions of the DSM, there has been a general trend to emphasize diagnosis as a process that examines symptoms in the context of the person's overall psychosocial functioning, experience of stressors, and relevant medical and physical conditions. There has been greater attention to variations in cultural patterns, norms, and the meaning that individuals attribute to their experiences. Even the concept of mental disorder is recognized to be overly simplistic because it implies an artificial division between physical and mental aspects of the person. It is helpful to restate the definition of mental disorder used in the DSM-IV (APA, xxi-xxii):

[A mental disorder] is conceptualized as a clinically significant behavioral or psychological syndrome or pattern that occurs in an individual and that is associated with present distress (e.g., a painful symptom) or disability (i.e., impairment in one or more important areas of functioning) or with a significantly increased risk of suffering death, pain, disability, or an important loss of freedom. In addition, this syndrome or pattern must not be merely an expectable and culturally sanctioned response to a particular event, for example, the death of a loved one.

Spiritual emergencies do meet the criteria in the first sentence (a clinically significant pattern in an individual, involving distress and risks). However, not all spiritual emergencies meet the criteria of the second sentence. Some spiritual emergencies are expectable reactions to dramatic life changes (such as diagnosis of a terminal illness, traumatic loss, or sudden opening to transpersonal awareness in peak or pit experiences). And most have a limited duration, as with other crises. A spiritual emergency includes the potential for growth in working through the process. In addition, there are peak and pit experiences that catalyze rapid spiritual growth but do not cause the debilitation of a crisis, and hence do not qualify as spiritual emergencies.

For example, a peak experience by definition involves intrinsically pleasant, even euphoric feelings rather than distress. In theory of stress, this is called *eustress*. But eustress is still stress, and too much of a good thing can cause overload and turn into distress. Eustress mobilizes excitement, enthusiasm, and creativity rather than anxiety, hopelessness, and despair. Since peak experiences may involve dramatic changes of states of consciousness and extraordinary thoughts and feelings, care must be taken not to confuse them with hallucinations or delusions.

Pit experiences by definition always involve intrinsically unpleasant feelings. But the associated psychosocial disruption may be manageable through a person's ordinary coping skills and resources. In this case, the pit experience would qualify as neither a spiritual emergency nor a mental disorder.

There is another important qualifier in the second sentence of the definition of a mental disorder. The syndrome or pattern must not be a *culturally sanctioned* response to a particular event. The authors state:

A clinician who is unfamiliar with the nuances of an individual's cultural frame of reference may incorrectly judge as psychopathology those normal variations in behavior, belief, or experience that are particular to the individual's culture. For example, certain religious practices or beliefs (e.g., hearing or seeing a deceased relative during bereavement) may be misdiagnosed as manifestations of a Psychotic Disorder. (p. xxiv)

This means that behaviors and beliefs held to be "normal" in one religious or cultural context could be viewed as "abnormal" in another context. When a practitioner does not share the spiritual framework of the client, there is an increased danger of biased and inaccurate diagnosis related to the ethnocentrism, religious assumptions, and theoretical beliefs of the practitioner. Diagnosis must take place with regard for the cultural, religious, and spiritual beliefs and practices of the person.

This matter of "normality" is complicated by the fact that every spiritual and cultural group has variations within it. It is quite possible that a person could have a valuable, life-enhancing peak experience that is deemed abnormal by members of his or her religious reference group. If the practitioner merely takes the position that the standard of normality of the group should be imposed on the person, then practice becomes nothing more than norm enforcement rather than spiritually sensitive helping. Maslow (1970) pointed out that religious organizations can promote and support peak experiences. But they also can inhibit and punish them, so spiritually sensitive dialogue with the client is crucial in helping him or her to sort this out. Assessment of the psychosocial impacts of participation in religious groups is discussed in Chapter 8.

In order to assist culturally and spiritually sensitive diagnosis, the DSM-IV offers information on cultural variations pertinent to particular disorders. For example, in the discussion of the cross-cultural diagnosis of schizophrenia, the authors of DSM-IV caution, "Ideas that may appear to be delusional in one culture (e.g., sorcery and witchcraft) may be commonly held in another. In some cultures, visual or auditory hallucinations with a religious content may be a normal part of religious experience (e.g., seeing the Virgin Mary or hearing God's voice)" (p. 281).

The advantage of such cautions is that practitioners are guided not to brand everyone who has a different experience of reality from their own as psychopathic. But notice the implicit bias in the language of DSM-IV: visionary experiences that are meaningful to people are still branded as hallucinations, albeit "normal" ones. How nice that mystics and visionaries are now considered culturally normative hallucinators rather than just plain hallucinators!

A *hallucination* is defined as "a sensory perception that has the compelling sense of reality of a true perception but that occurs without external stimulation of the relevant sensory organ" (p. 767). Hallucinations may occur in any sensory mode (auditory, gustatory, olfactory, tactile, visual, and somatic). This definition requires that the diagnoser know what *is* the nature of reality. This is a fundamental spiritual question. As we have seen in the review of religious and nonsectarian spiritual perspectives, there are many different views of the nature of reality, many of which contradict each other. Social workers (and all other helping professionals) are not trained to be master metaphysicians, and we certainly have no authority to dictate spiritual beliefs to clients, so we urge great caution in making any such judgments during assessment.

The same dilemma appears when trying to decide what constitutes a *delusion*. According to DSM-IV, a delusion is "a false belief based on incorrect inference about external reality that is firmly sustained despite what almost everyone else believes and despite what constitutes incontrovertible and obvious proof or evidence to the contrary. The belief is not one ordinarily accepted by other members of the person's culture or subculture (e.g., it is not an article of faith)" (p. 765).

But it is indeed an important question for people of all spiritual perspectives to distinguish between false (but apparently real) perceptions and genuine perceptions—*within the context of their own personal understanding of reality as it is influenced by personal experience and their cultural and spiritual group contexts.* It is not important for people to make this decision based on the social worker's understanding of reality. Because this is a complicated process, we will offer some considerations that social workers can use in dialogue with clients in evaluating transpersonal experiences.

Indeed, since social workers are committed to advocate for social justice, we cannot ignore the possibility that certain commonly held religious beliefs may in fact be delusional and detrimental, based on some other criterion of justice than simply "majority rules" the nature of reality. For example, during the period of slavery in the United States, most white people in this country believed that slavery was divinely justified. Many considered that African Americans and Indigenous peoples were subhuman and devoid of a soul, thereby rationalizing all manner of atrocities. Perhaps this was a form of mass delusion, serving the purposes of oppressors. Thank goodness that enough people dissented ("deviated") from this so-called normal belief so that in time it was overturned. We must ask ourselves: What kind of destructive mass delusions continue?

Ironically, in many Asian-originated spiritual systems, the common Western belief in the autonomy of an individual ego is considered itself to be a delusion at the heart of egocentrism, ethnocentrism, and environmental destruction. We mention this only to point out the difficulties and profundities that loom as soon as we try to make absolute judgments about the nature of reality in a professional helping context.

Here is a further wrinkle. DSM-IV excludes from the definition of *hallucination* "false perceptions" that occur during dreaming or falling asleep or just waking up. These are very common. Everyone dreams and most people remember dreams and near-sleep unusual perceptions some of the time. But, DSM-IV terms these "false" perceptions. This begs the question of whether there are distinct dream-world realities, for example. When we are within a dream, it is certainly real to us at the time (Jung's psychic reality). Indeed, the dream or near-sleep vision can be a source of tremendous spiritual insight that is much "truer" than our usual waking, ego-bound ways of viewing reality.

Further, there are many states of consciousness besides waking and dream states (Robbins, Chatterjee & Canda, 1998). A state of consciousness is an organized pattern and style of overall mental functioning at any given time (Tart, 1975). An *altered state of consciousness* is a pattern of mental functioning that is significantly different from the ordinary alert waking state. These include states associated with dreaming, deep relaxation, various types of meditation, biofeedback, sensory deprivation (e.g., fasting and isolation), sensory hyperstimulation (e.g., intense drumming or dancing), and psychoactive drug use (Achterberg, 1985; Bourguignon, 1979; Grof & Halifax, 1977; Masters & Houston, 1966; Pelletier & Garfield, 1976). Many kinds of altered states of consciousness are actively promoted in religious groups so that they give access to more profound understandings of reality, not "false" beliefs or "hallucinations." Perhaps the DSM-IV should recognize this wider variety of states of consciousness when making a distinction from hallucinations.

Actually, the DSM-IV has introduced some categories of spiritually oriented problems and mental syndromes that are unique to religious contexts. For example, Appendix I of DSM-IV includes a glossary of many culture-bound syndromes that are perceived as problematic within particular cultures but may not be recognized or present in others. Many of these have an explicit spiritual or religious connotation—for example, ghost sickness (among some Indigenous Americans), evil eye (*mal de ojo*) among Mediterranean people, spirit sickness (*shin-byung*) among Koreans, and *qigong* psychotic reaction among practitioners of a Chinese martial art.

Unfortunately, the descriptions are brief and often misleading. For example, *shin-byung* is described as a Korean folk label for a syndrome characterized by anxiety and somatic complaints leading to dissociation and possession by ancestral spirits. In fact, *shin-byung* is better understood as a culture-specific shamanic form of a spiritual emergency. The disorders associated with *shin-byung* are manifestations of a call by spirits (not necessarily ancestors) to a person to become a shaman. Therefore, it is not a mental disorder or syndrome, but rather a transformational spiritual crisis, which, when successfully resolved, leads to a new social role as shaman and to skills in applying transpersonal states of consciousness in this role (Canda, 1982).

Spiritual problems and crises that do not involve mental disorders can be categorized under a new V Code in DSM-IV: V62.89 Religious or Spiritual Problem (p. 685). It is described as follows:

> This category can be used when the focus of clinical attention is a religious or spiritual problem. Examples include distressing experiences that involve loss or questioning of faith, problems associated with conversion to a new faith, or questioning of spiritual values that may not necessarily be related to an organized church or religious institution.

Advocates for this new category distinguished between a religious problem and a spiritual problem (Lukoff, Lu & Turner, 1992, 1995; Turner, Lukoff, Barnhouse & Lu, 1995). According to them, a *religious problem* relates to distressing experiences pertaining to participation in formal religious institutions and adherence to their beliefs. Their examples include distress relating to changes in religious membership or belief, unusually intense adherence to religious beliefs and practices, loss or questioning of religious faith, guilt at committing a transgression against religious principles, and participation in destructive religious groups.

A *spiritual problem* relates to distressing experiences of a transpersonal nature or that involve powerful questioning of one's fundamental spiritual values that underpin the sense of self and reality. These include peak and pit experiences and spiritual emergencies. Their examples include distress associated with mystical experiences, near-death experiences, meditation-associated difficulties, and crises of meaning associated with terminal illness and addictions. These may or may not be related to participation in a religious institution. The differentiating factor is the transpersonal nature of the experiences that become distressing. The distinction in DSM-IV is simpler and less specific: religious problems pertain to religious institutional participation, and spiritual problems relate to spiritual issues outside a religious context.

For our purposes, one crucial distinction is between a spiritual emergence experience that leads to a crisis (which should be designated by the appropriate V Code) and that which contributes to a mental disorder. Another important distinction is between a spiritual growth experience or emergency that superficially resembles a mental disorder and bona-fide mental disorders. The Religious or Spiritual Problem V Code acknowledges that a religious or spiritual growth issue or crisis merits clinical assistance, but it is not pathologized.

However, as Lukoff (1985) pointed out, religious or spiritual problems may coexist and interact with mental disorders. So a person with schizophrenia, paranoid type who also grew up with an idea of a wrathful punishing God may have delusions of being persecuted by God. This would suggest that long-term treatment should address the mental disorder through appropriate combinations of medication, psychosocial support, and community-based case management. As the person with schizophrenia feels safe and coherent enough to engage in dialogue, the religious problem could be addressed through spiritually sensitive discussion and collaboration with the client's spiritual support system. This approach takes mental disorders and disabilities seriously, but it does not reduce the person to the disorder. Rather, the person is helped to deal with the disability as much as possible, and religious and spiritual strengths and resources are enlisted for this purpose.

Nelson (1994) cautioned against two extreme forms of argument. One extreme is represented by the antipsychiatry movement, which views all psychiatric diagnoses and treatments as arbitrary, coercive, and spiritually destructive. In some versions of this, mental disorders are seen as nothing more than social constructions that justify enforcement of social conventions. Psychoses are seen as mystical experiences that are misunderstood. In this view, pre-egoic or ego-confused experiences are misrepresented as trans-egoic experiences.

The other extreme argument is to say that all transpersonal experiences are nothing more than delusions and hallucinations, involving regression to pre-egoic modes of irrational functioning, flights of fantasy to avoid uncomfortable realities, or delusions related to inability to distinguish clearly between the egoic self and the environment. This mistake reduces trans-egoic experiences to pre-egoic (or confused egoic) experiences. Wilber (1995) calls these two errors *the pre/trans fallacy.*

Nelson presented a detailed examination of mental disorders in relation to transpersonal experiences and spiritual emergencies. He advocated for a holistic approach to assessment and treatment of people with chronic and persistent mental disorders from a transpersonal theoretical perspective. His book would be valuable for those who are working in the mental health field, especially regarding schizophrenia, bipolar disorder, and borderline personality disorder.

TOPICS FOR ASSESSMENT OF TRANSPERSONAL EXPERIENCES

In this chapter we have considered many assessment issues pertaining to spiritual emergence and spiritual emergencies, including differential diagnosis with regard to possible psychopathology. We have advocated for a spiritually sensitive approach to assessment that is client centered. The assessment process should help the client to tell her or his story of spiritual development in terms of her or his own spiritual perspective, unfettered by the presumptions of the social worker. Therefore, we present a series of topics that can be used in dialogue with clients to help them assess the nature and significance of the experience.

Describing the Immediate Situation

Initially, it is important to assess whether the client perceives the transpersonal experience as a spiritual emergency. Is it a peak or pit experience? If so, does it constitute a crisis? If not a crisis, the discussion can continue without a sense of urgency or danger.

If the client identifies the experience as a crisis, then a safety assessment is necessary immediately. Is the person able to communicate coherently? If the person is feeling overwhelmed, what can be done to provide a sense of security, reassurance, and support by professionals and loved ones? Is the person at risk of harm to self or others? Is there suicidal ideation, intent, or a suicide plan? Where there is immanent risk of harm, then protective measures should be taken until the person establishes sufficient emotional balance and cognitive function to enable continued therapeutic dialogue.

Once safety is assured, the story of the transpersonal experience can be explored in more detail. What occurred specifically? What was the physical place of the event? What precipitated the experience? Was it entirely spontaneous? Did it feel like a revelation or incoming of an insight or influence from a transcendent or supernatural source? Was it associated with a specific practice, such as prayer, meditation, visualization technique, or group ritual? What was the experiencer's state of consciousness? Were there any paranormal or mystical experiences? What senses were involved?

Identifying Predisposing Factors

What factors prepared the person to be open to this experience? What inner spiritual strengths and coping skills had the person developed that may have encouraged this experience? For example, is the person very introspective? Has he or she been generally preoccupied with spiritual questions and quests? What environmental resources has the person been using in support of spiritual development, such as spiritual reading material, religious group participation, being in touch with nature, feeling close to God? Are life stage developmental issues influencing this experience and its interpretation?

Are there any distressing predisposing factors, such as physical or mental disorders that could generate alterations of perception and consciousness? Has the person been experiencing intense distress, related to a life stage transition or psychosocial crisis? If yes, then medical and psychological assessment should rule out pathogenic hallucinations or delusions. Even if physical or mental disorders are involved in the experience, the possible meaningful aspects of the experience need to be explored.

Exploring Interpretations of the Event

How does the person interpret the meaning and significance of the experience? Were there important insights or messages within the experience? What values were conveyed? What images, symbols, metaphors, paradoxes, or parables best relay the nature of the experience? Are there religious or cultural stories familiar to the client that provide understanding? What are the implications of the experience for understanding and relating with oneself, other people, other beings, and ultimate reality? Are there immediate fruits of the experience, such as enhanced energy, creativity, insights into life problems, deepened sense of rapport?

If the experience has a strong negative tone, as in a pit experience sense of dread, or attack by demonic forces, then special care should be taken. Again, sense of safety should be ensured. What spiritual or religious practices and support systems could lend a sense of protection? Does the person wish to be referred to a religious specialist who can perform a necessary prayer or ritual for protection? What is the potential for resolution and growth through this negative experience?

Locating the Experience within a Complete Spiritual Development Narrative

If the person wishes to explore more deeply how this experience relates to his or her overall path of spiritual development, the time line for graphing spiritual emergence can be used to help illustrate the client's life story. First, identify other key spiritual turning points in life by date and mark them on a long sheet of paper to demarcate life phases. Consider how these turning points relate to gradual emergence experiences, gentle breakthroughs of awareness, or pit or peak experiences. Were any of these crises? How did they relate to life cycle events and stages of physical or psychosocial growth? Each of the significant spiritual turning point events could be assessed using the topics above.

Then long-term patterns of development can be identified by observing trends, themes, major characters, changes of spiritual styles, master stories, spiritually influential people and sources, key values, new or recurring symbols, and altered states of consciousness. The pattern of flow from pre-egoic through egoic to trans-egoic experiences and modes of consciousness can be identified.

What is the future potential implied by the current experience in relation to one's overall spiritual emergence story? Are there indications about possible changes of vocation? Is there any sense of what one should do next, in the near- or long-term future? In the case of a crisis, is there any indication of a light at the end of the tunnel? How can the learning of the past and present be applied to enhance one's future spiritual development?

SUMMARY

In this chapter, we have applied insights from many religious and non-sectarian spiritual perspectives to the assessment of spiritual development. We discussed occasions of gradual and rapid spiritual emergence; pit, peak, and plateau experiences; and spiritual emergencies. We considered the relation between spiritual development and stages of the life cycle. We examined similarities and differences between transpersonal experiences, spiritual crises, and psychopathology. We provided topics for dialogue with clients to help with assessment of transpersonal experiences and how they fit into one's overall life narrative.

We wish to emphasize the importance of a sense of humility before the mystery of spiritual development. First, there is often a sense of mystery, sacredness, destiny, or fate in the events and flow of spiritual emergence. People may even feel propelled by spiritual forces beyond understanding and drawn to spiritual realities beyond their ken. In our efforts to provide guidance for understanding and assessing spiritual development, we do not wish to diminish or discount this mystery. Rather, we wish to appreciate it.

There is also a practical reason for humility. The various theories of human development and functioning that have informed this discussion are not yet well enough developed conceptually or tested empirically for us to use them authoritatively. We believe it is appropriate that they be used only as guides to open up a spiritually sensitive dialogue with clients to help them to unfold their own stories.

EXERCISES

7.1. Assessing Your Own Spiritual Development

Before trying to assess clients' spiritual development, it is best to have a clear understanding of your own development. Self-understanding provides a basis for rapport with clients on their own spiritual journeys. In addition, it is best to practice the developmental assessment strategies in order to become familiar and comfortable with them before using them with clients.

Construct a spiritual emergence narrative for yourself. Follow the instructions in this chapter for graphing a spiritual development time line. Take into account the topics for assessment set out at the end of this chapter. Once the time line is graphed, write a spiritual autobiography, including past, present, and future potential and aspirations.

Adapt the time line idea for your own interests and style. Rather than drawing a time line, you could write an autobiographical essay. The time line and/or essay could be decorated with pictures, symbols, and colors that give vividness to the life story.

7.2. Assessing a Friend's Spiritual Development

Once you are familiar with this assessment process, identify a friend who would be interested to reflect on a selected spiritual emergence event with your assistance. Follow the topics for discussion indicated at the end of this chapter by focusing on the selected event and then putting it into the context of a spiritual development time line or essay.

7.3. Assessing a Client's Spiritual Development

Now you are ready to try this assessment process with a client who wishes your assistance in understanding his or her process of spiritual emergence. We recommend that you invite the client to tell his or her story in his or her own terms and symbols, in a manner appropriate to age and comfort level. Do not impose any assumptions about whether there are or should be peak or pit experiences or spiritual emergencies. Use the guidelines in Figure 7.1 to help you support the client in telling and illustrating the life story but not to constrain it.

CHAPTER EIGHT

UNDERSTANDING AND ASSESSING THERAPEUTIC PROCESS, SPIRITUAL ACTIVITIES, AND ETHICAL ISSUES

The way of the Creative
works through change and transformation,
so that each thing receives its true nature and destiny
and comes into permanent accord
with the Great Harmony.

The Book of Changes, Confucianism
(trans. Wilhelm & Baynes, 1976, p. 371).

INTRODUCTION

In this chapter, we provide a vantage on therapeutic process and spiritually based helping activities. First, we draw on cross-cultural studies of rituals to develop an understanding of transformational dynamics within the process of helping that can support spiritual development. Second, we present ethical guidelines for deciding when it is appropriate to address spirituality or religion and to incorporate explicit spiritually based helping activities. Third, we discuss issues of client participation in religious or spiritual groups, including identification of a client's spiritual propensity and assessment of psychosocial impacts of participation in spiritual groups.

SOCIAL WORK PRACTICE AS A TRANSFORMATIONAL PROCESS

Social workers often describe themselves as change agents. We promote beneficial changes for individual and family well-being as well as conditions of mutual support and justice in larger social systems. As we have seen in the previous chapter's discussion of spiritual development, spiritually sensitive practice involves creating conditions and activities that are conducive to growth and transformation for individuals and communities. This means that spiritually sensitive social work practice includes but is more than problem solving. It includes but is more than promoting coping, adapting, or recovery. In keeping with the strengths perspective, spiritually sensitive practice identifies people's talents, skills, capacities, and resources and mobilizes them in the service of both their immediate goals and their highest aspirations and potentials.

When change is transformational, it moves people forward on their spiritual paths. Transformational practice recognizes challenges and crises as opportunities for growth on a spiritual journey. This does not mean that a social worker should hold a presumption about what the client's aspirations should be. Rather, the spiritually sensitive social worker helps in a way that supports the potential for growth that is inherent within the client and supports the client to develop according to his or her own life path.

When we pay attention to the transformational dynamics within the helping process, we can flow with them like a rafter moving with the river current. The social worker does not originate the transformational energy, but he or she can steer and channel the raft of change along with it. By drawing on cross-cultural studies of transformational rituals for healing and life transition, we present a conceptual model for understanding and working with the transformational process. This model is a simplification, but as a guide, it can help us to flow more confidently on the river current of spiritual transformation.

Therapeutic Transformation and Ritual Studies

The cross-cultural study of rituals has yielded a great deal of insight into the ways in which people create dramatic, artistic, and religious formats to mark important life transitions. Contemporary ritual studies embrace many fields, ranging from anthropology to the dramatic arts and religious studies (Bell, 1992; Grimes, 1995; Heimbrock & Boudewijnse, 1990; Turner, 1992). These studies point out the great variety of rituals and their purposes. They caution against overgeneralization about universal patterns of action and symbolism in ritual process and urge us to be attentive to variations by culture, situation, purpose, gender, and other aspects of human diversity. However, they acknowledge that one of the remarkable commonalties among human beings is our tendency to mark important life transitions, such as a shift through a stage in the life cycle, changes in social status or role, and periods of personal and community crisis.

Rituals not only mark transitions; they also create them, celebrate them, and help us to pass through them safely. Indeed, many rituals of healing and helping can be thought of as rites of passage that help a person to pass from a condition of distress to a new condition of restored or enhanced life (Eliade, 1971; Frank, 1963; Kiefer & Cowan, 1979; Kiev, 1972; Lincoln, 1981; Scheff, 1979; Turner, 1965, 1969, 1974; Turner, 1992; Van Gennep, 1960; Wallace, 1966). Therefore, theory of ritual process provides us with keen insight into the workings of transformational process, which is so important in spiritually sensitive social work.

By drawing on this body of work, we present a model of therapeutic transformation that can guide our planning of activities in the helping process (adapted from Canda, 1988a). This model is a heuristic device that can lend insight and guidance for practice. It supplements more conventional models of the helping process by adding a focus on the potential for spiritual growth that is inherent within social work processes.

The Nature of Change and Therapeutic Transformation

Social work practice is designed to produce therapeutic change, that is, an enhancement of a person's or social system's situation. From the standpoint of spiritually sensitive practice, we recognize that each enhancement is a step in the life process of spiritual emergence, so we need to consider more carefully what we mean by these two key terms: *therapeutic* and *transformation*.

There is a significant nuance of the expression *therapy* that is generally omitted from common usage in social work. The Greek word *therapeutes* meant a healer who serves both the human and the divine (Hillman, 1975). So when we refer to *therapeutic* transformation, we do not restrict ourselves to thinking of social work as a form of psychotherapy, for social work's scope is much greater than that. Rather, we wish to emphasize a spiritual orientation to the helping process in all forms of social work practice. To improvise with Grof's term *holotropic,* discussed in the previous chapter, *therapeutic* transformation is change that moves people toward wholeness in relation with self, other people, the universe, and the ground of being itself, however we understand it.

By *transformation,* we mean a significant, relatively rapid change of condition, such as sudden leaps through peak and pit experiences. In general, especially as social work increasingly embraces brief modes of helping, such as solution-focused therapy, we are midwifing clients through transformational processes.

As we have seen in the discussion of spiritual emergencies, transformational experiences have great potential for enhancing a person's insight, vitality, sense of purpose, and way of life. However, getting to that point of breakthrough may depend on first going through a period of breakdown. Transformational processes often occur spontaneously, as in crises. Healing and helping rituals are procedures to help bring a person through the passage to enhanced life. Social work encounters with clients can be thought of as helping rituals.

We will divide the therapeutic transformation process into five phases. The preparation phase involves all that has gone before the helping encounter. Formal helping begins at contact with the social worker and moves through three phases: separation, flux, and aggregation. After formal helping, the person continues with life in a more spontaneous way, hopefully more resilient and reliant on his or her strengths and resources (congregation).

Phase One: Preparation (Pretherapy)

English idioms portray the transformation process vividly. In a time of crisis, we may say, "I am falling apart." This is the phase of crisis in which we feel overwhelmed and out of control. When this experience is intense, we may seek help from someone who can help us to "get it together." Our previous life experiences predispose us to perceive and respond to a crisis or life transition in a certain way. We are prepared by our learning of problem-solving strategies and acquisition of resilient qualities. When a challenge goes beyond our usual means and resources, we consult a professional helper. Then, formal helping beings.

Phase Two: Separation (Beginning Formal Helping)

In social work practice, we first welcome a person into the helping relationship. A space, such as an office or the client's home, is designated for a special kind of encounter dedicated to helping. We cue the person that she or he is being separated from the ordinary life situation in which he or she feels stuck. We indicate our intentions to help. We identify the person's story, troubles, aspirations. This is the phase of analysis, which literally means "to take apart." We deconstruct the situation and open up new possibilities. At this phase, it is important that the client be assured of respect, trust, and safety in the helping relationship. If he or she had been feeling overwhelmed by chaos, this phase of helping emphasizes restoration of a sense of protection, cognitive understanding, and hope for the future.

Phase Three: Flux

Disorder has its advantages. The very fact that a person's status quo is shaken up means that she or he is likely to be more amenable to change and growth. So as the helping process continues, it is important to open up more possibilities, new ways of looking at things, and unforeseen solutions and to summon up all the personal strengths and environmental resources that can support the change process. This means that the old rigid patterns need to be dismantled.

This is the phase of flux, in which maximum possibilities for creativity are opened up. Idiomatic expressions for this are being "neither here nor there" or being "betwixt and between." The anthropologist Victor Turner (1965, 1969, 1974) referred to this as the *liminal phase*, which literally means the "passageway phase." When we stand in a passageway, we are not in any particular room (which can feel ambiguous and disconcerting), but we have the possibility to move from one room to another (which can feel hopeful and empowering).

Turner pointed out that healing rituals and rites of passage emphasize two dimensions of this phase. One is the sense that ordinary personal or cultural programs, norms, and expectations are temporarily suspended. Many possibilities are opened up. People who are going through this antistructural process tend to form a sense of community bond or egalitarian mutual support, which he termed *communitas.* However, this lack of structure needs to be complemented by careful protection, support, and guidance by the helpers and healers. Creative chaos is complemented by supportive order, thus catalyzing the transformational process. The complementarity of antistructure and structure is similar to the concepts of morphostasis and morphogenesis in dynamic systems theory (Robbins, Chatterjee & Canda, 1998). *Morphostasis* means "form maintaining." It is the function of living systems that protects and restores the integrity of a living system, so that it can survive over time. *Morphogenesis* means "form creating." It is the function that adapts, changes, and creates new patterns in a living system, so that it can develop and grow over time. Morphostasis and morphogenesis are complementary and necessary aspects of the dynamic transformation process in living systems, called *homeokinesis.* Morphostasis alone results in stagnation. Morphogenesis alone results in chaos.

Phase Four: Aggregation

It is necessary but not sufficient to open up possibilities. If we are only deconstructed, we are left destroyed. It is critical that deconstruction be followed by reconstruction at an enhanced level of functioning and fulfillment. This is the third phase of helping, aggregation. In this phase, we help clients to incorporate insights, stabilize lifestyle changes, and work through these implications with significant others. This is the phase of "getting it together." A sense of closure is reached, and the client is helped to prepare for reentry into ordinary life. In effect, this three-phase helping process assists the client to rise above a constraining situation, journey to a peak of new possibilities, and then integrate this new learning at a plateau of enhanced living.

Phase Five: Congregation (Posttherapy)

When we achieve a sense of successful passage, our lives are again characterized by spontaneous creativity and enjoyment. We no longer have to rely on professional helpers (at least until another serious challenge), so we may say with satisfaction, "I feel as if I have it together." Ideally, we are able to incorporate the learning from the helping process into self-help and mutual support in ongoing life.

The Flow of Transformation

So far we have described the process of transformation with reference to individual growth over the course of an entire helping relationship. Whether the relationship lasts an hour, a day, weeks, or a year, it can be understood in terms of this flow from the spontaneous experience of life challenge through the helping process of separation, flux, and aggregation, and on to independent spontaneous living. Of course, a person may seek help through transformation many times throughout life, so this process would recur. In addition, within the total span of the helping process, there are many small transformational experiences. For example, each helping encounter proceeds through a rite of helping, from initial greeting, through therapeutic work, to planning for future work and closure of the session.

Within each helping encounter, there may be moments of powerful insights or catharses that break through habitual ways of thinking, feeling, and acting. The model of therapeutic transformation reminds us to be careful about these cathartic experiences. *Catharses* involve recalling and releasing painful memories and feelings. Therefore, social workers should evoke them only in the context of a safe and supportive environment. The released pain needs to be converted into creative energy that catalyzes growth. Cathartic episodes need to be processed and integrated emotionally, physically, intellectually, and spiritually so that a sense of closure is reached before concluding a session.

The division of the formal helping process into three phases is an artificial simplification of a flowing experience. We feel this flow in a musical composition that builds theme and rhythm, crescendos, and then resolves. We sense it in the plot of a story, in which a narrative world is first created, tensions are introduced, and then there is a denouement. Within each musical composition or story, as in all other transformational forms, there are many variations of this flow.

We can relate this model to the familiar stages of therapeutic group development, from group formation and norm establishment (separation), through conflict resolution and synergistic interactions (flux), to completion of goals and reaching closure (aggregation) (Anderson & Carter, 1990). And we know that in music and story, as well as therapeutic work, conflict, complications, and catharses can occur at any time. As each of these breakthrough events is worked through, the sense of dynamic energy is enhanced.

Using Metaphors and Stories of Transformation

This model of therapeutic transformation encourages us to draw on metaphors and stories, pertinent to clients, that demonstrate the spiritual growth potential inherent in their experiences. Once we identify the spiritual perspective of the client, we can ask her or him to identify symbols and master stories of transformation and crisis resolution that are inspirational and encouraging. For example, Christians may look to the story of the passion, death, and resurrection of Jesus. Jews may reflect on the exodus from servitude in Egypt. Hindus may consider the story from the Bhagavad Gita about the crisis of the hero Arjuna confronting battle and how the divine Krishna advised.

If no master stories of transformation are familiar to the client, this itself is an important indicator. It is much easier to wander aimlessly when we do not have any map to guide us at a time of feeling lost. In this case, especially if the client is not religious, nonreligious metaphors for transformation could be explored—for example, the butterfly emerging from a cocoon, the moon moving through its phases, or the passage from the coldness of winter to new vitality of spring.

In any case, it is important to personalize these metaphors and stories. Discussion with the client can explore how he or she has experienced transformation previously. One could ask the client to recall important dreams that depicted an experience of struggle and victory or resolution. Previous life experiences of challenge and courage can be recalled, identifying successful strategies and calling up reserves of resiliency and courage. People who have been inspirational for their ability to grow, overcome crises, and transform themselves and other people can be reflected on. When these are ancestors, relatives, and friends, a sense of spiritual kinship and solidarity can be mobilized. If these inspiring figures are deceased ancestors or sacred beings, clients may find insight by engaging in an inner dialogue with them, asking for guidance and support. If they are living spiritual helpers, relatives, or friends, clients can be reminded to connect with these significant people.

An Example of Transformational Practice

In spiritually sensitive practice, we should be especially attentive to these occasions of transformation, both at particular moments of breakthrough and in the overall process of helping. By supporting this transformational potential, we encourage the ongoing spiritual development of our clients.

The transformational power of social work can be greatly increased when it is possible to connect the client's personal experience with a spiritual tradition and community of support for the transformational process. The following fictionalized example is composed from several of my (EC) experiences with former clients.

Amy was experiencing stressors related to her personal spiritual development at the same time as dealing with disruptive behaviors of her teenage son and tensions with her husband. It happened that this client was a devout Catholic who practiced a form of meditation in a Catholic prayer group. I met with Amy and other members of her family over a period of several months, sometimes with Amy alone and sometimes with the family together.

Amy had a series of dreams during this period in which she was trapped in a house. In an early dream, she could look through a keyhole in the door to the outside and see a beautiful field. She longed to go out to this field but could not open the door. In another dream, the sense of family crisis was vividly portrayed by the fact that the house in which she was trapped was burning to the ground. These dreams were frightening and implied hopelessness and helplessness. However, the fact that Amy saw another world outside conveyed the possibility that there was an alternative, if only she could find out how to open that door.

Since Amy was familiar with meditation, we agreed to create a meditation experience that would explore the possibility of liberation from this burning house. She began with a prayer, according to her tradition, assuring her of divine protection and support. Amy relaxed, followed her breath, and centered awareness within herself. She visualized herself in the house. She then asked for divine guidance about how to find a way out. Suddenly she realized that there was a trap door in the floor and knew that she should go below.

Although she was nervous, she called on God for help. Feeling encouraged, she climbed down the dark stairway. Deep below, she discovered a cavernous illuminated room with a pool of water. As she approached, she noticed an old bearded man with a kindly and reassuring manner. The old man beckoned her to enter the water. She did so and felt renewed and strengthened, as though she had returned to her baptismal water of infancy. Afterward, the old man led her through a passageway that brought her up through a hole in the ground. She emerged into a beautiful sunlit field of flowers.

After this meditation journey, Amy felt that she rediscovered an inner reserve of spiritual vitality and strength as well as a more vivid sense of divine help. She felt confident that there would be a way out of her current crisis, although to get there would require the courage to go deep into a dark place of uncertainty.

As it happened, this dream occurred early in the season of Lent, in which Catholics (as other Christians) commemorate as a community the suffering, death, and resurrection of Jesus. Amy realized that she could become more intentional about linking her own experience of suffering and hope for resolution into the community church celebrations of communion, periods of fasting and reflection, scripture readings, and Stations of the Cross, all of which move the Catholic community collectively through the transformation process. Amy decided to use mutually reinforcing parallel processes between her own inner spiritual work and meditation, her therapeutic work, her daily family life, and her church community celebration of Lent.

The dreams, meditation experiences, and religious practices did not make Amy's problems and worries disappear suddenly and magically, but they did infuse her efforts with a sense of hope, strength, and support. She was not going through this alone or aimlessly. Rather, she was following a meaningful pattern of suffering, death, and resurrection within her own life, all with the support of her social worker, her spiritual community, her personal meditation practice, and experience of loving connection with God.

Social Work as Art and Drama

When we consider social work practice in the light of transformational ritual, we are reminded to pay attention to its aesthetic, emotive, and dramatic qualities. If we work in a bland square office and treat helping only as an analytical discussion or problem-solving activity, our helping will hardly be vibrant, beautiful, inspiring, or conducive to transformation. Symbols of transformation, inspirational people, gestures of caring, music, motion, and the arts can be embedded within a therapeutic narrative and drama of resilience, growth, and victory. In Chapter 9, we suggest how to help clients construct explicit rituals of transformation. But all forms and settings of social work practice can be enhanced in this way.

ETHICAL GUIDELINES FOR USING SPIRITUALLY BASED ACTIVITIES

The National Survey of NASW members identified a wide range of spiritually oriented helping practices employed by social workers. These include activities done directly with clients (e.g., prayer, meditation, or rituals), activities suggested to clients as "homework" assignments outside the session (e.g., reading of scripture or inspirational material, journaling), activities done by the social worker privately to prepare for practice (e.g., private prayer or meditation), and connecting with religious helpers and spiritual support systems (see Table 8.1). Note that a higher percentage of respondents indicated it is *appropriate* to use every spiritually oriented activity than those who actually did use them. For all but three activities (pray with a client, touch for healing purposes, and participate in the client's religious/spiritual rituals as a practice intervention), more than two-thirds of respondents believed it is appropriate to use them. Also, except for the three least often approved activities and dream assessment, more than half of respondents have performed these helping activities. This finding shows that most social workers are likely to recognize the usefulness and ethical appropriateness of a wide range of spiritually oriented practices. The three least approved practices are most directive and intimately involved with a client's personal life space and boundary, so it is understandable that workers would be cautious about them. Our ethical guidelines reflect these concerns.

Table 8.1
National NASW Survey: Practitioners' Views on Spiritually Oriented
Helping Activities

Question	Have Personally Done with Clients		Is an Appropriate Social Work Helping Activity (Intervention)	
	(%)	(n)	(%)	(n)
33. Use or recommend religious or spiritual books or writings	59.0	1,197	80.0	1,577
34. Pray privately *for* a client	57.9	1,167	70.6	1,344
35. Pray *with* a client	28.3	571	51.7	980
36. Use religious language or concepts	68.2	1,371	75.8	1,482
37. Use nonsectarian spiritual language or concepts	87.2	1,750	92.6	1,817
38. Recommend participation in a religious or spiritual support system or activity	81.3	1,639	87.5	1,728
39. Touch clients for "healing" purposes	14.6	296	24.4	472
40. Help clients develop religious/ spiritual rituals as a clinical intervention (e.g., house blessings, visiting graves of relatives, celebrating life transitions	63.3	1,281	81.3	1,591
41. Participate in a client's religious/ spiritual rituals as a practice intervention	18.2	369	37.6	720
42. Encourage the clients to do regular religious/spiritual self-reflective diary keeping or journal keeping	53.8	1,093	81.9	1,610
43. Discuss role of religious or spiritual beliefs in relation to significant others	80.7	1,637	90.3	1,784
44. Assist clients to reflect critically on religious or spiritual beliefs or practices	64.2	1,292	77.1	1,508
45. Help clients assess the meaning of spiritual experiences that occur in dreams	37.2	751	67.4	1,309
46. Help clients consider the spiritual meaning and purpose of his/her current life situation	71.0	1,432	83.2	1,635
47. Help clients reflect on their beliefs about what happens after death	71.8	1,454	87.3	1,728
48. Help clients consider ways their religious/spiritual support systems are *helpful*	94.1	1,910	97.4	1,941
49. Help clients consider ways their religious/spiritual support systems are *harmful*	70.9	1,427	87.0	1702

Overall, less than 9 percent of responders (n = 179) agreed that "integrating religion and spirituality in social work practice conflicts with the NASW Code of Ethics" or "social work's mission." Nearly 80 percent of responders believe that church-state separation does not prevent them from dealing with religion in practice. Nearly 91 percent believe it does not prevent them from dealing with nonsectarian spirituality in practice. This confirms that most social workers are already likely to feel that dealing with spirituality and religion in practice is consistent with professional values. There is also a recognition of the need for careful ethical reflection about it.

On the one hand, this finding demonstrates that there is a wide repertoire of helping activities that can be gleaned from religious and nonsectarian spiritual traditions and support systems. This makes practical sense, since there is much to learn from diverse traditions, often with histories spanning hundreds or thousands of years. As we have discussed, most Americans identify religion or spirituality as an important source of support. In addition, there is a wide and growing range of research that demonstrates beneficial impacts of participation in religious and spiritual practices and support systems. There are hundreds of studies suggesting that prayer and participation in spiritual support systems can aid physical healing and psychosocial resilience (Dossey, 1993; Matthews & Larson, 1995). Further, spirituality and religion are important aspects of both person and environment, so it would be inconsistent for practitioners to ignore them. Indeed, if a social worker avoided or denigrated the religious or spiritual beliefs and practices of a client, this could be construed as a form of discrimination that is prohibited by the NASW Code of Ethics.

But to use religious or explicit spiritually oriented helping activities remains controversial. For many people, even to consider this sets off fire alarm bells about personal discomfort, violating separation of church and state or client self-determination, blurring the boundary between social work and religious service, and imposing moralistic judgments.

We agree that it is very important to use explicit spiritually based practices on the basis of careful ethical reflection, but we do not see this as fundamentally different from ethical decision making about other practice activities. We believe that much of the smoke around the topic will dissipate when practitioners consider the issues according to basic professional standards of ethics and competency.

In order to assist readers in making ethical decisions, we offer some guidelines adapted and expanded from Canda's (1990a) ethical criteria for use of prayer in social work. First, we identify a range of options for activities. Then we suggest conditions under which these options may be appropriate. We offer these guidelines to help you engage in your own ethical decision making rather than as absolute standards. We hope that these guidelines promote further professional discussion and debate.

Options for Spiritually Based Helping Activities

In Table 8.2, the options for using spiritually based activities are ordered according to the degree to which the worker directly and explicitly uses them with a client, from least to most direct and explicit. Ranking activities in this order is helpful because it highlights the increasing level of care and caution that should be taken as we become more explicit and direct. This is so because there is more risk of infringing on clients' freedom and self-determination as we become more assertive and directive. Respondents in our National Survey reflected this concern. Only 35 percent of respondents agreed that they should introduce religion or spirituality by their own discretion; 52 percent felt that the client should first express interest.

The first option is *developing an implicit spiritually sensitive relationship and context.* By *implicit,* we mean that there is no overt reference to religion, spirituality, or transpersonal experiences in the helping situation. Neither the worker nor the client raises spiritual issues in an overt manner. For example, the presenting issues may be practical, like employment assistance or housing, or they may involve existential or transpersonal matters, but the client does not use explicitly religious or spiritual language to describe them.

It is not necessary to use overt religious or spiritual references in order to cultivate a spiritually sensitive relationship and context for helping. When the client is not interested in this or is put off by it, it is certainly better not to. But in our view, establishing at least an implicit spiritually sensitive relationship and context for helping is a prerequisite for competent practice of any kind. Genuine respect; empathy; rapport; compassion; alertness to transformative possibilities; incorporation of inspiring places, people, and symbols; building on clients' capacity for resilience, creativity, and mutual support; attending to the impacts of practice on clients and their social and natural environments; creating agencies and practice settings that are humane, empowering, and ecologically responsible—all of these qualities are essential to good practice.

The ethical issue here is one of risk incurred when not relating in a spiritually sensitive manner. The onus is on the worker to justify why one would not be spiritually sensitive, since neglecting to be so reduces the

Table 8.2
Ethical Considerations for Using Spiritually Based Activities in Social Work

Conditions for Determining When Activities Are Appropriate

A. Client has not expressed interest.
B. Client has expressed interest.
C. *Plus,* a spiritually sensitive relationship is well established.
D. *Plus,* worker has relevant qualifications for particular activities.

Options for Activities

1. Implicit spiritually sensitive relationship and context.
2. Private spiritually based activities by worker.
3. Referral to outside spiritual support systems.
4. Collaboration with outside spiritual support systems.
5. Direct use of spiritual activities by client's request.
6. Direct use of spiritual activities by worker's invitation.

Conditions Present	*Appropriate Options*
A ⟶	1, 2
B ⟶	1, 2, 3; 4 with caution
B and C ⟶	1, 2, 3, 4; 5 with caution
B, C and D ⟶	1, 2, 3, 4, 5; 6 with caution

Source: Adapted from Canda (1990a). Used with permission.

client to an "it" rather than a full human being. When administrators are not spiritually sensitive, workers become expendable human resources rather than respected and cherished colleagues. Spiritual neglect denies our responsibility as social workers for our part in the larger picture of social justice and human-nature interdependence. Therefore, an implicit spiritually sensitive relationship and context for practice is relevant under all practice conditions and circumstances.

Yet we wish to express an important caveat. There is a difference between being implicitly spiritually sensitive and acting on a hidden agenda. For example, if a transpersonally oriented social worker believed that all clients *should* view their crises as "opportunities for growth," this would lead to surreptitious or incompetent manipulations. If a person is overwhelmed with grief, despair, or anger, there is nothing worse than telling her or him, "Don't feel bad; in the long run you will grow from this." If the social worker had a favorite transpersonal technique, such as healing visualization, and sought every opportunity to insinuate it into practice, this would also be a problem for those for whom the practice is irrelevant or objectionable.

The second option, *private spiritually based activities by the worker*, refers to the social worker's use of religious or nonreligious spiritually based activities in his or her private life, as preparation and support for doing social work practice. For example, a worker might practice a form of relaxing meditation to relieve stress after a difficult day and to clarify the mind in preparation for practice. Some workers privately pray for their clients' well-being, believing that this supports their resilience and opens up a divine source of support for helping. These private activities do not infringe on the client and may enhance the worker's ability to help. So when the social worker is committed to a spiritual path and practice, it seems artificial and unnatural to exclude such private activities.

However, another caveat is in order. People pray for help and healing of clients because they believe this is effective in some way. Indeed, there are surprising medical experiments that indicate people may be influenced by prayer at a distance, even without their knowledge (Dossey, 1993). Whatever the empirical evidence, if a social worker believes that a client can be influenced by prayer or other spiritual helping practices, there is an important ethical consideration: Is it proper to influence clients without their informed consent?

Without the client's informed consent, spiritual techniques to manipulate the client are egocentric and presumptuous. If one were to pray for a specific outcome, such as that a client should undergo a religious conversion or become free of an affliction, this would imply that the social worker somehow had superior knowledge, foresight, and power over the client. What human can really know what is ultimately best for the client's spiritual development? What the worker ascertains to be an erroneous spiritual belief may really be the most appropriate place for the client to be. Even with seemingly good intentions, such as to relieve pain or distress, how can we know what role this affliction plays in the client's spiritual unfolding? A hidden manipulative agenda is certainly not what we mean by spiritually sensitive practice. In scientific research settings, covert experimental manipulation of people is highly suspect and is usually prohibited. We believe the same caution should be exercised with spiritual manipulation.

Some healing traditions recommend that helping prayer, without the client's permission, should be of an open, humble, and compassionate nature. For example, one might pray for the client's support and healing according to the client's own best interests and spiritual path. One leaves it to the wisdom of the divine and the choices of the client to work out the specifics.

The third option is *to refer the client to outside spiritually based social support systems.* These might include individuals, such as clergy, religiously based healers, friends, family members, spiritual mentors, or wise elders. These might include support groups such as religious communities, twelve-step programs and other nonsectarian spiritual mutual support groups, spiritual friendship groups, and groups for learning and practicing various types of meditation, prayer, ritual, and spiritually oriented physical disciplines, such as hatha yoga or t'ai chi ch'uan. Referral could also be to places and things, such as beautiful natural parks, retreat centers, and inspirational readings.

This option presumes that the client has expressed interest and that the referral is congruent with the client's beliefs and interests. It might involve helping the client to use a current support system more effectively, restore connection with a support that has been discontinued, or create a new support system. Competent referral also requires that the worker know to whom or what the client is being referred and that an assessment has been made that the outside support will serve the interests of the client. Follow-up should clarify that the contact has been made successfully and that it is working well for the client.

Option 4, *collaboration with an outside spiritually based social support system,* involves an active cooperative relationship between the spiritually based helper or support group and the social worker. In this case, the worker needs to have the commitment and skill to engage in cross-disciplinary and often cross-cultural teamwork. This will be described further in the section on multicultural teamwork in Chapter 9.

Option 5 is *direct use of spiritually based activities by the client's request.* By this we mean that the activities are used directly within the social work relationship and setting. This could be the case with forms of collaboration in which there is a multidisciplinary team operating within an organization, such as chaplains, social workers, nurses, and physicians in a hospice program. The social worker and the religious helper may function as cotherapists or coworkers. This option also includes the possibility that the social worker employ any of the spiritually based activities listed in Table 8.1 on his or her own with the client in the helping session. This presumes that the client has expressed interest and that a spiritually sensitive relationship is well established.

This situation may occur when a client requests a worker to pray with her or to help him design a ritual that would mark an important life transition. In community-based practice, social workers may interact with clients within the context of their religious support systems (Canda & Phaobtong, 1992), so this option requires an even greater degree of specialized training on the part of the worker. For example, if a client asks a social worker for advice about transpersonal experiences related to the practice of New Age channeling of spirit guides, the worker had better have relevant knowledge and skill, as well as comfort, to respond. Acting without relevant competency is a violation of the NASW Code of Ethics. If the social worker is not prepared, then referral or collaboration is an appropriate response.

It is also possible that a client may feel an immediate need for spiritual solace and support that can best come from a spiritual practice dear to him or her. Yet the worker may feel unprepared or uncomfortable engaging in this. For example, if a client invites a social worker to engage in Christian prayer to support the work at hand but the worker does not share that belief or practice, the social worker could offer to be with the client respectfully, with an attitude of quiet support, while the client prays. This response avoids a rude cutting off of the client. It also respects the beliefs and level of comfort and competence of the worker. It would certainly be inappropriate to share a spiritual activity without sincerity and honesty.

Option 6, *direct use of spiritually based activities by the worker's invitation*, is the most controversial and risky. In this situation, a client has not requested it, but the worker may assess that it would be helpful. Here, danger of abrogating the client's self-determination or inappropriate proselytization is greatest. For this reason, we consider this option feasible only if the client has expressed at least general interest in exploring spirituality in practice, a spiritually sensitive helping relationship and context are well established (including thorough assessment of the client's spiritual propensity), and the worker has specialized qualifications related to the spiritually based activity. In any case, we believe that caution should be exercised and that it is better to err on the side of caution.

This option is safest when the practice is nonsectarian in nature. For example, the social worker may be familiar with the mindfulness meditation technique, derived from Zen: quiet sitting, watching the breath, and awareness of the contents of one's thoughts and feelings without being attached to them (Keele, 1996). This technique could be applied without using any Zen-specific religious language or imagery. Similar practices are used in the systematic desensitization technique of behavior modification for teaching people to overcome phobic responses. Chapter 9 includes similar nonsectarian practices.

As another example, Jungian psychotherapists have often recommended a technique of symbol amplification to help clients explore the possible meanings of a dream symbol (Jung, 1963; Sandner, 1991). Suppose a person is going through a spiritual emergency. He feels that he is going through a major and tumultuous life change but is not sure of the direction. He is trying to sort out whether there is growth potential in the process. Then he dreams that he is being dismembered by spirits, who tell him that he must change his life or die. Although the dream is frightening, the man is intrigued by this message that the dismemberment may have something to do with his life purpose. Since he has no religious or cultural stories to explain this dream, it seems rather anomalous and confusing. In symbol amplification, the social worker could explore with the client the possible symbolic meanings of this dismemberment by spirits. It emerges that the client sees the possibility that the dream may be a portent of an important vocational transformation. In this case, the worker might describe the model of therapeutic transformation in relation to spiritual emergencies. She could suggest books that describe the symbolism of dismemberment and reconstruction of the self as part of a life transformation, as in many shamanistic cultures (Halifax, 1982). The client could read these books as part of a process of self-reflection, to determine whether any of these associations are significant to him.

In both examples, the social worker's invitation to the client is tentative, centered in the client's own beliefs and goals, and open to rejection by the client. We do not recommend introducing any religious practice without a foundation of interest expressed by the client.

Cross-Tradition Exchange of Spiritual Practices

The use of spiritually based helping activities in social work raises a social justice dimension of ethics in addition to the direct practice considerations we have addressed so far. The review of religious and nonsectarian spiritual traditions of service in Part II demonstrated a vast array of insights, institutions, and helping practices available to enhance social work practice. In some cases, these spiritually based practices may be applied by a social worker who was raised with them and has been authorized in a traditional manner by a spiritual community to employ them, for example when he or she is also a pastoral minister working with members of his or her congregation. However, we are often in situations in which the client and worker have different spiritual traditions. Appropriate use of, referral to, or collaboration with practices and support systems from the client's tradition may be necessary for spiritually sensitive and culturally competent practice. In addition, some social workers may seek to develop innovative theory and practices by learning from the wisdom of many different spiritual traditions. Finally, some social workers may be invited by teachers from spiritual traditions different from their own to learn the practices and to share them with others.

In all of these situations, we need to address some special ethical issues that relate to the macro sociopolitical context of spirituality and social work. On the one hand, we wish to promote a respectful dialogue and cooperation among and between spiritually diverse people. On the other hand, we wish to avoid the pitfalls of "superficial exploitive borrowing or misuse of spiritual activities" (Canda & Yellow Bird, 1996, p. 1). In order to assist in ethical reflection about cross-tradition exchange of spiritual practices, we consider how the exchange is done and what is the political relationship between individuals or groups involved in the exchange.

How the Exchange Is Done

There are six common kinds of exchange between people: banning, stealing, borrowing, sharing, selling, and gifting. The first two options, banning and stealing, occur in the context of overt exploitation and oppression. *Banning* means that a powerful individual or group prohibits a spiritual practice or belief of another group. For example, European American–dictated governmental and religious policies prohibited many traditional African and Indigenous spiritual practices in the United States for hundreds of years in the context of cultural oppression, colonialism, and slavery. Even today, some social workers attempt to ban, denigrate, or pathologize spiritual experiences and practices that they consider superstitious or irrational. Sometimes this takes on a legal struggle, as when human service administrators in Oregon punished an employee, a member of the Native American Church, for using peyote as a sacrament (Bullis, 1996), causing repercussions through the U.S. Supreme Court and Congress. Banning is clearly not consistent with the NASW Code of Ethics' principles of justice and nondiscrimination or with the principles of spiritually sensitive practice. The long history of spiritual banning and persecution, often of religious adherents who are people of color or politically marginalized groups, gives rise to a great deal of continuing suspicion toward people who want to engage in cross-tradition spiritual exchange.

Stealing means that we take without permission for the purpose of our own benefit at someone else's expense. For example, a social worker may admire a spiritual practice from another tradition and seek to appropriate it. However, appropriating something is not appropriate. Suppose a social worker wished to develop a ritual of forgiveness for a client overwrought with guilt. The social worker heard of the Catholic practice of the Sacrament of Reconciliation and thought it might be useful to adapt. So the social worker donned the garment of a priest, told the client to confess his sins, and then pronounced absolution. Any Catholic would think this ridiculous, if not offensive. The problem is not in learning about the dynamics of confession and reconciliation from Catholic tradition or in helping the client to work through feelings of guilt and to seek forgiveness. The problem is in mimicking the sacrament, taking a religion-specific form out of its religious context, and using it without proper training or authority. Likewise, from a Zen Buddhist perspective, no matter how enamored of Zen meditation, a social worker cannot legitimately proclaim him or herself a Zen Master (whether or not one is a Zen Buddhist).

Borrowing means that a social worker asks permission to use or adapt a spiritual activity in professional practice. Borrowing also implies that one return something. So, for example, I (EC) studied Korean percussion from a teacher in the shamanistic tradition of *nongak* (agricultural music) in 1976 and 1977 (Canda, 1993). I experienced that the music of drums and gongs, when employed in a meditative and ritual manner, can enhance therapeutic transformation for people. By incorporating my learning from this Korean teacher together with training in social work and cross-cultural religious studies, I developed a musical performance technique that can be applied in practice to facilitate transpersonal insights. As I was developing this technique, I corresponded with my Korean teacher to seek his advice and permission. In 1987, I was able to see him again shortly before his death. I told him in detail about what I was doing, and he gave me his encouragement. In return, he hoped that I would promote respect and understanding of Korean *nongak*.

Sharing is a mutual exchange of learning and support that benefits both parties directly. It is a collegial approach, in which people involved share knowledge and help. For example, in my (EC) work with Southeast Asian refugee communities, I developed panels to educate helping professionals about the varieties of traditional healing practices and systems available, such as acupuncture, herbalism, shamanic rituals, and Buddhist meditation. The panels were constructed of presenters from conventional helping professions and a variety of Southeast Asian backgrounds, including professional physicians and social workers as well as traditional shamans and monks. The purpose was to generate mutual knowledge and respect so that cross-referral and cooperation could be enhanced. This meant that people in the various religious, cultural, and helping perspectives came to learn from each other.

Selling means that a person gives spiritual help only in return for a reward. This is a controversial and complicated issue. Professional social workers usually sell their help; we expect to be reimbursed for services. On a practical level, we hope to make a living for ourselves and our loved ones through our work. In fact, state licensure boards may not even accept free (voluntary) service as professional activity worthy of recognition in qualification for licensure. Yet some people feel that selling spiritually based help (including social service) demeans it by attaching it to materialistic or selfish gain. For example, some Indigenous people consider it to be a violation of sacred trust to sell spiritually based helping and healing through professional service, workshops, and retreats (Bullis, 1996).

When spiritually sensitive social workers function in a professional paid capacity, we need to be mindful of this problem. Even if we are paid, we should have service as the first priority. Ideally, we want to work ourselves out of a job. Wouldn't it be wonderful if no one needed social workers any more! If we need to make a choice between profit and caring, caring comes first. In addition, we need to consider the feelings and wishes of recipients in regard to a specific practice. For example, if an Indigenous social worker is involved in a substance abuse treatment program for Native participants, it may well be appropriate for a qualified person to conduct a sweat lodge ritual for interested people going through the recovery program. But many Native people would consider it necessary to separate this from the formal secular helping and not to have a fee charged for the sacred ritual.

We also need to consider the risk of co-optation in professionalism. If we view our vocation as nothing more than a paying job or view our "spiritual" helping activity as nothing more than a new technical gimmick, then we lose the sense of sacredness in our service. Our capacity for radically compassionate action and justice may be compromised by limiting our work to pay, for, as the saying goes, "you shouldn't bite the hand that feeds you." This gives pause to consider why is it that the most noteworthy social reformers of this century, such as Mahatma Gandhi, Reverend Martin Luther King, Jr., Mother Teresa, and President Nelson Mandela, all did their most powerful work outside the confines of a formal paying job, often under extremely difficult and dangerous conditions.

Gifting means that a person gives without any expectation of return. Spiritual teachers of many different traditions have done this and made

their insights available to all. So we have an incredible array of spiritually based helping systems, strategies, and activities available for social
work. However, accepting a gift means being respectful to the giver. So
especially when spiritual practices are offered for help across cultural or
spiritual traditions, it is important that social workers use them according to the guidance, intentions, and highest purposes of those who contributed them.

Social workers are also encouraged to gift their services in the NASW
Code of Ethics. The first ethical principle, based on the value of service, is
to help people in need and to address social problems. Accordingly, the
code states, "Social workers are encouraged to volunteer some portion of
their professional skills with no expectation of significant financial return
(pro bono service)" (p. 5).

The Political Context of the Helping Relationship

Some of our examples indicate that ethical decision making requires taking into account the political context of the helping relationship between
worker and client. For example, if a European American social worker
wishes to explore the possibility of an Indigenous client's use of traditional spiritual practices, such as the sweat lodge purification ritual, the
political context cannot reasonably be ignored. Many Native people are
understandably suspicious when European Americans inquire about
their spirituality. The long history of insults, attacks, and prohibitions
against Native spirituality makes it understandable for the client to have
a healthy mistrust. Self-protection requires caution. Further, some First
Nations people feel that the current interest among European Americans
in Native spirituality can be problematic (Bullis, 1996; Canda & Yellow
Bird, 1996). Sometimes sacred teachings and rituals are taken out of context, adapted, and sold without due regard for the feelings and intentions
of Native people—a clear case of inappropriate appropriation. However,
we are not implying that social workers (including European Americans)
should not learn from other spiritual traditions, convert across religions,
or use new insights to help people. This is a matter of personal conscience
and religious freedom (Buhner, 1997). But we believe that when social
workers act in a professional capacity, we should consider the ethical and
justice issues we have described in order to be consistent with our Code
of Ethics.

We believe that special care and attention need to be used when the
historical relationship between cultural or religious groups represented
by worker and client has been one of oppression, colonialism, genocide,

slavery, racism, discrimination, exploitation, homophobia, sexism, classism, prejudice, or any other form of systematic harm. Even if an individual worker is not directly responsible for the systematic harm of present or past, the memory, wounds, and anger may still loom in the mind of the client. Posttraumatic stress, for both individuals and communities, takes a long time to process. Further, in keeping with our professional value to promote justice, the social worker has a special responsibility to work for the redress of wrongs and the empowerment of disenfranchised people.

For example, a Japanese American worker would need to be mindful of the possible sensitivity of a Korean American client, given Koreans' experience of Japanese colonialism. If a Mormon client is suspicious of a non-Mormon's inquiries about private spiritual practices and beliefs, again, one should not be surprised given the history of persecution of the Mormons. Of course, the specific action to be taken depends on the particular experiences, feelings, and attitudes of worker and client. But we recommend that the worker tread lightly, especially because spiritual matters can be so precious and private. Many times, the spirituality of an oppressed people is one of the last areas of traditional value and practice that has survived cultural persecution, and so it is protected carefully.

ASSESSING SPIRITUAL PROPENSITY

One of the first tasks in spiritually sensitive practice is to determine the spiritual propensity of clients. Then we can plan for ethically and culturally appropriate practice activities. In Chapter 2 we introduced the concept of spiritual propensity. Here we explain the concept in more detail and suggest ways to assess it in practice.

Assessment should be client centered. The client has the primary role in defining and interpreting the meaning and value of his or her spirituality. The client's experiences and behaviors should be understood within the context of his or her culture and spiritual perspective, and assessment should be ongoing and dynamic, since self-understanding and life circumstances continually change. Therefore, all our suggestions for assessment topics and questions are contingent on establishing a spiritually sensitive relationship and dialogue.

Spiritual propensity is the degree and manner for which spirituality is expressed for a person. There are two versions of this. *Religious propensity* (often called *religiosity*) refers to the degree and manner of expressions of a person's spirituality within religious institutional contexts. *Nonreligious spiritual propensity* refers to the degree and manner of expressions of a person's spirituality when there is no affiliation with a religious institution. There are also two styles of each of these: extrinsic and intrinsic. *Extrinsic spiritual propensity* means that the person's spiritual values, beliefs, and behaviors are primarily embedded in external religious or nonreligious social groups in conformance with group norms, consensus, and spiritual group leaders' directions. *Intrinsic spiritual propensity* also includes two possibilities: the person may have privatized his or her spiritual beliefs and practices and have no affiliation with a spiritual group, or the person may be committed to spiritual group membership and principles. In either case, he or she is able to apply spiritual principles flexibly in daily life and is relatively self-determined in spiritual decision making.

This results in a classification of four types of spiritual propensity (see Table 8.3). These types should not be taken as absolute categories, but rather as starting points for understanding the spiritual propensity of the client. The distinctions are useful because it is crucial first to identify a client's interest and patterns of participation in religious or nonreligious spiritual groups and activities, before planning explicitly spiritual practice activities. A client who is nonreligious should not be approached in a religious manner. A client who is religious would be more likely to be interested in religiously based social work practice, referral, or collaboration.

Table 8.3
Types of Spiritual Propensity

	Religious	Nonreligious
Extrinsic	Person's identity and orientation primarily tied to religious group membership and conformity	Person's identity and orientation primarily tied to nonreligious spiritual group membership and conformity
Intrinsic	Person's identity and orientation tied to religious group membership, but also is flexible, inclusive, and relatively self-determined	Person's identity and orientation privatized or tied to nonreligious spiritual group membership, but also is flexible, inclusive, and relatively self-determined

A client who has an extrinsic spiritual propensity is more likely to rely heavily on beliefs, values, and practices that are prescribed by spiritual reference groups and authority figures (whether religious or nonreligious). She or he will more likely be averse to social work practices that are prohibited or held suspect by the spiritual reference group. In contrast, a client who has an intrinsic spiritual propensity is more likely to be willing to engage in self-reflection, explore new spiritual insights, and try new spiritual helping activities, even if these are not officially approved by the spiritual reference group (whether religious or nonreligious).

Appendix A lists a series of questions for exploring a client's spiritual propensity. These questions are designed for a qualitative interview and dialogue format rather than a strict survey form. It is important that clients be given the option to identify one or multiple religious or spiritual orientations. It is also important for them to specify the denomination and spiritual community to which they belong, if any. In the case of multiple spiritual perspective affiliations, it is useful to ask the person to designate her or his primary affiliation.

In social work practice, we recommend a style of questioning that is based on the client's level of comfort and interest and encourages the client to alter the course of conversation in any way that is useful to him or her. Except for brief explorations about group affiliation or frequency of activities, questions should be open-ended. They should invite the client to tell her or his story on the client's own terms. The client should be instructed that he or she is welcome to answer or not answer any question, and can reword the question or respond to it in any way that seems useful.

The discussion guide in Appendix A addresses the following topics: spiritual group membership and participation; frequency, types, and helpfulness of spiritual activities; inspirational sources of support; and extrinsic or intrinsic styles of spiritual propensity. Questions about frequency and type of spiritual practices performed with spiritual groups, family members, and by oneself address the client's opinion about their relative helpfulness or unhelpfulness. Our National Survey of NASW Members showed that most practitioners are likely to attempt this. As Table 8.1 shows (items 48 and 49), most responders have helped clients to consider ways their religious or spiritual support systems are helpful (94 percent) or harmful (71 percent).

Regarding the questions about extrinsic or intrinsic styles, for questions 1, 3, and 9, generally the higher the rating is, the more likely is the style extrinsic. For questions 5 and 7, the lower the rating is the more likely is the style extrinsic. However, only the client's explanation and discussion can give an accurate and through sense of this.

ASSESSING PSYCHOSOCIAL IMPACTS OF PARTICIPATION IN SPIRITUAL GROUPS

Social workers may have an elevated concern about the possibility of harm for clients resulting from participation in unfamiliar or alternative spiritual groups, especially when the worker brands them as extremist, strange, or cultish. Unfortunately, discrimination and stereotyping are too often directed against new or alternative spiritual groups in the mental health and social work fields (Lewandowski & Canda, 1995; Robbins, 1995). For this reason, we do not use pejorative terms like *cult* or *superstition*. One person's cult is another's religious innovation; one person's superstition is another's dearly held belief. Our National Survey of NASW Members revealed that 35 percent of responders disagreed or strongly disagreed that it "is an interference with the client's right to self determination" to attempt to alter the client's belief system who is involved in a cult. Another 22.6 percent were neutral about this. Since religious discrimination is a direct violation of the NASW Code of Ethics, we are troubled by this finding. Perhaps, the word *cult* is so negatively charged that it provokes a negative attitude among practitioners. But this only strengthens the need to address this volatile issue.

Perhaps the best solution is to provide social workers with a guideline for assessing the possible psychosocial impacts of spiritual group participation that openly addresses the controversial issues, but does not rely on judgments about the validity of beliefs. For this purpose, we present here a simplified version of Lewandowski and Canda's (1995) guidelines for assessment of religious groups. We will consider the likely benefits and risks of participating in spiritual groups based on their type of organizational culture and salient topics to explore with clients in helping them to sort out whether they wish to begin, continue, or modify their relationship with a spiritual group. Note that this is one of the issues identified in the DSM-IV V Code for Religious or Spiritual Problem.

A *continuum of types of spiritual groups* can be developed by considering the range of leadership styles and recruiting methods that they employ. Lewandowski and Canda's model posits nine types. For our purpose, we will discuss only two extreme types as illustrations of the range that is possible.

Leadership style and recruitment style are key indicators of a spiritual group's organizational culture. *Leadership style* refers to the ways that leaders use authority to control access to resources, establish group norms, and exercise power. *Recruitment style* refers to the ways that new members are obtained and current members are retained or allowed to depart. By considering the relation between leadership style and recruitment style, we can form a continuum of spiritual group types: from totalitarian on one extreme to laissez-faire on the other extreme.

A *totalitarian spiritual group* is characterized by an authoritarian leadership style and an aggressive recruiting style. An authoritarian leader demands compliance of members, often supported by a rigid doctrinal system of which he or she is designated as the sole authority to interpret. This may be justified by the claim that the only way to salvation or enlightenment is through this group, and therefore the leader must protect the members at all costs. Members may be given a great deal of rewarding personal attention so that their needs and identity become closely meshed with the group and obedience to the leader. Aggressive recruiting means that the end of "saving" people justifies means of recruitment that may be coercive, deceptive, or manipulative. Members who wish to leave the group may be shunned as outcasts, or they may be held captive. Members may also be shunned when they no longer fit the purposes of the leader. In general, unauthorized communication with the outside world and critical reflection on the group's beliefs, values, and practices are discouraged.

An authoritarian spiritual group could be quite satisfying to members who seek clear moral and doctrinal guidelines and enjoy closely knit social ties. People with an extrinsic style of spiritual propensity are more likely to be satisfied with such a group. If a client belongs to such a group, as long as the group obeys the law and does no harm to its members, there is no ground for a social worker to discourage a client from participating in this type of group, although many social workers might be uncomfortable with it.

However, there are increased risks associated with restrictions of personal freedom and mobility. If a client reports that he is questioning the beliefs and practices of his spiritual group, the situation could be quite tense. The client may fear ostracism or even punishment if the group discovers his doubts. Authoritarian spiritual groups are also more likely to be suspicious of contacts with social workers, so the worker should use special care and caution if it is necessary to contact the group for referral or collaboration. If a client decides that she wishes to leave an authoritarian spiritual group, the worker may have to address feelings of fear, shame, and guilt engendered by the group. In addition, an authoritarian group is more likely to cut off contact with the doubting client completely, so separation and loss issues may have to be dealt with. In the case of authoritarian spiritual groups that are involved with criminal behavior, danger to both client and worker is intensified.

At the opposite extreme is a *laissez-faire spiritual group,* characterized by a collaborative leadership style and passive recruiting style. Collaborative leaders place emphasis on members' self-determination. They seek to earn members' respect and trust through meritorious behavior and example. They accept a variety of opinions but constructively challenge members to inquire and grow more deeply in their spiritual understanding. The collaborative leader puts priority on individual member satisfaction rather than group solidarity. Members may even share leadership roles in a flexible and egalitarian manner rather than having a fixed hierarchy of power and control. Recruitment selectively targets people who express interest in the group by their own initiative or through response to general advertisements. Members are free to leave the group or return as their needs and life circumstances change. Therefore, a wide range of variation among members may exist in the interpretation of and conformance with group doctrines, values, and practices.

A laissez-faire spiritual group may have special appeal to people who are very self-reliant, individualistic, and intrinsic in their style of spiritual propensity. Since many social workers emphasize values such as client self-determination and appreciation for diversity, they may be more comfortable with clients' participation in laissez-faire spiritual groups than authoritarian groups. However, the value depends on the client. The advantage of this type of spiritual group is that it provides a supportive social environment for spiritual belief and practice while allowing for maximum individual variation and freedom. The disadvantage is that it may not provide enough structured guidance for people who are still searching spiritually or who want a stronger sense of group solidarity and consensus.

Of course, there are many variations between these two extremes. The purpose of this typology is to help the client think about the nature of the spiritual group she or he is in, or wishes to explore, to consider the fit with his or her aspirations and needs and to weigh the possible desirable or undesirable consequences of participation. This leads to a set of further topics (listed in Table 8.4) that could be used in discussion with clients to help

Table 8.4
Topics for Assessing Spiritual Group Characteristics

Leadership style

Recruitment style

Nature of interpersonal relationships within the group

Impact of participation on family and friends

Degree of allowance for individual variety

Sources of authority for spiritual beliefs

Types of spiritual beliefs, values, and practices and congruence with
  personal commitments

Nature of relationship between the group and the environment

Adaptability of the group regarding changes in the environment

Allowance for members' departure from the group

Opportunities for support and assistance from the group

them examine the congruence between themselves, their loved ones, and the spiritual group (adapted from Lewandowski & Canda, 1995).

SUMMARY

In this chapter, we have provided suggestions for understanding and assessing spiritual aspects of the helping process in social work and participation in spiritual activities and groups. We also offered guidelines for ethical decision making about the use of spiritually based helping practices in social work settings. In the final chapter, we discuss specific spiritually explicit practice techniques that can be employed in social work practice.

EXERCISES

8.1. Social Work as a Transformational Process

Review the section on social work as a transformational process. Choose an example of your work with a client who went through a significant process of change with your assistance. In the overall helping process, how were the phases of separation, flux, and aggregation expressed? What were significant factors that prepared the client to work with you, and how did these predispose her or him to experience the helping process in a certain way? What did you do to help the client reach a sense of closure and prepare for integrating benefits into daily life? What stories or symbols of transformation were important to shed insight and guidance for the client? Were any important dreams or transpersonal experiences involved? Did any points of sudden breakthrough or catharsis catalyze the process? How did this transformation process support the client's total spiritual development? Given these reflections, what did you learn from this experience that could enhance your future work with this client or others?

8.2. Ethical Decision Making About Using Spirituality in Practice

Identify a past or current situation in which you have encountered an ethical question about whether to include an explicitly religious or nonreligious spiritual component in your practice. Use the guidelines in Table 8.2 to help you clarify what you should have done or what you plan to do in the future. How well do these guidelines work for you? Is there any way you believe they should be changed?

8.3. Cultural and Political Issues in Ethical Decision Making

Reflect on the types of practices that you currently use (if any) that have been inspired or learned from a spiritual tradition different from the one in which you were raised. Are there any issues of a cross-cultural, interreligious, or political nature that you feel you should pay more careful attention to? How have you obtained this practice? How do you demonstrate respect and support for the people or group from whom you received this practice?

8.4. Assessing Types of Intrinsic and Extrinsic Spiritual Propensity

Table 8.3 defines types of intrinsic and extrinsic spiritual propensity. What type do you feel best reflects yourself? Why? Now think of a client who you feel reflects another type. How does your difference of spiritual propensity affect your relationship? How can you find ways to work effectively across these differences?

8.5. Assessing Spiritual Propensity in Detail

Use the questions in Appendix A as a format for writing an autobiographical assessment of your own spiritual propensity. Then use the questions to interview a friend. These two activities will give you greater insight into yourself and your friend, and they will also help you decide how to adapt and use the guide for discussions with clients.

8.6. Assessing Psychosocial Impacts of Spiritual Groups

Review the section on psychosocial impacts of participation in spiritual groups and Table 8.4. If you participate in any type of spiritual group, religious or nonreligious, identify where you believe it would fit along a continuum from totalitarian to laissez-faire types. Review the topics in Table 8.4, and form a description of your group's organizational culture. Then consider to what extent there is a good fit between you and your group's characteristics. What implications are there for continuing, modifying, or discontinuing your participation in the group? This self-reflection exercise can help prepare you to engage in this type of reflection with a client if spiritual group participation is an issue in your work.

CHAPTER NINE

SPIRITUALLY SENSITIVE PRACTICE SKILLS AND TECHNIQUES

The world before me is restored in beauty.
The world behind me is restored in beauty.
The world below me is restored in beauty.
The world above me is restored in beauty.
All things around me are restored in beauty.
My voice is restored in beauty.
It is finished in beauty.

Healing Ritual Concluding Prayer, Diné
(Navaho) (cited in Sandner, 1991, p. 193).

INTRODUCTION

In this final chapter, we complete the framework for spiritually sensitive practice. We have come a long way, from defining central values and concepts, to portraying the wide range of religious and nonsectarian expressions of spirituality in social work, and to setting a context for understanding, assessing, and practicing spiritually sensitive social work. Now we present selected skills and techniques that are especially conducive to clients' spiritual growth.

Actually, all forms and types of social work activities can be consistent with spiritually sensitive practice when they are conducted within a framework of spiritually sensitive values and contexts for helping. Everything that furthers the spiritual fulfillment of people, individually and collectively, is spiritually sensitive *when the practitioner is aware of and intentional about this*. Again, this does not necessarily require that the practitioner speak explicitly about this with clients; this decision should be based on the best interests of clients. But it does require a keen spiritual vision of human capacity and possibility. This vision helps us to breathe new life into (literally, "to inspire") all our social work activities.

In this chapter, we provide practical suggestions on three topics of skill and technique: applying multicultural teamwork in practice with spiritual diversity, conducting helping activities that are conducive to individuals' transpersonal experiences and spiritual growth, and using these skills and techniques to support community involved social work practice. This will enable workers to build on clients' religious and spiritual strengths. In our National Survey, a high percentage of responders indicated that they met clients for whom religion (66 percent) and spirituality (86 percent) were strengths. A much smaller percentage met clients for whom religion (26 percent) and spirituality (18 percent) were a detriment.

MULTICULTURAL TEAMWORK FOR SPIRITUALLY SENSITIVE PRACTICE

The range and complexity of spiritual diversity in the United States is quite amazing. There are hundreds of different religions, many denominations of these, and numerous uncounted informal spiritual groups. In addition, there are complex variations of spirituality based on the interweaving of spiritual group affiliations, ethnicity, gender, sexual orientation, and many other aspects of human diversity. Further, each person, family, and community develops a distinctive pattern of spirituality in daily life by drawing on all these influences and by searching out personal paths of meaning and practice.

The intersections of spirituality, culture, and individual uniqueness create a practical challenge for spiritually sensitive practice. In effect, we need to apply the principles and techniques of cultural competence to spiritual diversity (Raines, 1996; Rey, 1997).

Culturally competent practice involves more than mere tolerance of diversity. It encompasses active appreciation for diversity and advocacy for empowerment and justice at both individual and collective levels. If this is to be more than rhetoric, human service organizations (including individual and group private practices) need to institute ongoing policies, programs, and procedures to address diversity (Canda, Carrizosa & Yellow Bird, 1995; Devore & Schlesinger, 1996; Green, 1995; Iglehart & Becerra, 1995; Lum, 1996).

There has been little practical advice published for how to develop a culturally competent way of dealing with spiritual diversity. We propose eight steps of spiritual diversity innovation to organize our suggestions for doing this. These are summarized in Table 9.1. We draw on suggestions given in the previously cited texts on culturally competent practice but focus the discussion on issues of spiritual diversity. Our suggestions are geared toward agency-based practice. They will need to be adapted by social workers in private practice by emphasizing community linkages and interagency cooperation to compensate for the limited resources and personnel available.

1. *Create an ongoing team within the human service organization for development, implementation, and monitoring of spiritually sensitive practice.* In our experience, most human service organizations do not have a formal plan for spiritually sensitive practice. Even if an agency has a plan to address cultural diversity, it is unlikely that spiritual issues have been a major focus. Although sectarian agencies are more likely to address religious issues than secular agencies, most do not have a formal plan for addressing spiritual diversity. This means that most agencies will have a great deal of work to do if they wish to incorporate a framework for spiritually sensitive practice. An ongoing formal team effort would be important for sustained innovation.

    Representatives from administrative and direct service staff in all agency departments should be involved. In addition, membership should include staff who have diverse spiritual perspectives and contacts with diverse types of religious and nonreligious spiritual groups in the community. This range of representation will make it more likely that the team can anticipate both agency-based and community-based issues.

Table 9.1
Eight Steps for Spiritual Diversity Innovation
in Human Service Organizations

1. Create an ongoing spiritual diversity team within the organization.
2. Designate a team coordinator.
3. Identify the range of spiritual diversity in the service area.
4. Include service recipient representatives in the innovation process.
5. Identify current competency among service providers regarding range of spiritual diversity among recipients and community.
6. Evaluate organizational policies, programs, and procedures for support of spiritually sensitive practice.
7. Establish a spiritual resource community directory.
8. Form cooperative cross-site service teams and partnerships, including religious and spiritual support systems and leadership.

Identification of staff's religious or spiritual group affiliation should be voluntary. The most important qualification is not simply group membership but rather enthusiasm for the task, personal familiarity with particular spiritual perspectives, and knowledge of how to contact and cooperate with community members who share these perspectives. If a cultural diversity committee already functions in the agency, its mission could be expanded to address religious and nonreligious spiritual diversity.

In private practice settings, the practitioner and partners (if any) would all need to be dedicated to this effort. So, in effect, the "team" would be solo or the entire group.

2. *Designate a staff person to coordinate the team and to oversee the overall process of innovation.* Responsibility for ongoing professional education and innovation about spiritual diversity should be shared by all staff. But the team and agency-wide efforts need to be coordinated by a designated person so that momentum does not fade. This should be a person with special interest (and, ideally, preparation) for addressing spiritual diversity. If there is already a staff person designated for cultural competence innovation, it might be feasible to have this person incorporate spiritual diversity or to cooperate with another team member who takes on spiritual diversity as a focus of work.

If there is no staff member with formal preparation to address spiritual diversity, it could be helpful for the team coordinator to go through the exercises in this book.

3. *Identify the range of spiritual diversity in the service area.* In order to plan a response to spiritual diversity, it is necessary to know what variety exists in the service area of the agency. It would be an overwhelming task to prepare to address the full range of spiritual diversity present in the United States. For local agencies, that is neither feasible nor necessary. A study of the current service recipients' spiritual propensities and perspectives should be done. If the agency keeps records of recipients' religious affiliations or other aspects of spirituality, these should be reviewed and a client population profile can be constructed. As a next step, a richer profile of spiritual propensity characteristics of service recipients can be developed by adapting a uniform intake assessment from selected questions provided in Appendix A.

A service consumer profile does not necessarily reveal the full range of perspectives in the service area, however. In order to be proactive and to prevent last-minute responses in emergencies, spiritual groups of all potential service consumers need to be identified. This can be done through existing demographic information that may be available from city government or university-based demographers. In lieu of this, a simple way to identify the range of religious groups is to refer to religious directory listings in city telephone books, newspapers, university telephone books, and national directories compiled by Melton (1992, 1993). Also, members of the spiritual diversity team can be asked about any groups with which they are familiar in the community.

A community profile of spiritual diversity can be developed by indicating the range of religious groups, including affiliated denominations, as well as important variations of spiritual communities pertaining to ethnicity, gender, sexual orientation, or other pertinent aspects of human diversity. Nonreligious spiritual groups can be identified by consulting with local experts on twelve-step programs, other self-help groups, and transpersonal approaches to therapy. Examples can be gleaned from Part II of this book.

4. *Include service recipient and community representatives in the innovation process.* People who are affected by decisions should be involved in making them. This important ingredient in empowerment and spiritually sensitive practice generally can bring a practical benefit to the agency, since staff cannot be expected to know or anticipate all the needs and goals of recipients and community members. Once the range of spiritual perspectives in the service area is identified, then representatives can be recruited as team members and consultants. In communities with a large number of different spiritual groups, it will not be possible to include representatives from every one. In that case, it is a good idea to seek representatives from highly contrasting perspectives. Representatives of community groups should be people who are formal or informal leaders, with a positive reputation among their constituents.

5. *Identify the current level and range of competency to address spiritual diversity among the service providers.* The spiritual diversity innovation team should conduct a study of agency staff people's level of interest and preparation for addressing spiritual diversity. Some staff may have specialized training in ministry, pastoral care, or academic religious studies. Some may have taken continuing education workshops and courses dealing with various aspects of spirituality in human service. Many will have developed personal familiarity pertaining to their own

religious or spiritual group affiliation. Staff who have formal experience with interreligious dialogue or clergy–social worker collaboration would be especially helpful.

Expertise in particular types of spiritual development issues or helping skills would also be desirable. For example, if a staff member has training and experience to help people deal with spiritual emergencies, this would be useful to know. Staff who are familiar with spiritual practices and therapeutic techniques that promote transpersonal experiences, such as meditation, could also be helpful.

A directory of agency staff expertise could be compiled from this study. In this way, relevant staff can be consulted on an as-needed basis for planning and implementation or for helping with a particular case.

All staff can be encouraged to engage in continuing education and reading to expand their competency to address spiritual diversity. As new areas of expertise are developed, those staff persons can be added to the directory. In our National Survey, 73 percent of social workers responding received no content on religious or spiritual issues in their social work education, so there is certainly a need to increase available education. But some social workers do have some training regarding this. In our survey, 5 percent of respondents had a religious educational degree, 41.5 percent had attended social work–related workshops or conferences in the past five years on religion or spirituality, and 55 percent had attended nonsocial work–related workshops or conferences on the topic. Yet most people had only attended five or less hours of spirituality- or religion-related workshops or conferences.

6. *Evaluate organizational policies, programs, and procedures for their responsiveness to spiritual diversity.* Part III of this book gives many suggestions for policies, programs, and procedures that are conducive to spiritual growth. Agency mission, goals, and objectives should be examined to identify the extent to which issues of spirituality and spiritual diversity are addressed formally or informally. If spiritual issues are not addressed sufficiently, modifications can be made. Policies, programs, procedures, and service activities should also be evaluated and modified.

7. *Establish a spiritual resource directory for the community.* The spiritual diversity innovation team can consult with representatives of service recipients and the community, as well as relevant staff, to develop a spiritual resource directory for the community. Information from Step 3 can be used to identify basic information about religious and spiri-

tual groups, including addresses, telephone numbers, and other contact information. It would be even more useful to identify specific contact people in these groups if frequent referrals and collaborations are likely.

8. *Form cooperative cross-site service teams and partnerships.* In many communities, it would be impossible for agency staff to have personal familiarity and expertise regarding the full range of spiritual diversity in the service area, but staff can be willing and able to engage in cooperation and mutual learning with other people in the community who do have the relevant knowledge. Teamwork begins within the agency and extends into the community.

When there are likely to be frequent occasions of referral and collaboration between agency staff and community-based spiritual groups, formal cooperative arrangements should be made. Spiritually based clergy, healers, and helpers can cross-train or at least meet together with social workers and other agency staff in order to learn about others' perspectives and procedures, to facilitate cross-referral and collaboration, and to establish ongoing partnerships that can be quickly and easily activated on a case-by-case basis. In practice settings in which sustained cooperation is necessary, as in refugee resettlement, hospice, substance abuse treatment, and health care, formal multisystem teams (including secular and religiously based service systems) can be established to coordinate community-wide planning and activity involving spiritual diversity.

Since cooperation with religious or spiritual leaders is an important component of multicultural teamwork, it is instructive to consider findings from the social work literature and our own National Survey on social workers' use of referral.

Clergy and social workers separately struggle to provide services for a variety of individual, family, and community problems. Helping could be enhanced through collaboration. For two decades roughly 40 percent of persons seeking help for personal and economic distress have preferred clergy over human service providers (Chalfant, Hellert, Rogerts, et al., 1990). A majority of people have routine to sporadic contact with a local or community church, whereas they have no such relationships with human service providers. Therefore, clergy are often clients' first contact for help and serve as gatekeepers to other service resources (Henderson, Gartner, Greer, & Estadt, 1992).

Loewenberg's (1988) review reported that secular social workers made more frequent referrals to clergy than did religious social workers. He speculated that religiously oriented social workers may feel more comfortable discussing the religious aspects of a client problem situation. In contrast, Furman and Chandy's (1994) research found that although 25 percent of randomly surveyed social workers involved the client's pastor or religious leader in the helping process, religious social workers tended to do this more often.

Collaboration between social workers and clergy can avoid duplication of services. It can also integrate psychological and theological perspectives, which allows for more breadth and depth in the healing process (Danylchuk, 1992) while providing an opportunity to develop creative models of service delivery (Turner, 1984).

Furman, Fry, and Fontaine (1997) studied the propensity of referral between social workers and clergy in an upper midwestern state. The random samples consisted of 640 social workers and 876 clergy who represented major Christian denominations. Forty-one percent of the social workers had referred individuals with marriage and family problems to clergy, 30 percent had referred individuals with mental or physical health problems to clergy, and 50 percent had referred individuals with religious and spiritual problems to clergy. More clergy had referred their congregational members to social workers. Sixty-four percent of the clergy members had referred congregational members with marriage and family problems, and 39 percent had referred individuals with mental or physical health problems to social workers. Clergy were not asked if they had referred congregational members with spiritual and religious issues to social workers. Fifty-seven percent of the clergy and 50 percent of the social workers said that barriers such as conflicting values, issues of confidentiality, and differing religious belief systems prevented them from making referrals.

A clearer picture emerges from our National Survey. Seventy-one percent of the responding social workers had referred a client to a clergyperson or other religious or spiritual leader. Considering just the 71 percent who had referred, 44 percent felt that problems concerning differences of beliefs or values between social workers and religious or spiritual leaders would prevent referrals.

Again considering only those 71 percent who had referred clients to clergy, 63.7 percent felt that a social worker's lack of trust or confidence in religious or spiritual leaders would prevent referring clients to them. Then social workers were asked to conjecture if they felt that a religious or spiritual leader's lack of trust or confidence in social workers may prevent referral, and 69 percent felt that this was sometimes or always the case. Referral to clergy or spiritual helpers was not significantly related to the social worker's personal religious or spiritual practices. However, social workers who believed that their differences from clergy could prevent referrals were less likely to make referrals.

These findings reinforce our contention that social workers and religious or spiritual helpers need to become more familiar with each other, earn each others' trust, and develop ongoing collaboration (Furman, Perry & Goldade, 1996).

SPIRITUAL GROWTH–ORIENTED HELPING TECHNIQUES

Our National Survey showed that a large percentage of social workers use a wide range of spiritually oriented helping techniques. Also, the spiritual perspectives on service offer many other helping techniques. In Table 9.2, we list examples of the religious and nonsectarian helping activities available to social workers. The next section of the chapter provides a more detailed introduction to the practice of some of these techniques to encourage greater use of these valuable ways of helping.

We have selected helping techniques according to several criteria. First, they explicitly *promote spiritual development in individuals.* They help clients move in a sense of healing and wholeness on their chosen path toward ultimacy, however they understand that. Second, their practice *results in an immediate perception of benefit,* in the forms of clarified awareness of self and others and generally a reduction of tension and distraction. Third, they are *conducive to transpersonal awareness and experiences.* Fourth, they are so *basic to being human* that there are versions in most, if not all, religious traditions. For example, all people breathe and all religious traditions recognize the significance of intentional, careful breathing. Indeed, many languages have words that can mean spirit, vital force, and breath—for example, *spiritus* (Latin), *ruach* (Hebrew), *pneuma* (Greek), and *prana* (Sanskrit).

Fifth, the techniques are *nonsectarian in form.* Sixth, they *can be linked to specific religious versions* of the practice if a client so desires. Sixth, they *can be applied to many different practice situations.* Seventh, they are *simple and easy to learn.* Eighth, they *do not require formal training or supervision* unless they are taken to a refined level or are practiced in the context of a specific religious or spiritual tradition. Ninth, they *involve low risk to clients.*

We will present some general contraindications and cautions. Then we will present four ingredients of many spiritually oriented therapeutic practices: paying attention, intentional breathing, equipoise, and consistency. These are prerequisites for the other spiritual exercises to be described:

Table 9.2
Examples of Spiritually Oriented Helping Activities

Practice with and by Individuals, Families, and Groups

Active imagination
Art, music, dance, and poetry therapies
Assessing spiritual emergencies
Assessing spiritual propensity
Biofeedback
Caring for the body
Cooperation with clergy, religious communities, and spiritual support groups
Cooperation with traditional healers
Creating a spiritual development time line and narrative
Developing and using multicultural teams
Developing mutually beneficial human-nature relationships
Developing or participating in rituals and ceremonies
Dialoguing across spiritual perspectives
Differentiating between spiritual emergencies and psychopathology
Dissolving inner chatter and distractions
Distinguishing between religious visions and hallucinations or delusions
Dream interpretation
Exploring family patterns of meaning and ritual
Exploring sacred stories, symbols, and teachings
Family brainstorming
Focused relaxing
Forgiveness
Guided visualization
Intentional breathing
Journaling and diary keeping
Meditation and prayer
Mindful paying attention
Nature retreats
Physical disciplines for spiritual cultivation, such as hatha yoga or t'ai chi
Reading scripture and inspirational materials
Reflecting on beliefs regarding death and afterlife
Reflecting on helpful or harmful impacts of religious participation
Win-win solution making

Practice with and by Organizations and Communities

Advocacy for spiritual sensitivity in health and social service policy
Almsgiving and donations
Cooperation with clergy, religious communities, and spiritual support groups
Cooperation with traditional healers
Creating a spiritually sensitive administrative approach
Developing and using multicultural teams

Table 9.2 (continued)
Examples of Spiritually Oriented Helping Activities

Developing mutually beneficial human-nature relationships
Developing or participating in rituals and ceremonies
Dialoguing across spiritual perspectives
Exploring sacred stories, symbols, and teachings of spiritual communities
Lobbying and social activism by religious groups
Reflecting on beliefs regarding death and afterlife
Voluntary agency assistance to redress poverty and justice issues
Win-win solution making

focused relaxing, caring for the body, doing ritual and ceremony, and practicing forgiveness. These last four kinds of activities can then be tailored to
specific purposes and spiritual beliefs as needed. Of course, when clients
are interested in religion-specific spiritual practices, this can be incorporated into practice according to the ethical guidelines described in Chapter
8. In describing these nonsectarian practices, we draw on several works
(Bullis, 1996; Canda, 1990a; Cooper, 1992; Hanh, 1987; Kabat-Zinn, 1990;
Keefe, 1996; Krill, 1990; Osterkamp & Press, 1988).

General Contraindications, Cautions, and Indications

Any practice, no matter how ordinary or common, can lead to unexpected
and sometimes difficult experiences. Especially if a client is on the verge
of a crisis or spiritual emergency, any practice that opens up awareness
to the inner world of deep feelings or loosens the ego boundary can catalyze a major breakthrough. For example, a deep relaxation exercise could
put a person in touch with a repressed traumatic memory. This could
result in a valuable cathartic experience. But as we pointed out in regard
to therapeutic transformation, people sometimes need support for breakdown to lead to breakthrough. It is important that practitioners keep this
in mind. One must be alert, obtain feedback from the client about
progress, and offer support and opportunity to work things through as
necessary.

We presume that the social worker is following the ethical principle of
competency in all of this. The NASW Code of Ethics requires that practitioners have established competency before applying any particular helping activities. So none should "try out" any of these spiritually oriented
practices on clients without first having significant personal experience

and, if possible, formal training with them. Therefore, we introduce the practices as exercises for the reader to do before considering using them with clients.

If a client has a serious physical or mental condition that involves fragile health or psychological instability, special precautions should be taken. For example, if someone has a back injury, then therapeutic massage that involves any vigorous touch should be done only by a specially trained person, such as a physical therapist or chiropractor. Of course, these practices could be very beneficial in relieving or coping with physical illness, injury, or disability, but care and skill are necessary.

In the case of mental disorders or personality disorders, keep in mind a simple principle: *Generally adults should have a well-established ego before it is safe to transcend it.* Promoting transpersonal (trans-egoic) experiences does not mean destroying the ego or denigrating it. So, for example, if someone already is confused about who he or she is, it would not make sense to use a relaxation technique for the purpose of dis-identifying with the individual body and mind (Assagioli, 1965). If a person is experiencing uncontrollable and unpleasant hallucinations, it would not be wise to induce further altered states of consciousness.

However, the simple practices described here could also be helpful in dealing with mental disorders. For example, people with anxiety disorders could learn relaxation techniques. People experiencing depression could learn to do meditative self-affirmations. People coping with certain types of schizophrenia might be able to ground themselves and relieve hallucinatory or delusional episodes through paying-attention exercises. A person with bipolar disorder might benefit from paying-attention exercises and relaxation, so that he or she can be more alert to the beginning of mood swings in order to take preventive action (such as adjusting medication) and in order to reduce the extremes of the swings. Our point is that special care and training on the part of the practitioner are needed to attend to acute or chronic physical or mental distress or disability (Nelson, 1994).

In general, it is helpful to choose spiritual practices that build on clients' strengths and provide a balancing complement to their problematic extremes. For example, highly introspective clients would likely be comfortable with quiet sitting, while the same activity might be frustrating to an extrovert. The extrovert might be more comfortable with body-focused therapies or paying-attention exercises done during physical activity.

Someone's problematic extreme could be balanced by learning a new skill. For example, a person who is extremely introverted might use introspective meditation defensively to avoid dealing with physical issues or social interactions, but this would not help her or him to integrate whatever benefits come from meditation into daily life. So physical exercise routines, such as hatha yoga or t'ai chi, might help the person to integrate spiritual learning with the physical and social realms.

We have to be very respectful of clients' spiritual beliefs and related attitudes about spiritual practices. For example, some theologically conservative Christians believe that forms of systematic relaxation or guided visualization are tantamount to brainwashing or demonic tricks. As always, our practice decisions need to be client centered. We have to find out what the client believes about these things.

Although it is unlikely with the exercises we describe here, it is possible that someone may report an unusually intense or frightening experience that goes beyond the understanding, worldview, or experience of the social worker. An obvious example would be a sense of attack by evil forces. Our advice is this: Don't pretend you know what you are doing, and don't minimize or discount the experience. Take it very seriously, whatever your own belief system. If this experience is clearly a symptom of a mental disorder, then obtain the needed medication or other support needed. But such an experience can occur in situations that have nothing to do with mental disorders. If necessary, refer to or collaborate with a competent spiritual support person or religious leader who shares a perspective similar to the client's. And also, take care of yourself.

I (EC) recall an emotionally charged consulting visit to a mental health center dealing with this. Staff asked me and a colleague to talk with staff about an increasing incidence of clients who claimed to have been traumatized in satanic rituals, a controversial and complex subject (Melton, 1993; McShane, 1993; Peck, 1983; Robbins, 1997). Official satanic organizations disavow violence, and police investigations have not uncovered any wide satanic conspiracies, as have often been alleged. But the bottom line was that many staff felt frightened, highly distressed, and at a loss.

The major issue that emerged was that different staff people were experiencing similar frightening things. They were worried that somehow they could be under physical or even magical attack. They were confused about the possible reality of the clients' reported experiences and the demonic forces that were possibly involved. But they had not been talking to one another out of fear of embarrassment or sounding unprofessional. During the discussion, it became clear that various staff people found ways of dealing with the stress that made sense within their own religious beliefs and personal styles. Talking openly relieved the feelings of isolation and strangeness. Staff decided that they needed to be more open with each other, to help each other ventilate and process feelings, to share effective coping strategies, and to give each other affirmation and support. These are excellent recommendations for any practitioners in stressful working conditions.

On the other hand, techniques that open oneself up to transpersonal experiences could lead to amazingly wonderful but surprising events, such as peak experiences and revelations. Even positively perceived peak experiences can shake the foundations of one's sense of self and reality. If a peak experience generates a spiritual emergency, then the social worker certainly needs to help the client work this through to a plateau of enhanced living.

Basic Exercises

Paying Attention

The simple act of attention has a healing and restoring effect. When we notice something, we are affected by it. When we pay attention to ourselves, we are alert to our thoughts, feelings, sensations, and intuitions. When we pay attention to others, we can perceive them accurately and empathize. When we pay attention to the world, the amazing quality of each moment becomes clear. When we notice very carefully, we discover new things and we experience even very familiar things freshly and vividly. Paying attention is a practice that is always available.

A simple exercise to start is to pay attention to any common object. Suppose you are ready to eat an orange. Before beginning, look at it closely. Notice the subtle colors of its peel. Do not assume what it looks like. Note every shade of color, every rumple. Touch it and note its texture. Smell it. Then open the peel as if you are opening a gift. Allow yourself to be surprised by what is wrapped within. Be vividly aware of the pungent smell, the soft liquid texture, the veins running through the flesh. Then, taste. Move the piece of orange around in your mouth to sense it with every part of your tongue. Discover the variations of flavor that come with each piece. If you do this, you will discover a new kind of orange, even if you have eaten a thousand of the same kind before.

Now apply this learning to all aspects of life. While walking, savor the walk. While talking, savor the talk. While showering, savor the shower. While keeping company with a loved one, savor the company. Each moment is so precious, yet it immediately disappears. Our enjoyment of life can be greatly enhanced by such a simple thing as paying attention.

A more difficult version of this exercise is to pay attention to some uncomfortable sensation. We suggest you start with something mild. Suppose you feel tired from a long day of work. Try lying down in a comfortable position, and pay attention to all the details of what it feels like to be tired. Soon the tiredness will be relieved. If not, this tells you to attend even more carefully to your need for rest.

It is important that paying attention be done gently and nonjudgmentally. Especially if you are paying attention to a painful feeling or sensation, regard yourself gently, lovingly, and soothingly. If you pay attention with harshness, anger, or self-condemnation, you will surely intensify the negative experience.

Intentional Breathing

We often take breathing for granted unless our oxygen is cut short by lack of air in a stuffy room or a respiratory problem. When we pay attention to breathing, more benefits emerge. Of course, it is perfectly natural to breath automatically most of the time. But taking periods through the day to watch the breath and settle into it can instantly relieve stress and clarify the mind.

In intentional breathing, we first pay attention to the fact that we are breathing. This practice is easiest to begin by setting aside several minutes without demanding activity. Just notice that you are breathing. Notice the rate of breaths in and out. How deep or shallow are the breaths? How do the abdomen and chest move? Find a position in which you are not physically strained, such as sitting upright or lying down. Notice how changes of posture affect your breathing.

Now, take in a gentle but deep breath from the abdomen. Bring in the breath to a comfortable extent; then release it slowly and gently for about twice the length of time as the inhalation. Notice how your body and mind feel, already calming and clearing of distractions and distress.

Take ten breaths in and out like this. You may find it helpful to pause slightly between each inhalation and exhalation. After ten breaths, rest for a few moments in a sense of peace and calm. Let your breathing settle into a gentle natural rhythm. Now return to your previous activity, but bring with you the rest and clarity from this breathing exercise.

If you notice an increase of distractions or uncomfortable sensations, that is a cue that you should pay attention to this. As soon as you can, take care of whatever physical, mental, emotional, or spiritual issues arose. And when you do, try beginning with three intentional relaxing breaths.

Equipoise

Another basic ingredient of many spiritual practices is mental and physical balance. The body and mind are kept in a poise free of strain or exaggerated motions. Even in some vigorous physical practices, like trance dancing or ritual drumming, the body needs to be moved in a way that does not strain or harm it. Otherwise you will be worse off afterward. There are exceptions—practices that are designed to induce transpersonal experiences rapidly or to sacrifice one's comfort for others' spiritual well-being, such as enduring extreme austerities or intense physical stimulation and pain—but they require special guidance and support (Achterburg, 1985).

Generally, balance of body and mind are important qualities to prepare for spiritual practices. Literally, the body can be held in postures that are balanced and free of strain. The mind can be poised in a state that balances relaxation with alertness. This combination encourages moving into altered states of consciousness, such as deeply relaxed introspection or heightened awareness of the environment.

It is easy for most people to begin this practice by sitting in a comfortable position. Many people find it comfortable to sit on a low cushion with legs crossed. Some people prefer to sit on a comfortable chair, with ankles crossed. In either case, it is best, when possible, to keep the spine straight (but not forced) and to find a natural balancing point. This is aided by being sure that there are solid points of rest for your body: your seat on the cushion or chair and your legs or feet on the floor. Hands can be folded in the lap. The head rests in a balanced way atop the neck and shoulders.

Adjust the posture for your own comfort and body type. When you find a sense of physical equipoise, you will notice that it is easier to calm the mind. The breath will also flow more smoothly.

Consistency

In order to become proficient at any practice, consistency is necessary. Also, while there are immediate beneficial effects of these practices, benefits accumulate and grow with consistent repetition, so it is best to set aside a quiet place and time at least once every day, for at least ten minutes, to practice these exercises. Actually, the exercises fit nicely together. You can combine them by finding a comfortable, balanced posture, intentionally breathing, and paying attention to your experience. Once you become familiar with this, you will be able to move into a relaxed but alert state very quickly, within a few moments. Then you can extend the complete practice into your daily activities more easily. When sitting at a boring meeting, try finding a comfortable posture and pay attention to your breath. Soon the meeting will become more interesting (or at least bearable). When sitting with a client, try these exercises to help you listen and respond more accurately, empathetically, and intuitively. The ideal is to infuse all of life with these qualities of attention, breath (inspiration), and equipoise.

Further Practices

The basic exercises provide a foundation that can be applied to many other practices conducive to spiritual growth. We discuss four such practices that can be further applied to various purposes in social work practice.

Focused Relaxing

Once you have learned to combine paying attention with intentional breathing and equipoise, you have begun focused relaxing, which is a combination of focus and relaxation. The mind is neither wandering aimlessly nor tightly controlled. The body is neither limp nor strained. Most people find that sitting is the easiest posture for focused relaxing, because lying down increases the risk of falling asleep. But once one learns the technique, it can be used with any posture, depending on the purpose. Many people find it comforting to begin with a brief affirmation of intention or prayer that centers one in a sense of goodwill and protection.

There are some common techniques for maintaining focus. One is to follow the breath. You might try counting on each inhalation: one . . . two . . . three . . . up to ten, and then start over again. If you lose count, it may be that your attention has wavered. Go back to one.

A common mistake in focused relaxing is being too impatient or judgmental. All you need to do is let yourself be relaxed. It is natural for people to settle into relaxation when given the chance. There is no need to force yourself. Suppose you notice that you have lost count. Then, in your mind, you complain to yourself for being so distracted. That is a sure way to become more distracted. Just return to one. Or you become tense because you are not yet relaxed enough. Just return to one.

Another common focusing technique is to use a word or brief phrase that you repeat to yourself silently. Often this is termed a *mantra*, from Hindu and Buddhist traditions, but there are versions in all religious meditation traditions. It is often best if you choose a word or short phrase that fits you well. It may have a special spiritual significance to you, it may come from a spiritual teacher or tradition, or it may have no literal meaning. It should be short enough so that you can harmonize its repetition with the inflow and outflow of breath. For example, breathe in *peace,* breathe out *for all.*

If any distracting or disturbing thoughts, feelings, or sensations arise, just be gently aware of them; remind yourself that you will remember them if important after the session so you can attend to them. Then let them go. Best results are obtained with a minimum of ten to twenty minutes at a sitting.

Another important ingredient of focused relaxing is *purpose,* to focus the direction and specific use of the relaxed state. There are three common directions for focus: outward, inward, and at the boundary.

If you want to clarify your awareness of the outside world, an outward focus of awareness will affect your technique. In quiet sitting, outward-focused techniques include keeping your eyes open and gazing gently at an attractive or significant but mild stimulus, such as a candle flame, a symbol, or a meaningful picture. One could listen to music or natural sounds that are inspiring. One could chant aloud a focusing word or phrase. Outward focus can also be used to enhance walking, driving, or any other physical or social activity.

If you want to enhance awareness of your inner thoughts, feelings, sensations, intuitions, or stillness and quiet, then it would be helpful to close the eyes, or keep them only slightly open, and to avoid loud or distracting sounds. Use an inner focus, such as the breath or a silent focusing word.

You might wish to cultivate an awareness that is not fixed in either the internal or external world but is restfully clear between them. In this case, you can follow the breath or a focusing silent word, keep the eyes gently and slightly open, and let your attention rest at the border between inside and outside yourself. For example, you could rest your gaze at a spot on the floor a foot or two in front of you, without fixing on the spot but also without losing awareness of it.

Purpose also directs what you want to accomplish with your chosen practice. Actually, it is often very restful not to try to accomplish anything, but just to dwell in the peace of the experience. But we might have a particular helping or healing purpose in mind as well that could lead to other adjunct techniques. In this case, focused relaxation is a gateway into some other practice. Here are several examples.

Inward-directed focus can prepare one for various kinds of self-discovery. There are many learning exercises in this book based on *self-reflection.* So inward-focused relaxation can clarify awareness of one's feelings, thoughts, sensations, and intuitions and the reasons behind them through introspective self-reflection. It can also prepare one to explore the creativity of imagination. For example, in the Jungian *active imagination* technique, the person relaxes and pays attention to the spontaneous flow of images and inner dialogue in relation to some important life theme. One might seek out conversation with an inner guide, or an important inspirational figure, to seek advice. In the Jungian form of practice, these are conversations with deep and wise aspects of the transpersonal True Self. Active imagination can be applied to *exploring the meaning of dreams* as well by reentering the dream situation and letting the dream play out further, or by engaging in dialogue with the dream figures.

One could also use inward-focused relaxation to prepare for religion-specific forms of *prayer* that involve getting in touch with the divine within yourself. Some forms of *contemplation* or *meditation* involve going within oneself into an experience of quiet and stillness that involves no contents of thought, feeling, or sensation. In theistic traditions, this may be described as a communion with the God beyond all images of God.

Outward-focused relaxation can lead directly into self-reflective *journaling* or diary keeping, reading of *inspirational books or scriptures*, or *artistic expressions* such as poetry, drawing, dance, or musical performance. When applied in therapeutic contexts, these practices can help clients open up many sources of insight into self, one's life situation, and creative ways of solving problems, working through crises, or growing.

In-between focused relaxation has the advantage that it can prepare one for activities that move in either direction, inward or outward. Of course, any directional focus can prepare one for any type of activity if you shift direction while continuing the experience of clarity. Indeed, focused relaxation is an excellent skill to incorporate into the following practices.

Caring for the Body

Although we often say that as social workers, we want to deal with the whole person, bio-psycho-social (and now spiritual) aspects in all, we too often neglect the body (as well as the spirit). Clients who feel stressed, hurt, and confused may tend to neglect their bodies, so caring for the body is an important ingredient in holistic spiritually sensitive practice. In some religious traditions, this notion is embodied in such expressions as, "The body is the temple of the divine." Whatever our beliefs, we know that we cannot live without the body, so let us make the best of it.

Everyone has occasions when they crave caring attention to their bodies. For example, at a time of illness or dying, the body is especially tender and in need of care. At such times, if we are able, we should tend to our own bodies with the same kind of careful paying attention as we use to prepare for focused relaxation. Indeed, practice in focused relaxation can help put us in touch with inner reserves of resilience, and it can relieve pain and distress. When our loved ones or clients are physically distressed, we can help them to find the physical comfort and care they need. We intend that this go beyond the technical aspects of medical care. Medical treatments can be given with caring attention. Caring attention is the more fundamental medicine.

We also suggest that caring for the body is a practice that should be done every day, whatever the state of physical health. This promotes overall well-being and helps to prevent stress. There are many such practices possible—for example, *regular exercise, sports activities, walking in beautiful places,* following a *healthy eating pattern, growing and eating your own vegetables,* taking a *relaxing shower or bath.* One could learn *physical exercise* systems that have an explicit spiritual orientation, such as t'ai chi or hatha yoga. There are many types of body therapies that can be received from trained professionals (or loved ones), such as *therapeutic touch* and *massage.* Any type of physical care can be conducive to spiritual growth when it involves paying caring attention and is placed within the context of the person's spiritual aspirations.

We need to make a cautionary note on body therapies that involve touching clients because of the great potential for misuse or abuse. Even a simple gesture intended as a sign of friendliness, such as touching a client's shoulder, can be an unwanted intrusion. In some cultures, touching the head is considered rude and jarring. More intimate kinds of touch, like massage, are even riskier. If a social worker wishes to incorporate these practices within his or her own work (rather than making referrals), it is important to have clear, explicit, informed consent from clients. It is also crucial to be sure that psychodynamic issues do not complicate and confuse the meaning of touch if both psychotherapy and massage are combined. Touching clients for healing purposes was the least used or approved helping activity in our National Survey. This is a little-explored area in social work so far. A quotation regarding physical contact from the NASW Code of Ethics (p. 13) is noteworthy here:

> Social workers should not engage in physical contact with clients when there is a possibility of psychological harm to the client as a result of the contact (such as cradling or caressing clients). Social

workers who engage in appropriate physical contact with clients
are responsible for setting clear, appropriate, and culturally sensitive boundaries that govern such physical contact.

This statement is ambiguous as to what specific types of contact may
be prohibited, but it is clear that the onus is placed on the social worker
to establish competency, minimal risk for the client, and a good rationale
for the practice.

Doing Ritual and Ceremony

Victor Turner (1965), an anthropologist, made a helpful distinction
between ritual and ceremony. *Ceremony* refers to celebrations and confir-
mations of existing situations and conditions. *Ritual* refers to procedures
that bring about a fundamental transformation of existing situations and
conditions. We will use the terms in this way.

Laird (1984) pointed out that some people do not have well-established
rituals or ceremonies to celebrate important life events and to encourage
transitions. For example, there is no ritual to mark the passage from adolescence to adulthood that is generally accepted by most Americans. There
are some religious rituals, such as Jewish bar mitzvah and bat mitzvah
(Kahn, 1995), that can help a person to make a clear statement of identity
and to have that affirmed and supported by others. But all too often adolescents may take up activities that are not necessarily beneficial in order
to claim adult status, such as smoking or drinking alcohol. For another
example, divorce is a major life transition for many married people, but
the legal and economic rituals marking this change are not set up to help
people grow through the process.

The opposite problem is when people have a ritual or ceremony that
is too routinized, rigid, or taken for granted. It no longer has a sense of
meaning or power. So Laird suggested that social workers may sometimes
be called on to help clients to celebrate accomplishments and move
through critical life passages safely.

Further, the model of therapeutic transformation explored in Chapter 8
suggests that all social work practice situations promoting change can be
viewed as a form of ritual. We can enliven them by applying ritual techniques to them in an explicit manner.

Designing a ritual or ceremony can be emotionally moving and enjoyable.
It links self-reflection and dialogue with significant people whom you
wish to be present. It can involve joining with existing ritual and ceremonies in one's spiritual group to find affirmation and support there. It

can involve renewing lost ties to a spiritual group, to rediscover a community of spiritual caring. It can involve creating an entirely new or personally tailored event, suited to private and particular beliefs and circumstances. Actually performing the ritual or ceremony, especially with a sense of support from loved ones, spiritual mentors, the community, and (if believed) sacred or supernatural beings, can be a powerful event cherished for a long time.

In order to clarify this, I (EC) would like to give an example from a former student who was a social worker for a Lutheran Social Services agency during the 1980s. He had established a peer support group for Cambodian refugee youth who had been resettled as unaccompanied minors. These youth were dealing with many compounded stressors related to loss of homeland, family, and friends; experience of the genocidal "killing fields"; the dangerous and uncertain flight from Cambodia; extended stay in refugee camps; and cross-cultural transition in the United States.

Over the course of support group meetings, it became clear that the youth needed to tell their stories for healing, not only to each other but to the general public. Speaking the truth, including the pain, was an important step in honoring the memories of loved ones lost, releasing the traumatic pain, and moving on. The group meetings became a multimedia event. Participants told stories, drew pictures, wrote stories, and spoke to newspaper reporters. The social worker recognized that a dramatic ritual of transformation was unfolding and documented this in records kept for the youth participants. But there was still a lot of pain and much hope for the uncertain future to address. The youth were Buddhist, and so they asked to have a Cambodian Buddhist monk visit them to perform a formal religious ritual of healing. They worked with the social worker and the monk to tailor a ritual that focused all the energy of healing from the entire process.

The youth found a beautiful location for the ritual in a field. They dug a hole in the ground. Into the earth they symbolically placed all their pain, grief, and loss. The monk prayed for their help and blessed the process. Then the youth planted a sapling in the hole, so that new life would grow up from it. This tree symbolized their new life in the United States in which they would continue to honor their culture of origin and their memories, but would also forge a new identity and way of life. This ritual simply yet powerfully represented their healing transformation. This example beautifully reflects the guidelines we have offered for ethical use of religiously based activities and multicultural teamwork.

Lynda Paladin, a friend of mine (EC), went through an extremely difficult time following the death of her husband, David, an inspired Navajo painter and spiritual teacher whose artwork had become known worldwide (Hillerman, 1987–1988). He was appreciated for his volunteer service for Indigenous prisoners, outreach to non-Native people, and generally compassionate attitude. Lynda was closely involved with David's art and all aspects of his life. When he died, she felt a terrible loss and disorientation. In order to help herself work through this, she recalled her learning about ritual and spirituality from her time with David. She designed a ritual to help her honor David's memory and spirit and to help her move into a new phase of life. Then she wrote a book to help others address similar life transitions (Paladin, 1991). In order to help you to design helping rituals or ceremonies for yourself or your clients, we include a list of suggestions influenced by Lynda's guidelines (see Table 9.3).

Note that Lynda Paladin used the term *ceremony* in the sense that we mean *ritual*. We do not wish to make too much of this distinction. Ritual and ceremony need not be mutually exclusive; we see this as a matter of emphasis. But we think it can be helpful to be clear about the general purpose of your event. For example, if you wish to design a ceremony, your event will emphasize themes and symbols of celebration, confirmation, appreciation, dedication, affirmation, and continuation. If you wish to design a ritual, your event will emphasize themes and symbols of transformation, movement, discontinuity, and newness. At the conclusion of a ritual, it would be important to have a ceremonial ending that confirms and celebrates the change.

Practicing Forgiveness

Forgiveness of self or others can be an important step in releasing pain and preoccupation with feelings of guilt, shame, or anger toward oneself and anger and hostility toward others (Garvin, 1998). Therapeutic forgiveness does not mean "forgive and forget," because it is often impossible and undesirable to forget an injustice or outrage. We need to learn from our mistakes and also move on. We need to take proactive stands against indignity or injustice against ourselves and others, but without being stuck in an adversarial mentality and way of life. Indeed, forgiveness can open up energy and insight for more effective action.

"Forgiveness is conceptually defined as letting go of the need for vengeance and releasing associated negative feelings such as bitterness and resentment" (DiBlasio, 1993, p. 163). It has been described as a powerful therapeutic intervention (Fitzgibbons, 1986).

Table 9.3
Suggestions for Designing Ritual or Ceremony

1. **Identify Your Intention**
   - What ideals, values, accomplishments, relationships, or events do you want to celebrate and affirm?
   - What situations, relationships, or events do you want to change?
2. **Symbolize Your Purpose and Hope**
   - Find or create images, stories, or objects that represent whatever you want to celebrate or change.
3. **Symbolize the Process of Celebration or Change**
   - Consider the actions you would like to perform that will represent the process of affirmation or transformation.
   - What inspirational stories and persons can be recalled as models for the actions you will perform?
4. **Create a Meaningful Time and Place**
   - Where do you wish to perform the ritual or ceremony that will be safe, empowering, and significant?
   - Choose a time during which you will be undisturbed and that will be significant.
5. **Invite Participants**
   - Invite supporters and loved ones to participate.
   - Are there nonhuman beings you would like to be present, such as favorite animals or plants?
   - Are there ancestors, spirits, or other sacred forces you would like to invite and symbolize their presence with objects or images?
6. **Open the Ritual or Ceremony**
   - Mark the beginning as a special event, with music or dramatic actions.
   - State your intentions and purpose.
   - Welcome all participants.
7. **Enact the Celebration or Transformation**
   - Carry out the symbolic actions of celebration or change.
8. **Make a Commitment to the Future**
   - Reflect on the insights for your continuing growth and lifestyle.
   - Make a commitment to act on these insights in daily life.
9. **Give Gratitude**
   - Thank all the participants and sacred forces who supported you in this event.
10. **Close the Ritual or Ceremony**
    - Use music, symbolism, or dramatic action to bring the ritual or ceremony to a close.
    - Provide a reminder or memento for yourself and participants to bring out of the ritual or ceremony.

DiBlasio (1993) found that clinicians with strong religious identification were more receptive than less religious clinicians to the idea of forgiveness in clinical practice (DiBlasio, 1993, p. 167). However, DiBlasio and Proctor (1993) found that a majority of clinicians they studied had a favorable impression of forgiveness and that their personal level of religiosity was not a factor in whether forgiveness was used as a therapeutic intervention.

Studzinske (1986) listed reasons a client may not wish to work on forgiveness. These included lack of time and energy, refusal to let go of the pain, fear of being perceived as weak, preoccupation with the wrongdoer's guilt, and a bias against forgiveness because of its association with religious traditions. Additionally Smede (1996) posited that some people mistakenly believe that if they forgive, they must reunite with the offender. Therefore, it is important to assess whether clients wish to work on forgiveness.

We asked two questions that dealt with forgiveness issues in our National Survey. Sixty percent of the respondents indicated that it is important to help clients assess whether they wish to work on forgiveness, and 74 percent of the respondents use techniques in their practice that deal with forgiveness. This finding suggests that many respondents use techniques in practice that relate to forgiveness without assessing whether the client wishes to do so. This puzzling result calls for a reminder of the importance of assessment and matching a helping technique to the client's preference.

Regarding forgiveness of self, Krill (1990) made a helpful distinction between appropriate and inappropriate feelings of guilt. In practice, a client can be encouraged to reflect on feelings of guilt without self-punishing judgmentalism. This opens the possibility for distinguishing between appropriate guilt (i.e., remorse for one's harmful acts) and inappropriate guilt induced by harsh evaluations of self, low self-esteem, or blaming by others. Honest acknowledgment of appropriate guilt can shift a person from self-defeating preoccupation with mistakes to constructive acts of acceptance of self, correction of mistakes, and restitution. Recognition of inappropriate guilt can lift the weight of blame and open up energy and insight for positive self-concept and refusal to accept inappropriate judgments from self or others.

Regarding forgiveness of others, Holmgren (1993) identified four key elements: an injured person who must do the forgiving; the offender's act must be considered to have an element of willful wrongdoing, negligence, or recklessness; the aggrieved must overcome his or her negative feelings and overcome any resentment toward the offender; and the aggrieved must reach a point at which he or she internally accepts the offender as a person.

According to Worthington and DiBlasio (1990) it is necessary to evaluate whether the client has sufficient ego capacities to seek or grant forgiveness. These ego capacities include the ability to empathize with his or her offender and demonstrate remorseful attitudes. Holmgren (1993) said that the aggrieved must complete a series of tasks that are central to his or her self-esteem and self-respect before he or she can forgive. Worthington and DiBlasio (1990) emphasized that when clients demonstrate defensive posturing and continuous denial, they are not ready to work on forgiveness. Additionally, DiBlasio (1993) stated that whether forgiveness is appropriate depends solely on the beliefs, feelings, attitudes, and decisions of the aggrieved person. If the client does not wish to forgive the offender, then the client's right to self-determination must be respected.

Hope (1987) characterized the process of forgiveness as being a central process in therapy and related it to the relationship between the client and therapist. When the therapist models an accepting attitude toward the client, it is perhaps this experience of being valued in the present in spite of the obvious shortcomings and failures in the past that provokes clients into forgiving their pasts and developing a more forgiving attitude in the present.

We would like to suggest that the activities of focused relaxation can help clients to get in touch with painful feelings gently, in the process of working through to forgiveness. The social worker could also help an interested client to design a ritual of forgiveness for self or others at an appropriate time. If the client participates in a religious tradition or spiritual practice with an established ritual for forgiveness, an authorized spiritual helper could be involved in the process through referral or direct collaboration.

SPIRITUALITY AND MANAGED CARE

Much social work practice takes place in the context of managed care systems, restrictive insurance policies, and government-based standards of utilization review with concomitant pressures toward short-term, technocratic ways of service. To the extent that these pressures are inimical to spiritually sensitive practice, social workers need to be active in movements for health care reform, mental health policy reform, and advocacy with insurers and third-party reimbursers. Actually, some third-party payers are supporting holistic and complementary approaches to health care, such as acupuncture and stress management programs. Accreditation standards for hospitals and hospice programs include spiritual needs. We can work creatively with these trends to find ways to incorporate spiritually oriented helping activities.

Even when short-term modalities of service are required by managed care, that does not preclude spiritually oriented helping. For example, brief solution-focused therapies are very consistent with both a strengths perspective and spiritual growth issues (Hoyt, 1996). There are many therapeutic activities derived from humanistic, existential, and transpersonal theories that are conducive to rapid breakthroughs in spiritual awareness, such as holotropic breathwork (Grof, 1988; Krill, 1978, 1990). Many helping activities in this book can be taught to clients to be done as self-directed "homework" outside of paid sessions (e.g., focused relaxation and journaling).

Managed care pressures can be an incentive to find ways for clients to work on solutions and growth in their home and daily life settings, free from the often stultifying confines of hospitals, mental health centers, and social work agencies. For instance, a medical social worker could assist a person with a chronic physical illness to access home-based health care and to draw on the loving, beautiful, and supportive qualities of family, friends, spiritual support groups, the natural environment, and activities such as meditation, prayer, or ritual.

Finally, spiritual sensitivity can pervade all situations and modalities of practice. Clients can be treated with humanity, compassion, and concern for justice in managed care or any other setting. This depends on the quality of the helping relationship more than on any particular technique.

SPIRITUALITY AND COMMUNITY-INVOLVED PRACTICE

We do not have the space in this book to deal with community-based social work practice in detail. We chose to focus on social work practice at the micro level because that is where most social workers practice. However, we have woven meso and macro level issues throughout our discussion of practice, recognizing that there cannot be, nor should there be, a dichotomy between them (see table 9.2). Effective micro practice needs to take into account the larger systems. Indeed, the hallmark of social work is its commitment to both individual well-being and social justice. Because this is so important, we conclude this book with some thoughts about the implications of our framework for spiritually sensitive practice regarding community.

Spirituality is not just a private matter. As we use the term *spirituality*, it cannot be considered merely a private matter. Human beings are relational beings. We live only because of our interrelatedness with other people and all other beings. Certainly there is a private dimension of spiritual experience, some of which we may never share openly with others. But even that could not exist without others. Individual spirituality grows in the field of community: family and friends; religious institutions or nonsectarian spiritual social groups; neighborhoods and cities; cultures and nations; ecosystems of plants, animals, stones, air, sunlight, moonlight, and clouds; the planet earth; the cosmos; and perhaps, as many believe, communities of spiritual beings and the divine Ground of Being Itself. Many religious traditions of service acknowledge and honor this relatedness, and it would be well for us to do so also. We need to develop social welfare practices and policies that benefit all beings in the global community and planetary ecology.

Spiritual development is a motion toward coresponsibility. As we grow in our awareness of this interrelatedness, we realize with gratitude our fundamental reliance on others. Our capacity for empathy and our zeal for justice ripen. We experience that our own well-being cannot be separated from the well-being of others. Our sense of compassion extends from self and those familiar to us, out to others of different cultures, religions, and ways of life, and out to other beings. A principle of coresponsibility guides us.

On a practical level, *spiritually sensitive helping requires a supportive context of organizations and communities,* so we need to attend to the way our human service organizations are structured. We need to examine programs, policies, and procedures for the extent to which they humanize and support people's highest aspirations and transpersonal potential. We seek modes of social change that nonviolently promote solutions for the benefit of all involved, including the nonhuman beings with whom we share this planet.

Spirituality and religion are closely connected with contemporary social policy development. Therefore, we need to be astute about the use and abuse of spirituality in the political process (Canda & Chambers, 1994; Ressler, 1998). Since social policies determine key social values and the distribution of resources, we need to examine them for whether they empower people and support them on their individual and collective spiritual paths. The value and moral dimensions of policymaking are spiritual. They are best examined explicitly and openly in the context of public dialogue and critical reflection, lest particular spiritual agendas dominate and harm people who are less influential in the policymaking process. Some politicians and activists openly appeal to divine sanction, religious authorities, and politically charged religious groups to bolster their positions and sway the public.

In order to avoid this danger, as well as to incorporate the positive insights of careful spiritual reflection, we recommend that social workers assist people of diverse and contrasting spiritual perspectives to become active in the policymaking process (Canda & Chambers, 1994). We can also work to create settings and processes for policy debate based on win-win strategies and the value of mutual respect. We view the ideal policy-making process as a societal movement toward creating conditions that are conducive to all people's spiritual development.

Collective action for social justice comes from the solidarity of full persons. Accomplishing large-scale social change requires many people working together, so it is crucial that each person in the effort work out her or his spiritual development. If a person feels spiritually empty, his or her energy and motivation for justice, especially in the mode of nonviolence, will be hard to sustain.

In 1979, I (EC) had a conversation with two African American activists that stuck with me and has guided me through my career in social work since then. They have long been active in the civil rights movement. They were personal friends and associates of Rev. Dr. Martin Luther King, Jr. I met them when I was a graduate student in religious studies at the University of Denver, before I went into social work.

They told me of their heady times at the peak of the civil rights movement. When the movement was going strong, there was tremendous collective energy and mutual support. Charismatic leadership, group enthusiasm, and optimism carried them along. But after Rev. King and Malcolm X were killed, the movement lost some steam and direction. Hopes and dreams began to waver. Some of the group momentum and energy seeped away. But the need for justice and social change continued. They said that many, like them, went through a period of discontent and emptiness. They needed new energy and inspiration to help them keep on.

They realized that they had overrelied on outside forces and group momentum to sustain them and that their spiritual centers were not strong and vibrant enough to sustain them. So they took some time to reconnect with their spirituality, nurture it, and gain new perspective. This spiritual rejuvenation not only restored energy and direction for their continuing international peace and justice work; it also deepened their grounding in compassion as a guide to their action.

They pointed out the wisdom of black spirituals, the hymns of divine praise and human liberation, so important in the African American community. These hymns sustain individuals in a religious community. They tap a power for perseverance over the long haul. And they do this by joining spirituality and justice in a spirit of celebration.

Their story reminds us to stay in touch with our inner spiritual center as we go out to do our work in the world.

SUMMARY

In this book, we have offered a framework of values, concepts, knowledge, and activities that are conducive to spiritually sensitive social work practice. Our framework springs out of our profession's mission to promote the well-being of individuals as well as social justice. But by recalling our profession's original commitment to the whole person—bio-psycho-social and spiritual—we hope we have extended the range of that vision. We hope that this book encourages you to continue your inner work on spiritual development to inspire your service on behalf of others. We hope also that this book helps you to extend the range of your service vision to take in people of all religions, spiritual paths, cultures, and ways of life, and, further, all the beings with whom we coexist.

By way of concluding, we would like to convey our appreciation to you for reading this book. We designed the book so that reading it would usher you through your own transformation process, your own journey of spiritual development. We appreciate your willingness to participate.

As we know from the nature of therapeutic transformation, the end is the beginning. So we leave you with a parting wish:

> May any benefit you received
> from reading this book
> ripple throughout your life
> like a pebble dropped into a pond.
>
> And may the ripples of benefit extend
> to all those whom you serve
> to all people whom you meet
> and to all beings
> with whom you share this life.

EXERCISES

9.1. Putting the Skills to Practice

This chapter presents an introduction to practice skills and techniques by giving explanations about how to do them. We recommend that you try these exercises yourself. Do them repeatedly until you feel comfortable to use them with clients. Seek additional reading and instruction from experienced practitioners as needed. We list the exercises here. Start with one exercise and practice it thoroughly. Then try another.

A. Designing a multicultural teamwork approach for spiritually sensitive practice (see Table 9.1)
B. Paying attention (p. 295)
C. Intentional breathing (p. 296)
D. Equipoise (p. 297)
E. Consistency (p. 297)
F. Focused relaxing (p. 298)
G. Caring for the body (p. 300)
H. Doing ritual and ceremony (see Table 9.3)
I. Practicing forgiveness (p. 304)

9.2. Taking a Macro Perspective

In the section "Spirituality and Community-Involved Practice," we emphasized the inseparability between personal well-being and collective justice. We invite you to review each of the five major points (in italics). Also, review the second section of Table 9.2. Now reflect on your own social work practice. Identify at least one way you can extend your spiritually sensitive practice into macro arenas through involvement with community collaboration, community organizing, or social policy formation.

DISCUSSION GUIDE FOR ASSESSING SPIRITUAL PROPENSITY[1]

For the purpose of discussion, I am defining *spirituality* as the human search for life meaning, morally fulfilling relationships, and an understanding of the reality that has greatest significance to you. This may or may not involve belief in a God or supernatural aspect of the world. I am defining *religion* as an organized set of beliefs, values, and practices, shared by a community, that focuses on spirituality. Therefore, a person's spirituality may or may not be expressed through a religion. So when I use the term spiritual, I include religious and nonreligious possibilities.

Considering these definitions, I am interested to learn about your experiences about spirituality and religion. Please feel free to answer or not answer my questions in any way that is comfortable to you. We can also change the terms and definitions of spirituality and religion if you wish. Please describe what spirituality, religion, and faith mean to you, if anything. I am interested in hearing your story in your own words.

(Pause for client's response.) Thank you very much. Now I would like to follow up with some more specific questions.

Spiritual Group Membership and Participation
1. Do you belong to or participate in any spiritual groups?
2. If so, please name them.
3. Would you describe these as religious or nonreligious? Please explain.
4. If your spiritual group affiliations and participation have changed during your lifetime, please explain.
5. What are the major beliefs and values of these groups?

[1]Note: Please refer to the guidelines in Chapter 8 (pp. 273–276).

6. Would you be interested in exploring how your spirituality or religion might be related to our work together? Please explain.

7. If you do not participate in any spiritual groups, do you have other ways of expressing spiritual needs or interests? Please explain.

Frequency, Types, and Helpfulness of Spiritual Activities

1. How often do you attend a place for spiritual practice, such as a church, temple, mosque, or a ceremonial site in nature? Please describe these places.

   Daily?   Weekly?   Monthly?   Yearly?   Very Rarely?   Never?

2. What kinds of spiritual activities do you perform together with a spiritual group? These might include forms of prayer, meditation, ritual, ceremony, reading sacred texts, telling and listening to inspirational stories or speeches, or participating in social support groups. Please describe them.

3. In what ways do you find these activities helpful or unhelpful?

4. How often do you perform spiritual activities together with your family at home?

   Daily?   Weekly?   Monthly?   Yearly?   Very Rarely?   Never?

5. What kinds of spiritual activities do you perform together with your family at home? Please describe them.

6. In what ways do you find these activities helpful or unhelpful?

7. How often do you perform spiritual activities by yourself?

   Daily?   Weekly?   Monthly?   Yearly?   Very Rarely?   Never?

8. What kinds of spiritual activities do you perform by yourself? Please describe them.

9. In what ways do you find these activities helpful or unhelpful?

Inspirational Sources of Support

1. Who have been your most important spiritual friends and mentors? Please describe them.

2. What are the most significant stories, teachings, or symbols that give you guidance? Please describe them.

3. What have been the most profound and moving experiences that gave you a sense of peace, wisdom, or grace? Please describe them.

4. When you have been at a time of crisis previously, what spiritual supports helped you most? Please describe them.

5. When you have been at a time of great satisfaction and joy, what spiritual supports contributed most? Please describe them.

Extrinsic/Intrinsic Styles of Spiritual Propensity
1. How often do you agree with the teachings and values of your spiritual groups?

    Never?   Rarely?   Sometimes?   Usually?   Always?

2. Please explain and give examples.
3. How comfortable are you with the activities and style of your spiritual groups?

    Not at all?   Not Much?   Somewhat?   Very much?   Completely?

4. Please explain and give examples.
5. If you ever disagree or are uncomfortable with any aspect of your spiritual groups, how often do you tell people?

    Never?   Rarely?   Sometimes?   Usually?   Always?

6. Please explain and give examples.
7. How much are your spiritual principles and practices integrated into your daily life outside of spiritual group participation?

    Not at all?   Very little?   Somewhat?   Very much?   Completely?

8. Please explain and give examples.
9. When you meet someone from a different spiritual perspective from your own, how often do you feel that you should help that person to change to your perspective?

    Never?   Rarely?   Somewhat?   Usually?   Always?

10. Please explain and give examples.

METHODOLOGICAL SUMMARY FOR NATIONAL SURVEY OF NASW MEMBERS ON SPIRITUALITY IN PRACTICE

This national study explored the views of NASW members in direct practice regarding their professional use of religion and spirituality. The questionnaire defined *religion* as "an organized, structured set of beliefs and practices shared by a community, related to spirituality" and *spirituality* as "involving the search for meaning, purpose, and morally fulfilling relations with self, other people, the encompassing universe and ultimate reality, however a person understands it." According to these definitions, spirituality also can be expressed through religious forms but is not limited to them.

The 105-item questionnaire included items for demographic, educational background, and practice information; past and current religious or spiritual affiliation and involvement; ideological measures of types of belief in a divinity or a personal God; and items regarding forgiveness, the DSM-IV, referral to clergy, and attitudes about "cults." A newly developed scale separating religion from spirituality was used to assess social workers' agreement with raising these topics in practice. Additionally, the survey requested information about spiritually based "helping activities" that social workers used in their practice and that they felt were appropriate to use. Other items explored possible conflicts between religion and spirituality with the social work mission, the Code of Ethics, and separation of church and state.

A random sample of 8,000 practicing social workers was selected from NASW membership lists and stratified by states into four U.S. Census Bureau Regional Divisions (Northeast, Midwest, South, and West). Two thousand questionnaires were mailed to each area. The resultant 1,069 returned questionnaires provided a 26 percent overall response rate with a sampling error of plus or minus 2.2 percent at the 95 percent confidence interval. The demographic characteristics of the sample so closely align with NASW demographic data (Gibleman & Schervish, 1997) that it is likely the sample closely reflects the total membership.

RELIABILITY AND SCALING

Many items were treated as categorical rather than continuous variables, so attempts to combine items into reliable scales were initiated with this investigation. Thus, other than the fact that selected items were used in previous investigations (Bullis, 1993; Dudley & Helfgott, 1990; Sheridan et al., 1991, 1992), this instrument has no track record. Evidence was sought through exploratory principal components analysis regarding whether items referring to religion or spirituality could be combined to form scales.

Evidence for separate religion and spirituality factors (scores) was contradictory. The factor structure supported only one scale, which seemed to pertain to transcendent values in social work practice, across items worded in terms of either spirituality or religion [λ (lambda) = 14.16, percent of inter-item variance explained = 64.3]. However, if separate scales are constructed of the religion-versus-spirituality items, then subjects rated spirituality items (SPIR) significantly higher than religion items (REL) (mean MSPIR = 3.78, S.D. = 0.87; MREL = 3.33, S.D. = 1.01).

Coefficient alphas were calculated for scales made up of religion items (R), spirituality items (S), and a combined religion-spirituality scale (RS). The R alpha turned out to be .97, while those for S and RS were .96 and .97, respectively. These data suggest that at least spiritually based and religiously based items measure a trait we have called RS (religion/spirituality). An examination of the items suggests that this trait deals with spirituality and religion as they manifest in social work practice. The high coefficient alphas suggest that the religion and spirituality items may be useful in future investigations as measurement scales.

Validity

Several sets of items were culled from past research, where their utility was at least established though the peer review process (Bullis, 1993; Dudley & Helfgott, 1990; Sheridan et al., 1992; Sheridan, Wilmer & Atcheson, 1994). Reworkings of items from past studies and newly developed items were subjected to content and wording analysis by thirteen members of a university social work department. Items that faculty members found conceptually confusing (validity) or difficult to understand (reliability) were reworked in the light of their comments. Reviewers were asked to comment on whether items tapped attitudes of social workers toward religion, spirituality, and social work practice. The instrument evolved over several weeks and permutations until we were satisfied with content validity.

Given that the religion and spirituality items could reliably be combined into a scale (or scales), it is possible to use this scale as an initial check on the criterion-referenced/concurrent validity of some of the other items. If the combined RS scale is in fact tapping fundamental attitudes of social workers toward raising these issues in their practices, then the scale should covary with other items where the content is related.

For example, RS correlated positively with the number of religious/spiritual helping activities reportedly performed ($r_{xy} = .44, p < .001$) and with the number of religious/spiritual activities nominated as appropriate for use with clients ($r_{xy} = .46, p < .001$). Social workers reporting a higher level of personal spiritual involvement are more willing (and perhaps able) to introduce religion and/or spirituality into their practice. The RS scale was significantly correlated ($r_{xy} = .242, p < .001$) with items related to respondents' personal religious and spiritual practices.

A check on the discriminant validity of the R scale (and thus R items) can be conducted by comparing the scores of atheists and agnostics with those of Christians. Christians scored significantly higher on the R scale ($M = 3.45$, S.D. $= .961$ versus agnostics/atheists $M = 2.84$, S.D. $= 1.01$; $t, df = 187.2, = 6.95, p < .001$), suggesting that those identifying themselves with a specific religion also responded to items dealing with religion in a predictable manner. It also means that Christians are significantly more likely to discuss the topic of religion with clients than are agnostics or atheists.

REFERENCES

Abe, M. (1995). A Buddhist view of human rights. In A. A. An-Na'im, J. D. Gort, H. Jansen & H. M. Vroom (Eds.), *Human rights and religious values: An uneasy relationship?* (pp. 144–153). Grand Rapids, MI: William B. Eerdmans Publishing Company.

Achterberg, J. (1985). *Imagery in healing: Shamanism and modern medicine.* Boston: Shambhala.

Aldridge, M. J., Macy, H., & Walz, T. (n.d.). *Beyond management: Humanizing the administrative process.* Iowa City, IA: School of Social Work, University of Iowa.

Al-Krenawi, A. (1996). Group work with bedouin widows of the Negev in a medical clinic. *Affilia, 11*(3), 303–318.

Amato-von Hemert, K. (1994). Should social work education address religious issues? Yes! *Journal of Social Work Education, 30*(1), 7–11, 16–17.

American Psychiatric Association. (1994). *Diagnostic and statistical manual of mental disorders* (4th ed.). Washington, DC: Author.

Anderson, R. E., & Carter, I. (1990). *Human behavior in the social environment: A social systems approach* (4th ed.). New York: Aldine de Gruyter.

Anderson, R. (1996). *Magic, science, and health: The aims and achievements of medical anthropology.* Fort Worth, TX: Harcourt Brace.

Angel, L. (1994). *Enlightenment east and west.* Albany: State University of New York.

Ansel, E. (1973). T'shuva—parallels to the existential growth process. *Jewish Social Work Forum, 10*(2), 36–47.

Assagioli, R. (1965). *Psychosynthesis: A collection of basic writings.* New York: Penguin.

Axinn, J., & Levin, H. (1982). *Social welfare: A history of the American response to need* (2nd ed.). New York: Harper & Row.

Banerjee, M. M. (1997a). Strengths despite constraints: Memoirs of research in a slum in Calcutta. *Reflections: Narratives of Professional Helping, 3*(3), 36–45.

Banerjee, M. M. (1997b). Frozen feta cheese lasagna with crushed hot peppers. *Reflections: Narratives of Professional Helping, 3*(4), 44–54.

Barry, W. A., & Connolly, W. J. (1982). *The practice of spiritual direction.* New York: Seabury Press.

Baum, R. M. (1993). Homosexuality and the traditional religions of the Americas and Africa. In Arlene Swidler (Ed.), *Homosexuality and world religions* (pp. 1–46). Valley Forge, PA: Trinity Press International.

Beane, W. C., & Doty, W. G. (Eds.). (1975). *Myths, rites, symbols: A Mircea Eliade reader.* New York: Harper & Row.

Bell, C. M. (1992). *Ritual theory, ritual practice.* New York: Oxford University Press.

Bellah, R. N. (1991). *Beyond belief: Essays on religion in a post-traditional world.* Berkeley, CA: University of California Press.

Benson, P. L., Donahue, M. J., & Erickson, J. A. (1993). The faith maturity scale: Conceptualization, measurement, and empirical validation. In M. L. Lynn & D. O. Moberg (Eds.), *Research in the social scientific study of religion* (Vol. 5, pp. 1–26). Greenwich, CT: JAI Press.

Benton, J. F. (1981). A theology of charity for Christian social agencies. *Social Thought, 7*(4), 2–13.

Berl, F. (1979). Clinical practice in a Jewish context. *Journal of Jewish Communal Service, 55*(4), 366–368.

Bhattacharya, V. (1965). Swami Vivekenanda's message of service. *Social Welfare, 12*(1), 1–3.

Biestek, F. P. (1956). Religion and social casework. In L. C. DeSantis (Ed.), *The social welfare forum* (pp. 86–95). New York: Columbia University Press.

Bigham, T. J. (1956). Cooperation between ministers and social workers. In F. E. Johnson (Ed.), *Religion and social work* (pp. 141–154). New York: Institute for Religious and Social Studies, Harper and Brothers.

Black, P. N., Jeffreys, D. & Hartley, E. K. (1993). Personal history of psychosocial trauma in the early life of social work and business students. *Journal of Social Work Education, 29*(2), 171–180.

Blofeld, J. (1988). *Bodhisattva of compassion: The mystical tradition of Kuan Yin.* Boston: Shambhala.

Borenzweig, H. (1984). *Jung and social work.* New York: University Press of America.

Bourguignon, E. (1979). *Psychological anthropology.* New York: Holt, Rinehart and Winston.

Brackney, B., & Watkins, D. (1983). An analysis of Christian values and social work practice. *Social Work and Christianity, 10*(1), 5–20.

Bradford, K. A. (1969). *Existentialism and casework.* New York: Exposition Press.

Bragdon, E. (1990). *The call of spiritual emergency: From personal crisis to personal transformation.* San Francisco: Harper & Row.

Brandon, D. (1976). *Zen in the art of helping.* New York: Delta/Seymour Lawrence.

Brandon, D. (1979). Zen practice in social work. In D. Brandon & B. Jordon (Eds.), *Creative social work* (pp. 30–35). Oxford: Basil Blackwell.

Braude, A. (1997). Women's history is American religious history. In Thomas A. Tweed (Ed.), *Retelling U.S. religious history* (pp. 87–107). Berkeley: University of California Press.

Breton, M. (1989). Liberation theology, group work, and the right of the poor and oppressed to participate in the life of the community. *Social Work with Groups, 12*(3), 5–18.

Brinkerhoff, M., & Mackie, M. (1993). Nonbelief in Canada: Characteristics and origins of religious nones. In W. E. Hewitt (Ed.), *The sociology of religion: A Canadian focus* (pp. 109–131). Toronto: Butterworths.

Brower, I. C. (1984). *The 4th ear of the spiritual-sensitive social worker.* Union for Experimenting Colleges and Universities. Ann Arbor, MI: University Microfilms International, 8500785.

Brown, J. E. (Ed.). (1971). *The sacred pipe: Black Elk's account of the seven rites of the Oglala Sioux.* New York: Penguin Books.

Brown, L. B. (Ed.). (1994). *Religion, personality, and mental health.* New York: Springer-Verlag.

Buber, M. (1957). *I and thou.* (Trans. Ronald Gregor Smith.) Edinburgh: T. & T. Clark.

Bubis, G. B. (1980). The Jewish component in Jewish communal service—from theory to practice. *Journal of Jewish Communal Service, 56*(3), 227–237.

Bubis, G. B. (1981). Professional trends in Jewish communal practice in America. *Journal of Jewish Communal Service, 57*(4), 304–311.

Buhner, S. (1997). *One spirit/many peoples.* Boulder, CO: Roberts Rinehart Publishers.

Bullis, R. K. (1993). *Religious/spiritual factors in clinical social work practice: An examination of assessment, intervention and ethics.* Unpublished doctoral dissertation, Virginia Commonwealth University.

Bullis, R. K. (1996). *Spirituality in social work practice.* Washington, DC: Taylor & Francis.

Burtonin, H. P., Laughlin, J., & Chakravarty, A. (Eds.). (1975). *The Asian Journal of Thomas Merton.* New York: New Directions.

Cain, R. (1996). Heterosexism and self-disclosure in the social work classroom. *Journal of Social Work Education, 32*(1), 65–76.

Canda, E. R. (1982). Korean shamanic initiation as therapeutic transformation: A transcultural view. *Korea Journal, 22*(11), 13–26.

Canda, E. R. (1983). General implications of shamanism for clinical social work. *International Social Work, 26*(4), 14–22.

Canda, E. R. (1988a). Therapeutic transformation in ritual, therapy, and human development. *Journal of Religion and Health, 27*(3), 205–220.

Canda, E. R. (1988b). Conceptualizing spirituality for social work: Insights from diverse perspectives. *Social Thought, 14*(1), 30–46.

Canda, E. R. (1988c). Spirituality, religious diversity, and social work practice. *Social Casework, 69*(4), 238–247.

Canda, E. R. (1989a). Religious content in social work education: A comparative approach. *Journal of Social Work Education, 25*(1), 36–45.

Canda, E. R. (1989b). Religion and social work: A response to Sanzenbach. *Social Casework, 70*(9), 572–574.

Canda, E. R. (1990a). An holistic approach to prayer for social work practice. *Social Thought, 16*(3), 3–13.

Canda, E. R. (1990b). Afterword: Spirituality re-examined. *Spirituality and Social Work Communicator, 1*(1), 13–14.

Canda, E. R. (1990c). Spiritual diversity and social work values. In J. J. Kattakayam (Ed.), *Contemporary social issues* (pp. 1–20). Trivandrum, India: University of Kerala.

Canda, E. R. (1991). East/West philosophical synthesis in transpersonal theory. *Journal of Sociology and Social Welfare, 18*(4), 137–152.

Canda, E. R. (1993). Gripped by the drum: The Korean tradition of *nongak. Shaman's Drum, 33*, 18–23.

Canda, E. R. (1995a). Bodhisattva, sage, and shaman: Exemplars of compassion and service in traditional Korean religions. In H. Kwon (Ed.), *Korean cultural roots: Religion and social thoughts* (pp. 31–44). Chicago: Integrated Technical Resources.

Canda, E. R. (1995b) (Ed.). Spirituality: A Special Issue. *Reflections: Narratives of Professional Helping, 1*(4), 1–81.

Canda, E. R. (1997a). Does religion and spirituality have a significant place in the core HBSE curriculum? Yes. In M. Bloom & W. C. Klein (Eds.), *Controversial issues in human behavior in the social environment* (pp. 172–177, 183–184). Boston: Allyn & Bacon.

Canda, E. R. (1997b). Spirituality. In Richard L. Edwards (Ed.), *Encyclopedia of social work 19th Edition Supplement* (pp. 299–309). Washington, DC: National Association of Social Workers.

Canda, E. R. (Ed.). (1998). *Spirituality and social work: New directions.* Binghamton, NY: Haworth Pastoral Press.

Canda, E. R. & Canda, H. J. (1996). Korean spiritual philosophies of human service: Current state and prospects. *Social Development Issues, 18*(3), 53–70.

Canda, E. R., Carrizosa, S., & Yellow Bird, M. (1995). *Cultural diversity in child welfare practice: A training curriculum for cultural competence,* revised. Lawrence, KS: University of Kansas, School of Social Welfare.

Canda, E. R., & Chambers, D. (1994). Should spiritual principles guide social policy? Yes. In H. J. Karger & J. Midgley (Eds.), *Controversial issues in social policy* (pp. 63–70, 74–78). Boston: Allyn & Bacon.

Canda, E. R., & Phaobtong, T. (1992). Buddhism as a support system for Southeast Asian refugees. *Social Work, 37*(1), 61–67.

Canda, E. R., Shin, S., & Canda, H. (1993). Traditional philosophies of human service in Korea and contemporary social work implications. *Social Development Issues, 15*(3), 84–104.

Canda, E. R., & Yellow Bird, M. J. (1996). Cross-tradition borrowing of spiritual practices in social work settings. *Society for Spirituality and Social Work Newsletter, 3*(1), 1, 7.

Capozzi, L. (1992). Nonviolent social work and stress reduction: A Gandhian cognitive restructuring model. *Spirituality and Social Work Journal, 3*(1), 13–18.

Capps, W. H. (1995). *Religious studies: The making of a discipline.* Minneapolis, MN: Fortress Press.

Caroll, M. M. (1998). Social work's conceptualization of spirituality. In Edward R. Canda (Ed.), *Spirituality in social work: New directions* (pp. 1–13). Binghamton, NY: Haworth Pastoral Press.

Casteneda, C. (1968). *The teachings of Don Juan: A Yaqui way of knowledge.* New York: Ballantine.

Castex, G. M. (1994). Providing services to Hispanic/Latino populations: Profiles in diversity. *Social Work, 39*(3), 288–296.

Cataldo, C. (1979). Wilderness therapy: Modern day shamanism. In C. B. Germain (Ed.), *Social work practice: People and environments* (pp. 46–73). New York: Columbia University Press.

Cave, D. (1993). *Mircea Eliade's vision for a new humanism.* New York: Oxford University Press.

Chalfant, H. P., Beckley, R. E., & Palmer, C. E. (1987). *Religion in contemporary society* (2nd ed). Palo Alto, CA: Mayfield Publishing Company.

Chalfant, H. P., Heller, P. L., Rogerts, A., Brioner, D., Aguirre-Hochbaum, S., & Farr, W. (1990). The clergy as a resource for those encountering psychological distress. *Review of Religious Research, 31*(3), 305–315.

Chenault, V. (1990). A Native American practice framework. *Spirituality and Social Work Communicator, 1*(2), 5–7.

Chesler, M. A. (1991). Participatory action research with self-help groups: An alternative paradigm for inquiry and action. *American Journal of Community Psychology, 19*(5), 757–768.

Clark, J. (1994). Should social work education address religious issues? No! *Journal of Social Work Education, 30*(1), 11–16.

Coggins, K. (1990). *Alternative pathways to healing: The recovery medicine wheel.* Deerfield Beach, FL: Health Communications.

Coleman, P. (1980). *Christian attitudes to homosexuality.* London: SPCK.

Coles, R. (1990). *The spiritual life of children.* Boston: Houghton Mifflin.

Coles, R. (1993). *The call of service.* Boston: Houghton Mifflin.

Comstock, G. D. (1993). *Gay theology without apology.* Cleveland, OH: Pilgrim Press.

Consiglio, W. E. (1987). *Spirit-led helping: A model for evangelical social work counseling.* St. Davids, PA: North American Association of Christians in Social Work.

Constable, R. T. (1983). Values, religion, and social work practice. *Social Thought, 9*(4), 29–41.

Constable, R. (1990). Spirituality and social work: Issues to be addressed. *Spirituality and Social Work Communicator, 1*(1), 4–6.

Cooper, D. A. (1992). *Silence, simplicity, and Solitude: A guide for spiritual retreat.* New York: Bell Tower.

Corbett, J. M. (1997). *Religion in America* (3rd ed.). Upper Saddle River, NJ: Prentice Hall.

Costas, O. E. (1991). Hispanic theology in North America. In L. M. Getz & R. O. Costa (Eds.), *Struggles for solidarity: Liberation theologies in tension* (pp. 63–74). Minneapolis, MN: Fortress Press.

Coughlin, B. J. (1970). Religious values and child welfare. *Social Casework, 51*(2), 82–90.

Cowley, A. (1993). Transpersonal social work: A theory for the 1990s. *Social Work, 38*(5), 527–534.

Cowley, A. S. (1996). Transpersonal social work. In F. J. Turner (Ed.), *Social work treatment: Interlocking theoretical approaches* (pp. 663–698). New York: Free Press.

Cowley, A. S., & Derezotes, D. (1994). Transpersonal psychology and social work education. *Journal of Social Work Education, 30*(1), 32–41.

Cox, J. L. (1996). *Expressing the sacred: An introduction to the phenomenology of religion.* Harare, Zimbabwe: University of Zimbabwe Publications.

Crim, K. (Ed.). (1981). *The perennial dictionary of world religions.* San Francisco: HarperSanFrancisco.

Cromey, R. W. (1991). *In God's symbol: Christian witness to the need for gay/lesbian equality in the eyes of the church.* San Francisco: Alamo Square Press.

Curiel, H. (1995). Hispanics: Mexican Americans. In R. L. Edwards (Ed.), *Encyclopedia of social work* (19th ed.) (pp. 1233–1244). Washington, DC: NASW Press.

Daly, M. (1973). *Beyond God the father: Toward a philosophy of women's liberation.* Boston: Beacon Press.

Danylchuk, L. S. (1992). The pastoral counselor as mental health professional: A comparison of the training of AAPC fellow pastoral counselors and licensed clinical social workers. *Journal of Pastoral Care, 46*(4), 382–391.

Dasgupta, S. (1986). Gandhi and the new society. *Social Development Issues, 10*(1), 1–10.

Dass, R., & Gorman, P. (1985). *How can I help? Stories and reflections on service.* New York: Knopf.

Davis, C. F. (1989). *The evidential force of religious experience.* New York: Oxford University Press.

De Bary, W. T. (Ed.). (1969). *The Buddhist tradition in India, China and Japan.* New York: Vintage Books.

De La Rosa, M. (1988). Puerto Rican spiritualism: A key dimension for effective social casework practice with Puerto Ricans. *International Social Work, 31*(4), 273–283.

De Mallie, R. J. (Ed.). (1984). *The sixth grandfather: Black Elk's teachings given to John G. Neihardt.* Lincoln, NE: University of Nebraska Press.

De Silva, P. (1995). Human rights in Buddhist perspective. In A. A. An-Na'im, J. D. Gort, H. Jansen, & H. M. Vroom (Eds.), *Human rights and religious values: An uneasy relationship?* (pp. 133–143). Grand Rapids, MI: William B. Eerdmans Publishing Company.

Deck, A. F. (1989). *The second wave: Hispanic ministry and the evangelization of cultures.* New York: Paulist Press.

Delgado, M. (1977). Puerto Rican spiritism and the social work profession. *Social Casework, 58*(8), 451–458.

Delgado, M. (1988). Groups in Puerto Rican spiritism: Implications for clinicians. In C. Jacobs & D. D. Bowles (Eds.), *Ethnicity and race: Critical concepts in social work* (pp. 34–47). Silver Spring, MD: National Association of Social Workers.

Delgado, M., & Humm-Delgado, D. (1982). Natural support systems: Source of strength in Hispanic communities. *Social Work, 27*(1), 83–89.

Deloria, V., Jr. (1994). *God is red: A native view of religion.* Golden, CO: Fulcrum Publishing.

Denton, R. T. (1990). The religiously fundamentalist family: Training for assessment and treatment. *Journal of Social Work Education, 26*(1), 6–14.

Derezotes, D. S., & Evans, K. E. (1995). Spirituality and religiosity in practice: In-depth interviews of social work practitioners. *Social Thought, 18*(1), 39–56.

Devore, W., & Schlesinger, E. G. (1996). *Ethnic sensitive social work practice.* New York: Merrill.

DiBlasio, F. A. (1993). The role of social workers' religious beliefs in helping family members forgive. *Families in Society, 74*(3), 167–170.

DiBlasio, F. A., & Proctor, J. H. (1993). Therapists and the clinical use of forgiveness. *American Journal of Family Therapy, 21*(2), 175–184.

Dixon, S. L. (1979). *Working with people in crisis: Theory and practice.* St. Louis, MO: C.V. Mosby Company.

Doore, G. (Ed.). (1988). *Shaman's path: Healing, personal growth, and empowerment.* Boston: Shambhala.

Dossey, L. (1993). *Healing words: The power of prayer and the practice of medicine.* San Francisco: Harper.

Dowdy, T. E. (1991). Invisibility and plausibility: An analysis of the relationship between forms of privatization and individual religiosity. In M. L. Lynn & D. O. Moberg (Eds.), *Research in the social scientific study of religion* (Vol. 3, pp. 89–114). Greenwich, CN: JAI Press.

Dudley, J. R., & Helfgott, C. (1990). Exploring a place for spirituality in the social work curriculum. *Journal of Social Work Education, 26*(3), 287–294.

Dupre, L. (1987). Mysticism. In *The encyclopedia of religion* (pp. 245–261). New York: Macmillan.

Duran, K. (1993). Homosexuality and Islam. In Arlene Swidler (Ed.), *Homosexuality and world religions* (pp. 181–197). Valley Forge, PA: Trinity Press International.

Dynes, W. R., & Donaldson, S. (Eds.). (1992). *Homosexuality and religion and philosophy.* New York: Garland.

Edwards, D. G. (1982). *Existential psychotherapy: The process of caring.* New York: Gardner Press.

Eliade, M. (1959). *The sacred and the profane: The nature of religion.* New York: Harcourt, Brace & World.

Eliade, M. (1963). *Myth and reality.* (W. R. Trask, Trans.). New York: Harper & Row.

Eliade, M. (1964). *Shamanism: Archaic techniques of ecstasy.* Princeton, NJ: Princeton University Press.

Eliade, M. (1971). *The myth of the eternal return, or, cosmos and history.* (W. R. Trask, trans.). Bollingen Series, no. 46. Princeton: Princeton University Press.

Eppsteiner, F. (Ed.). (1988). *The path of compassion: Writings on socially engaged Buddhism.* Berkeley, CA: Parallax Press.

Erikson, E. H. (1962). *Young man Luther: A study in psychoanalysis and history.* New York: Norton.

Erikson, E. H. (1963). *Childhood and society* (2nd rev. ed, enl.). New York: Norton.

Erikson, E. H. (1968). *Identity: Youth and crisis.* New York: Norton.

Erikson, E. H. (1969). *Gandhi's truth: On the origins of militant nonviolence.* New York: Norton.

Erikson, E. H. (1982). *The life-cycle completed.* New York: Norton.

Eskenazi, D. (1983). God concepts and community structure. *Journal of Jewish Communal Service, 59*(3), 217–227.

Esposito, J. L. (1991). *Islam: The straight path.* New York: Oxford University Press.

Famighetti, R. (Ed.). (1995). *The world almanac and book of facts, 1996.* New York: World Almanac Books.

Faver, C. (1986). Religion, research, and social work. *Social Thought, 12*(3), 20–29.

Fischer, L. (1950). *The life of Mahatma Gandhi.* New York: Harper & Row.

Fitzgibbons, R. P. (1986). The cognitive and emotive uses of forgiveness in the treatment of anger. *Psychotherapy, 23*(4), 629–633.

Fowler, J. W. (1981). *Stages of faith: The psychology of human development and the quest for meaning.* San Francisco: Harper & Row.

Fowler, J. W. (1984). *Becoming adult, becoming Christian: Adult development and Christian faith.* San Francisco: Harper & Row.

Fowler, J. W. (1996). *Faithful change: The personal and public challenges of postmodern life.* Nashville, TN: Abingdon Press.

Frank, J. D. (1963). *Persuasion and healing.* New York: Schocken Books.

Frankl, V. E. (1969). *The will to meaning: Foundations and applications of logotherapy.* New York: World Publishing Co.

Franklin, R. M. (1994). The safest place on earth: The culture of black congregations. In J. P. Wind & J. W. Lewis (Eds.), *American congregations* (Vol. 2, pp. 257–284). Chicago: University of Chicago Press.

Frey, L. A., & Edinburg, G. (1978). Helping, manipulation, and magic. *Social Work, 23*(2), 89–93.

Fromm, E. (1966). *Marx's concept of man.* New York: Frederick Ungar Publishing Co.

Furman, L. D., Perry, D., & Goldade, T. (1996). Interaction of evangelical Christians and social workers in the rural environment. *Human Services in the Rural Environment, 19*(2/3), 5–8.

Furman, L. E. (1994). Religion and spirituality in social work education: Preparing the culturally sensitive practitioner for the future. *Social Work and Christianity: An International Journal, 21,* 103–115.

Furman, L. E., & Chandy, J. M. (1994). Religion and spirituality: A long-neglected cultural component of rural social work practice. *Human Services in the Rural Environment, 17*(3/4), 21–26.

Furman, L., Fry, S., & Fontaine, C. (1997). Social Workers and Clergy: Collaborators or Competitors, NASW National Conference, Baltimore, MD, October 4–6.

Furuto, S. M., Biswas, R., Chung, D. K., Murase, K., & Ross-Sherif, F. (Eds.). (1992). *Social work practice with Asian Americans.* Newbury Park, CA: Sage.

Gandhi, A. (n.d.). *M. K. Gandhi's wit and wisdom.* Nashville, TN: Gandhi Institute.

Garcia, I. (1987). *Justice in Latin American theology of liberation*. Atlanta, GA: John Knox Press.

Garland, D. S. R. (Ed.). (1992). *Church social work: Helping the whole person in the context of the church*. St. Davids, PA: North American Association of Christians in Social Work.

Garvin, C. (Ed.) (1998). Special issue: Forgiveness. *Reflections: Narratives of Professional Helping, 4*(4), 1–72.

Gatza, M. (1979). The role of healing prayer in the helping professions. *Social Thought, 5*(2), 3–13.

Gelman, S. R., & Schall, D. J. (1997). Jewish communal services. In R. L. Edwards (Ed.), *Encyclopedia of social work* (19th ed., 1997 suppl.) (pp. 169–178). Washington, DC: NASW Press.

Getz, L. M., & Costa, R. O. (Eds.). (1991). *Struggles for solidarity: Liberation theologies in tension*. Minneapolis, MN: Fortress Press.

Gibleman, M., & Schervish, P. H. (1997). *Who we are: A second look*. Washington, DC: NASW Press.

Gieben, S. (1980). *Christian sacrament and devotion*. Leiden, Netherlands: E. J. Brill.

Golan, N. (1981). *Passing through transitions*. New York: Free Press.

Gorsuch, R. L. (1983). *Factor analysis*. Hillsdale, NJ: Erlbaum.

Graham, J. R., & Al-Krenawi, A. (1996). A Comparison study of traditional helpers in a late nineteenth century Canadian (Christian) Society in Toronto, Canada and in a late twentieth century bedouin (Muslim) Society in Neger, Israel. *Journal of Multicultural Social Work, 4*(2), 31–45.

Gravely, W. B. (1973). *Gilbert Haven: Methodist abolitionist*. Nashville, TN: Abingdon Press.

Greeley, A. M. (1989). *Religious change in America*. Cambridge, MA: Harvard University Press.

Greeley, A. M. (1995). *Religion as poetry*. New Brunswick, NJ: Transaction Publishers.

Green, J. W. (1995). *Cultural awareness in the human services: A multi-ethnic approach*. Needham Heights, MA: Allyn & Bacon.

Griffin, D. R. (Ed.). (1988). *Spirituality and society: Postmodern visions.* Albany, NY: State University of New York Press.

Grimes, R. L. (1995). *Beginnings in ritual studies* (rev. ed.). Columbia, SC: University of South Carolina Press.

Grof, S. (1988). *The adventure of self discovery.* Albany: State University of New York Press.

Grof, S., & Grof, C. (Eds.). (1989). *Spiritual emergency: When personal transformation becomes a crisis.* Los Angeles: Tarcher.

Grof, S., & Grof, C. (1990). *The stormy search for the self.* New York: G. P. Putnam's Sons.

Grof, S., & Halifax, J. (1977). *The human encounter with death.* New York: Dutton.

Gross, R. (1994). Buddhism. In Jean Holm & John Bowker (Eds.), *Women in religion* (pp. 1–29). New York: Pinter Publishers.

Gutierrez, L. (1994). Beyond coping: An empowerment perspective on stressful life events. *Journal of Sociology and Social Welfare, 21*(3), 201–219.

Gutierrez, L. (1988). *A theology of liberation: History, politics and salvation.* Maryknoll, NY: Orbis Books.

Gutierrez, L. (1990). Working with women of color: An empowerment perspective. *Social Work, 35*(2), 149–153.

Halifax, J. (1982). *Shaman: The wounded healer.* New York: Crossroad.

Hanh, T. N. (1987). *The miracle of mindfulness: A manual on meditation* (rev. ed.). Boston: Beacon Press.

Harding, V. (1990). *Hope and history: Why we must share the story of the movement.* Mary Knoll, NY: Orbis Books.

Haynes, A. W., Eweiss, M. M. I., Mageed, M. A., & Chung, D. K. (1997). Islamic social transformation: Considerations for the social worker. *International Social Work, 40,* 265–275.

Heimbrock, H., & Boudewijnse, H. B. (Eds.). (1990). *Current studies on rituals: Perspectives for the psychology of religion.* Amsterdam: Rodopi.

Helminiak, D. A. (1996). *The human core of spirituality: Mind as psyche and spirit.* Albany, NY: State University of New York Press.

Henderson, D. C., Gartner, J. D., Greer, J. M. G., & Estadt, B. K. (1992). Who sees a pastoral counselor? An empirical study of client characteristics. *Journal of Pastoral Care, 46*(2), 210–217.

Hess, J. J., Jr. (1980). Social work's identity crisis: A Christian anthropological response. *Social Thought, 6*(1), 59–69.

Hewitt, W. E. (Ed.). *The sociology of religion: A Canadian focus.* Toronto: Butterworths.

Hick, J. H. (1990). *Philosophy of religion* (4th ed.). Englewood Cliffs, NJ: Prentice Hall.

Hillerman, A. (1987–1988). The shamanic art of David Chethlahe Paladin. *Shaman's Drum, 11*, 32–37.

Hillman, J. (1975). *Re-visioning psychology.* New York: Harper & Row.

Hollenback, J. B. (1996). *Mysticism: Experience, response, and empowerment.* University Park, PA: Pennsylvania State University Press.

Holm, J., & Bowker, J. (Eds.) (1994). *Women in religion.* New York: Pinter Publishers.

Holmgren, M. R. (1993). Forgivness and the intrinsic value of persons. *American Psychological Quarterly, 30*(4), 341–352.

Hope, D. (1987). The healing paradox of forgiveness. *Psychotherapy, 24*(2), 240–244.

Hoyt, M. F. (Ed.). (1996). *Constructive therapies 2.* New York: Guilford Press.

Iglehart, A. P., & Becerra, R. M. (1995). *Social services and the ethnic community.* Boston: Allyn & Bacon.

Imbrogno, S., & Canda, E. R. (1988). Social work as an holistic system of activity. *Social Thought, 14*(1), 16–29.

Imre, R. W. (1971). A theological view of social casework. *Social Casework, 52*(9), 578–585.

Jain, N. (1965). Zakat: A Muslim way of helping the needy. *Social Welfare, 12*(1), 4–5.

James, W. (1982). *The varieties of religious experience.* New York: Penguin Books.

Johnston, W. (1995). *Mystical theology: The science of love.* London: HarperCollins.

Johnstone, R. L. (1992). *Religion in society: A sociology of religion* (4th ed.). Englewood Cliffs, NJ: Prentice Hall.

Jones, C., Wainwright, G., & Yarnold, E. (Eds). *The study of spirituality.* New York: Oxford University Press.

Jones, L. N. (1991). The organized church: Its historic significance and changing role in contemporary African American experience. In W. J. Payne (Ed.), *Directory of African American religious bodies* (pp. 1–19). Washington, DC: Howard University Press.

Joseph, M. V. (1975). The parish as a social service and social action center: An ecological systems approach. *Social Thought, 1*(2), 43–59.

Joseph, M. V. (1987). The religious and spiritual aspects of social work practice: A neglected dimension of social work. *Social Thought, 13*(1), 12–23.

Joseph, M. V. (1988). Religion and social work practice. *Social Casework, 60*(7), 443–452.

Joseph, M. V. (1989). Response to Sanzenbach. *Social Casework, 70*(9), 574–575.

Joy, M., & Neumaier-Dargay, E. K. (Eds.). (1995). *Gender, genre, and religion: Feminist reflections.* Waterloo, Ontario, Canada: Wilfrid Laurier University Press.

Jung, C. (1938). *Psychology and religion.* New Haven, CT: Yale University Press.

Jung, C. G. (1953). *The structure of the unconscious.* Princeton, NJ: Princeton University Press.

Jung, C. (1959). *The concept of the collective unconscious.* Princeton, NJ: Princeton University Press.

Jung, C. (1963). *Memories, dreams, reflections*. New York: Random House.

Kabat-Zinn, J. (1990). *Full catastrophe living: Using the wisdom of your body and mind to face stress, pain, and illness*. New York: Delta.

Kahn, N. E. (1995). The adult bat mitzvah: Its use in the articulation of women's identity. *Affilia, 10*(3), 299–314.

Kalton, M. C. (Ed. and Trans.). (1988). *To become a sage: The ten diagrams on sage learning by Yi T'oegye*. New York: Columbia University Press.

Karenga, M. (1995). Making the past meaningful: KWANZAA and the concept of Sankofa. *Reflections: Narratives of Professional Helping, 1*(4), 36–46.

Kauffman, W. (1956). *Existentialism from Dostoevsky to Sartre*. Cleveland: World Publishing Company.

Keefe, T. (1975). A Zen perspective on social casework. *Social Casework, 56*(3), 140–144.

Keefe, T. (1996). Meditation and social work treatment. In F. J. Turner (Ed.), *Social work treatment: Interlocking theoretical approaches* (4th ed.) (pp. 434–460). New York: Free Press.

Keith-Lucas, A. (1985). *So you want to be a social worker: A primer for the Christian student*. St. Davids, PA: North American Association of Christians in Social Work.

Keith-Lucas, A. (1994). *Giving and taking help* (rev. ed.). St. Davids, PA: North American Association of Christians in Social Work.

Kiefer, C. W., & Cowan, J. (1979). State/context dependence and theories of ritual. *Journal of Psychological Anthropology, 2*(1), 53–83.

Kiev, A. (1972). *Transcultural psychiatry*. New York: Free Press.

King, N. (1965). Some perspectives on theology and social work. In P. C. McCabe & F. J. Turner (Eds.), *Catholic social work: A contemporary overview* (pp. 6–27). Ottawa: Catholic Charities Council of Canada.

King, U. (Ed.) (1987). *Women in the world's religions, past and present*. New York: Paragon House.

Koenig, T. L., & Spano, R. N. (1988). Taoism and the strengths perspective. In Edward R. Canda (Ed.), *Spirituality in social work: New directions* (pp. 47–65). Binghamton, NY: Haworth Pastoral Press.

Kreutziger, S. S. (1995). Spirituality in faith. *Reflections: Narratives of Professional Helping, 1*(4), 28–35.

Krieger, D. J. (1996). Methodological foundations for interreligious dialogue. In Joseph Prabhu (Ed.), *The intercultural challenge of Raimon Panikkar* (pp. 201–223). Maryknoll, NY: Orbis Books.

Krill, D. F. (1978). *Existential social work.* New York: Free Press.

Krill, D. F. (1979). Existential social work. In F. J. Turner (Ed.), *Social work treatment: Interlocking theoretical perspectives* (pp. 147–176). New York: Free Press.

Krill, D. (1986). *The beat worker: Humanizing social work and psychotherapy.* Lanham, MD: University Press of America.

Krill, D. F. (1988). Existential social work. In R. A. Dorfman (Ed.), *Paradigms of clinical social work* (pp. 295–316). New York: Brunner/Mazel.

Krill, D. F. (1990). *Practice wisdom: A guide for the helping professional.* Newbury Park, CA: Sage.

Krill, D. F. (1995). My spiritual sojourn into existential social work. *Reflections: Narratives of professional helping, 1*(4), 57–64.

Krill, D. F. (1996). Existential social work. In F. J. Turner (Ed.), *Social work treatment: Interlocking theoretical approaches* (4th ed.) (pp. 250–281). New York: Free Press.

Laird, J. (1984). Sorcerers, shamans, and social workers: The use of ritual in social work practice. *Social Work, 29*(2), 123–128.

Lal, P. (trans.) (1967). *The Dhammapada.* New York: Farrar, Straus & Giroux.

Lantz, J. (1993). *Existential family therapy: Using the concepts of Victor Frankl.* Northvale, NJ: Jason Aronson.

Lau, D. C. (trans.) (1970). *Mencius.* New York: Penguin Books.

Leashore, B. R. (1995). African Americans overview. In R. L. Edwards (Ed.), *Encyclopedia of social work* (19th ed.) (pp. 101–115). Washington, DC: National Association of Social Workers.

Lee, J. (1994). *The empowerment approach to social work practice.* New York: Columbia University Press.

Lehmann, A. C., & Myers, J. E. (1997). *Magic, witchcraft, and religion: An anthropological study of the supernatural* (4th ed.). Mountain View, CA: Mayfield Publishing Company.

Leiby, J. (1985). Moral foundations of social welfare and social work: A historical view. *Social Work, 30*(4), 323–330.

Lessa, W. A., & Vogt, E. Z. (Eds.). (1972). *Reader in comparative religion: An anthropological approach* (3rd ed.). New York: Harper & Row.

Lewandowski, C. A., & Canda, E. R. (1995). A typological model for the assessment of religious groups. *Social Thought, 18*(1), 17–38.

Lincoln, B. (1981). *Emerging from the chrysalis: Studies in rituals of women's initiation.* Cambridge: Harvard University Press.

Lincoln, Y. S. (1995). Emerging criteria for quality in qualitative and interpretive research. *Qualitative Inquiry, 1*(3), 275–289.

Lincoln, Y. S., & Guba, E. G. (1985). *Naturalistic inquiry.* Beverly Hills, CA: Sage.

Linzer, N. (1979). A Jewish philosophy of social work practice. *Journal of Jewish Communal Service, 55*(4), 309–317.

Lippy, C. H., & Williams, P. W. (Eds.). (1988). *Encyclopedia of American religious experience: Studies of traditions and movements.* New York: Charles Scribner's Sons.

Loewenberg, F. M. (1988). *Religion and social work practice in contemporary American society.* New York: Columbia University Press.

Logan, S. (1990). Critical issues in operationalizing the spiritual dimension of social work practice. *Spirituality and Social Work Communicator, 1*(1), 7–9.

Logan, S. L. (1996). *The black family: Strengths, self-help, and positive change.* Boulder, CO: Westview Press.

Logan, S. L. (1997). Meditation as a tool that links the personal and the professional. *Reflections: Narratives of Professional Helping, 3*(1), 38–44.

Logan, S. L., Freeman, E. M., & McRoy, R. G. (1990). *Social work practice with black families: A culturally specific perspective.* New York: Longman.

Lukoff, D. (1985). The diagnosis of mystical experiences with psychotic features. *Journal of Transpersonal Psychology, 17*(2), 155–181.

Lukoff, D., Lu, F. G., & Turner, R. (1992). Toward a more culturally sensitive DSM-IV: Psychoreligious and psychospiritual problems. *Journal of Nervous and Mental Disease, 180*(11), 673–682.

Lukoff, D., Lu, F. G., & Turner, R. (1995). Cultural considerations in the assessment and treatment of religious and spiritual problems. *Cultural Psychiatry, 18*(3), 467–485.

Lum, D. (1996). *Social work practice with people of color: A process stage approach* (3rd ed). Pacific Grove, CA: Brooks/Cole Publishing.

Luoma, B. (1988). An exploration of intuition for social work practice and education. In Edward R. Canda (Ed.), *Spirituality in social work: New directions* (pp 31–45). Binghamton, NY: Haworth Pastoral Press.

Lyon, W. S. (1996). *Encyclopedia of Native American healing.* Santa Barbara, CA: ABC-CLIO.

Macy, J. (1991). *Mutual causality in Buddhism and general systems theory.* Albany: State University of New York Press.

Marshall, J. (1991). The spiritual dimension in social work education. *Spirituality and Social Work Communicator, 2*(1), 12–15.

Marty, M. E. (1980). Social service: Godly and godless. *Social Service Review, 54*(4), 4463–4481.

Marty, M. E., & Appleby, S. (Eds.). (1991). *Fundamentalisms observed.* Chicago: University of Chicago Press.

Maslow, A. (1968). *Toward a psychology of being* (2nd ed.). New York: D. Van Nostrand.

Maslow, A. (1969). The farther reaches of human nature. *Journal of Transpersonal Psychology, 1*(1), 1–9.

Maslow, A. (1970). *Religions, values and peak experiences.* New York: Viking.

Masters, R. E. L., & Houston, J. (1966). *The varieties of psychedelic experience.* New York: Delta.

Matthews, D. A., & Larson, D. B. (1995). *The faith factor: An annotated bibliography of clinical research on spiritual subjects, Vol. 3: Enhancing life satisfaction.* Rockville, MD: National Institute for Healthcare Research.

Matthews, D. A., Larson, D. B., & Barry, C. P. (1993). *The faith factor: An annotated bibliography of clinical research on spiritual subjects.* Rockville, MD: National Institute for Healthcare Research.

McCabe, P. C. (1965). Sectarian social work—necessity or luxury. In P. C. McCabe & F. J. Turner (Eds.), *Catholic social work: A contemporary overview* (pp. 28–43). Ottowa: Catholic Charities Council of Canada.

McGee, E. (1984). The transpersonal perspective: Implications for the future of personal and social development. *Social Development Issues, 8*(3), 151–181.

McLaughlin, C., & Davidson, G. (1994). *Spiritual politics.* New York: Ballantine.

McShane, C. (1993). Satanic sexual abuse: A paradigm. *Affilia, 8*(2), 200–212.

Melton, J. G. (1991). *The churches speak on: Homosexuality.* Detroit, MI: Gale Research.

Melton, J. G. (1992). *Religious bodies in the United States: A directory.* New York: Garland Publishing.

Melton, J. G. (Ed.). (1993). *Encyclopedia of American religion.* Detroit, MI: Gale Research.

Merton, T. (1968). *Conjectures of a guilty bystander.* Garden City, NY: Image Books.

Meystedt, D. M. (1984). Religion and the rural population: Implications for social work. *Social Casework, 65*(4), 219–226.

Mickey, P. A. (1991). *Of sacred worth.* Nashville, TN: Abingdon Press.

Midgely, J. (1990). The new Christian right, social policy, and the welfare state. *Journal of Sociology and Social Welfare, 17*(2), 89–106.

Midgely, J., & Sanzenbach, P. (1989). Social work, religion, and the global challenge of fundamentalism. *International Social Work, 32*(4), 273–287.

Miller, C. (1980). Commitment, ideology, and skill. *Journal of Jewish Communal Service, 57*(1), 30–36.

Miller, T. (Ed.). (1995). *America's alternative religions.* Albany: State University of New York Press.

Mokuau, N. (1990). A family-centered approach in native Hawaiian culture. *Families in Society, 7*(10), 607–613.

Morris, B. (1987). *Anthropological studies of religion: An introductory text.* New York: Cambridge University Press.

Morris, C. S. (1991). African Americans and Methodism. In W. J. Payne (Ed.), *Directory of African American religious bodies* (pp. 238–247). Washington, DC: Howard University Press.

Murray, P., & Murray, L. (1996). *The Oxford companion to Christian art and architecture.* Oxford: Oxford University Press.

Nabigon, H., & Mawhiney, A. (1996). Aboriginal theory: A Cree medicine wheel guide for healing First Nations. In F. J. Turner (Ed.), *Social work treatment: Interlocking theoretical approaches* (4th ed.) (pp. 18–38). New York: Free Press.

Nakashima, M. (1995). Spiritual growth through hospice work. *Reflections: Narratives of Professional Helping, 1*(4), 17–27.

National Association of Social Workers. (1996). *The NASW Code of Ethics.* Washington, DC: NASW.

National Conference of Catholic Charities. (1983). *A code of ethics.* Washington, DC: Author.

Nelson, J. E. (1994). *Healing the split: Integrating spirit into our understanding of the mentally ill* (rev. ed.). Albany: State University of New York Press.

Netting, F. E. (1982a). Secular and religious funding in church-related agencies. *Social Service Review, 56*(12), 586–604.

Netting, F. E. (1982b). Social work and religious values in church-related agencies. *Social Work and Christianity, 9*(1–2), 4–20.

Netting, F. E. (1984). Church-related agencies and social welfare. *Social Service Review 58*(3), 404–420.

Netting, F. E., Kettner, P. M., & McMurty, S. L. (1998). *Social work macro practice* (2nd ed.). New York: Longman.

Netting, F. E., Thibault, J. T., & Ellor, J. W. (1990). Integrating content on organized religion into macropractice courses. *Journal of Social Work Education, 26*(1), 15–24.

Neusner, J. (1979). *The way of Torah: An introduction to Judaism* (3rd ed.). North Scituate, MA: Duxbury Press.

Newsome, C. G. (1991). A synoptic survey of the history of African American Baptists. In W. J. Payne (Ed.), *Directory of African American religious bodies* (pp. 226–237). Washington, DC: Howard University Press.

Niebuhr, R. (1932). *The contribution of religion to social work.* New York: Columbia University Press.

Nielsen, N. C., Jr., et al. (1993). *Religions of the world* (3rd ed.). New York: St. Martin's Press.

Nussbaum, D. (1983). Tsedakah, social justice, and human rights. *Journal of Jewish Communal Service, 59*(3), 228–236.

Oakley, V. (1955). *Cathedral of compassion: Dramatic outline of the life of Jane Addams, 1860–1935.* Philadelphia: Press of Lyon and Armor.

Ortiz, L. (1991). Religious issues: The missing link in social work education. *Spirituality and Social Work Journal, 2*(2), 13–18.

Osterkamp, L., & Press, A. (1988). *Stress: Find your balance* (rev. ed.). Lawrence, KS: Preventive Measures.

Ostrov, S. (1976). A family therapist's approach to working with an Orthodox Jewish clientele. *Journal of Jewish Communal Service, 63*(2), 147–154.

Otto, R. (1950). *The idea of the holy* (2nd ed.). (J. W. Harvey, Trans.). London: Oxford University Press.

Paden, W. E. (1992). *Interpreting the sacred: Ways of viewing religion.* Boston: Beacon Press.

Paden, W. E. (1994). *Religious worlds: The comparative study of religion.* Boston: Beacon Press.

Paladin, L. S. (1991). *Ceremonies for change: Creating rituals to heal life's hurts.* Walpole, NH: Stillpoint.

Pals, D. L. (1996). *Seven theories of religion.* New York: Oxford University Press.

Pandey, R. S. (1996). Gandhian perspectives on personal empowerment and social development. *Social Development Issues, 18*(2), 66–84.

Paris, P. J. (1995). *The spirituality of African peoples: The search for a common moral discourse.* Minneapolis, MN: Fortress Press.

Parr, R. G., & Jones, L. E. (1996). Point/Counterpoint: Should CSWE allow social work programs in religious institutions an exemption from the accreditation nondiscrimination standard related to sexual orientation? *Journal of Social Work Education, 32*(3), 297–313.

Patel, I. (1987). *Vivekananda's approach to social work.* Mylapore, India: Sri Ramakvishna Math.

Paulino, A. M. (1995a). Death, dying, and religion among Dominican immigrants. In J. Parry & A. R. Shen (Eds.), *A cross-cultural look at death, dying, and religion* (pp. 84–101). Chicago: Nelson Hall Publishers.

Paulino, A. (1995b). Spiritism, santeria, brujeria, and voodooism: A comparative view of indigenous healing systems. *Journal of Teaching in Social Work, 12*(1/2), 105–124.

Payne, W. J. (Ed.). (1991). *Directory of African American religious bodies.* Washington, DC: Howard University Press.

Peck, M. S. (1983). *People of the lie: The hope for healing human evil.* New York: Simon & Schuster.

Pelletier, K., & Garfield, C. (1976). *Consciousness East and West.* New York: Harper & Row.

Pepper, A. R. (1956). Protestant social work today. In F. E. Johnson (Ed.), *Religion and social work* (pp. 17–27). New York: Institute for Religious and Social Studies, Harper and Brothers.

Peters, F. E. (1982). *Children of Abraham: Judaism/Christianity/Islam.* Princeton, NJ: Princeton University Press.

Proudfoot, W. (1985). *Religious experience.* Berkeley: University of California Press.

Raines, J. (1996). Toward a definition of spiritually-sensitive social work practice. *Society for Spirituality and Social Work Newsletter, 3*(2), 4–5.

Ramirez, R. (1985). Hispanic spirituality. *Social Thought, 11*(3), 6–13.

Randour, M. L. (1987). *Women's psyche, women's spirit: The reality of relationships.* New York: Columbia University Press.

Rapp, C., Shera, W., & Kisthardt, W. (1993). Research strategies for consumer empowerment of people with severe mental illness. *Social Work*, *38*(6), 727–735.

Reamer, F. G. (1992). Social work and the public good: Calling or career? In P. Nelson Reid & P. R. Popple (Eds.), *The moral purposes of social work* (pp. 11–33). Chicago: Nelson-Hall Publishers.

Reid, P. N., & Popple, P. R. (Eds.). (1992). *The moral purposes of social work: The character and intentions of a profession.* Chicago: Nelson-Hall Publishers.

Rennie, B. S. (1996). *Reconstructing Eliade: Making sense of religion.* Albany: State University of New York Press.

Ressler, L. (1992). Theologically enriched social work: Alan Keith-Lucas' approach to social work and religion. *Spirituality and Social Work Journal*, *3*(2), 14–20.

Ressler, L. (1998). The relation between church and state: Issues in social work and the law. In Edward R. Canda (Ed.), *Spirituality in social work: New directions* (pp. 81–95). Binghamton, NY: Haworth Pastoral Press.

Rey, L. D. (1997). Religion as invisible culture: Knowing about and knowing with. *Journal of Family Social Work*, *2*(2), 159–177.

Robbins, S. P. (1995). Cults: In *The encyclopedia of social work* (19th ed.) (pp. 667–677). Washington, DC: National Association of Social Workers Press.

Robbins, S. P., Canda, E. R., & Chatterjee, P. (1998). *Contemporary human behavior theory: A critical perspective for social work.* Boston: Allyn & Bacon.

Roberts, K. A. (1995). *Religion in sociological perspective* (3rd ed.). Belmont, CA: Wadsworth.

Roof, W. C. (1993). *A generation of seekers: The spiritual journeys of the baby boom generation.* San Francisco: HarperSanFrancisco.

Russel, R. (1998). Spirituality and religion in graduate social work education. In E. R. Canda (Ed.), *Spirituality and social work: New directions.* Hazleton, PA: Haworth Press.

Saleebey, D. (Ed.). (1997). *The strengths perspective in social work practice* (2nd ed.) New York: Longman Publishers.

Salomon, E. L. (1967). Humanistic values and social casework. *Social Casework, 48*(1), 26–31.

Sandner, D. (1991). *Navaho symbols of healing.* Rochester, VT: Healing Arts Press.

Sanzenbach, P. (1989). Religion and social work: It's not that simple. *Social Casework, 70*(9), 571–572.

Scharper, P. J. (1975). The theology of liberation: Some reflections. *Social Thought, 1*(1), 59–66.

Schecter, M. (1971). A value system model in Jewish social welfare. *Jewish Social Work Forum, 8*(2), 5–22.

Scheff, T. J. (1979). *Catharsis in healing, ritual and drama.* Berkeley: University of California Press.

Schuhmacher, S., & Woerner, G. (Eds.). (1994). *The encyclopedia of Eastern philosophy and religion: Buddhism, Hunduism, Taoism, Zen.* Boston: Shambhala.

Seow, C. L. (1996). *Homosexuality and Christian community.* Louisville, KY: Westminster John Knox Press.

Seplowin, V. M. (1992). Social work and karma therapy. *Spirituality and Social Work Journal, 3*(2), 2–8.

Shafranske, E. P. (Ed.). (1996). *Religion and the clinical practice of psychology.* Washington, DC: American Psychological Association.

Sharma, A. (Ed.). (1994). *Today's woman in world religions.* Albany: State University of New York Press.

Sharma, S. (1987). Development, peace, and nonviolent social change: The Gandhian perspective. *Social Development Issues, 10*(3), 31–45.

Sheridan, M. J. (1997). If we nurtured the soul of social work. *Society for Spirituality and Social Work Newsletter, 4*(2), 3.

Sheridan, M. J., & Bullis, R. K. (1991). Practitioners' views on religion and spirituality. *Spirituality and Social Work Journal, 2*(2), 2–10.

Sheridan, M. J., Bullis, R. K., Adcock, C. R., Berlin, S. D., & Miller, P. C. (1992). Practitioners' personal and professional attitudes toward religion and spirituality: Issues for education and practice. *Journal of Social Work Education, 28*(2), 190–203.

Sheridan, M. J., Wilmer, C. M., & Atcheson, L. (1994). Inclusion of content on religion and spirituality in the social work curriculum: A study of faculty views. *Journal of Social Work Education, 30*(3), 363–376.

Simkhovitch, M. K. (1950). The settlement and religion. In L. M. Pacey (Ed.), *Readings in the development of settlement work* (pp. 136–142). Freeport, NY: Books for Libraries Press.

Simos, B. G. (1979). *A time to grieve: Loss as a universal human experience.* New York: Family Service Association of America.

Simpkinson, C., Wengell, D., & Casavant, J. (Eds.). (1994). *The common boundary graduate education guide: Holistic programs and resources integrating spirituality and psychology.* Bethesda, MD: Common Boundary.

Singh, R. N. (1992). Integrating concepts from Eastern psychology and spirituality: A treatment approach for Asian-American clients. *Spirituality and Social Work Journal, 3*(2), 8–14.

Siporin, M. (1982). Moral philosophy in social work today. *Social Service Review, 56*(4), 516–538.

Siporin, M. (1983). Morality and immorality in working with clients. *Social Thought, 9*(4), 10–27.

Siporin, M. (1985). Current social work perspectives on clinical practice. *Clinical Social Work Journal, 13*(3), 198–217.

Siporin, M. (1986). Contribution of religious values to social work and the law. *Social Thought, 12*(4), 35–50.

Siporin, M. (1990). Welcome to the Spirituality and Social Work Communicator. *Spirituality and Social Work Communicator, 1*(1), 3–4.

Smede, L. B. (1996). *The art of forgiving: When you need to forgive and don't know how.* New York: Ballantine Books.

Smith, E. D. (1995). Addressing the psychospiritual distress of death as reality: A transpersonal approach. *Social Work, 40*(3), 402–412.

Smith, E. D., & Gray, C. (1995). Integrating and transcending divorce: A transpersonal model. *Social Thought: Journal of Religion in the Social Services, 18*(1), 57–74.

Smith, J. E. (1994). *Quasi-religions: Humanism, Marxism and nationalism.* New York: St. Martin's Press.

Smith, R. (1961). Spiritual, ethical and moral values for children in foster care. *Child Welfare, 40*(1), 20–24.

Sneck, W. J., & Bonica, R. P. (1980). Attempting the integration of psychology and spirituality. *Social Thought, 6*(3), 27–36.

Sobrino, J. (1988). *Spirituality of liberation: Toward political holiness* (R. R. Barr, Trans.). Maryknoll, NY: Orbis Books.

Solomon, B. (1987). Empowerment: Social work in oppressed communities. *Journal of Social Work Practice, 2*(4), 79–91.

Spencer, S. (1956). Religion and social work. *Social Work, 1*(3), 19–26.

Spero, M. H. (1981). A clinical note on the therapeutic management of "religious" resistances in Orthodox Jewish clientele. *Journal of Jewish Communal Service, 57*(4), 334–341.

Spero, M. H. (1987). Identity and individuality in the nouveau-religious patient: Theoretical and clinical aspects. *Journal of Social Work and Policy in Israel, 1*, 25–49.

Sprafkin, B. R. (1970). Sectarian services in a time of crisis. *The Jewish Social Work Forum, 7*(1), 36–45.

Starhawk. (1979). *The spiral dance: A rebirth of the ancient religion of the Great Goddess.* San Francisco: Harper & Row.

Steltenkamp, M. F. (1993). *Black Elk: Holy man of the Oglala.* Norman, OK: University of Oklahoma Press.

Studzinski, R. (1986). Remember and forgive: Psychological dimensions of forgiveness. In C. Floristan & D. Duquoc (Eds.), *Forgiveness.* Edinburgh, Scotland: T. & Clark Ltd.

Sullivan, P. (1994). Should spiritual principles guide social policy? No. In H. J. Karger & J. Midgley (Eds.), *Controversial issues in human behavior in the social environment* (pp. 69–74). Boston: Allyn & Bacon.

Sullivan, W. P. (1992). Spirituality as social support for individuals with severe mental illness. *Spirituality and Social Work Journal, 3*(1), 7–13.

Swidler, A. (Ed.). (1993). *Homosexuality and world religions.* Valley Forge, PA: Trinity Press International.

Takaki, R. (1993). *A different mirror: A history of multicultural America.* Boston: Little, Brown.

Tart, C. T. (1975). Science, states of consciousness, and spiritual experiences: The need for state-specific sciences. In Charles T. Tart (Ed.), *Transpersonal psychologies* (pp. 9–58). New York: Harper & Row.

Thurman, R. A. F. (1996). Human rights and human responsibilities: Buddhist views on individualism and altruism. In I. Bloom, J. P. Martin, & W. Proudfoot (Eds.), *Religious diversity and human rights* (pp. 87–113). New York: Columbia University Press.

Tillich, P. (1962). The philosophy of social work. *Social Service Review, 36*(1), 13–16.

Timberlake, E. M., & Cook, K. O. (1984). Social work and the Vietnamese refugee. *Social Work, 29*(2), 108–114.

Towle, C. (1965). *Common human needs* (rev. ed). Washington, DC: National Association of Social Workers Press.

Townshend, J. (1988). Neo-shamanism and the modern mystical movement. In G. Doore (Ed.), *Shaman's Path: Healing, personal growth, and empowerment* (pp. 73–83). Boston: Shambhala.

Turner, E. (1992). *Experiencing ritual: A new interpretation of African healing.* Philadelphia, PA: University of Pennsylvania Press.

Turner, R., Lukoff, D., Barnhouse, R. T., & Lu, F. G. (1995). Religious or spiritual problem: A culturally sensitive diagnostic category in the DSM-IV. *Journal of Nervous and Mental Disease, 183*(7), 435–444.

Turner, V. W. (1965). Betwixt and between: The liminal period in rites of passage. In W. A. Lessa & E. V. Vogt (Eds.), *Reader in comparative religion: An anthropological approach* (3rd ed.). New York: Harper & Row.

Turner, V. W. (1969). *The ritual process: Structure and anti-structure.* Ithaca, NY: Cornell University Press.

Turner, V. W. (1974). *Dramas, fields and metaphors: Symbolic action in human society.* Ithaca, NY: Cornell University Press.

Tyson, K. (1995). *New foundations for scientific social and behavioral research: The heuristic paradigm.* Boston: Allyn & Bacon.

United States Catholic Conference. (1994). *Catechism of the Catholic church.* Liguori, MO: Liquori Publications.

Van Gennep, A. (1960). *The rites of passage.* M. B. Vizedom & G. L. Caffee, trans., with introduction by S. T. Kimball. Chicago: University of Chicago Press.

Van Hook, M. P. (1997). Christian social work. In R. L. Edwards (Ed.), *Encyclopedia of social work* (19th ed. 1997 suppl.) (pp. 68–77). Washington, DC: National Association of Social Workers.

Van Kaam, A. (1983). *Fundamental formation.* New York: Crossroad.

Van Os, H. (1994). *The art of devotion in the late Middle Ages in Europe: 1300–1500.* Princeton, NJ: Princeton University Press.

Van Soest, D. (1996). The influence of competing ideologies about homosexuality on nondiscrimination policy: Implications for social work education. *Journal of Social Work Education, 32*(1), 53–64.

Vardey, L. (Ed). (1995). *Mother Teresa: A simple path.* New York: Ballantine Books.

Wallace, A. F. C. (1966). *Religion: An anthropological view.* New York: Random House.

Walsh, R. N. (1990). *The spirit of shamanism.* New York: G. P. Putnam's Sons.

Walz, T., Sharma, S., & Birnbaum, C. (1990). Gandhian thought as theory base for social work. *University of Illinois School of Social Work Occasional Paper Series I.* Urbana-Champaign: University of Illinois.

Warner, M. (1976). *Alone of all her sex: The myth and the cult of the Virgin Mary.* New York: Pocket Books.

Watson, K. W. (1994). Spiritual emergency: Concepts and implications for psychotherapy. *Journal of Humanistic Psychology, 34*(2), 22–45.

Watts, F., & Williams, M. (1988). *The psychology of religious knowing.* Cambridge, England: Cambridge University Press.

Weber, P. J., & Jones, W. L. (1994). *U.S. religious interest groups: Institutional profiles.* Westport, CT: Greenwood Press.

Weisman, E. R. (1997). Does religion and spirituality have a significant place in the Core HBSE curriculum? No. In M. Bloom & W. C. Klein (Eds.), *Controversial issues in human behavior in the social environment* (pp. 177–183). Boston: Allyn & Bacon.

Weitzmann, K. (1978). *The icon: Holy images—Sixth to fourteenth century.* New York: Braziller.

Welwood, J. (Ed.). (1992). *Ordinary magic: Everyday life as spiritual path.* Boston: Shambhala.

White, B. W., & Hampton, D. M. (1995). African American pioneers in social work. In R. L. Edwards (Ed.), *Encyclopedia of social work, 19th edition* (pp. 101–115). Washington, DC: NASW Press.

Wikler, M. (1977). The Torah view of mental illness: Sin or sickness? *Journal of Jewish Communal Service, 53*(4), 338–344.

Wikler, M. (1986). Pathways to treatment: How Orthodox Jews enter therapy. *Social Casework, 67*(2), 113–118.

Wilber, K. (1980). *The Atman project: A transpersonal view of human development.* Wheaton, IL: Quest.

Wilber, K. (1993). *Grace and grit: Spirituality and healing in the life and death of Treya Killiam Wilber.* Boston: Shambhala.

Wilber, K. (1995). *Sex, ecology, spirituality: The spirit of evolution.* Boston: Shambhala.

Wilber, K. (1996). *A brief history of everything.* Boston: Shambhala.

Wilhelm, R., & Baynes, C. F. (trans). (1967). *The I Ching or book of changes* (3rd ed.). Bollingen Series, no. 19. Princeton, NJ: Princeton University Press.

Williamson, W. B. (Ed.). (1992). *An encyclopedia of religions in the United States.* New York: Crossroad.

Wilson, S. J. (1980). *Recording guidelines for social workers.* New York: Free Press.

Worthington, E. L., Jr., & DiBlasio, F. A. (1990). Promoting mutual forgiveness within the fractured relationship. *Psychotherapy, 27* (2), 219–223.

Wulff, D. M. (1991). *Psychology of religion: Classic and contemporary views.* New York: Wiley.

Yellow Bird, M. J. (1995). Spirituality in First Nations story telling: A Sahnish-Hidatsa approach to narratives. *Reflections: Narratives of professional helping, 1*(4), 65–72.

Zimdars-Swartz, S. L. (1991). *Encountering Mary: Visions of Mary from La Salette to Medjugorje.* New York: Avon Books.

FOR FURTHER INFORMATION ON SPIRITUAL DIVERSITY IN SOCIAL WORK

For information on a newsletter, professional networking and conferences:

Robin Russel, Ph.D., Director
Society for Spirituality and Social Work
School of Social Work
University of Nebraska–Omaha
Omaha, NE 68182

For information about technical research design for the 1997 National Survey of NASW Members on Spirituality in Practice (see also Appendix B):

Leola Dyrud Furman, Ph.D.
Department of Social Work
University of North Dakota–Grand Forks
Grand Forks, ND 58202

For information on interdisciplinary education in social work and religious studies:

Edward R. Canda, Ph.D.
School of Social Welfare
University of Kansas
Lawrence, KS 66045

INDEX